THE RICH GET RICHER

About the Author

Dennis Braun is Professor of Sociology at Mankato State University in Minnesota. He received his B.A. and M.A. degrees at the University of Minnesota, and earned a Ph.D. in Sociology at the American University in Washington, D.C. Professor Braun is the author of three other books in sociology, including *Patterns of Living: Social Indicators and Quality of Life in Minnesota,* and numerous papers on the use of statistical methods in social science. He has worked with the U.S. Census Bureau, and is currently involved in developing statistical database applications for use with personal computers.

THE
RICH
GET
RICHER

The Rise of Income Inequality in the
United States and the World

Denny Braun

Mankato State University

NELSON-HALL PUBLISHERS
Chicago

Project Editor: Dorothy Anderson
Text Designer: Tamra Campbell-Phelps
Cover Painting: R. C. Nichols, *Pillory*

Library of Congress Cataloging-in-Publication Data

Braun, Denny
   The rich get richer / Denny Braun.
      p.   cm.
   Includes bibliographical references.
   ISBN 0-8304-1226-3.—ISBN 0-8304-1264-6 (pbk.)
   1. Wealth—United States. 2. Income distribution—United States.
3. Wealth—Brazil. 4. Income distribution—Brazil. 5. Wealth.
6. Income distribution.   I. Title.
HC110.W4B73   1991
339.2′0973—dc20   90-35294
                                                              CIP

Manufactured in the United States of America

10   9   8   7   6   5   4   3   2

TM   The paper used in this book meets the
minimum requirements of American
National Standard for Information
Sciences—Permanence of Paper for
Printed Library Materials, ANSI
Z39.48-1984.

DEDICATED TO:

Cathy Calkins Braun
(*Mi Esposa, Amante, y Amiga*)

CONTENTS

PREFACE

The world-wide debt crisis, together with the economic slide that the United States has experienced within the global economy, has been the subject of countless books and articles within the past decade. This book does not attempt to turn over such already plowed ground. Rather, my goal is to show how such international and domestic forces have worked to reduce real income and drive up relative income inequality on a personal level. Economic expansion by multinational corporations and bank loans from industrial countries to Third World countries have been called "development." The research here indicates the stark opposite. Where penetration by corporations from industrial countries in poor nations has occurred, actual declines in meeting basic human needs have been the result. Only small minorities have seen their real incomes go up, while the great bulk of the people in less developed countries (LDCs) have become more impoverished or seen their incomes stagnate.

While income cuts took place in poor nations, most people in the United States did not benefit either. The record overseas investments of American corporations led to capital flight, depriving our industries at home of urgently needed investment (deindustrialization), and loss of high paying manufacturing jobs. The bottom line has been a great increase of income inequality within America and a severe erosion of the U.S. middle class. The rich have become much wealthier in the past two decades, but especially during the 1980s. A drastic slash in the nation's social safety net also set in during the 1970s and reached epidemic proportions under Reaganomics during the 1980s. The poor grew even more desperate as they saw their real income deteriorate at an even faster pace. U.S. defense spending nearly reached wartime levels, which further drained resources away from productive manufacturing. Commercial research and development has dropped like a rock, making our industrial exports more dated and of inferior quality. Fiscal policies pursued by the federal government during the past decade have been like salt poured on a wound. Unheard of trade deficits, budget gaps, and personal/corporate debt have piled up as a result. Despite the false appearance of economic growth, the pillars of the American economy have become rotten with neglect.

Yet not all sectors of the economy nor all groups within the United States have witnessed declining income. We also need not feel helpless in the face of declining income. There is still hope to reverse the growth of inequality within America. We do not have to be victims. To accomplish this, a number of strategies and plans to stop the income decline are suggested in the final chapter. These include ideas for basic change at the global, national, and personal level.

To help build a greater awareness of the income slide and the dangers it entails, a major attempt is made in this book to reach out to a broad audience of concerned citizens. *The Rich Get Richer* is hopefully not just another academic tome. I have actively sought to avoid difficult professional concepts and overly complex explanations. A major goal has been simplicity in an effort to build understanding.

At times, attempting to write an easily understood book on income inequality with enough academic substance to give it weight seemed impossible. I owe a great deal to my wife, Cathy, who served as audience and gently constructive critic. Although it seems almost mandatory for an author to express thanks to a spouse, words simply cannot convey Cathy's help in this enterprise. She was a source of emotional support as well as intellectual aid, when the faceless statistics took on a life of their own. She was at my side when we were mugged in Rio, feeling the fear, anger, and compassion that firsthand contact with desperate income inequality breeds.

Also rendering support were Dave Paxson, Johannes Postma, Bob Lowe, and Mark and Kathy Kennedy. Important technical assistance in making maps was provided by my son, Dennis. My colleague Steve Buechler provided a much appreciated critique of portions of this manuscript. Karen Purrington in our Sociology Department helped gather materials, took care of travel details, and coordinated office help. Mankato State University assisted my efforts through faculty research grants. For my talks with Brazilian economists, I owe thanks to J. Ray Kennedy (Center of Brazilian Studies, School of Advanced International Studies, Johns Hopkins University), and especially to Professor Edmar L. Bacha (Pontificia Universidade Catolica do Rio de Janeiro) in helping me to network with his colleagues. I owe a special debt of gratitude to José Marcio Camargo of this university for consenting to a fairly lengthy interview. Regis Bonelli and his staff at the Instituto de Planejamento Economico e Social in Rio de Janeiro also provided invaluable assistance and insight into Brazilian income inequality as well. Finally, material and findings from Helga Hoffman at the United Nations (Office of the Director General for Development and International Economic Cooperation) were very useful.

I have relied heavily upon government documents, congressional studies, and federal data for analysis of American income inequality. Congressmen David Obey (Wisconsin) and Gerry Sikorski (Minnesota) were quite helpful in locating information for this purpose. A tremendous amount of assistance for this effort came from Congressman Tim Penny (Minnesota) and his staff, who located and forwarded material that would have been difficult to get otherwise. Tim Penny has been an outspoken advocate in combatting world hunger in his activities in Congress. David Obey has been in the forefront of numerous efforts to deal with the increasing levels of low income and poverty within the United States. Although none of these congressmen necessarily endorse the conclusions reached in my book, I am confident that they share a common concern in striving to preserve an equitable and just society for all Americans. If this book is at all successful in helping to bring about this worthy purpose, I will be extremely grateful.

1

WHY INCREASING INEQUALITY IS A DANGER TO US ALL

It seems that people have always argued about how resources in society are shared. Discord usually centers around whether the share we get is an equitable and fair reward for our hard work, effort, and sacrifice. One school believes that those who receive more must somehow deserve their higher incomes. Another view generally sees society as basically unfair. Scarce resources are passed out on the basis of inheritance from the very well off to their offspring. This view asserts that persons in a ruling class or powerful elite maintain their positions of influence by use of coercion, oppression, naked aggression, and force. Such an elite preys upon the weak of society in maintaining and increasing its intrenched, high position.

This privileged class is often accused of cruel indifference to suffering in the masses it dominates. A famous quote attributed to Marie Antoinette just prior to the bloody French Revolution in the eighteenth century, starkly illustrates this attitude. The story is told that as queen of France at the apex of an incredibly opulent and decadent court society, she was informed that the peasants had no bread, that they were literally starving to death. Her alleged offhand quote, "Let them eat cake," earned her a place of infamy within history.

There is evidence that she never voiced such incredible indifference.[1] Yet, if her lack of concern may not have stemmed from genuine cruelty, Marie Antoinette was ignorant regarding the true condition of the poor within French society. Being so out of touch with her starving subjects literally cost her her head! The parallel message for any society with an economic elite which bleeds the very financial life from its citizenry ought to be crystal clear. To continue—through chicanery, fraud, and naked force—to steal from the poor to enrich those who are already abundantly wealthy carries an eventually extreme penalty. To follow a

1

path of economic gluttony, while those around us literally starve, all but guarantees some form of French Revolution for contemporary society.

The Shrinking Middle Class

A more subdued but similar debate has been simmering within the popular press in the United States for most of the 1980s. Two interrelated threads which are not easily separated continue to reappear as major themes: (1) America has lost its economic dominance and leadership among the nations of the world; (2) Principally as a result of our country's precipitous decline, middle- and low-income Americans are less well off than what was promised in the economic reforms of the Reagan administration.

It is especially around the issue of a "shrinking middle class" that the debate has been fiercely fought. Concern was initially kicked off in 1982 with the publication of Bluestone and Harrison's book *The Deindustrialization of America*.[2] The authors documented a decline in employment within unionized smokestack and goods-producing industries along with a parallel growth in nonunionized high technology and service-producing industries. Critics have surmised from these developments that the middle class is disappearing. A bipolarization of the earnings structure can be the only result. The substantially higher pay of manufacturing jobs has been replaced with low-paying service-sector jobs—the McDonaldization of the work force.

Early commentary by the mass media threw cold water on any notion that structural causes in the American economy could be to blame. *U.S. News and World Report,* for example, cited demographic trends as the primary cause for declining family income (the growth of new households; baby boomers glutting the job market and depressing wages; increasing divorce resulting in poor, female-headed households; etc.).[3] *Newsweek* presented some brief counterevidence to reject this notion,[4] while the business community's *Forbes* magazine descended to the level of blaming the victim, concluding that "the most important contributor to the poverty statistics . . . is the fact that so many unmarried teenagers choose to have children they cannot support."[5] The same judgmental tone is echoed in a later article in *Forbes* as well:

> So the statistics may be telling us more about families than about
> economic failure. If couples get divorced, if unmarried teenagers in
> a Chicago slum have babies, if a flood of inexperienced workers join
> the work force, that will drive down the income statistics. But it
> doesn't in itself mean the economy is falling apart.[6]

Thankfully, less biased and more thoroughly objective articles were still being published in the popular press.[7] An article in *Business Week* briefly reviewed the evidence to date, concluding that the income erosion was probably real but that to dismiss it as "merely" demographic was of little solace to a young family just getting its start.[8] The author concludes that unless economic growth produces an equitable distribution of benefits, something is deeply wrong with democratic capitalism. A finely balanced *Time* magazine article skirted around any firm opinions, but did underline the importance of a healthy middle class:

> Any substantial decline of the middle class—even if it is partially psychological—would be ominous for the U.S. as a whole. It is the middle class whose values and ambitions set the tone for the country. Without it the U.S. could become a house divided in which middle Americans would no longer serve as a powerful voice for political compromise. . . . Virtually everyone agrees that America needs to maintain its middle class.[9]

Not surprisingly, the debate has been fanned by the flames of presidential election politics. In 1988, Republican contender George Bush claimed that the newly created 17 million jobs within the United States over the past six years paid an average of $22,000 per year. His Democratic opponent Michael Dukakis charged that within the same period the average weekly wage of jobs lost in this country was $440, and that replacement jobs paid an average of one-third less than the ones lost. The *Washington Post* believes both candidates were playing fast and loose with different statistics:

> A look at the data shows there is some evidence that bolsters the Democratic argument, even if it doesn't prove Dukakis' arithmetic. . . . The proportion of jobs providing relatively low wages appears to have grown, notably among workers who work year-round and full time. Meanwhile, wages for the entire work force have failed to rise above inflation during the 1980s; by some measures, real wages have declined. . . . And industries such as steel and autos, which pay well almost uniformly, have been among the biggest job losers, while industries such as retailing and restaurants—which almost uniformly offer low pay—have been among the biggest gainers, BLS data show.[10]

A Declining Consumer Base

Barbara Ehrenreich adopts a similar theme of growing income inequality in a *New York Times Magazine* article, pointing out that in the area of consumer goods we have already become a two-tier society.[11] The middle is disappearing from the retail industry (Korvettes, Gimbels) while remaining middle income retailers such as Sears and Penney scramble to reposition for a more upscale market. The stores and chains that prosper tend to serve clientele at either extreme of the income spectrum: Bloomingdale's and Saks for the affluent; K mart and Woolco for the underclass. While this may initially appear frivolous to those of us who are not involved with marketing, it should also be remembered that America is probably the most consumer-oriented country in the world. No one knows for sure what types of reaction could ensue if today's relatively plentiful flow of goods becomes tomorrow's trickle. Moreover, the newly working poor who now staff the shops in malls may have their class-consciousness expanded as they sell to the wealthy luxury goods they themselves can no longer possibly afford. The outcome may be political extremism, perhaps a greater alignment with either the radical left or reactionary, militant right. Indeed, Ehrenreich concludes her article with penetrating insight:

> Everyone has a stake in creating a less anxious, more egalitarian society. . . . The greatest danger is not that a class-conscious, left-leaning political alternative will arise, but that it will not. For without a potent political alternative, we are likely to continue our slide toward a society divided between the hungry and the overfed, the hopeless and the have-it-alls. What is worse, there will be no mainstream, peaceable political outlets for the frustration of the declining middle class or the desperation of those at the bottom. Instead, it is safe to predict that there will be more crime, more exotic forms of political and religious sectarianism, and ultimately, that we will no longer be one nation, but two.[12]

A Threat to Democracy

Is this overly dramatic? Can we expect a fundamental alteration in the American way of life, a threat to our basic democratic institutions if economic inequality gets worse? One is tempted to dismiss popular media articles as sensationalistic and exaggerated, no matter how persuasive they seem. Yet recent evidence from sociology indicates that political extremism and violence does result when income inequality increases. The ability of a given society to meet the basic needs of its citizens would seem a major indicator of its health and staying power. The very foundations of democracy may depend upon a government's ability to maintain the economic well-being of its population. In some recent research, Edward Muller analyzed over fifty countries where income inequality data existed. It was discovered that the death rate from political violence in countries (regime repressiveness, coups, revolutions, disappearances, etc.) actually goes up as income inequality increases.[13] As a result, countries which follow a strategy of development which ignores distributional equality are more likely to experience higher levels of mass political violence. On the international scene, this is called the "Brazil Model"—named after the country so closely identified with rapid accumulation of wealth through efforts to aid rich landowners and industrialists while virtually ignoring the welfare of the poorer masses. The parallel within the United States to Reaganomics "trickle-down" theories or "Voodoo" economics needs no elaboration.

Further development of this research, examining the impact of stable democracy upon income inequality, led Muller to an even more important discovery:

> A very strong inverse association is observed between income inequality and the likelihood of stability versus breakdown of democracy. Democracies . . . with extremely inegalitarian distributions of income . . . all experienced a breakdown of democracy (typically due to military coup d'etat), while a breakdown of democracy occurred in only 30 percent of those with intermediate income inequality. It did not occur at all among democracies with relatively egalitarian distributions of income. This negative effect of income inequality on democratic stability is independent of a country's level of development. . . . Indeed, level of economic development, considered by many scholars to be the predominant cause of variation in the stability of democratic regimes, is found to be an irrelevant variable once income inequality is taken into account.[14]

In essence, no matter how wealthy a country becomes, it is still vulnerable to political violence and instability if its distribution of income is fundamentally unequal. Conversely, even if a country is relatively poor, democratic institutions will survive and flourish if income is distributed in a fair manner. It may have become a cliché to state that the very survival of democracy is dependent upon how a government treats its citizens, but concrete evidence now gives new meaning to this axiom.

Deteriorating Family Life

We thus have a multitude of reasons for being concerned with the prevention and amelioration of income inequality, both within our own society and those of our neighbors in this one-world community we are part of. If survival of basic democratic institutions in our own country or world unrest still seem remote or unlikely, there is much reason for worry closer to home. Beginning in 1973 and continuing through 1987, the average real wage of American workers declined by 13.8 percent.[15] To maintain living standards in much of the 1970s and 1980s, women have increasingly entered the labor force. Although there are many positive consequences to this trend, an unrecognized fact is that the doubling of female participation in the labor force since 1940 is equivalent to a 20 percent increase in the average family's paid workweek. People work more and have less time for leisure or family activities because of economic deterioration. Frank Levy unleashes a truly terrifying statistic which sharply illustrates just how bad the situation really is for newly formed families. The typical father of today's baby boomer faced housing costs that were equivalent to about 14 percent of his gross monthly pay; in 1983 a thirty–year–old man had to allocate a staggering 44 percent of his income for house payments. Indeed, Levy reports that for males in previous generations, the average increase in earnings was 30 percent between ages forty and fifty. By 1983, however, this had actually changed to a *minus* 14 percent for men who turned forty in 1973.[16] Despite more women working, increasing proportions of younger families are being frozen out of the housing market.

Disaster can also ensue with divorce, which has grown sharply within the past several decades. For example, disposable income falls 73 percent for ex-wives within a year of the divorce, whereas it rises by 42 percent for ex-husbands.[17] While the "feminization of poverty" can be easily documented statistically,[18] such trends bode poorly for the children who are assigned to the custody of these women, which happens in 90 percent of the cases. A study done by Danziger and Gottschalk shows that American families with children have lost a large amount of real income irrespective of which of the five income groups they were in— but that families with children in the lowest group lost proportionately more income.[19] On the whole, the share of national income going to American families with children declined by nearly 20 percent between 1973 and 1984.

Looming Economic Depression

A chilling picture is offered by Ravi Batra, an economist on the faculty at Southern Methodist University, who presents evidence tying in growth of wealth inequality with economic depressions. His thesis is that especially deep depressions (where unemployment, for example, reaches 25 percent) have occurred periodically since the American Revolution when the growth of wealth inequality reaches a magnitude where it destabilizes our basic economy.[20] Before explaining his conclusions in detail, it is important to note that wealth and income inequality are not the same, although they are related.[21] Basically, income inequality derives from mostly job-related earnings, although other sources of income can be very important (alimony and child support; rent; interest on savings; stock dividends; transfer payments such as Aid to Families with Dependent Children (AFDC), Social Security, Medicare, etc.). Wealth income is almost totally derived from ownership in stocks, bonds, and capital goods within the United States—i.e., it is the *capitalist* dimension of our society.

An average citizen may have some wealth equity, such as a house or IRA or pension investment, but the great majority do not own stocks—where the comparison becomes one of giants and dwarfs. For example, the top 1.0 percent of all U.S. families own 60.3 percent of all corporate stock in the country.[22] The inequality in wealth within our society—what we receive in income plus the worth of the assets we own—is very much more lopsided than that of income alone. Analysis indicates that when families are ordered by wealth, the top 10 percent of families hold 70 percent of all net wealth; when families are looked at in terms of income, the top 10 percent of family units own 50.1 percent of net wealth. Either picture shows extreme disparities, but the differences are even higher when wealth is measured rather than only income. Indeed, the top 1.0 percent of families own nearly one-fourth of all net wealth in the United States, although they receive only a mere 11 percent of all money income! What this means is aptly explained by Kerbo:

> There is some correlation between wealth and income but . . . at the lower end of the income scale we find that increases in income bring only small increases in wealth. This is because with higher income more money remains (after purchasing necessities) to purchase things that can be held as wealth (such as a home or corporate stock). But at the higher end of the income scale we find a significant jump in wealth. Quite simply this is because substantial wealth often brings higher income. . . . In other words, we find that the causal relation between income and wealth becomes reversed as we reach higher levels of income and wealth—great wealth brings a high income. And as we find that great wealth is more likely to be inherited in the United States today, . . . we find that the base of many high incomes today is also inherited.[23]

The role of inheritance plays a crucial role in Batra's theory of wealth inequality causing economic depression. He points out that great inequality in wealth does not develop overnight, but mainly from inheritance. Thus, it usually takes one or two generations before its distribution becomes critically unequal—making depressions thankfully more rare in the American experience (generally, a sixty-year cycle). It should be noted, however, that the rate of wealth concentration is likely to be curvilinear—increasing at astronomical rates just before the onset of depression. Batra notes that in 1922, 1.0 percent of U.S. families owned 31.6 percent of national wealth—but that just seven years later this had risen to 36.3 percent.[24] Although this may not seem on the surface to be a startling figure, it represented the highest concentration in history for our country, and a gigantic leap in the concentration of wealth from the typical glacial pace that the rates change.

The wealth inequality causes two other factors to come into play which set the stage for panic and depression: speculative fever and shaky loans made to higher-risk customers. The number of persons with no or few assets rises because of increasing income disparity; because of this, the borrowing needs of the poor are more pronounced. The banks, in their turn, are now awash in deposits from the very rich; they cannot afford to pay interest on the deposits without lending them out. Therefore, as the concentration of wealth increases, the number of banks with less credit-worthy loans also rises. This increases the potential number of bank failures if panic ensues (over two thousand banks suspended operation in 1931 alone). But what could kick off a rush on the banks?

> A side effect of the growing wealth disparity is the rise in spec-
> ulative investments. As a person becomes wealthy, his aversion to
> risk declines. As wealth inequality grows, the overall riskiness of
> investments made by the rich also grows. It essentially reflects the
> human urge to make a quick profit. It means margin or installment
> buying of assets and goods only for resale and not for productive
> purposes. It means, for instance, increasing involvement of investors
> in futures markets. When others see the rich profiting quickly from
> speculative purchases, they tend to follow suit. . . . Speculative fe-
> ver tends to feed on itself, and by the time the general population
> rushes to join the bandwagon, the venture is usually nearing its last
> stage. . . . Eventually even those normally too cautious for such
> ventures are tempted by "easy" profits.[25]

Batra emphasizes that the speculative fever cannot begin in the absence of wealth disparity, since it is only the very rich who can afford to take such heady risks with potentially high but uncertain return. It is the concentration of wealth—great inequalities in the distribution of income—that is the centerpiece for his assertions. He ultimately concludes that high wealth disparity is responsible both for the surge in speculative mania and the fragility of the banking system. The real cause of great depressions is extreme inequality in the distribution of wealth.

One could argue against this negative scenario by stressing the real divergence between wealth and income, but it should be remembered that the two are closely related. Extreme wealth always ends up generating extremely high income. Thus, inequality within the U.S. income distribution picture is an indicator of whether this growth in wealth inequality has reached the blast-off stage in its rate of growth. This point is quite important because accurate and recent wealth data is much harder to get than income data.[26] One source of wealth estimation is estate tax records, which are only filed after the person dies. Although inheritors' wealth can be estimated from such archives, there is an obvious lag of up-to-date information. As we shall see later, income information is gathered and published yearly by the Census Bureau. It is thus possible to trace income inequities and their immediate consequences in our society more readily than analyzing disparity in wealth holding, which takes on a more historical, ex post facto character. Since Batra's work shows the rate of wealth concentration steepening so abruptly just before the onset of depression, income data would be the only means to estimate whether this was happening before the event actually takes place.

How Much Is Enough? Social Justice and the Very Rich

Lastly, an important reason for being greatly concerned with the distribution of income is simply a matter of social justice. It can well be asked, "How much is enough?" In essence, what extremes of income disparity are we willing to tolerate in our society? The answer, of course, will lie in the eye of the beholder and will no doubt be greatly influenced by that person's relative position on the income spectrum. The point is rarely asked in American society, but it should be. In addition to worrying about the deterioration of the middle class, there has been a very real growth of poverty, homelessness, and what is now being described as an emergent, persistent "underclass" in our society.[27] There are many who will undoubtedly argue that it is the inalienable right of every American to earn as much as he or she can get in a "free" and "open" competitive market economy. Time does not permit a refutation of this position, although any good sociology textbook on social stratification will do the job.[28] Simply put, the game is fixed in advance, with the wealthy and influential determining the rules of access and reward (income) within U.S. society. Most of us operate in a limited market of educational and employment opportunity (so we can hopefully avoid McDonald's in favor of McDonnell Douglas), but we are excluded from large incomes because we failed the first litmus test—being born as sons and daughters to the truly wealthy in our society. It is these offspring who are doubly blessed, both because of the money they will inherit and because of the advantages which accrue to their social class that will permit them to take over the helms of our major corporations and banks in the future— eventually giving them still higher incomes.

How much is enough? *Forbes* magazine proudly monitors the pulse of corporate America by publishing salaries of its leading executives each year. In recent data dealing with the top 800 corporations in America, total compensation is listed for the chief executive officer (CEO) in 1987.[29] Despite the October market collapse of 1987, when the Dow-Jones Industrial Average lost over 500 points in a single day, it was still a good year for nearly all of these corporate giants. A full 273 CEO's earned $1 million or more, while the median compensation for all 800 was $762,253—an 8 percent increase over 1986.[30]

It is important to point out that total compensation for these corporate executives includes much more than just a salary figure—although this is usually quite generous as well. The top twenty corporate executives in terms of total compensation are listed in table 1.1. *Salary plus bonus* includes cash and deferred salary and bonus payments, as well as director's fees and commissions. *Other* includes payments from long-term compensation plans, restricted stock awards, thrift plan contributions, etc. One can easily see that a huge source of compensation comes directly from stock ownership, which includes holdings of the chief executive officer (CEO), his wife, and children (other family members, parents, and foundations were not included, which probably *understates* the magnitude of the stock gains since this is a common ploy in keeping IRS payments down).[31] *Stock gains* in this category thus include net value realized in shares or cash from the exercise of stock options or stock appreciation rights granted in previous years.

At over $60 million total compensation, Charles Lazarus of Toys "Я" Us led the pack of exorbitantly high-paid chief executives, followed in second place by Jim Manzi of Lotus Development at $26 million. Lee Iacocca, whose name has become a household word because of his frequent nice-guy, "just an average Joe" advertising appearances as Chrysler's CEO, wrapped up third place in the mega-million dollar sweep stakes with $17,656,000. Assuming that these executives get about four weeks of vacation per year like the rest of us, and that they are hardworking (putting in an average of 60 hours per week to give them a generous estimate), Lazarus actually earned $20,845 per hour, followed by Manzi at $9,145 and Iacocca at $6,130! It is impossible to spend money at the rate many of these executives rake it in. Even the average CEO compensation of the top 800 was nearly $265 per hour. A person can only eat so many meals per day, own so many cars, live in so many houses, buy so many suits ad nauseam with this deluge of money! What do they do with it? As shown in the previous discussion, they invest it in stocks so they can realize even greater profits!

The singularly important point to note is that many of these top executives "earn" in only a few hours what it takes the rest of us an entire

TABLE 1.1   Total Compensation of Forty Highest Paid Chief Executives in the United States: 1987 (in thousands of dollars)

Company	Executive	Salary + Bonus	Other	Stock Gains	Total
1. Toys "Я" Us	Charles Lazarus	3,594	30	56,410	60,034
2. Lotus Development	Jim Manzi	941	40	25,356	26,337
3. Chrysler	Lee Iacocca	1,491	2,706	13,459	17,656
4. LIN Broadcast	Donald Pels	950	22	16,428	17,400
5. Reebok International	Paul Fireman	15,424	4	———	15,427
6. Squibb	Richard Furlaud	1,405	745	11,891	14,040
7. General Electric	John Welch, Jr.	2,057	———	10,574	12,631
8. State St Boston	William Edgerly	657	4	9,455	10,116
9. Unisys	Michael Blumenthal	1,278	271	8,433	9,983
10. Community Psych	James Conte	925	51	7,640	8,617
11. Anheuser-Busch	August Busch III	1,455	16	6,525	7,997
12. GenCorp	A. William Reynolds	808	6,908	———	7,716
13. Time Inc	J. Richard Munro	1,288	———	6,125	7,413
14. Walt Disney	Michael Eisner	6,730	12	———	6,742
15. Masco	Richard Manoogian	1,025	30	5,116	6,171
16. Wal-Mart Stores	David Glass	488	29	5,569	6,085
17. Pfizer	Edmund Pratt Jr.	1,249	———	4,820	6,068
18. EI du Pont	Richard Heckert	1,418	60	4,481	5,959
19. Brunswick	Jack Reichert	1,155	4,707	———	5,862
20. Sara Lee	John Bryan Jr.	1,251	588	3,949	5,788
21. Bear Stearns	Alan Greenberg	5,712	———	———	5,712
22. Exxon	Lawrence Rawl	1,207	59	4,257	5,523
23. Temple-Inland	Clifford Grum	665	2	4,534	5,201
24. Ogden	Ralph Ablon	1,389	113	3,651	5,153
25. Potlatch	Richard Madden	865	11	4,106	4,981
26. Albertson's	Warren McCain	771	22	3,930	4,723
27. TRW	Ruben Mettler	1,061	32	3,530	4,623
28. Kraft	John Richman	1,200	19	3,288	4,506
29. Amdahl	John Lewis	898	774	2,805	4,477
30. Seagate Tech	Allan Shugart	1,264	———	3,213	4,476
31. VF	Lawrencee Pugh	1,075	———	3,366	4,441
32. Gillette	Colman Mockler Jr.	890	45	3,489	4,423
33. Reliance Group	Saul Steinberg	4,272	36	———	4,308
34. Eli Lilly	Richard Wood	1,009	335	2,876	4,220
35. Columbia S & L	Thomas Spiegel	3,860	239	———	4,099
36. Union Pacific	Andrew Lewis Jr.	1,200	48	2,753	4,000
37. NCR	Charles Exley Jr.	1,001	2	2,898	3,901
38. USX	David Roderick	1,364	———	2,484	3,848
39. Ford Motor Co	Donald Petersen	3,730	50	———	3,779
40. Progressive	Peter Lewis	1,606	30	1,979	3,615

year to make! Are we to conclude that these men (only three of the 800 are women) possess talents and skills so rare as to warrant such extravagant pay? Are the jobs they perform and the positions they command so crucial to the country's well-being that they somehow deserve these exorbitant sums? It is reasonable to point out the other side of the coin as well: by awarding such lavish sums to top corporate executives the message is also unmistakably being communicated to us that the tasks we may perform within our economy are relatively unimportant in the scheme of things.

Are these corporate executives really worth the money they receive? Surprisingly, even the business magazine *Fortune* thinks not.[32] In a sophisticated multiple regression study,[33] compensation analysis revealed that *rational* factors one could expect to be used as justification for CEO pay accounted for only 39 percent of the variation in ultimate compensation. In essence, almost two-thirds of corporate executive pay for the largest 170 U.S. industrial and service corporations cannot be logically accounted for. The good news was that among the rational factors examined which should figure as important in predicting executive pay, the corporation's financial performance was the most salient. Other, less important objective factors driving up executive pay were larger size of company, higher risk for corporations in volatile markets, and absence of governmental regulation of the industry (transportation and utility companies pay lower because of this).

On the other hand, factors which ought to matter in total compensation were found to have no relationship to CEO pay, such as the age of the executive or whether the corporation's board of directors came from within or outside of the company. The most remarkable finding was that it did not matter how much corporation stock was owned by the CEO in predicting "rational pay." The study found a multitude of executives who were lavishly awarded with stock options, who were even permitted to swap old option shares for newer, lower priced shares when the corporation's market performance was dismal.

How much is enough? In the last decade CEO pay in general has increased at a 12.2 percent compound annual rate, which is double the 6.1 percent rate for U.S. production workers. In 1988, the salary and bonus payments to CEOs in a survey of America's top 100 companies were up 14.4 percent over 1987—a rate triple that of inflation.[34] The really big gains have come from a rising tide of stock options, which netted 40 percent more than in 1987 for an average of $917,000 per corporate executive. The *Wall Street Journal,* describing this increase in stock options, points out that they tend to be used as rewards even when the company's stock does not do well. One example given was Archer-Daniels-Midland, which last year canceled options given to its executives at $23.875 per share and replaced them with an equal number at $19 per share. In this way, despite the poor performance of the companies they head up, corporate honchos are still protected in their profit-taking. They can cash in at any time and walk away with a tidy sum. So much for incentive!

Moreover, American corporate executives are greatly overpaid in comparison to CEOs outside of the United States.[35] For example, the CEO of a billion-dollar-a-year U.S. corporation receives an average $983,000 compared to the much more distant second place for French corporations of the same size ($577,000), followed by the Swiss ($468,000), West Germans ($403,000), British ($342,000), and Japanese ($330,000). Even when stock options are excluded from total compensation and only base pay and bonuses are used to make the comparison, since West Germany and Japan use them more sparingly, CEOs in these two countries still make only 65 percent of what American CEOs receive. Put simply, most European and Japanese managers believe that an organization suffers when the CEO receives an astronomical multiple of the average employee's pay. A European corporation's chief executive officer typically receives pay that is six to eight times that of an entry-level professional employee, whereas the ratio is 14 to 1 in the United States. An eloquent summary of these findings helps us take a step toward answering the question, "How much is enough?"

> Some would even say that CEO pay at its most stupendous is just wrong. Plato, apparently the world's first compensation consultant, suggested that the highest paid person in the community should earn no more than five times the lowest. Management writer Peter Drucker relates approvingly that J. P. Morgan raised that ratio to around twenty and maintained it in his enterprises. There is nothing scientific about those numbers, but they reflect a society's instinctive sense of fairness. . . . The CEO's fortunes should rise and fall with his company's. But at many corporations the board has adopted only half the principle. The CEO gets a terrific reward when the company does well . . . but he still gets a pretty good reward when it does badly.[36]

Finally, in case you have not yet concluded that there is never enough for the very rich in our society—whether they are the chief executives of America's largest corporations, scions of the country's wealthiest families, or major recipients of the great bulk of stock dividends parceled out every year—there is further disquieting news that "the rich get richer." The last available data from the U.S. Internal Revenue Service, which uses 1982 tax returns, reveals the country to have 410,000 millionaires.[37] This represents an increase from 180,000 only six years before, or a growth rate of 38 percent per year! In the same six-year period, the inflation rate came to about 9.4 percent—meaning that the number of millionaires was increasing at a rate four times that which would normally be expected.

The real issue is not whether income has become more unequally distributed within the United States, but rather just how bad the situation is. There are many who would argue that such a trend is both necessary and desirable for a society to develop economically (especially with reference to Third World countries), that the poor are always with us,[38] that the pace of change is glacial and consequently irrelevant, that the pattern will reverse itself when certain demographic trends play themselves out, and so on. All of these points will be addressed in subsequent sections and, in most cases, refuted. The economic news is exceedingly and undeniably bad, so it makes little sense to fiddle with rationalizations while Rome burns. Nonetheless, there may still be time to attempt to turn the decline around, before many of the tragic consequences described above come to pass. A framework to accomplish this will be offered in the concluding section.

It is also the intention of this book to describe income inequality between and among populations, rather than only address the trends revealing economic deterioration. It is a fact of life that if one area in the world or a given country is doing poorly, prosperity will also be found elsewhere. Different countries of the world will be compared on income inequality, as well as U.S. regions, states, and even counties. Looking at income inequality both geographically and descriptively will help in isolating common factors which tend to produce it or, conversely, to promote greater egalitarianism in the distribution of income. Before turning to these tasks, however, the next chapter will review some of the theories advanced to explain income inequality between and within societies. Such an exercise can provide a better perspective with which to understand the mass of studies dealing with income inequality. In our contemporary era of information overload, an adequate theoretical grounding can help us avoid overlooking the forest because of the trees.

2

THE BATTLEGROUND OF IDEOLOGY: THEORIES AND UNDERLYING VALUES SURROUNDING THE EXPLANATION OF INCOME INEQUALITY

This chapter looks at a variety of reasons why some groups receive more income than others. Why do some nations seem to be blessed with great affluence while others suffer under the curse of poverty and underdevelopment? There are many ideas which seek to account for the vast income difference, prevalent in the past and which are still with us today. Unfortunately, sharp disagreement between scholars is more often the rule than the exception. Many of these differences stem from competing values and beliefs. All involve attitudes about what is right and just in a society, and what is unfair and basically wrong with the system we live in.

Most theories eagerly claim to know the ultimate truth about how wealth is passed out. Thus, there is a very real danger when studying income inequality that ideological and political overtones will bias our view. Yet social reality is complex. This will guarantee that one theory alone will never have an absolute and final answer explaining why some are more equal than others. In truth, all theories do have some basic values which are often unexpressed. Such values greatly affect how we view inequality and the system that generates and maintains it. In essence, these ideas do carry with them implied assumptions about whether income inequality may be "good" or "bad." All theories can be said to have underlying value assumptions and ideological premises accepted as axioms of truth.

Because of this, certain theories regarding income inequality will be more easily accepted than others. This is especially likely when they are based upon beliefs which are dear to our country. The values and beliefs surrounding capitalism provide the starting foundation in the United States upon which inequality is viewed. One common American view is that poor people deserve their lowly place in our perfectly functioning, competitive market system. Those who suffer from low income are by definition somehow "not plugged into the system." This may be caused by a number of things: lack of education, outmoded job skills, low contacts, poor information about labor markets, personal laziness, moral depravity, and so forth.

In essence, relative failure to achieve a decent income within our society is seen as somehow due to personal failure. Few people believe that low income could be caused by environmental conditions. Recent research on attitudes of Americans about their economic position in life is eye-opening. There is a marked tendency to see lack of advancement and success as one's own fault.[1] It is assumed without question by most people that the United States is the land of opportunity where anyone can succeed by applying a little effort. The system or structure is seen as basically sound, so that personal shortcomings must be to blame for those classes of people who do not benefit from it. It is this type of social bias that we must guard against as we try to come to grips with income inequality.[2]

There are basically two major sides to the debate surrounding income inequality.[3] The *conservative* position holds that economic inequality is both necessary and functional. The *radical* view sees inequities as neither fair nor just. The two opposing views separate on a number of different points. Conservatives believe that the system of distribution we now have is just. The system rewards those who are most deserving (especially by individual effort and hard work), so that defending the status quo in society works to protect the interests of all.

Radicals view the existing distribution of wealth as unjust. The powerful simply expropriate more riches by means of force, coercion, inheritance, discriminatory tax laws, and other unfair methods. As part of this scheme, governments are said to work on behalf of the wealthy to maintain the interests of the rich over those of the common people. Thus, conflict within society is inevitable because of the unfair means of distribution. An exorbitant degree of inequality may in this way be damaging to the functioning of a nation and the well-being of its inhabitants.

Reality lies somewhere in between for most societies. Thus, it is probably more helpful to think of nations in positions along a continuum of income inequality. The specific causes of a country's stratification system will undoubtedly vary through time and by region. Income inequality may be due to coercion and traditional inertia. It may also stem from the operation of a competitive free market. More likely, inequality will result from a combination of both. There are elements of truth to both radical and conservative thought, as we shall discover as we go along. Analysis gets muddied too often by simply insisting that one model is correct while the other is false. Thus, Princeton University Professor Robert Gilpin simply labels theories of inequality as "ideologies." They form intellectual acts of faith that cannot be proved.[4] He believes such theories are based upon assumptions about people and society that cannot be put to a fair and impartial test.

Marx and Capitalism

Concern about ideological bias is very justified. Americans, as an example, can get hysterically anticommunist. There tends to be a total rejection of anything termed "Marxist" without any evaluation.[5] Much of this compulsive overreaction stems from both fear and ignorance. We have been in a cold war with Russia and other communist nations since 1947. Many in the United States may find it threatening that over one-third of the world's population are living under communist governments. This includes China, with over one billion people. Yet most Americans still have no idea what Marx had to say about inequality, economics, and the role of social classes in society.

Some would find it surprising, for instance, that Karl Marx admired a number of things about capitalism in modern nations. Marx wrote at the dawn of heavy industrialization in the mid-1800s. On the basis of Europe's experience, he concluded that capitalism was a truly dynamic, modernizing force. It would soon wipe out any older, rigid, and autocratic systems of inequality.[6] Capitalism meant doom for the nobility and aristocracy of feudal regimes. He regarded the technology of capitalism as far superior and efficient to the way work had been previously organized. Ironically, this would eventually lead to the downfall of capitalism.

At the base of Marxian thought is how people in a society organize their work. Early bands set up their means of production by hunting and gathering. There was fairly equal sharing within a communal arrangement. Systems of slavery were next, in which the means of production were determined by ownership of human beings. A feudal order came next. Here the means of production became centered around ownership of land by the nobility. Rent was paid by serfs returning a portion of their harvest to the aristocracy. Finally, the era of capitalism overthrew the old feudal arrangement. The new means of production has become primarily industrial, owned in the form of factories and capital by a small class of entrepreneurs called the bourgeoisie. For the most part, the rest of society forms the proletariat or working class who must sell their labor to the factory owners in order to survive.

A major component of Marxism is the idea of unequal exchange. Briefly, the exploitive nature of capitalism is obvious from the subsistence wages paid to workers, which are greatly below the value of the actual products they manufacture. The difference between the wage paid to labor for manufacturing the product and the much larger value of what it is actually worth is "surplus value" that is taken by the capitalist for profit. This profit is so excessive that it can only be spent by reinvestment in more industrial expansion. This is true especially in the purchase of capital goods such as factories and machines, which again add to the buildup of more profit at a later time. Thus, capitalism is by its very nature inherently expansionary. It produces a thirst for new markets and continuous investment in new industries. The wage earning class gets larger when previously undeveloped areas are industrialized.

Central to all societies—regardless of how each economy is organized—are two classes of people: the haves and the have-nots. Whether these be free man and slave, lord and serf, bourgeoisie and proletariat, etc.—they are always in the nature of oppressor and oppressed, and invariably in periodic conflict with one another. In essence, each historical era is marked by rather extreme inequality and thus carries within itself its own demise—in Marxian terms "the seeds of its own destruction." Feudalism gave birth to early capitalism. Basically, it arose by the forming of towns, trade, and craft production. The new business class soon successfully challenged the power and privileges of the landed nobility.

And so it is to be with the contemporary era of capitalism. It is the very efficiency and relentless, growing energy of the capitalist system that may breed its own downfall. Early capitalism was marked by fierce wars of survival between industrialists. Often this led to hostile takeovers, mergers, and business failures. The eventual outcome left a few big firms in control of most of the industry. It is under monopoly capitalism where the proletariat are gathered *en masse* to man the giant factories. As ownership becomes ever more concentrated in fewer hands, more and more people are forced into wage labor to survive. The remaining firms, engaged with each other in a death struggle for survival, cut all possible costs of production in their drive for greater profit. Wages paid to labor are slashed to bare subsistence as greater work demands and larger quotas are instituted. Incomes start to shrink. Workers begin to realize that they are oppressed. Since they work and live in the same place, organization for resistance is comparatively easy. Strikes and violence all become normal as open war against factory owners sets in. Such clashes grow more virulent and bloody until revolution takes place. At this point the proletariat forcibly takes over the means of production. A new socialist state is ushered in that ultimately will be replaced by the perfect communist society. Income will then be divided on this basis: "from each according to his ability, to each according to his need." In a word, those who have greater need for income will be given more from the state.

The end point is clearly utopian. Yet Marx has been unfairly criticized for predicting a perfectionist outcome. Actually, he had little to say

about ultimate communism, preferring to dwell upon the more pronounced traits of capitalism in his day. A more valid weak point is that
communist revolutions did not occur in modern states. The world instead witnessed agrarian and nonindustrial countries such as Russia,
China, Cuba, and Vietnam become communist. In advanced capitalist
countries, workers have been less militant and have been able to win
major concessions from giant corporations.[7] This took place while a
healthy middle-income sector arose. The predicted increases in poverty
simply failed to materialize. In fact, many were helped when deprivation
and want did arise. Welfare capitalism came about in an effort to provide
a safety net for the poor. This was something Marxists clearly believed
would never happen!

Another flaw of Marxism is its mono-determinism. It tends to see
everything in society as ultimately caused by the mode of production.
Marx believed the very ideas and ideology of capitalist society were
formed and controlled by the bourgeoisie. He included such areas as
intellectual theory, science, art, and even religion. His famous quote—
"Religion is the opiate of the masses"—essentially stems from this line
of reasoning. By this he meant that religious dogma supports values of
the upper class at the expense of the lower class. Poor laborers were
urged by the clergy to remain docile and obedient in order to reap true
riches in heaven.

For Marx, all aspects of society are reduced to the economic. He
virtually ignored the role and potential power of the state, which he saw
only as a pawn serving capitalist interests. Neo-Marxists today argue
that the state does have an independent power with some free rein apart
from the corporate class.[8] A major defect of Marxism is its failure to see
the role of political factors in international relations.[9] For example, national rivalries occur regardless of common economic systems. The hatred between Russia and China, between Vietnam and China, and between Vietnam and Kampuchea are prime examples.

A Capitalist Viewpoint: The Market Mechanism in Sociology

The role of values as an independent force in their own right is often said
to be neglected in Marxist theory. Max Weber was a contemporary
scholar to Marx. Weber is thus frequently touted as supplying a refutation to Marxian thought. Weber's "Protestant Ethic and the Spirit of
Capitalism" argued that the values within religion could change the way
the economy works.[10] For example, early Calvinists would look to material success and prosperity as a sign of grace from God. This would
subtly impel them toward more industriousness in a self-fulfilling prophecy. In actuality, however, Weber built very closely upon Marxian con-

cepts. This was very true in his definition of social class within "Class, Status, and Party." [11] Weber largely agreed with Marx that class is determined by the ownership of economic property. As such, class ultimately determines a person's life chances—including even health and longevity. But Weber added a component to the definition of class that is similar to today's description of a market system. Weber pointed out that a person could better his class position by taking advantage of opportunities for income—essentially the skill level a person has in his occupation. The implied idea is that a person could advance in social class by training for skilled, highly paid occupations.

Within sociology, the idea that a market economy is at the bottom of much of today's work world was carried to an extreme by Davis and Moore. [12] They believed that rewards (essentially income) for a given occupation were set by its functional importance. In other words, how does the job increase the survival and well-being of society? More important positions must carry with them higher rewards to induce the most talented persons in that society to train for such jobs and to perform adequately in them. In the end, inequality in rewards is positive, functional, and inevitable in any society.

This explanation of income inequality has been sharply criticized. The attack was very hostile with respect to the underlying market mechanism which is said to reward us on the basis of merit. A major question is: who determines what jobs are more important than others in a society? [13] On the surface, the answer seems very simple—work which pays more must be more important. A moment's reflection shows this to be circular thinking. In essence, if we argue that pay is dependent upon importance, then importance cannot be dependent upon pay! The theory is very conservative and status-quo oriented. It assumes that given income inequalities must be rational and deserved because those with top-paying jobs would not receive the salaries they get if they did not deserve them. Nothing is said about the role of power in perpetuating or increasing income inequality. For example, Kerbo believes

> the greater the rewards received by individuals or groups, the greater their ability to make sure they continue receiving such rewards, and even more rewards, no matter what function they serve for society. [14]

Carried to its logical extreme, the theory should lead to perfect equality in the distribution of wealth. [15] In a market economy, if labor is free to move to higher paying jobs, such occupations should attract a surplus of workers—leading to a decline of income for these jobs. Positions paying low salaries would also attract fewer workers, which should ultimately lead to higher wages to entice more people to enter them. Frankly, perfect mobility does not exist in society because many are barred from even starting the race to begin with. There are many curbs to the effort to build scarce skills. Serious gaps in educational quality and opportunity have been shown to exist. At the same time, mediocre offspring of wealthy families receive the best training that money can buy. Their connections for job and business networking become plus marks in the race for more pay. A review of eleven panel studies which looked at jobs and earnings of American men found the same thing: family background explains about half of the difference in men's work success.[16] The most important single predictor of a son's occupational status is his father's occupational status. Put in money terms, 57 percent of economic status is due to family background.[17] A man born into the top five percent of family income had a 63 percent chance of earning over $25,000 per year in 1976 (being in the top 17.8 percent of family income). But a man born into the bottom 10 percent of family income had only a 1.0 percent chance of attaining this level.

Lastly, even if one were to seriously accept the market explanation underlying functional theory, we are still left with the question: How much is enough? If, for example, we believe a medical doctor is actually functionally more important than a garbage collector, how much more should the doctor be paid? Ten times more? Twenty times more? Does a ratio of 20 to 1 mean that the doctor is twenty times more important than the garbage collector? One can see how easily this line of reasoning tends to end in subjective bias.

Capitalism Continued: The Market in Economics

A neoclassical economist will see the health of a free market as crucial.[18] Many western economists believe it is in the very nature of humans to be self-seeking, to barter, and to trade for goods and security. Such activity will lead to the natural evolution of a market which will set prices of goods by the laws of supply and demand. Individual consumers will respond to price changes, buying at the lowest price with all other things (e.g., quality) being equal. Firms must grow by greater innovation and more efficiency to remain viable. This drives the whole system ever upward to achieve greater and greater levels of wealth and productivity. Progress means increasing per capita wealth. The fact that some groups or persons will not benefit as much from a country's growth in affluence is seen as unfortunate but also unavoidable. In short, some persons will contribute more to the economic productivity of society than others. As a result, more productive people will be more amply rewarded. Only a few will risk more in the hope of getting an even larger amount of money.[19] Income inequality is thus seen as both rational and positive. It serves as a reward for those who contribute the most and as a way to urge others to try harder. The end result, in this view, can only be to advance the whole system as we all work to achieve higher productivity.

How do we achieve higher productivity? A basic part of classic economics is human capital.[20] The theory is that people will voluntarily defer income. They will invest in themselves by staying out of the labor market while going to school. The results work to enhance their skills and lifetime earning potential. Immediate sacrifices are made. Yet persons will see such costs balanced by greater pay in the long run. The model assumes perfect rationality and a good knowledge of the labor market. Equality of education and similar native talent are also basic assumptions of this model. Finally, money income is viewed as the main motivator pushing us into given jobs in an open, competitive labor market where wages are flexible.

Obviously, this scenario does not exist in reality. Just a decade ago the average pay of an American college professor was less than the average wage of a coal miner or an auto worker.[21] Perhaps some of this income rift can be explained by unions. Noneconomic rewards may also work to get people to take lower paying jobs. Yet such factors as intrinsic job interest or an opportunity to work for social justice cannot be safely used to prove the theory. To begin with, people will vary quite a bit in the value they attach to psychic rewards in lieu of pay. Taken to the extreme, as Osberg points out, this argument quickly becomes absurd:

> If one really believed in the theory of compensating differentials, one could, for example, argue that a Mississippi sharecropper with a money income of $8,000 and a New York office worker earning $35,000 are equally well off, since the sharecropper has nicer weather and lives in a more tightly knit community.[22]

Although noneconomic traits play some part in what line of work a person may enter, there is no proof that such psychic rewards cause income inequality. It is hard to actually test such values since they are so vague and amorphous by their very nature.[23] On a broader level, market theory errs in its basic assumption. There is some doubt about the idea that economically equal actors behave in a rational manner within a free and competitive exchange. We know that the exchange is seldom free or equal. Elements of coercion, vast power differences due to monopoly, and politics all get in the way to "rig the game" in advance.[24] A major fault stems from classical economists who fail to recognize that the economy functions within a very real social class system. The same criticism of being fixated on one major variable said to explain all things, leveled at Marxist theory, can be applied as well to market economics. Many contemporary economists behave as if everyone enters the starting block as equals in a fair game of competitive prowess. Unfair disparities caused by inheritance and favoritism toward the well off are too easily ignored. Generalized class bias promoting the interests of the wealthy seem not to exist. Capitalist economists simply fail to see the havoc caused by market forces. This is especially true of the grossly unequal distribution of wealth and income among societies. The unquestioned orientation of classical economics is geared toward maximizing profit for persons and firms, which is assumed to benefit everyone in the long run. The economic status quo becomes the conservative bedrock of market theory. Stability and equilibrium form the frame of its foundation.

Rather than having such absolute free choice with an equal starting point, it is more realistic to point out that people do make limited choices. Some options simply do not exist for certain segments of the population. In essence, unless we are lucky enough to come from a wealthy background, alternatives can be more restricted for us. Even for those with outstanding academic talent, an education at Harvard would be simply unavailable. Its average yearly cost of about $20,000 makes it impossible for poor and middle-class Americans to attend this university. The point is that we still have the choice to go to college, but the option of attending a higher quality Ivy League university is simply not there for most of us. It then follows that we alone cannot be completely responsible for our position on the income distribution. This is exactly the reverse of what market economics would have us believe.

As a case in point, one study estimates that over 80 percent of American workers are members of "internal labor markets."[25] This is a system where pay and assignment of workers is set by administrative rules and bureaucratic procedures. Wages are determined by custom and patterns which have spontaneously evolved from the past. Such pay scales have been gradually codified and set through labor/management agreements. Wide pay differences from one department to another may exist in jobs that have the same responsibility and work difficulty. The system may not be rational, but it is seen as fair and just by workers because this is the way it has always been.

Much of the skill within the internal labor market is gained by on-the-job training. One employee informally helps to train another. The knowledge upon which a person's income may be based is thus obtained in a work-setting group whose norms may operate outside of official company policy. In short, social skills and congeniality may determine much of our income over and above any formal educational preparation we went through to get the job in the first place! Lester Thurow believes that 60 percent of U.S. employees derive all their work skills on the job.[26]

The labor market which acts to set our income is really a market where supplies of trainable labor are matched with training opportunities. It is the job openings that exist rather than the formal training we undergo that determines our pay. The locus of this "choice" is firmly trapped by the decision of a given corporation to create openings or by a particular industry to expand. Once we are hired at the entry level, we must further pilot our way among the shoals of management and coworkers to ingratiate ourselves. Success will mean our coworkers' willingness to impart the informal skills leading to higher pay. A major point is that if you are outside the internal labor market, you are simply shut out!

We have been endlessly told that the best way to increase our earnings is through more formal education. But many doubts exist that raise questions about the effectiveness of this strategy. Some argue that the major function of education is to screen workers for future jobs.[27] In a society based upon credentials, having a master's degree is more important than having a bachelor's degree. This is quite apart from the actual skills needed on the job. Access to better jobs will be restricted to those with higher levels of education, even if more advanced education is not needed to perform the work. Thus, the norm for landing the really good jobs changes rapidly. Whereas a decade ago this may have meant earning a bachelor's degree in Business Administration, it now means a master's degree (M.B.A.). *Education then becomes a necessary but not a sufficient force in getting a better paying job.* The basic minimum to qualify for any decent job in today's society would be a baccalaureate degree, but achieving this level of education will not necessarily get you a nice job. Not having a college degree, on the other hand, is a guarantee of poor employment. If more education actually did produce greater real income, the explosion in college education since World War II should have reduced income differences. This it clearly has not done.[28] Although there is some room for debate, it seems that education has little or no impact upon earnings.[29] At best, the effect of education upon income is very different among business firms and industrial contexts. In the end, there is no guaranteed payoff.[30]

The Dual Economy thesis forms another attack which undermines the rational functioning of the market economy.[31] A great deal of American wage research is tainted by the individualistic bias within market theory. That is, a person's starting place within the system and eventual lifetime earnings are claimed to be a reflection of that worker's basic value to the system. From this perspective, income inequality due to earnings is caused by our personal attributes (or lack of them) such as education, achievement motivation, commitment to work, etc. Thus, variables used to explain income differences tend to focus upon characteristics of individuals such as work experience, amount of formal education, age, and the like.

A better explanation would focus upon industrial characteristics as they change workers' earnings. A core industrial sector of huge monopolistic firms which arose in the era of early capitalism is commonly described by Dual Economy supporters.[32] This is always compared to a periphery made up of smaller firms operating in an open, competitive environment. Bluestone provides an excellent summary of these basic differences:

> The core economy includes those industries that comprise the muscle of American economic and political power. . . . Entrenched in durable manufacturing, the construction trades, and to a lesser extent the extraction industries, the firms in the core economy are noted for high productivity, high profits, intensive utilization of capital, high incidence of monopoly elements, and a high degree of unionization. . . . The automobile, steel, rubber, aluminum, aerospace, and petroleum industries are ranking members of this part of the economy. Workers who are able to secure employment in these industries are, in most cases, assured of relatively high wages and better than average working conditions and fringe benefits. . . . Concentrated in agriculture, non-durable manufacturing, retail trade, and sub-professional services, the peripheral industries are noted for their small firm size, labor intensity, low profits, low productivity, intensive product market competition, lack of unionization, and low wages. Unlike core sector industries, the periphery lacks the assets, size, and political power to take advantage of economies of scale or to spend large sums on research and development.[33]

In the end, there are two American labor markets which are created by a sector's dominant technology. The primary labor market is made up of well paid jobs. These jobs carry reasonable security, good fringe benefits, and nice working conditions. Such work is typical of industries geared toward long, stable production runs. The secondary labor market is made up of subcontractors, service workers, secondary manufacturers, and suppliers. The welfare of these firms springs directly from the well being of the primary industries. Thus, such jobs are marginal and low paying. They tend to be unstable and haunted by poor working conditions. Many minorities—especially blacks, Hispanics, foreign born, and some women—tend to be thrown into this area. The job experience of the work force in this market is branded by low pay and poor prospects for advancement. Morale is low. Insecurity, absenteeism, and turnover are very high. Certain categories of workers find themselves trapped in

this job market for a variety of reasons. Its existence is guaranteed because of fixed conditions that must be met for capitalist economies to do
well. Overproduction, business slowdowns, seasonal shifts, and technological changes can lead to bouts of unemployment for those who hold
jobs here.[34]

Since the sector one works in has a large effect upon pay, differences
in the impact of personal traits such as education will also be present.
Core industries with minutely tuned wage scales will use education to
assign individuals to specific jobs that they are said to be "trained for."
In the peripheral sector, there is a smaller and simpler opportunity structure with fewer differences between jobs. Thus, individual traits such as
education, skill, motivation, and so forth will play a much smaller role
in earnings. The Dual Economy theory thus offers an alternative to the
individualistic bias present in the human capital/market explanation of
income inequality.

Analyzing data representative of the U.S. work force in 1975–76,
Beck and his colleagues found major differences between the two sectors,
especially with regard to pay. Core workers earned over $3,000 per year
more than periphery workers. Core workers also showed many more
gains: better education, more high status occupations, more full-time
work, and higher levels of workers in unions. Lastly, they were more
likely to be male and white—which explains some of the gap in earnings
with the periphery. The effect of these variables upon earnings is quite
important, so they were held constant through regression analysis. The
researchers were still able to conclude that workers in the periphery
would receive over $1,000 more per year compared to core workers. This
was apart from the effects of sex, age, race, education, and occupation.
Their study ends with a strong message to those seeking to explain income inequality using market level explanations:

> What does all this mean? It means that we should be very suspicious
> of any attempts to build models of occupational or earnings pro-
> cesses in industrial society which consist exclusively of individual
> level variables. Our analysis suggests that the rules which govern the
> distribution of socioeconomic benefits to individual workers are not
> uniform across all sectors of the economy. Analysts in the human
> capital and status attainment tradition have tended to interpret in-
> come and status differences as due to the application of a fixed set of
> rates-of-return to different mixes of individual background charac-
> teristics, skills, and experience. We have shown that these rates are
> not fixed, and that one important determinant of their variability is
> a distinction between core and periphery sectors derived from the
> theories of the structure of industrial capitalism. In our view these

findings constitute a challenge to models of the social and economic order which underlie the human capital and status attainment research traditions.[35]

Of Marx and Markets: The Dynamics of International Political Economy

Market explanations of how much income people receive in a society are not a result of the rational "choices" they might make to "earn" higher pay. The social structure we are born into and our family class position can give us a head start. The schools we attend and the values we learn from our parents, teachers, and friends affect our later pay packet. What part of the dual economy we may land in, plus aspects of the internal labor market (social factors on the job) work to set wages. Our sex, age, and race also enter into the equation of what income we will eventually receive. Despite what we have previously learned, there is one crucial point to remember. The idea that the system is basically fair and that we receive income in direct proportion to the real value of our labor is simply not true! This does not mean that self effort has nothing to do with the income we receive in life. As noted above, it is necessary to get a college degree in the right field to qualify for a decent job in today's labor market. There are some things we must do to remain generally competitive and in the running to quality for a middle-class income. Riches do not beckon to us all, however, if we somehow earn the right college degree from one of the more prestigious universities. It matters less what innate abilities we are lucky enough to have, such as high intelligence, or how hard we work on the job. What really matters is the social structure of the economy and labor market that we attempt to plug into.

Americans may have some trouble seeing the impact and great importance of structural variables. Our training from early childhood includes learning values which fit a competitive labor market system. We have come to believe that our personal economic well-being is due only to our own work and effort.[36] For example, a 1988 Gallup Poll found that an overwhelming majority of Americans (71 percent) rejected the idea that U.S. society is divided into two groups, the "Haves" and the "Have Nots." On the other hand, 73 percent in Great Britain believe that the United Kingdom is so divided![37] For those Americans not recognizing a class polarization, the largest group believes that it is "lack of effort that is more often to blame if a person is poor." Only one-third see poor circumstances as a cause of poverty and want.

One reason for the popularity of such beliefs is that there is little talk within schools or the media about how large-scale economic forces serve the interests of the wealthy. A more penetrating query would look at how multinational corporations are tied in with U.S. financial policy. Defense spending, initiatives (or their absence) in basic research and development, funds for education, and so forth cannot fail to have some effect on our personal financial situation. Many studies show a large and direct upper-class bias among top government officeholders.[38] Extravagant contributions to political action committees (PACs) have proven payoffs for wealthy individuals and corporations.[39] Economic elite dominance of semi-official policy research groups (Council on Foreign Relations, Trilateral Commission, Committee on Economic Development, to name a few) works to sway top federal decisions.[40] We have known for quite some time that intensive Congressional lobbying by big business can have repercussions for our economic and physical well-being.[41] The rear-guard actions fought against corporations to reduce physical pollution, to increase car safety, and to recognize hazards of smoking all serve as major examples.

What should be kept in mind is that there is little we can do on a personal level to increase the pay we earn. Perhaps we cannot even keep our current income from going down. The real power which skews the distribution of income stems from more macro-oriented variables. These can include major moves of multinational corporations, the political and economic drama between nations, changes in domestic labor and business laws, the level of defense spending, and so forth. It is this point that is the most damning flaw of market explanations for income growth and distribution.

The unproven assumption is also made by free-market advocates that increasing affluence in any nation will ultimately benefit all of its citizens. This is the bottom line behind the questionable idea of supply side "trickle-down." Reaganomics has now dominated American society for nearly a decade. After this experience, can we still really believe that "a rising tide lifts all boats"? Is it not by now obvious that there is a need for some democratic control over how any increase in wealth is to be more fairly divided? The dubious assumption is made too often that it is possible for the economic pie to keep growing without limit. It is too easily accepted that the American model of development can be repeated in other nations willing to make the necessary sacrifices to follow our lead.

It is certainly true that there is an inherent tendency for market-driven economies to expand rapidly. Marx wrote admiringly of the many ways in which capitalism tended to organize and improve industry. But it always ended up with periodic gluts of over-production, which then led to economic downturns. It was this very efficiency that led capitalist industries to expand in an insatiable search for new markets to sell their goods, which in turn led to greater profits for the owners. Again, in turn, this led such owners to invest in even more productive facilities. But Marx foresaw only collapse. In the long run, over-production would lead to a satiation of markets. Slack demand for goods, less need for manufacturing, a spurt in unemployment of workers, further poverty, and eventual violence would well up within a sinking economy.

A great defect of Marx was his focus only upon domestic economies, although to be fair this was the *modus operandi* of his day. What developed after his death was a profound globalization of world markets that had reached epic proportions by the start of World War I. By 1917 Lenin had published his first extension of Marx in *Imperialism*.[42] His book described a world economy led by giant industrial combines working closely with huge banking interests. In effect, Lenin's revision of Marx argues that industrial nations had escaped working-class revolutions and were able to enjoy a higher standard of living because of overseas imperialism. By seizing colonies, capitalist economies were able to get rid of extra goods manufactured at home. They could also import cheap raw materials for their own firms while investing any added profit in their various spheres of influence. In this stage of advanced capitalism, the world becomes one great battleground for markets, profit, and global dominance. Inequality between nations continues and may even get worse. But this is not only because of colonial exploitation. The advanced countries are also not equal in their ability to compete with one another. The international contest of wills arising among them breeds instability, political change, and war. Gilpin nicely summarizes the meaning of the new revisions:

> In Marx's critique of capitalism, the causes of its downfall were economic; capitalism would fail for economic reasons as the proletariat revolted against its impoverishment. . . . The actors in this drama (were) social classes. Lenin, however, substituted a political critique of capitalism in which the principal actors in effect became competing mercantilistic nation-states driven by economic necessity. Although international capitalism was economically successful, Lenin argued that it was politically unstable and constituted a war-system.
>
> In summary, Lenin argued that the inherent contradiction of capitalism is that it develops the world and plants the political seeds of its own destruction as it diffuses technology, industry, and military power. It creates foreign competitors with lower wages and standards of living who can outcompete the previously dominant economy on the battlefield of world markets. Intensification of economic and political competition between declining and rising capi-

talist powers leads to economic conflicts, imperial rivalries, and eventually war.[43]

Lenin can be criticized, of course, for being as deterministic as Marx. Lenin's rigid view allows no other scenario to result from the expansion of market forces other than cataclysm. But no matter how the revolutionary scene plays out, humans still stand accused of being inherently self-centered. They may continue to fight over scarce resources under communism as much as under any other system. From witnessing the horrors of Stalinism to those of the Khmer Rouge in Kampuchea, we hear a ring of truth to this point. It is also a fact that Lenin ignored the existence of state autonomy as much as Marx. It is possible that a government will pursue national goals that are not in the best interest of its top economic class. Nevertheless, many of the inherent tendencies that Marx and Lenin identified as typical of capitalist market economies are quite valid. There is an undeniable urge to expand through trade, export capital, investment, and technology in an effort to get more profit. It thus creates a true world economy. The outcome of this process has yet to be fully grasped. Its operation has spawned two contending perspectives of the world economy. Each claims to show a greater impact than the other on the level of personal income we receive.

Toward a World System: Development and Dependency Theories

A recent analysis has both similarities and differences with respect to ideas advanced by Marx and Lenin.[44] The Modern World System theory of Immanuel Wallerstein seeks to explain today's inequality by paying heed to the past.[45] The idea of an emerging global economy we now hear so much about is not new. Simply put, much as with the wrong belief that all persons start the race for income equally, the same is true of nations. Many countries start from a better position in a world economic hierarchy, which largely causes higher levels of income for its citizens. Those in poor countries are doomed to remain in poverty since they must compete with many initial disadvantages. One such drawback is a result of their nation's low rank within a global economic pecking order.

Wallerstein begins to build his theory by posing a distinction between a single "world economy" versus a "world empire." The single world economy forms a global division of labor made up of many nations with separate governments. The world empire is built upon a single, dominant state made up of many national economies which do not mesh very well with one another. In the past, much of the world has been organized from time to time under empires via military dominance (e.g., the Roman Empire). By the end of the sixteenth century, however, there had arisen in Europe a new type of commercial capitalism which was resistant to world empire. This newly emerging world economy was to have an even greater global impact than world empire.

Wallerstein describes a number of countries in northwestern Europe as a "core" to this world economy system. England and Holland came to dominate Latin America and Eastern Europe, which were said to occupy a "periphery." Midway between these two extremes are nations of the "semi-periphery" (Mediterranean Europe, including Spain and Portugal). Such nations are somewhat free and are not completely subjugated by the economic system. Nevertheless, they lack enough power to become truly influential on an international level. The basic pivot to this world economy is trade. The global market arises by exchanging manufactured goods from core countries with raw materials from periphery countries. The major division of labor is now seen from a world perspective and not as internal to a particular country. The gap between factory owners and wage laborers in Marxist thought is less important. The major actors on the world stage become nation states, although the ideas of surplus value and exploitation still operate. In the modern world there is now one mode of production which all nations engage in: production of goods for sale and profit on the world market. The basic underlying point is that a world market has emerged as an all powerful force. The system integrates all nations *economically* through global trade, production, and a new division of labor among nations.

As always, some nations are more equal than others. Powerful economic actors within each state, while pursuing profit in this single world market, seek to influence their governments to dominate and distort the market to their benefit. Business interests within core nations seek easy access to cheap raw materials from periphery countries. They also try to build a guaranteed market for their manufactured goods within the borders of these poor nations. The strong countries of the core joust with one another in colonization, in military sallies, in diplomacy, and in drawing up trade treaties. But none are influential enough in the end to completely dominate the world market.

Different areas of the world end up specializing in different economic roles for a variety of reasons. The world geographic division of labor is for the most part dependent upon resources. This is very true for the extraction of raw materials. The time that an area joined the world system also dictates relative power. Recent arrivals tend to be weaker and more easily exploited. The geographic division of labor has two consequences. First, rings form across nations among parties with the same economic interests. Economic elites often align with one another despite their national home base. Second, core economic elites try to influence and control what happens in other countries. A nation in the core has an advantage here since it generally has an advanced and highly productive home economy. A country in the periphery does have some modern attributes such as mines, ports, and plantations that specialize in raw material export. But a traditional sector of tribes and subsistence agriculture also exists along with the modern sector. A country in the periphery is export oriented because of core influence and demand. As a result, its own internal economy is poorly developed and dependent upon imports from core countries. Its government is consequently weak and is often subjected to great influence from the outside by core countries. Because of this outside force, local manufacturing is not allowed to develop. Core firms fear that the market for selling their manufactured goods would be lost if local businesses were allowed to develop. In Wallerstein's view, the march toward the creation of a total world economy made up of all nations on earth is unavoidable.

The Modern World System theory has been further refined by Chase-Dunn and Rubinson to include these elements:

1. Unequal exchange is a permanent feature of the system. The basic rank of nations within the core, periphery, and semi-periphery will remain the same despite any other type of change. Shifts in trade goods, manufacturing, newly discovered resources, and advances in technology have no effect on this world hierarchy. Productivity always remains high within core nations. More capital ends up flowing into them because of unfair trade advantages. Goods bought from periphery nations never make up for the unequal inflow. A core country has highly advanced plants, machines, and plenty of money to invest to ensure greater profit. Its human capital in the form of a well educated and skilled labor force is also very high. Although productivity and wages may go up in the periphery, they will also do so in the core as well. The core is simply able to drain more money from peripheral lands because core nations are powerful enough to control world prices for goods peripheral countries export. Hence, there are higher rates of exploitation and lower rates of capital buildup in the periphery.

2. While there are many political nations in the system, there is only one world market. The states vary in terms of power, and they tend to both compete and make deals with one another based upon their economic self-interest.

3. There are different forms of production relationships, with free-wage labor in the core and different types of coercion or forced labor in the periphery. Governments often work to prevent unions from forming in less developed countries. Their goal is to keep the average wage quite low at the urging of core countries.

4. Although inequality in power between core and periphery tends to remain constant, its form will shift through time. From the end of World War II to about 1970, the structure of political control was more relaxed because all economies were growing. Dominance was set in motion more along the lines of economic multinational corporate influence. In times of economic contraction, such as today, attempts to influence the periphery are less subtle and much more direct. Fear engendered by saber-rattling and military force are time-honored traditions. Economic brow-beating is an old standby. Clandestine paramilitary ventures and secretly organized coups have unfortunately become too common. All such indirect sanctions brought to bear against periphery nations are meant to keep them within the system and in their "proper" place. Above all, core nations are fans of "free trade" since they have the competitive advantage and power to set world prices in their favor.

5. A single top power can emerge among the core nations. This country may occupy a central position within the world economy for a time. The example of the United States after World War II is a case in point. At that time, America had the only intact economy left over from the devastation of war. There is also a tendency for other core nations to emerge and overtake the head power (Japan). Much of this is caused by the huge overhead the hegemonic power must spend to keep world stability through military and political means. This erodes its own ability to continue investing in itself in order to stay competitive through advancing technology. Competition eventually gets worse between core countries as the lead power fades. Military conflict and trade wars usually result until another strong power emerges to keep the economic peace.

6. The world economy is prone to periods of expansion and contraction. The long-term trend, however, is one of continued growth. Rarely does a downturn go back to an earlier low point in these economic waves. During such skids, military conflict and trade wars again tend to prevail.

7. The system results in greater riches for all participants. This does not mean that all benefit equally, as will be seen in the next chapter. There are some who argue that periphery countries would be better off without being part of the world system. Core nations tend to become more wealthy. Another trend toward massing of capital in huge banks or corporations also develops, which feeds more expansion of business firms.

8. The number of nations participating in the world system tends to grow. Much of this is a result of the decolonization of previously subjugated countries. A growth in core dominance of newly freed countries results from investment loans and the location of branch plants in foreign lands.

9. The tendency for the system to expand is now over. As the entire globe is now "spoken for," competition between core countries for dominance of the periphery has increased.[46]

Although there are similarities to some Marxian ideas, the modern World System theory is different—especially with regard to the dynamics of social class. For example, social classes cut across national boundaries in a system very different from that envisioned by Marx. In the not-too-distant past, core economic elites would often enter into quiet agreements with core labor interests. The two groups worked with economic elites in peripheral countries to exploit the labor and resources of peripheral countries. It is this unholy alliance that has prevented the "international proletarization of the working class." Marx had predicted a growth in working-class consciousness that was to develop on a worldwide basis. The past collusion of core labor with economic elites acted to defy this notion.

It is with semi-periphery countries of the system that some hope remains for independent economic growth and development. It is within these nations that there is a mix of core and periphery activities. Due to such advantages as natural resources and internal markets, a chance does exist for these countries to grow freely:

> Because of the mix of core and periphery activities, dominant classes tend to have very opposing interests. . . . Thus it is often the case that the state apparatus itself becomes the dominant element in forming the power block that is able to shape the political coalitions among economic groups. . . . This may take either a leftist or a rightist political form. Those upwardly mobile countries that rely on alliances with core powers tend to develop rightist political regimes (e.g., Brazil since 1964) while those that attempt autonomous development move toward the left (e.g., China and the Soviet Union). Whether leftist or rightist, upwardly mobile semi-peripheral countries tend to employ more state-directed and state-mobilized development policies than do core countries. . . . Anti-imperialist movements may take state power and try to mobilize for development (e.g. Angola, Cuba, Vietnam, Mozambique, Cambodia, etc.), but the development of core-type activities requires resources that small periphery countries most often do not have. Internal market size, natural resources, and sufficient political will to isolate the country from core powers are necessary if such anti-imperialist mobilization is not to become either an isolationist backwater or a CIA countercoup. Those areas that escape the system but do not economically develop are soon reconquered (e.g., Haiti, Ghana, Chile).[47]

Only within the semi-periphery is it possible to avoid the collusion that occurs across nations between economic elites within core and periphery countries—and then not always. A national consensus that is strongly opposed to core domination can develop. Such a fear can breed an alliance between domestic capitalists and labor in semi-periphery countries. This partially explains why many socialist movements have come to power in Russia and China rather than in the periphery, where conditions for workers and peasants are actually worse. In the end, however, it is the very isolation of such leftist movements within the semi-periphery that works to stabilize the exploitation of the periphery by the core. According to Wallerstein, the contamination is then quarantined to an area where it can do no harm while still keeping in place the overall status quo of world economic inequality.[48] In this way, periphery countries remain rigidly locked up within a system of subordination and subservience.

A drawback to the modern World System theory has been its vagueness as to which nation belongs to what category. Snyder and Kick examined 118 countries to divide them into core, periphery, and semi-periphery status.[49] In doing so, four types of international networks were looked at: (1) the net value of trade between countries (exports minus imports); (2) military interventions into other countries; (3) diplomats posted within other countries; (4) joining international treaties. The authors believe their method has tapped the power dimension within World System theory:

> Theories of imperialism typically emphasize the domination of the world economy by core powers . . . and the use of threat of superior armed forces as the means of ensuring economic domination. We also consider that diplomatic exchanges constitute a salient form of information flow in the world system. For sending nations, diplomatic missions provide regular and ostensibly reliable information concerning local economic opportunities, political conditions, etc. in the host country. Such missions may also facilitate trade agreements and sometimes serve as a base for attempts to manipulate local conditions. . . . Finally, we included the treaty data on the rationale that they would address networks of defense commitments or reflect attempts by some nations (e.g., core powers) to legitimate potential military intervention in others (peripheral countries).[50]

It is important to note that locating a nation within the three-tier ranking of the modern World System is not only done by use of economic terms. Of the four criteria used by Snyder and Kick, only the information on superior trade advantage could be called economic. The

other three networks have less direct financial results. This distinction
will have some bearing when developmental models of income inequality are discussed below. Snyder and Kick did go on to measure the impact
of World System position on subsequent economic growth for the 118
countries. They looked at change in Gross National Product per capita
(GNP) from 1955 to 1970. Strong support for modern World System
theory was evident from their results. In essence, they report the "cost"
of location in a peripheral or semi-peripheral nation is roughly $500 per
capita over this fifteen-year period. A full *forty-two countries had a per capita
GNP of less than this amount* in 1986![51] Core countries always experienced
greater economic growth, and at a faster pace, than peripheral or semi-
peripheral countries.[52]

More recent research by Kenneth Bollen also indicates that the position a country occupies within the World System theory is predictive
of whether democratic institutions will flourish or not.[53] This finding
stayed the same whether a nation was affluent or poor. But affluence was
important in encouraging democracy in and of itself. Taken in conjunction with Snyder and Kick's findings, what this means is that peripheral
and semi-peripheral countries are less democratic than core nations.
They are also poorer, but they will not develop economically as fast as
core countries because of their World System position. Since they are less
well off, they will also be less democratic. Yet since they are less democratic, there will be less encouragement of economic development. In
essence, peripheral countries are truly locked into a Catch-22 situation.
They seem doomed to endless subservience, political tyranny, and a
swamp of economic backwater.

Bollen also looked more in depth at nations out of the norm. He
concluded that Snyder and Kick's original list of nations contained six
misclassifications. Bollen's new ranking is the most recent and has been
widely accepted within sociology as the most accurate (see table 2.1).
Unfortunately, it continues to be based upon information originating as
far back as 1965. World System theorists would argue that this really
does not matter, since change occurs very slowly within the system—if
at all. This point is basically an assumption, however, that must be
proven. Chase-Dunn will publish a new book very soon that may revise
the dated typology.[54] He has promised to discuss in this new work the
latest studies done in the area, which will hopefully spur a number of
new research initiatives.

A glance at table 2.1 shows the complete dominance of European
countries together with the United States and Canada in the lineup of
core countries. Japan is the only Asian core country, while Yugoslavia is
the only country from the Eastern European or communist world. Such
a situation has resulted in the criticism that the theory is ethnocentric,

being ultimately Euro-centered. It is hard to agree that any bias stems merely from Anglo scholars with a narrow focus based only upon their own experiences. Ranks were drawn up by using a number of objective dimensions of power. More recently, the end product of world economic inequality is increasingly being posed as a North-South question. Such a polarity takes note of the immense power these core countries have within the system.[55]

Scholars of what has become known as the Dependency school of-

TABLE 2.1   Position of Countries into Core, Semi-Periphery, and Periphery Within Modern World Systems Theory: 1965

Core	Semi-Periphery	Periphery	
Australia	Argentina	Afghanistan	Laos
Austria	Bulgaria	Albania	Liberia
Belgium	Burma	Algeria	Libya
Canada	Cuba	Benin	Madagascar
Denmark	Cyprus	Bolivia	Mali
France	East Germany	Brazil	Malta
Greece	Finland	Burkina Faso	Mauritania
Italy	Hungary	Burundi	Mexico
Japan	India	Cameroon	Mongolia
Luxembourg	Iran	Central African Rep.	Morocco
Netherlands	Ireland	Chad	Nepal
Norway	Israel	Chile	New Zealand
Sweden	Jordan	China	Nicaragua
Switzerland	Kenya	Colombia	Niger
United Kingdom	Lebanon	Congo	Nigeria
United States	Malaysia	Costa Rica	Panama
West Germany	Pakistan	Czechoslovakia	Paraguay
Yugoslavia	Peru	Dominican Republic	Poland
	Philippines	Ecuador	Rwanda
	Portugal	Egypt	Saudi Arabia
	Rumania	El Salvador	Senegal
	South Africa	Ethiopia	Sierra Leone
	South Korea	Gabon	Somalia
	Spain	Ghana	Sudan
	Sri Lanka	Guatemala	Syria
	Turkey	Guinea	Taiwan
	Uruguay	Haiti	Thailand
	U.S.S.R.	Honduras	Togo
	Venezuela	Iceland	Trinidad and
		Indonesia	Tobago
		Iraq	Tunisia
		Ivory Coast	Uganda
		Jamaica	Vietnam
		Kampuchea	Yemen
		Kuwait	Zaire

fer a view of this structure from the eyes of intellectuals within the periphery (most of whom are Latin Americans). Dependency theory actually developed before modern World System theory was created, but it does fit quite nicely within the World System framework. A Brazilian economist named Dos Santos is the best known advocate of this approach.[56] He points out that the world is in its third period of dependency today (the prior two being colonialism and imperialism). Today's world has seen money spent by multinational corporations in areas which cater to the internal markets of less-developed countries (LDCs). Simply put, the possibility for economic growth in an underdeveloped country depends on having the money to buy machinery and raw materials not available within that nation. Yet the foreign dollars needed for industrial growth must come from exports of raw materials. This in turn increases the power of elites who have long been in control of these businesses. Such elites have no interest in seeing local industry increased. They may perhaps even see such development as a threat to their continued influence. It is also true that in many countries these very export businesses are themselves owned and controlled by foreign capital, so that high profits return to the home bases of multinational firms. Trade relations take place in a highly monopolized international market anyway, tending to lower the price of exported raw materials. In such a system, advanced industrial countries can simply raise the prices of industrial products to ensure greater profits. A chronic budget deficit with which to finance development results. This occurs because so much capital is drained off from poor countries by multinationals. These countries are thus forced into repeated borrowing from core nations in order to continue economic expansion:

> Foreign capital and foreign "aid" thus fill up the holes that they themselves created. The real value of this aid, however, is doubtful. . . . The gravity of the situation becomes even clearer if we consider that these credits are used in large part to finance North American investments, to subsidize foreign imports which compete with national products, to introduce technology not adapted to the needs of underdeveloped countries, and to invest in low-priority sectors of the national economies. The hard truth is that the underdeveloped countries have to pay for all the "aid" they receive.[57]

The net effect when foreign capital penetrates an underdeveloped country is to freeze it at the existing level. More gains become impossible. All benefits now go to foreign firms who get red carpet treatment from governments who wish to persuade them to make new investments. Dos Santos calculates that for each dollar entering Latin America as investment, $2.70 leaves in the form of loan repayments, interest charges, profit to corporations, and the like.[58] Not only does growth stagnate, conditions may actually *worsen!* Politics and the day-to-day running of government come under the thumb of multinationals. Income inequality increases between the ever richer political, military, and industrial elites and the mass of workers. Real wages are lowered through intimidation of unions, which in turn limits labor's purchasing power. This acts to retard the development of an internal consumer market which could spawn new businesses. Job creation is further reduced by bringing in high-tech production techniques with less labor demand. Most importantly, however, the profits which return abroad to core firms also carry away much of the economic surplus that the country could use to invest in itself. The unavoidable result is backwardness, misery, and social marginality wherever dependent capitalism is introduced. It rewards only a narrow segment of society while stopping true economic growth. The never-ending pile-up of trade deficits in turn generates greater exploitation through more loan and investment dependence.

A number of criticisms have been leveled at World System and/or Dependency theories. A weakness to these ideas is their lack of logically related points that researchers can test.[59] When conflicting results appear in dependency studies, supporters tend to quickly fall back on rhetoric to explain away the findings that do not fit. The study of dependency between nations tends to be haunted by ideological bias.[60] To be fair, however, such a criticism can also be applied to Development theory (discussed below). No theory is ever completely removed from ideological bias, even if it claims to be free of such values.

World System theory tends to ignore internal forces acting within a country that could lower income inequality. Nationalist movements and political conflict are of this ilk. The facts of history upon which the World System was built are open to challenge as well.[61] The theory cannot explain the "success cases" within the periphery as some of these countries (Taiwan, South Korea) have gone into economic hyperdrive within the last decade or two.[62] New forces such as strong and free state governments have risen in the periphery, which allow national growth to be started and kept going on its own.[63] It is also claimed that certain parts of capitalism are progressive, which may at the least make economic growth possible in LDCs.[64] Lastly, the theory is also accused of trying to explain three different outcomes (underdevelopment, marginalization, and dependent development) by using the same independent variable (the nature and shape of the world economy).[65]

Capitalism in Retreat: World Markets and
Development Theory

The flip side to World System/Dependency theories is a clear, no-nonsense form of market capitalism. Development theory claims that only good things will result for nations as a global free market economy comes to predominate within our world. The market is seen as supplying a tireless engine for economic growth to Third World countries. Enthusiastic fans of international capitalism make no apologies for its pervasive effect and influence upon poor countries. They particularly see its long-range impact as leading to real income growth for the people within these countries.

It is surprising, therefore, that there is no single comprehensive theory of the effects of development upon income distribution.[66] A major area of consensus, however, does exist. All seem to agree about the need to remove political and governmental roadblocks to the operation of free markets. In a sense, this is the bottom line to Development theory which gets universal support. The major assumption is that an interdependent world economy based upon free trade, export specialization, and an international division of labor will produce economic growth within nations. Developed nations invest money, knowledge, and business skills in LDCs. They help LDCs establish industries that are suited to their particular natural resources. Trade will then order itself in a natural way so that goods, capital, and technology flow in the most efficient manner possible.

If a country fails to develop, the fault does not lie with the operation of the international market system. Frequently the blame can be laid at the feet of poor national leadership, obstacles due to traditional culture, a poor rate of domestic savings, etc. In a word, the ultimate task of economic development must rest with each nation alone. It is precisely those nations which have followed marketing prescriptions most aggressively that have benefited the most (Hong Kong, Singapore, Taiwan, South Korea). For the earth's economic basket-cases, the real reason for continued poverty is lack of integration into the world market. Nations unfortunate enough to be poor year after year tend to rely upon irrational state policies which impede functioning of the free market. In this view, the poor are poor because they are inefficient—not because they are being bullied by core countries. The similarity to Functional theory at this point is stunning. Both views conservatively assume it is the fault of economic actors—whether individuals or nations—that is the cause for poverty. It is not due to the way the system works, which is seen as basically just and fair.

A high per capita Gross National Product is always seen as the mark of success in the Development model. Many areas of the periphery have witnessed their per capita GNPs rise at historically high rates since World War II[67] and even during the past century.[68] Many studies conclude, however, that the chasm in per capita income between poor and rich countries is actually growing wider in real dollars. In the twenty-five years from 1950 to 1975, for example, the absolute GNP income gap *doubled* between LDCs and developed countries (including the "miracle economies" of Taiwan and South Korea). Assuming that these rates continue, the great majority of developing countries will never catch up to the developed countries. It is possible, however, for sixteen LDCs to close the gap within one thousand years.[69] It would take China, with one-fifth of the world's population, over 2,900 years to close the gap! In terms of relative wealth, the total income of the world's poor countries declined from 4.3 percent of what was made by industrialized countries in 1950 to a mere 2.5 percent in 1980.[70]

Development theorists argue, however, that economic growth must by its very nature be unequal since it does not start in every part of the economy at the same time. Economies grow by using more and better technology. But only a limited number of people can be transferred from the older techniques of subsistence agriculture to newer industrial modes at one time. The remainder must wait their turn. While they do so, they are likely to fall behind.[71] Simon Kuznets has explained the reasoning behind the apparent contradiction of economic growth in a nation and increasing income inequality. He states that as economies mature in LDCs, factors come into play such as rapid population growth, more industry, and a surge of people moving to cities.[72] These forces at first act to lessen the well-being of lower income groups and to raise general income inequality. As development later gets going at a faster pace, social and political factors emerge to improve the poorer sector of the economy. These can include unions, populist political parties, or even a new savvy about urban living gained through experience. The upper income group at the same time now experiences less spectacular growth than under early industrialization. Hence, after a certain threshold is reached, income inequality begins to decline once again. This formula has been called the inverted-U hypothesis. The importance of Kuznets's hypothesis cannot be overestimated. It has been at the center of nearly all research and discussion of economic development that was to follow.

Development scholars go so far as to argue that this initial surge in the share of income going to an upper industrializing elite is desirable. Since this group saves more, it will also invest more.[73] Thus, the entire population will benefit from subsequent economic growth. That this is a twin of supply-side Reaganomic conservative arguments is quite obvious. Within the United States, it has been claimed that allowing the rich to receive more income via lower taxes with less governmental interference will lead to increased investment and economic growth. Development theory also states that growing nations must first go through a stage of more income inequality at the outset before things improve for everyone.[74]

The politics within which economic growth takes place is all but neglected in this theory. Influential domestic and international elites form the financial status quo. Since their power is unchallenged, such interests can set the rules of the game which form the stairway to economic success.[75] Development theory has been seen as ethnocentric and biased in favor of a particular economic path (market-driven capitalism). It is biased in its Western assumption that democracy is needed for growth to occur. The belief in never-ending progress which can occur only through clear historical stages is both dogmatic and naive.[76] The assumption that it is necessary for poor countries to pass through a long transitional period of worsening inequality is open to question. The belief that economic growth will inevitably lead to greater income and less inequality continues to be seriously debated. One particularly eloquent critic points out that

> Economic growth, in itself, does not guarantee that the masses of people will benefit from the growth, still less that they will benefit equally. . . . There has, indeed, been considerable economic growth in recent decades. Gross global product increased from $1 trillion in the late 1940s to more than $6 trillion in 1975, and to more than $9 trillion in 1978. Most of the newly created wealth, however, continues to be appropriated by the wealthy classes in capitalist countries. At the other end of the pole, in the classes which produce that wealth, particularly those in nations of the periphery, abject poverty, starvation, disease, and illiteracy abound and even increase. In just one of the decades (1963–73) of rapid economic growth, the number of "seriously poor" people in the capitalist periphery is estimated to have increased by 119 million people to a total of 1.21 billion seriously poor people. . . . This represents fully 45 percent of the population of the entire capitalist world in 1973. And even in the wealthy core countries . . . there still remain vast inequalities of wealth and power, hard core poverty sectors and marginalized populations.[77]

Development theory tends to downplay or completely ignore adverse reactions such as the above. Other negative results are the rise of cutthroat business practices, the destruction of older trades, and geographical polarization. A speed-up in population growth caused by a lower death rate can also increase the drain on resources.[78] There is more and more evidence to show that the conversion of agriculture from subsistence farming to export-driven agribusiness results in pauperization. A decline in living standards and outright starvation occur within many Third World countries following this path.[79] Indeed, the very nature and intent of development "aid" has been seriously challenged as too inadequate. Aid is often disguised militarism. It has provided the means and motive for LDC dictators to remain in power to do the bidding of core elites.[80] The end result is a system of very shaky loans to LDCs for projects of dubious purpose. Unneeded dams and nuclear reactors always seem to top the Third World wish list of grandiose projects. Many experts believe these loans will never be fully paid back.[81] Even interest payments due on these huge debts cannot be paid by some periphery nations, forcing them to borrow more from the International Monetary Fund (IMF) to service their debts.

The price for this gracious gesture on the part of core countries is the introduction of austerity programs into recalcitrant nations. "Remedies" are cuts in the value of their currencies and a drastic rollback in government funds. The axe tends to fall very hard especially where money is spent on social programs. Yet slashes in the military budget are never made. Higher taxes, caps on wages for labor, and selling off government operations to private businesses fill out this bleak portrait of want.

Despite such brutal austerity, *development has simply not been working for LDCs.*[82] For Latin American countries, as an example, new capital inflow (aid and investment) was $38 billion in the 1982–1985 period. But during the same time the area paid back $144 billion in debt service to core countries. In April of 1987 the General Agreement on Tariffs and Trade (GATT) released figures showing the share of world trade for LDCs had declined from 28 percent in 1980 to 19 percent by 1986. Developed countries increased their share of world trade from 63 percent to 70 percent in the same period. Put differently, in 1980 developed countries bought 29 percent of their imports from LDCs and 66 percent from each other. By 1986 they bought only 19 percent of their imports from these poor countries but 77 percent from each other.[83]

The crucial question that is never asked is what kind of development are we about? Development for whom, and with what kind of consequences? The most desirable outcome is always seen as growth in Gross National Product (GNP) per capita, but what does this actually mean? George sees a great many drawbacks to this model:

Industrialization is frequently its centerpiece, sometimes export agriculture relying on industrial inputs. The rich countries of the
North nearly always built up their own industries on a strong agricultural base; the model conveniently forgets this and favors instant
industrialization over food security. . . . The model is costly. It neglects resources that the local environment could provide and the
skills that local people could supply, counting rather on imports, at
escalating prices. It neglects not only peasants but anyone who does
not belong to a thin layer at the top of society, identified as the
"modernizing" elements. . . . The model is outward looking. It
never seeks to enhance the specific, generic, original features of "undeveloped" countries and their peoples, treating them rather as if
they were a kind of undifferentiated clay to be moulded to the standard requirements of the world market and of world capital, to the
uniform tastes of international bureaucrats and national ones trained
in their image. Hunger is one result. People who . . . cannot become
consumers in the global food system will not get enough to eat.
Militarization is another. Masses of miserable people with little to
lose are prone to revolt. Armed forces (including the police) in third
world countries are used as often internally as against outsiders.
Debt is a further outcome of the mal-development model. Elites
borrowed to put it into practice and now expect their poorer com-
patriots to bail them out.[84]

Ultimately, it can be seen that growth in GNP per capita is too
narrow and rigid a measure of economic development. While there may
be growth, it is questionable whether there are any beneficial consequences for the masses in Third World countries. Reviews of studies on
the way development works has found that any benefits to growth that
may occur have been unevenly parceled out. Development has simply
failed to raise the low income which the bulk of Third World inhabitants
suffer from.[85] In essence, this brings us back to our major concern about
income inequality. The alleged "economic development" or growth that
is said to have occurred can obscure the real issue: How fairly is the pie
divided? As we shall see in the next chapter, differences between countries are monumental. Given the fact that income inequality is so widespread in our world, is it possible to cut the pie any differently?

In the end, we are still left with the age-old question of who is
essentially correct in the description of income inequality. All of the
theories described have a semblance of validity to them—being composed of both strong and weak points. And as any wise person knows,
no one has a complete corner on the truth. A number of studies will be
looked at in the next few chapters about the validity of World System
and Dependency theories versus Development ideas. But controversy
rages here as well. Criticisms over the nature of the data, methodological

bias, misspecification of concepts, and fuzzy hypotheses abound. In the end, there are no easy answers.

There is widespread agreement today regarding the use of the core/periphery/semi-periphery division proposed by World System theory. Beyond this, consensus rapidly breaks down. It seems that economists largely tend to opt for the Development perspective, probably because they take as their starting point the existence of a functioning, free market system. My discipline of sociology nearly always looks at the types of inequality found within and among societies. Power and position become major causal variables determining who gets how much of what. These are the lenses to my theoretical glasses. It is a focus which leads me to see World System theory as yielding a more valid picture of contemporary American economic life and the global division of labor. Hopefully, the studies to be discussed plus analysis of my own data will convince you that this image of America and the world is more accurate than market forces.

Lastly, I must admit to a strong reaction to one important plank of Development theory—the axiom that income inequality must get even worse before it gets better. Although some data indicates a link between growth of income and a reduction in income inequality, the evidence has not been taken at different points in time. In short, we are asked to accept on blind faith that currently developing nations which show greater income inequality today will have less of it in the future. This is mainly based on evidence which states that such a process has already happened for advanced industrial nations. Whether this has actually been the case or not is another question. At least one researcher has found no change in the rate of income inequality in the state of Wisconsin over the past one hundred years.[86] But even if this were true, World System theorists would be correct to argue that today's core nations were able to develop their economic lead in a bygone age with much less challenge from other countries. This was at a time when the earth was not so finite, when frontiers beckoned, lands were open to exploration and settlement, entirely new trade routes were established, and so forth. The peripheral nations of today live in a much more constrained world than that of the United States two hundred years ago. Presently, possibilities are much more limited. The leg irons to free choice have become more the rule than the exception.

The idea that periphery countries must experience more inequality before true economic development can take place is belied by at least one example, that of modern-day Taiwan. After World War II this country began its long economic ascendancy from a base of tremendous inequality. But as general affluence went up—income inequality steadily went down.[87] Even if Taiwan or a few other nations similar to it are dismissed as mere anomalies, the idea that LDCs must somehow "bite the bullet" of growing income inequality is highly suspect. No one ever talks about how much inequality there needs to be, nor for how long. Ultimately, we get back to the same question raised in Chapter 1: "How much is enough?" At what level are pain and suffering, starvation and unmet basic human needs permissible in a world with a few affluent nations but where the majority of humans experience true want? In the end, the Kuznets hypothesis and Development theory reflect a conservative justification and rationalization of the global income inequality status quo. The implication of the theory is self-serving for the rich, while it carries a perennial message to the poor. You too—they seem to say—can be as wealthy as we are if you only grit your teeth, sacrifice, save your pennies, and work hard for us at subsistence wages. In the meantime, the rich core countries reap profits from the "sweat off the brows" of poor countries. LDCs are told that if they only keep their nose to the grindstone— some financial nirvana will await them in a vague and distant future.

The conservative bias within Development theory is the same as the right-wing bias within functional, human capital, and supply-side economic arguments. All of these explanations essentially accuse those actors who do not do well of ineptitude. The operation of the system they "compete" in is seen as fair and without many problems. The "rational" marketplace is claimed to be an impartial arbiter which rewards those who prove to be the most talented and/or hardworking. All the while, the weak and incompetent are also being "weeded out" through the inexorable force of competition. None of the theories give serious attention to a fact of life we all know to exist from common, everyday experience: those who have, get. It is a wealthy and privileged economic elite which gets special treatment, benefits, and help. Favoritism also allows them to perpetuate and enhance their high position. This is true whether the economic actor is a rich person or a wealthy social class within a given nation. It is also the case for core countries within the Modern World System.

The end result is that system variables are the most important forces which shape income inequality. Income does not grow because individualistic efforts of improvement are made by a factory worker here or an impoverished Third World country there. This is not to say that we are completely powerless as individuals. Joining together for collective action still remains a personal choice. Nor can we afford to be complacent about honing skills along human capital lines as lone job seekers. Moreover, nations who completely ignore market forces do so at great peril. But these realities should not fog the tremendous unfairness built into the system at the start. The society we are in acts to reward those with an initial power advantage in much greater proportion than the unfortunates who are poor and downtrodden to begin with. It is this reality that is often glossed over, ignored, or forgotten within American society when opposing ideas about income inequality are looked at. Yet system bias is the driving force behind the allocation of either riches or rags to all participants within our domestic and global economies.

3

ECONOMIC INEQUALITY AROUND THE WORLD

The overall degree of global income inequality is extremely lopsided. The top 1.0 percent of income recipients in the world receives about 15 percent of worldwide income, while the top 5 percent of recipients gets 40 percent of all income. At the other extreme, the poorest 20 percent of the world's population gets only 1.0 percent of global income![1] Given this incredible degree of inequality as a starting point, fierce debate exists on whether today's poor nations can ever have any real economic growth. Yet there is almost complete agreement that income differences between countries are currently way too high. Nearly all those who review the international financial scene call for an end to the gross inequities in wealth that are now frozen among the nations of the world. The answers needed to fix such an unfair income schism are less easy to come by. To begin this feat, we need to see how such huge differences between the economies of modern nations came about in the first place.

A good starting place would be the Bretton Woods (New Hampshire) conference which took place with America and its European allies in 1944, shortly before the end of World War II. Before the killing even ended, it was felt by all allied nations that America had the only healthy and intact economy left. War-torn Europe had been laid to waste and its industrial might was in smoldering ruins. It looked as if old trade patterns were gone for good. Fears of a postwar decline were very high. There was even deep worry that Europe would no longer be able to feed itself:

> It was hard to procure raw materials and even harder to find machinery or parts. Railways were destroyed, bridges bombed, harbors blocked. In 1946 there was only one passable bridge over the Rhine, and one over the Elbe. The French ports of La Rochelle, Calais, Boulogne, Dunkirk, and Toulon were virtually unusable. Much of

49

Holland was flooded with salt water; canal systems everywhere had been closed or diverted. A flourishing black market in every imaginable product from ball bearings to synthetic fibers vastly complicated the task of restoring production. The sole source for most goods was the U.S., the only major country to have escaped the war's devastation. Machines and agricultural products that once had come from Germany now came from the U.S. . . . The devastation was so overwhelming, the problems of reconstruction so difficult, that it was not certain for several years that the world would recover.[2]

Such was the economic power vacuum that America found itself in at the end of the war. The major point of agreement among all countries signing the Bretton Woods accord was a desire for economic growth. Nations badly wanted to avoid the stagnant trade, declines in business, and high unemployment which had cursed the Depression decade of the 1930s. In order for recovery to come about, the ravaged countries of Europe (including Germany) had to have the means to buy American goods. The United States was to supply the dollars needed for rebuilding by such efforts as the Marshall Plan. In short, America was to spend whatever money was needed to feed growth in the world economy.

The dollar became the only global currency upon which the value of all other types of money was pegged. In this successful quest for world economic order, each nation agreed to keep the value of its own money within 1.0 percent of its par value to the dollar at the time of the agreement. European countries had to buy extra dollars, but only if the United States ran a trade deficit in its effort to buy goods from the allies. In this system of fixed currency exchange, The U.S. Federal Reserve became the world's banker and the dollar became the bedrock of the international monetary system—at least for a while.

A second major area of consensus from Bretton Woods was a "Yes" vote for free world trade. The protectionism in vogue before World War II had all but destroyed trade between countries. Nation after nation had been dragged down by each other as their economies sank. A common ploy was to stop buying foreign goods when times were bad. Trade barriers were built for the protection of home markets during the Depression. Yet all suffered as a result.

The new system was to prevent this from happening again by means of the General Agreement on Trade and Tariffs (GATT). Before GATT, nations would usually deal with each other on a one-to-one basis. Their aim was to reduce or remove trade tariffs between each other. As an example, Canada might agree not to attach a duty fee to American computer chips if the United States were to do the same with imports of Canadian wood products. Yet such bilateral pacts are impractical. Since there is such a huge number of goods being traded between a large number of countries, the deals get to be very complex. GATT imposed some order on this chaos by using these same tariff cuts for all other nations as well. In a word, the system brought strong pressure to bear for open, free trade between all nations. Its effect was to improve the running of the world economy via the marketplace.

A third popular idea in the Bretton Woods pact was multi-lateralism. Global institutions such as the International Monetary Fund (IMF) and the International Bank for Reconstruction and Development (World Bank) were created to get as many nations as possible involved in world trade. The first goal of the IMF was to help bankroll the recovery of European nations. Today it continues to govern balance-of-payment problems, but it is also now deeply involved with Third World growth. By contrast, the intent of the World Bank from the start was to help LDCs by funding investment projects with low interest loans.

For at least two decades, the system worked well with few major problems for both America and its allies. Western Europe spurted to new heights of growth. Between 1949 and 1963, for example, industrial production tripled in Austria, Italy, Germany, and Greece while doubling in Denmark, Finland, France, the Netherlands, and Norway.[3] The United States had over half of all the productive capacity in the world at the end of the war. With this base and the privilege of having the dollar as the only legal path of exchange, our country was able to invest in other nations with great ease and under immensely favorable conditions. American business funded a massive buildup in new foreign plants which produced goods for later U.S. imports.

> One corporation alone, General Electric, increased its overseas capacity fourfold, from twenty-one foreign plants in 1949 to eighty-two in 1969. The proportion of total plant and equipment investment located outside the United States doubled in the metal and machinery industries. . . . By the early 1970s, nearly one-third of annual U.S. automobile company investment was being placed abroad. The widespread plants, mines, distribution centers and offices of the multinational corporations made up entire production systems linked on a global scale. . . . During the 1960s, the productive capacity of the American economy nearly tripled, even after accounting for inflation. This meant uninterrupted, unparalleled, and unprecedented economic expansion from the end of the 1961 (Eisenhower) recession to the 1969–70 (Nixon) crash. It was a period in which economists declared the business cycle obsolete and families saw their real income grow by a third. Exports to overseas markets and production abroad were more than matched by an enormous burst of growth in the home market. . . . Growth of . . .

discretionary incomes of working families provided an opportunity for business to develop and market a wide range of new consumer goods and services. The postwar suburbanization of middle-class households, itself in part an aspect of this explosive consumerism, set the scene for the proliferation of shopping centers, tract-housing projects, and a seemingly endless array of services related to the automobile, from drive-in restaurants to drive-in movies.[4]

America raked in money! Such a scale of affluence and wealth had never been seen before in the world. We became the envy of nearly every other country. Although the United States has since met severe economic trials, huge income gaps will remain between our nation and others if only because of this postwar miracle. Due to postwar growth, core countries of the Modern World System will continue to earn higher income than nations of the periphery and semi-periphery.

But what of the Third World countries? What has become of the poor nations that are at times euphemistically called Less Developed Countries (LDCs)? How did they fare under the international new deal which sprang forth from the Bretton Woods agreement? In a word, growth for some of these countries proved just as healthy. For a short time it was as phenomenal for a few LDCs and equal to the high pace of increase for Europe, America, and its vanquished enemies Japan and Germany.[5] In this hemisphere, countries such as Mexico and Brazil chased explosive, outward-oriented growth rates. During the past two decades, they were at first successful in their try to gain large profits from exports. The Newly Industrialized Countries (NICs) of East Asia, especially the "Four Tigers" of Hong Kong, Singapore, South Korea, and Taiwan, had phenomenal growth. Much of this has been due to their dramatic penetration of the U.S. market. A full 37 percent of American imports come from these four countries.[6] The astounding success of Japan is also the Horatio Alger story of the late twentieth century. There is some evidence to indicate that the average Gross National Product (GNP) per person in LDCs has grown faster in recent years than for countries of the core.[7] In the 1945–55 period, the total GNP for all Latin American countries went up by nearly 5 percent per year while GNP per person increased 2.4 percent annually.[8] Both figures were much larger than those for the United States during the same period.

There is another side to this coin. Despite higher growth rates in GNP totals, the actual gap in real dollars between rich and poor lands in GNP per person has actually gone up. The latest World Bank figures (table 3.1) are misleading in this way due to the use of a weighted average to account for population size within each country. The inclusion of only one nation—China—with over one billion people sharply skews the inequality picture. With China's entire population added in, it seems as if low-income countries are actually doing better than industrial nations. Yet it could be argued that a better unit of study should be the state. Some may also feel that China should be kept out of any discussion of development to begin with. It has been removed from any Western expansion until only recently. A major contrast turns up even when it is left in as one unweighted case among the thirty-three countries with low

TABLE 3.1   Average GNP Per Capita and Average Annual Growth Rate for Countries by Level of Income: 1986

Income Level of Country	GNP Per Person			
	1986 Dollars		Average Annual Percent Growth (1965–86)	
	By Population	By Country	By Population	By Country
Low-Income Economies[a] ($120–$420)	$ 270	$ 265	3.1	.59
Lower Middle-Income Economies[b] ($460–$1570)	750	891	2.5	2.18
Upper-Middle-Income Economies[c] ($1,810–$7,410)	1,890	3,242	2.8	3.27
High-Income Oil Exporters[d] ($6,950–$14,680)	6,740	11,840	1.8	1.70
Industrial Market Economies[e] ($4,860–$17,680)	12,960	11,274	2.3	2.38

a. Ethiopia, Bhutan, Burkina Faso, Nepal, Bangladesh, Malawi, Zaire, Mali, Burma, Mozambique, Madagascar, Uganda, Burundi, Tanzania, Togo, Niger, Benin, Somalia, Central African Republic, India, Rwanda, China, Kenya, Zambia, Sierra Leone, Sudan, Haiti, Pakistan, Lesotho, Ghana, Sri Lanka, Mauritania, and Senegal.

b. Liberia, Yemen PDR, Indonesia, Yemen Arab Rep., Philippines, Morocco, Bolivia, Zimbabwe, Nigeria, Dominican Republic, Papua New Guinea, Ivory Coast, Honduras, Egypt, Nicaragua, Thailand, El Salvador, Botswana, Jamaica, Cameroon, Guatemala, Congo, Paraguay, Peru, Turkey, Tunisia, Ecuador, Mauritius, Colombia, Chile, Costa Rica, Jordan, Syria, and Lebanon.

c. Brazil, Malaysia, South Africa, Mexico, Uruguay, Hungary, Poland, Portugal, Yugoslavia, Panama, Argentina, South Korea, Algeria, Venezuela, Gabon, Greece, Oman, Israel, Trinidad and Tobago, Israel, Hong Kong, Singapore.

d. Saudi Arabia, Kuwait, and United Arab Emirates.

e. Spain, Ireland, New Zealand, Italy, United Kingdom, Belgium, Austria, Netherlands, France, Australia, West Germany, Finland, Denmark, Japan, Sweden, Canada, Norway, United States, and Switzerland.

income (GNPs per person of $270 to $420 in 1986). The early conclusion is reversed. The annual growth rate in GNP per person declines from 3.1 percent to .6 percent for low-income countries, and from 2.5 percent to 2.2 percent for the thirty-three lower-middle-income nations. The percentage figure *rises* from 2.3 percent to 2.4 percent for the nineteen industrial market economies. In essence, *the developed countries did largely outperform LDCs both in GNP per person and the percent increase of GNP per person between 1965 and 1986.*[9]

It is true that some LDCs have shown great promise. Yet most countries in the periphery have not shared such success equally. There are over one hundred countries in what could be called the Third World. All are arrayed along an income spectrum running from dire poverty in Sub-Saharan Africa to levels nearing relative affluence. Some GNP increases are not likely to last very long. Many are the product of boom-and-bust business cycles. For example, Mexico expanded the drilling and export of oil to meet a thirsty demand during the lucrative market caused by the OPEC embargo. The market came crashing down a few years later as the world oil glut developed. Currently there is also a severe drop in the world economy. This threat may still bring on financial collapse for all countries, whether core or periphery. The global economic recession has already had a disastrous effect on many nations during the 1980s. Although many incomes in the United States have been changed as a result of the decline, most Americans are still unaware of any ill effects.

The gap between LDCs and developed countries is quite complex. Yet it is a safe bet that absolute income differences have become worse. The latest GATT figures show that the share of world trade for LDCs dropped from 28 percent in 1980 to 19 percent by 1986.[10] Even before this period, the average per capita income gap between low income countries and industrialized countries increased from $3,677 to $9,403 between 1950–80.[11] Thus, while poor countries saw average income climb only from $164 to $245, income of industrial countries soared from $3,841 to $9,648. Whereas in 1950 LDCs earned 4.3 percent of the world's total income, this had gone down to only 2.5 percent in 1980.

Table 3.2 lists GNP per person in 1986 dollars and its increase from 1965 to 1986 for nations by position in the Modern World System.[12] A clear hierarchy can be seen between the three groups of nations in average 1986 GNP per person. The eighteen countries of the core lead with a mean GNP per person of $11,467, followed by twenty-two countries of the semi-periphery ($2,545) and fifty-nine nations of the periphery ($1,573).[13] There are also large gaps in growth of GNP per person that follow theoretical expectations. Core nations show the highest increase per year (2.6 percent), followed by the semi-periphery (2.5 percent) and the periphery (1.5 percent).

TABLE 3.2   Average GNP Per Person and Average Annual Growth Rate for
Countries by Modern World System Position: 1986

World Position	GNP Per Capita	Average Annual Percent Growth
Core		
Yugoslavia	$ 2,300	3.9%
Greece	3,680	3.3
Italy	8,550	2.6
United Kingdom	8,870	1.7
Belgium	9,230	2.7
Austria	9,990	3.3
Netherlands	10,020	1.9
France	10,720	2.8
Australia	11,920	1.7
West Germany	12,080	2.5
Denmark	12,600	1.9
Japan	12,840	4.3
Sweden	13,160	1.6
Canada	14,120	2.6
Norway	15,400	3.4
Luxembourg	15,770	4.1
United States	17,480	1.6
Switzerland	17,680	1.4
Group Average for Core	$11,467	2.63%
Semi-Periphery		
Burma	$ 200	2.3%
India	290	1.8
Kenya	300	1.9
Pakistan	350	2.4
Sri Lanka	400	2.9
Philippines	560	1.9
Peru	1,090	.1
Turkey	1,110	2.7
Jordan	1,540	5.5
Malaysia	1,830	4.3
South Africa	1,850	.4
Uruguay	1,900	1.4
Hungary	2,020	3.9
Portugal	2,250	3.2
Argentina	2,350	.2
South Korea	2,370	6.7
Venezuela	2,920	.4
Cyprus	4,360	NA
Spain	4,860	2.9
Ireland	5,070	1.7
Israel	6,210	2.6
Finland	12,160	3.2
Group Average for Semi-Periphery	$ 2,545	2.50%

TABLE 3.2   (*Continued*)

World Position	GNP Per Capita	Average Annual Percent Growth
Periphery		
Ethiopia	$ 120	0.0%
Burkina Faso	150	1.3
Nepal	150	1.9
Zaire	160	−2.2
Mali	180	1.1
Madagascar	230	−1.7
Uganda	230	−2.6
Burundi	240	1.8
Togo	250	.2
Niger	260	−2.2
Benin	270	.2
Somalia	280	−.3
Central African Republic	290	−.6
Rwanda	290	1.5
China	300	5.1
Sierra Leone	310	.2
Sudan	320	−.2
Haiti	330	.6
Ghana	390	−1.7
Mauritania	420	−.3
Senegal	420	−.6
Liberia	460	−1.4
Yemen, PDR	470	NA
Indonesia	490	4.6
Yemen Arab Republic	550	4.7
Morocco	590	1.9
Bolivia	600	−.4
Nigeria	640	1.9
Dominican Republic	710	2.5
Ivory Coast	730	1.2
Honduras	740	.3
Egypt	760	3.1
Nicaragua	790	−2.2
Thailand	810	4.0
El Salvador	820	−.3
Jamaica	840	−1.4
Cameroon	910	3.9
Guatemala	930	1.4
Congo	990	3.6
Paraguay	1,000	3.6
Tunisia	1,140	3.8
Ecuador	1,160	3.5
Mauritius	1,200	3.0
Colombia	1,230	2.8
Chile	1,320	−.2
Costa Rica	1,480	1.6

TABLE 3.2   (Continued)

World Position	GNP Per Capita	Average Annual Percent Growth
Syria	1,570	3.7
Brazil	1,810	4.3
Mexico	1,860	2.6
Poland	2,070	NA
Panama	2,330	2.4
Algeria	2,590	3.5
Gabon	3,080	1.9
Malta	3,450	7.7
Trinidad and Tobago	5,360	1.6
Saudi Arabia	6,950	4.0
New Zealand	7,460	1.5
Iceland	13,410	3.1
Kuwait	13,890	− .6
Group Average for Periphery	$ 1,573	1.45%

Not Classified: Bhutan, Bangladesh, Malawi, Mozambique, Tanzania, Zambia, Lesotho, Zimbabwe, Papua New Guinea, Botswana, Oman, Hong Kong, Singapore, and United Arab Emirates.

The world map in figure 3.1 depicts GNP per person for the upper and lower 25 percent of countries. It is apparent that most of the low-income nations are concentrated in Africa (figure 3.2). Of the twenty-nine low-income nations in the bottom 25 percent of GNP per person (under $375 per year), nearly three-fourths are located in Africa. There are nearly three times the number of low-income countries in this continent than would be expected on the basis of chance. At the other end, Europe captures the regional honors for the largest percent of countries with high GNPs ($4,900 per year or more). The region has twice as many nations in this coveted position as would normally be expected (figure 3.3). We shall see later, however, that low income among nations is more than just a regional problem. GNP per person is only a gross average. This crude figure can hide large numbers of poor people, even in rich countries.

In summary, sharp income differences between nations continue at very high levels and seem to be increasing. This is aside from the fact that some growth has taken place in LDCs with respect to their overall GNP levels. In making comparisons through time and between countries, the presence or absence of only a few countries can greatly affect the outcome. Although countries such as India or China are fairly poor, their sheer numbers weigh heavily in making comparisons. The use of socialist countries in comparing GNP per person can also lead to strange results. Any big change in China alone may end with dramatically shift-

FIGURE 3.1: Global GNP Per Person in 1986

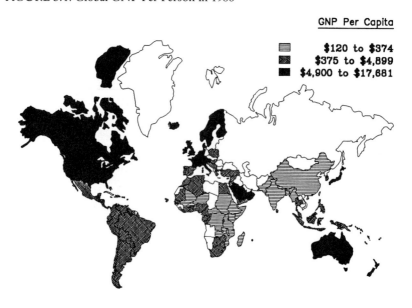

FIGURE 3.2: GNP Per Person in Africa, 1986

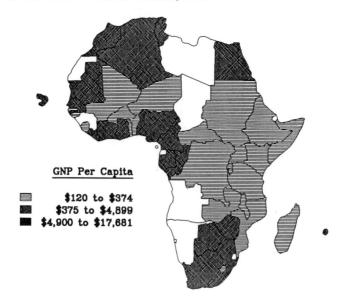

FIGURE 3.3: GNP Per Person in Europe and Asia, 1986

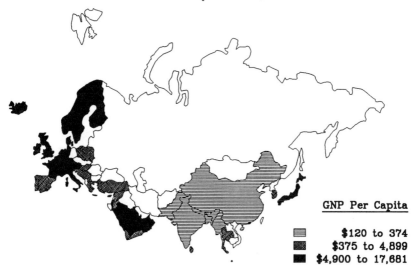

GNP Per Capita

$120 to 374
$375 to 4,899
$4,900 to 17,681

ing cycles. If China is included, for example, there has been no change in world income inequality from 1950 to 1977.[14] Theoretically and practically, however, communist countries have been only a minimal part of the emergent world economy after World War II. To keep such nations in a study of free market development is arguable. For noncommunist countries, there has been an unmistakable increase of income inequality occurring during the quarter century after the war:

> The 1950s and early 1960s exhibit a relative stability, possibly a slight decline in inequality; between 1964 and 1972 there was a substantial worsening; finally, during 1972–1977 there was again no trend. . . . For the period as a whole distribution seems to have worsened somewhat. . . . The share of the upper-middle deciles rose by 1.8% of total income, with 1.3% coming from the bottom six deciles and only 0.5% from the richest 10%. . . . The decline in share of world GNP over 1950–1977 was most marked for the lowest deciles, reaching almost 20% for the first decile.[15]

In the end, the relative incomes of most people in the free market world have become much worse over the postwar economic "expansion." Only when communist China is included among the statistics does this picture change. Yet even here the income gap gets better only in the sense that today's inequality is no worse than it was in 1950. The average person did not become worse off, but neither was there improvement. The income shifts that did occur acted to impoverish the poor even more.

A decline in real income of 20 percent set in for the poorest 10 percent of income recipients.[16]

Albert Berry and his associates were able to break down the sources for the world's decline in relative income. Faster population growth among the poorest LDCs slowed emerging equality. So did a lag in India's economic growth. Since India is the second highest in sheer numbers and among the most poor of all nations, it is a severe drag on overall global growth. U.S. growth in per person GNP was below that of the entire world. When this is added to the increase in real incomes for Organization of Petroleum Exporting Countries (OPEC) and newly industrialized countries, the trend to a larger gap in world income is eased. All told, U.S. growth in real GNP per person during the period was 6.7 percent *below* the worldwide norm of 2.8 percent increase per year. The only other areas of the world with a worse record than the United States were the subcontinent made up of India, Pakistan, Sri Lanka, and Bangladesh (-20.5 percent); poor African countries (-25.2 percent); and Argentina, South Africa, and Uruguay (-18.5 percent). The communist countries of China (63.8 percent), USSR (40.7 percent), and East Europe (50.3 percent) did much better. Not surprisingly, newly industrialized countries had per person GNP increases 50.6 percent above the norm, while Japan led all national groups with an increase of 193 percent above the average. Even our closest allies of Canada, France, Italy, the United Kingdom, and West Germany managed to ring in real GNP increases per head that were 21.5 percent above average. One fact stands out. The stark reality is that the United States fell behind nearly all other industrialized countries in its per person GNP growth rate. Had our GNP level not been so high to begin with, this situation would have been even more extremely urgent than it actually is.

The Debt Crisis and World Recession

Much of this worsening economic scenario has sped up dramatically during the 1980s. Today it is often referred to as the "debt crisis." This can be a loaded term, however, suggesting that LDC borrowing is out of control. An image exists of wanton poor nations that seek to recklessly expand their economies overnight. This single leap from marginal subsistence to modern industrialism is to be helped by loans from the core. While some LDCs may have such a utopia in mind, the depiction smacks of blaming the victim. Certainly the World Bank and its sanction-wielding IMF twin are not hesitant to cry for austerity. Such programs are viewed as an indispensable aid to increasing national income through more exports. In its last report, the World Bank has continued to push for cuts in public spending and subsidies as a means of deficit reduction.[17] The message is clear and unmistakable: most of today's global fiscal crisis is laid at the feet of poor countries who simply do not have the discipline to balance their own budgets.

Notice that officials, bankers, politicians, and economists in core nations never urge LDCs to simply stop borrowing money. The crux of the problem may lie with prolific and careless lending on the part of core nations. More than half of the World Bank's lending capital is supplied by core countries.[18] It is these very countries, especially the United States, that decide who gets how much of what. Such largesse is in turn always awarded to the LDCs who conform most closely to IMF mandates. The impact of these development loans is very questionable, since many of the projects are geared toward high technology uses which need an elaborate support structure. The necessary supplies and technical expertise for many of these projects are never available in the host country. Of course, such crucial imports are ready for purchase from core nations who make the loans. A recent example can be found in the plan to open Mexico's Laguna Verde nuclear power plant in Vera Cruz. The plant has now been put through its first startup despite the fact that it is situated between two geological faults and within ten miles of an active volcano. The General Electric reactors it uses have serious design flaws for which GE is being sued in the United States.[19]

When oil prices quadrupled during the mid-1970s, LDCs were urged by core banks and OPEC depositors to borrow heavily. The goal was to fuel a buildup of industry and business to feed exports. In this way, the heavier cost of oil imports could be more easily paid by increased profits. Such plans assumed that core countries like the United States would be willing to import more goods from the periphery. All parties to the musical-aid game also took for granted that the variable rate interest on their loans would remain the same. Neither assumption was ever met. The second price increase of 1979 wreaked havoc upon Third World economies. Input costs for manufacturing and agribusiness went wild, spinning out of control. For the 1974–82 period, non-oil LDCs paid for $345 billion worth of oil when the bill would normally have been $85 billion before the price hike.[20] By then, many LDCs were trapped in the vicious circle of hopeless debt. They had to borrow even more money to pay for higher oil imports in order to produce more goods for export to pay off their debts!

The second blow came from a sharp drop in the demand for their goods. A glut of products on the world market rapidly developed, with panic sales at bargain basement prices. Many more factors add to the vulnerability of poor countries on the export treadmill:

Compounding the problem is the limited range of goods that the debtors can offer, which pits one against the other. African coffee producers compete not only against other Africans but against Latin Americans as well. The least developed economies are dependent on one, two or three agricultural or mineral raw materials, and it is folly to tell them to diversify in their present capital starved condition. . . . Third World commodities are further undermined by substitution. Every time the industrial countries think that the price of some raw material is out of line, they introduce a substitute that they can produce without recourse to outside suppliers. Sugar is a flagrant case. . . . As for non-agricultural raw materials, more efficient Western industries are using fewer mined metals, employing more synthetics. . . . Glass fibre as a substitute for copper wire in the telecommunications industry is one example. When Third World countries struggle to sell a limited range of goods in the face of shrinking demand, over-supply and plunging prices are the predictable results. Markets . . . simply cannot swallow unlimited quantities of foods or textiles or transistors.[21]

With so much of the national budget going to increased energy costs, less was left over for other consumption in many parts of the world. To make matters worse, the United States began to sharply raise its interest rates. This acted to siphon off much capital from the Third World that would normally have gone for investment and local consumption. The high interest rates meant that more now had to be paid on development loans taken out at initially lower rates. The end result has been a hemorrhaging of money from LDCs to the advanced industrial countries. For Latin America alone, new capital inflow in terms of aid and investment came to $38 billion between 1982–85. Yet the region paid back $144 billion in debt servicing.[22] By 1985 the per person product in Latin America was 9 percent lower than in 1980. Effects have varied from one country to another, but they are all variations along a continuum from bad to worse. The per person economic output in Brazil fell 12 percent in four years, while its inflation rate increased at an annual level of 200 percent. Brazil still owes $100 billion of debt to foreign banks. Brazil's 40 percent unemployment rate has set the stage for eventual default. With nearly two-thirds of its people undernourished, the cumulative effect takes on the size of utter disaster.[23] Output, real wages, consumption, and profits have all fallen throughout Latin America:

Per person output in 1986 was almost 8 percent lower than in 1980, the last year before the crisis. Unemployment grew at an annual average rate of 6.3 percent in the first five years of the crisis. . . . In Mexico real wages fell 5 percent between 1979 and 1984. Private consumption stagnated in Mexico. In Brazil, it fell from a healthy

9.1 percent average . . . to an anemic 2.2 percent. In Argentina, private consumption actually fell at an annual rate of 1.2 percent from 1980 to 1985. . . . Private investment declined: 9.1 percent per year in Mexico, 5.5 percent in Brazil, and 13.8 percent in Argentina.[24]

The natural response to these conditions on the part of LDCs is to cut back on imports from other countries. This acts to improve the balance of trade so that they can pay back their loans. The tragedy is that many of these imported goods are also essential for Third World economic and physical well-being. Orders for medicine, food, books, machinery, spare parts, fertilizer, and the like have been cut to the bone. Quality of life becomes a thing of meaning only to rich nations in the core.

Export profits of core countries who ship to LDCs have also dried to a trickle. Between 1981–85, total exports from the United States to Latin America fell by over $11 billion. This made up 55 percent of the total drop in all our exports. Import cutbacks by Mexico alone accounted for a full one-fourth of the drop.[25] The strong message is that the United States and other core countries do not live in a vacuum. We are tied to the fate of Third World countries. When they fail to prosper, we ultimately do so as well.

The idea may still be held that the United States has benefited from the problems of our poor neighbors. To a small extent this is true. Yet the costs far outweigh the advantages in the grand scheme of things. To put it more bluntly and in different terms, we are living on borrowed time. The sand within our economic hourglass has all but reached the bottom! In 1981 the United States was in a strong position as a lender nation when our country held over $140 billion in foreign assets (more than any other country). Incredibly, the United States had slipped deeply into red ink by as early as 1985. By that year we had become a debtor nation to the tune of $107 billion.[26]

The United States had become the world's largest debtor. . . . The United States was borrowing approximately $100–120 billion net each year and foreign holdings of American government securities soared. Projections of future borrowing indicated that by the end of the decade, the American foreign debt could reach $1 trillion. The world's richest country in less than five years had reversed a century-long trend and become the world's most indebted nation. . . . By the mid-1980s, the evidence supporting the relative decline of the American economy had become overwhelming. In the early 1950s, the United States, with 6 percent of total world population, accounted for approximately 40 percent of the gross world product; by 1980, the American share had dropped by half to approximately

22 percent. Whereas the United States in the early postwar period produced 30 percent of world manufacturing exports, by 1986 its share had dropped to a mere 13 percent. American productivity growth, which had outpaced the rest of the world for decades, declined dramatically from a growth rate of 3 percent annually in the early postwar years to an incredible low of 0.8 percent in the 1970s. As American productivity lagged behind that of other advanced economies, particularly Japan, West Germany, and the NICs, the result was a less competitive economy and a substantial lowering of the American standard of living. In capital formation, technological leadership, and the quality of the labor force (human capital), the United States was falling behind in a growing field of industrial competitors.[27]

Appalling as all this may seem, the story actually gets worse! Our foreign debt situation is the same as debt on all other levels. Total household, corporate, and consumer debt has risen 60 percent between 1982 and 1987.[28] In 1986, household installment credit debt reached 16.5 percent of total personal income—a postwar record.[29] By 1984 the proportion of total farm debt to net farm income had hit a postwar record and has been rising ever since. Corporate business debt took $1 out of every $7 earned during the 1960s. It rose to $1 for every $3 in the 1970s, soon reaching today's crescendo of half of all earnings. Our federal budget deficit will have tripled as of 1989 from its $1 trillion base in 1980.[30] In 1987 the interest payment on the former federal debt was greater than that year's budget deficit. In effect, our government has been borrowing new money to pay interest on old debts.

To make matters worse, much of this money is not owed to U.S. banks or is not in the form of treasury notes owned by American citizens. The debt payoff is increasingly going to foreign powers. Annual interest paid out to foreigners on the U.S. debt has doubled since 1980 and now amounts to $24 billion per year.[31] The Japanese have been bankrolling the massive increase in U.S. debt for a number of reasons. To begin with, they have had the money to do so. The economic success of Japanese industrial development since the end of World War II has been breathtaking to see. They have used different means to subsidize heavy manufacturing (steel and autos) and high-tech industry (especially electronics) to develop an export economy. Japan has also gone to great lengths to protect its local business markets from foreign penetration. It has encouraged personal savings at very high rates while aggressively marketing its products around the globe. Japan had undeniably usurped the top American position of world creditor by the mid-1980s. At a time when the net asset value of the United States was plunging into the red, Japanese trade surplus was the largest in the world. In 1970, seven American banks ranked among the globe's top twenty-five in terms of assets. By the end of 1987, Citicorp was the only U.S. bank in this chosen circle (tenth place). Today, the ten largest banks in the world in terms of deposits are Japanese with no U.S. banks in the top twenty-five.[32] Much of the investment coming from these banks has been in the form of U.S. Treasury bond purchases.[33]

Two other reasons led Japan to feed America's spendaholic deficit binge. We are without doubt Japan's best customer. In the five years since 1982, Japanese exports to the United States more than doubled.[34] Preserving our financial health keeps their labor force fully at work. The other magnet which drew foreign money and investment to the United States was the decision by the Federal Reserve to increase interest rates to all-time highs. This was part of an effort to curb the massive inflation endemic to the 1970s. While the result was to produce the severest U.S. and world economic tailspin since the Depression, it did work to stabilize prices. Money from rich and poor countries alike gushed in from around the world. Our interest rates were off the charts in comparison to other countries. Since the U.S. political climate was both conservative and stable, the mix formed an attractive investment package.

The massive inflow of capital to America also took away needed cash from LDCs for their own development. Profits from local firms in poor nations ended up in U.S. banks, rather than being recycled into their own economies. While money flowed to the United States, it was less available in other lands to purchase goods produced in LDCs. This made the recessionary problems caused by the OPEC oil price hikes much worse. Even within the United States, however, our newfound wealth failed to be put to productive use. Rather than using the money to reinvest in our own aging and badly outmoded industries, it has been frittered away. Much of it was spent for nonproductive mega-mergers between avaricious U.S. corporations. This has been the major reason behind the long-term corporate debt alluded to earlier.

Most of the money was also spent on the largest peacetime military buildup the world has ever witnessed:

Spending for defense more than doubled, from $134 billion in 1980 to $282 billion in 1987, in the process coming to consume nearly 60 cents out of every personal and corporate dollar raised by the federal government though income taxes. Even after accounting for inflation, this amounted to an average growth rate of over 7 percent a year—nearly three-and-a-half times the real growth rate of GNP. . . . As a result of all of this defense activity, more and more American manufacturers were becoming increasingly dependent on the Pentagon as a customer for their wares.[35]

The result of this massive arms buildup caused a short-term growth in GNP. Some jobs were created within the United States. While employment in defense-related work grew by less than 4 percent per year just prior to the buildup, this expanded to 20 percent under the Reagan presidency. There was a 45 percent increase within the private sector as well, which could be laid at the feet of the newly fattened military calf. During the first five years of Reagan's tenure in office, 1.2 million new jobs were added to the defense-related payroll.[36] The result of such an incredible military spending spree is cancerous. Like so-called banana republics, many American industries have become almost helpless in their dependence upon the defense budget. They are very vulnerable, along with the entire American economy, if any major downturn were to occur. Much of the fee for America's research and development effort is now aimed at esoteric and impractical ends. Products are made that we all fervently wish will never be used. While the United States develops stealth bombers and writes reams of SDI (Star Wars) software that critics claim will never work, our competitor nations develop computers, VCRs, high-resolution color TV sets, and more such goods for real people who want to buy these products! We have cut our own throat by worsening the ability of the United States to trade and to produce consumer goods. Most experts feel that the direct application of this exotic military hardware to the commercial market is quite limited or nonexistent. Since the United States was forced to borrow heavily in order to finance the buildup, interest rates were driven up around the world. This depleted capital for LDC investment while also forcing them to pay more on their variable interest rates. The worldwide recession was made worse. An already anemic consumer market within the developing world was weakened even more. Lastly, some believe that the results of all of these changes enabled the United States to cunningly levy a hidden military tax upon the Third World.

The other side to the imposing United States debt crisis is the effect of Reaganomic tax cuts. Not only did they fail to stimulate the economy (other than in military areas), even more red ink was spilled. The nation refused to follow the Hollywood script. Rather than save, as it was supposed to do, the public went into debt at even higher rates. Total spending on new manufacturing plants and equipment actually declined as it also did for firms outside of primary industry. Labor productivity, which was supposed to increase as a result of greater investment in new technology, took a deep dive and was actually negative by 1985.[37]

The last factor underlying American debt has been the rapidly developing trade gap between the United States and the rest of the industrialized world. By now there can be no doubt that a global economy is a reality in today's world. The United States, Japan, West Germany, and a few other core nations form its decorative centerpiece. Yet, the economic performance of the United States during the 1980s has been at best questionable. At worst it is akin to a hidden, Titantic-like disaster about ready to strike the iceberg of fiscal irresponsibility. We have a junkie-like addiction to borrow beyond our means. The Japanese have been enabling our addiction to debt by lending us money for our "fix." Together with the global recession and resulting glut of goods on the world market—the United States has emerged as the "buyer of last resort" among all nations. We are the only country with the means and the desire to bury ourselves in a deluge of imported goods. Indeed, our free market rhetoric almost demands that we abandon any strategy of nationalistic consumption ("buy American"). Any planned industrial development is seen as an ogre to the American way of life. Instead, as a nation we have favored the laissez-faire free-for-all that leaves cheaper imported goods on our doorstep.

The high value of the dollar, sparked by the Federal Reserve's unheard of increase to a 21 percent prime lending rate, made American exports far too costly for the rest of the world. This killed any chance of selling our goods abroad. The fall in oil prices lessened the ability of OPEC nations to buy products. The rising debt and interest payments of Third World countries destroyed their purchasing ability. As a result, demand for imports in the developing world actually fell by $100 billion in four years. The strategy pursued by nearly every other country—except the United States—was to push exports while cutting imports. In a time of recession, this is known as "putting your house in order." America went the other way! For the 1980–85 period, U.S. imports rose 35 percent while our exports fell 3 percent. Japan during the same period increased exports by 35 percent while slashing imports by 8 percent. The result was massive and immediate: a burgeoning trade debt that has shown no sign of ending. It is still too high, even with our government's success in reducing the value of the dollar. The trade deficit has been on a stubborn course of increase since 1981. The latest data show it at a negative $170 billion in 1987.[38] According to a recent study by New York University's Institute for Economic Analysis, the size of the deficit has cost the United States a loss of 5.1 million jobs in manufacturing.[39]

The point of all of this comes down to basically one assertion: the so-called Reagan economic recovery is basically false. Although there are cosmetic repercussions, such as the creation of jobs in defense-related industries, what little growth that did occur has been due to the onset of ruinous debt. The fact that we have been able to get away with this for so long has been due to our past position of chief economic power for the world. We have been badly abusing this privilege since 1971 when Nixon declared that our country would no longer pay out in gold for U.S. dollars held by other nations. Despite the loss of real productivity and many sick industries, the United States has gone on a spending binge while the rest of the world has been prudently dieting or even forced into starvation. The American public has not even begun to perceive the bad results, the facts of which were carefully kept from voters during the 1988 presidential election. In a new book by Harvard economist Benjamin Friedman, the author points out that the net federal debt after eight years of Reagan amounts to $2.1 trillion, or forty-three cents for every dollar of national income. Prior to his assuming office, this debt was twenty-six cents for every dollar—a rate that was two-thirds lower. Friedman concludes that unless the nation acts quickly to reverse the accumulating debt, "today's voters and their children will pay the consequences in the form of a diminished standard of living and a far different role for America in world affairs."[40] Princeton University professor Robert Gilpin also warns us of the dire consequences:

> First, the competitive position of important sectors of the American economy has been permanently damaged and the structure of the entire economy has been distorted. Second, repayment of the immense external debt and the associated interest payments will absorb a large share of America's productive resources for many years to come; these costs will substantially lower the standard of living for a considerable period, even if defense expenditures are considerably curtailed. And third, the newly acquired preference of Americans for foreign goods and the expansion of productive capacity abroad have decimated many industries in which the United States once had a strong comparative advantage; America will be required to develop new products and industries if it is to regain even part of its former competitive position in world markets. The task of reversing the trends toward deindustrialization will be difficult and very costly . . . the United States had indulged itself in over-consumption and underinvestment for too long. Americans were consuming the source of their national wealth and that of other societies as well rather than putting it into productive investments. . . . For a time, the United States was able to mask its decline . . . through foreign borrowing, especially with the financial assistance of the Japanese. . . . Despite the cries of a few Cassandras, the false prosperity of the Reagan "economic miracle" hid from the American people the reality of their true situation and the fact that they were prospering only on other people's money. The country as a whole failed to appreciate the historic meaning of the budget deficit and its long-term implications for the society.[41]

Austerity, Income Inequality, and the Third World

Those within the Third World are aware of all of the trends discussed so far. Many of their intellectuals and leaders have earned Harvard Ph.D.s in economics or M.B.A.s to better plan the modernization of their own nations. One thing our contemporary world does not lack in this age of telecommunications, satellites, cheap jet travel, fax machines, and computer modems is instantaneous, up-to-date information. Third World leaders cannot help but know of the disarray (if not decrepitude) existing within the American house of finance. There is thus deep resentment when our country blithely demands fiscal austerity for developing countries while turning a blind eye toward our own economic chaos. Such an arrogant pose shows ignorance at best, if not outright hypocrisy. Yet the message from the World Bank and IMF, almost wholly under U.S. tutelage, continues to be ground out. Developing countries are admonished to stop their outrageous public spending on "questionable" programs designed to meet social needs. They are sanctimoniously told to trim their budgets in the provision of human services. They are lectured without mercy to make goods for export to the world market. Pressure to cut local consumption by ending food price subsidies, barring unions, lowering and/or putting caps on wages are usual parts of the IMF package. Removal of price controls and letting the costs rise for electricity or transportation form still another part of the typical "adjustment" scheme. The plan calls for higher taxes. Interest rates go up in an effort to end runaway inflation. The big picture we are left with in this group portrait is sacrifice and poverty for LDCs. Can there be any question that a shift takes place in income from the poor toward the wealthy? Bankers now come right out and say they want to do this in order to encourage savings and to drive down wasteful local consumption.[42]

What is never discussed is the dwindling market for all of these goods. No one talks about what happens when the economic pie actually gets smaller. Conflict will rear up in a nation when its piece of the economic action is less. The spread of income within any society is marked by rancor, hostility, and intense bitterness even during the best of times. Unfortunately, during epochs of decline there is an even greater tendency for the strong to prey upon the weak as they try to keep their same income coming in. *As inequality gets worse **between** nations, income inequality **within** nations also tends to grow.*

Susan George cites the case study of Jamaica as a typical example of how an IMF austerity program works on its target population.[43] Jamaica's economy is dominated by bauxite and sugar exports as well as tourism. Foreign investment by aluminum companies in this nation was heavy in the 1950s and 1960s. By the 1970s this industrial initiative had dried up. Jamaica was left to wrestle with oil price hikes and world recession at the same time. A brief fling with a socialist government brought further decline as foreign firms began to flee the country. To meet rising costs while its export revenues declined, Jamaica increased its borrowing. It raised its foreign debt from $150 million in 1971 to $813 million by 1976. By that year, Jamaica was forced to restructure its debt along IMF adjustment policies. By 1980 the Fund demanded a $300 million cut in state spending (26 percent of the previous year's budget) which resulted in the layoff of 11,000 public sector employees. Because it was so compliant and as a reward for voting its socialist government out of office in 1980, the Reagan administration chose to make Jamaica a showcase example of free market, conservative economic development. Financial aid went through the roof. Between 1981 and 1984 this country was lent $495 million from the United States, more than twice the amount of aid it had received in the last twenty-four years. Yet the reinvestment still failed to ignite the economy. Since by then the IMF/World Bank had allocated $900 million to Jamaica, it demanded its pound of flesh to service the new loans. Further austerity cut all food subsidies, public investment fell by 30 percent, and real income was slashed by nearly one half in a period of two years. While water, telephone, and electricity rates all went up by 100 percent in 1984, local food production fell 13 percent in the same year. This was at a time when the minimum wage was not allowed to rise above $8.95 per week. George correctly pinpoints the major result as the destruction of this nation's ability to meet basic human needs:

> "The shrinkage of the 'social wage' which occurred throughout 1981–85 had a further regressive effect on income distribution, dumping most of the welfare costs of adjustment on the doorstep of the worst off in the society." But this is exactly what the IMF wants. According to Fund doctrine, "redistribution of income" (read "more to the rich, less to the poor") will result in higher profits, which in turn will result in higher investment and thus create jobs so that people can earn more money, etc., etc. That is the theory. In practice, though there certainly has been "redistribution," the rich have invested their windfall not in job creation but simply in speculation (a lot in real estate) or even more simply in foreign bank accounts. Here, once more, is a classic case of the banks getting their money back twice—in payments on the debt made at the expense of the poor and, simultaneously, in the form of cash deposits that they can then reloan ad infinitum, or at least until something cracks. Jamaica is unlikely to struggle back to . . . prosperity through IMF measures.[44]

Horror stories such as these are common. Yet, we are still dealing with income inequality at the level of lone nations with only a few selected case studies. Although such accounts tend to be rich in detail and suggest paths for more research, they may still not be representative of the majority of less-developed countries. The experience of Jamaica suggests that dark forces are deeply felt in LDC economies, but it is hard to generalize from only a few examples. While Jamaica's story may be typical, we cannot be sure until all nations are examined together. In such research, a focus is needed on their income inequality and how this varies with development and their position within the modern World System.

Such an analysis was conducted at about the same time Jamaica's economy came under the knife of IMF austerity. A study of thirty-two countries led to strong evidence that government spending reduces income inequality.[45] This is particularly true for funds spent on "social wage" items as social security, government-owned enterprises, and expenditures meant to prime the economy. For every 10 percent increase in direct government spending, there is an associated decrease of 3.6 percent in income inequality. The United States, with the highest unemployment rate of 6.7 percent among these nations, had one of the lowest government expenditure rates at 21 percent of GNP. Sweden, with one of the highest government spending rates (39.1 percent of GNP), had an unemployment rate of only 1.5 percent. Put differently, while government spending was twice as high in Sweden, unemployment was four times as low. The conclusion is obvious. If you slash government spending and its safety net of ways to meet basic human needs, then income inequality will skyrocket. What is most compelling about this study is an added finding that sharply challenges IMF and World Bank wisdom. All other things being equal (GNP per person and direct government spending), an increase in economic growth does not lessen the degree of income inequality in these countries.

"Trickle down" does not work! It is a bad joke perpetrated on poor countries to justify enriching already corpulently wealthy elites. All the while, the majority are deprived of even the food needed to keep alive. There is conclusive evidence that local consumption plummets when income inequality goes up within LDCs.[46] Among twenty poor nations in 1975–79, it was found that more income inequality was associated with less money spent on personal needs. Austerity leads to suffering, deprivation, and the destruction of local consumer markets at home.

Another study of eighteen Latin American countries for the 1965–81 period did show a better balance of payment resulting from the introduction of austerity programs. Yet the scholars found the improvement was more artificial than real. Conditions got better despite lack of improvement in the trade balance. They also found outright declines that took place in the balance of goods, services, and income available within these nations. The signing up for an IMF austerity package served as a "seal of approval" which allowed docile countries to obtain further loans from private banks. It was a fresh influx of money rather than real recovery that led to healthier looking balance of payments for poor nations. All of this took place while inflation ran wild as a by-product of IMF austerity. Their most important finding was a consistent weakening of income for laborers and workers, i.e., a relentless, growing poverty. The decline in the social wage and real income of workers results because the IMF helps core nations dominate the periphery by use of judicious loans:

> This is partly because, as argued previously, the cooperation of local elites can be obtained by sparing them the burdens of adjustment. This rise in surplus—given no general effects on growth rates—should lead to an increase in profitability sufficient to attract the private capital inflows demonstrated. This inflow may allow a rosy picture of balance of payments improvement, but beneath it lies worsening income distribution, exacerbated social tension, and little or no improvement in the inflation, current account, and growth fundamentals. . . . After riots induced by the IMF-recommended price increases left 60 dead, 200 wounded, and 4,300 arrested, the planning minister of the Dominican Republic rejected (temporarily) the IMF pact commenting that "It is not that we are unwilling to put our own house in order. It is that we want to keep our house and not let it go up in flames." Economic policymakers both inside and outside the Fund should recognize that the [demonstrated] inequitable apportionment of adjustment burdens . . . cannot persist without letting societies "go up in flames." The design of stabilization policies to replace the unfair and often ineffective Fund policies should be the object of new research.[47]

The latest violence sparked by an IMF austerity plan in a Third World country came to Venezuela in March of 1989. It was largely due to "adjustments" suggested by the IMF, such as a currency devaluation, an increase in loan interest rates, and a series of price increases. Because of heavy payments to service Venezuela's external debt of $33 billion— fourth largest behind Brazil, Mexico, and Argentina of all Latin American countries—the average real wage in this nation has fallen by 38 percent since 1983.[48] Venezuelans saw the price for fuel increase by 80 percent and for public transportation by 50 percent almost overnight. The price hikes sparked rioting among the country's already destitute population, eventually leaving 347 officially listed as dead (Caracas newspapers have estimated the dead at over 600); 1,000 injured; and 2,000 arrested. The severity of the outbreak led to unusual candor by Venezuela's newly elected President Carlos Andres Perez. Although seen by many as being in the pocket of international bankers, Perez showed no hesitation in placing the blame: "The crisis Latin American nations are undergoing has a name written with capital letters—foreign debt."[49] He went on to fault the industrialized nations for giving little or no help to support democratic governments. His claim is true. Venezuela saw the proportion of money going to service its debt, as a percentage of its export earnings, increase from 4.2 percent in 1970 to 37.4 percent in 1986 (nearly an 800 percent increase). Adding to this picture have been debt service increases of 234 percent for Brazil, 24 percent for Argentina, 52 percent for Chile, 66 percent for Columbia, and 140 percent for both Ecuador and Bolivia.[50] In a word, the drain has been horrendous.

Income Distribution and Available Data

Comparing different countries on the spread of internal income is very different from comparing nations on the level of GNP per person. A high GNP per person is often falsely seen as a high level of wealth. Yet it is possible for a country to have a high level of GNP and a very high degree of internal income inequality. It is not enough to ask what level of average wealth exists without also asking how the economic piece of pie that a country gets is itself divided up within its borders. Brazil is often held up as a model of economic development. Its GNP per person in 1986 was $1,810—enviable by Third World standards. Just over one half (50.6 percent) of this income, however, was being captured by the highest 10 percent of all households. Only 2 percent of all income went to the poorest 20 percent of all households! South Korea is an equally successful LDC nation with a GNP per person ($2,370) roughly equivalent to Brazil's. South Korea shows only 27.5 percent of its income going to the top 10 percent of all households, while 5.7 percent of all income ends up in the poorest fifth of all households.[51] In essence, economic "development" is very questionable if only a small minority of the population benefits. Much of the concern for income inequality must be looked at in terms of how it is spread out within countries. Without this, average GNP is very misleading.

Unfortunately, the quality of existing data which looks at the internal distribution of income in nations is weaker and less complete than GNP per person figures. The main sources for the income distribution data have been gained from sample surveys. Even within developed countries there is a risk of bias resulting from how the sample is selected. There is always a chance that the sample will not somehow be a good proxy for the entire population. Within LDCs this problem can be more severe due to a number of factors: nomadic groups, hard-to-reach regions, fear of government officials using such information to increase a household's tax burden, failure to include nonmoney income such as food, etc.[52] Comparing inequality of family incomes between Third World nations with developed countries may not yield valid results because even the very definition of what a family is can vary widely from one country to the next.[53]

Nearly all analysts wish to use estimates that are close together in time, based on large and representative national samples, and which tap the same unit (most frequently, the household). Figures released from the World Bank in their latest report come closest to this ideal.[54] All estimates are within ten years of a 1980 benchmark (only eleven of forty-six countries in this data set are earlier than 1975), while all are based upon household estimates. Muller feels that data sets gathered within eleven years of each other are roughly the same.[55] Thus, the income distribution results in table 3.3 should be the best and most up-to-date figures available for households in the world. An obvious flaw to this data, however, is its underrepresentation among LDCs in comparison to core nations.

Table 3.3 can be more easily understood if we think of all households that receive income as occupying a continuum. It will go from the lowest income to the highest income. The third column in table 3.3 thus says that for the Netherlands, the lowest 20 percent of all households receive only 8.3 percent of all the income distributed in that country. The fourth column states that 36.2 percent of all income goes to the households in the top 20 percent of all households. The fifth column says that 21.5 percent of all income went to the top 10 percent of all households. There are three quintiles (segments of 20 percent each) that have been left out of the table to improve simplicity, but which would give a more complete picture of the income distribution. It is not really necessary to look at these other three quintiles to get a clear idea of the skewed nature of income data. It is apparent that the poorest 20 percent of all households receive much less than 20 percent of all the income. At the other end, the richest 20 percent of all households receive much more than 20 percent of all income distributed. Japan, one of the most equal of all countries, shows only 8.7 percent of all its national income going to the poorest 20 percent of households. Almost 40 percent of all its income ends up in the wealthiest 20 percent of all households.

Such patterns are typical of all countries to some degree. If the data were to be divided into even finer groups of 1.0 percent each, the resulting graph would show a large hump among the lower-middle income range with a long tail trailing off to the right. This skewing vividly shows the high incomes that go to only a small proportion of the popu-

TABLE 3.3   Household Income Distribution within Countries by Modern
World System Position

Country and World Position	Household Gini and (Percent Rank)	Percent of income going to households		
		Lowest 20 Percent	Top 20 Percent	Top 10 Percent
Core				
Netherlands	.2664 (2.0)	8.3	36.2	21.5
Belgium	.2722 (4.1)	7.9	36.0	21.5
Japan	.2773 (6.1)	8.7	37.5	22.4
Switzerland	.3002 (10.2)	6.6	38.0	23.7
West Germany	.3037 (12.2)	7.9	39.5	24.0
Yugoslavia	.3111 (18.4)	6.6	38.7	22.9
Norway	.3118 (20.4)	6.0	38.2	22.8
Sweden	.3205 (24.5)	7.4	41.7	28.1
United Kingdom	.3219 (26.5)	7.0	39.7	23.4
Denmark	.3260 (28.6)	5.4	38.6	22.3
United States	.3359 (32.7)	5.3	39.9	23.3
Canada	.3376 (34.7)	5.3	40.0	23.8
France	.3530 (36.7)	5.5	42.2	26.4
Italy	.3595 (38.8)	6.2	43.9	28.1
Australia	.3975 (53.1)	5.4	47.1	30.5
Average	.32 (23.3)	6.6	39.8	24.3
Semi-Periphery				
Hungary	.2800 (8.2)	6.9	35.8	20.5
Ireland	.3108 (14.3)	7.2	39.4	25.1
Finland	.3108 (16.3)	6.3	37.6	21.7
Spain	.3176 (22.4)	6.9	40.0	24.5
Israel	.3261 (30.6)	6.0	39.9	22.6
South Korea	.3713 (42.9)	5.7	45.3	27.5
India	.4022 (55.1)	7.0	49.4	33.6
Sri Lanka	.4114 (57.1)	5.8	49.8	34.7
Portugal	.4141 (59.2)	5.2	49.1	33.4
Argentina	.4345 (65.3)	4.4	50.3	35.2
Philippines	.4451 (69.4)	5.2	52.5	37.0
Venezuela	.4874 (73.5)	3.0	54.0	35.7
Malaysia	.4947 (75.5)	3.5	56.1	39.8
Turkey	.4949 (77.6)	3.5	56.5	40.7
Kenya	.5452 (89.8)	2.6	60.4	45.8
Iran	.5489 (91.8)	3.4	62.7	47.4
Peru	.5612 (95.9)	1.9	61.0	42.9
Average	.42 (55.6)	5.0	49.4	33.4
Periphery				
New Zealand	.3791 (44.9)	5.1	44.7	28.7
El Salvador	.3957 (49.0)	5.5	47.3	29.5
Egypt	.3964 (51.0)	5.8	48.0	33.2

TABLE 3.3   (*Continued*)

Country and World Position	Household Gini and (Percent Rank)	Percent of income going to households		
		Lowest 20 Percent	Top 20 Percent	Top 10 Percent
Thailand	.4180 (61.2)	5.6	49.8	34.1
Indonesia	.4242 (63.3)	6.6	49.4	34.0
Trinidad & Tobago	.4348 (67.3)	4.2	50.0	31.8
Costa Rica	.4816 (71.4)	3.3	54.8	39.5
Senegal	.5031 (79.6)	5.5	60.9	45.4
Colombia	.5105 (81.6)	4.0	58.5	43.5
Mexico	.5155 (83.7)	2.9	57.7	40.6
Mauritius	.5229 (85.7)	4.0	60.5	46.7
Ivory Coast	.5496 (93.9)	2.4	61.4	43.7
Panama	.5642 (98.0)	2.0	61.8	44.2
Brazil	.5994 (100.0)	2.0	66.6	50.6
Average	.48 (73.6)	4.2	55.1	39.0
All Nation Average	.41 (50.0)	5.3	48.2	32.4

lation. A more graphic picture than this has been used to describe the "typical" income distribution:

> Jan Pen (1971) paints a fascinating "word picture" of the income distribution of individuals when he likens it to a parade of people whose height is proportional to their income and who all must pass a certain point in an hour. It takes 48 minutes before one sees marchers of average heights (income) and the parade grows with agonizing slowness until giants of 27 feet loom up at 1 minute to go. From then on, their height increases with dizzying rapidity—in the last few seconds of the march come businessmen and executives 100 feet tall while the final marcher (a multimillionaire) is some thousands of feet high.[56]

The data show that world position has much to do with the degree of income inequality within a nation. Among core countries, 6.6 percent of all income goes to the poorest 20 percent of all households—compared to 5 percent in the semi-periphery and 4.2 percent in the periphery. *Within the poorest of countries, the poorest of households receive less income!* Hope for persons of the Third World dims with this fact. As a nation becomes less wealthy, the poorest segment of the population suffers even more than within wealthier countries. The opposite is true for the richest 10 percent of all households. Within core countries they get 24.3 percent of all income, compared to 33.4 percent in the semi-periphery and 39 percent in the periphery. Again, as nations become less well-off, the rich actually receive more income than do the rich in the wealthiest of countries. Apparently there is some truth to the old adage that "the rich get richer, but the poor get children." [57]

What is a *fair* distribution of income? Harking back to the original question raised in the first chapter, we again ask, "How much is enough?" Unfortunately, comparing income distributions puts us into a more subjective, relative range. It is obvious that all national income distributions are somewhat unfair. All do not share equally. That some of this may be due to intrinsic factors goes without saying. Hard work, motivation, risk taking, getting more education, and finding skilled employment are all crucial in the race for income. Yet major doubts about human capital must remain in the face of such huge differences between nations in income inequality.

Even among core nations, the large differences between countries suggest that other forces are at work to produce greater or lesser income inequality. The United States, for example, shows the lowest 20 percent of households to be the "poorest" among all core nations. Only 5.3 percent of all our income goes to this group. Japan has the most well-off bottom quintile with 8.7 percent of its household income being claimed by this group. At the other extreme, however, the United States actually shows a "modest" 23.3 percent of all income going to the richest 10 percent of all households. This is in contrast to 30.5 percent for Australia. All of these comparisons within the core pale into insignificance, however, when distributions within the periphery are examined. Without doubt, Brazil has the worst recorded picture of income inequality in the world. While only 2 percent of all income goes to the poorest 20 percent of its households, over one-half of all income ends up in the hands of the richest 10 percent of its households!

But what is the right statistic to look at? Should we be concerned with the bottom 10 percent of all households? The richest 20 percent? The elite top 5 percent? What about the quintiles left out of the picture? A society can have both a high percent of income going to the bottom quintile and a low percent to the top 20 percent, yet still be greatly unequal. This will occur if a high percent of income is found in the fourth quintile (60–79 percent range), a low percent in the second quintile (20–39 percent range), or both. In short, the picture can become very muddy if all five quintiles are compared between all forty-nine countries. Even if we were to follow this analytical avenue, it might not lead us to any clear conclusions. We would still be left with the task of sorting out and deciding which quintile or portion thereof (e.g., top 10 percent) we felt was the most important.

Gini Ratios to the Rescue: A Single Measurement of Income Inequality

While it is acceptable to look at both ends of the income distribution in comparing countries, there is an easier way to describe all of a nation's income inequality at one time. We can theoretically draw a graph showing what a perfectly equal income distribution for a population would look like. Figure 3.4 looks at family income inequality within the United States as of 1987 (the most recent data available). Perfect equality would here be seen in the 45-degree diagonal line A to C. What this shows is that 20 percent of all families receive 20 percent of all income, 40 percent of families receive 40 percent of all income, etc. up to 100 percent. A distribution such as this, of course, does not exist in reality. It is the departure from this perfectly equal state of income distribution we are interested in. This also can be plotted in a curve using quintiles or deciles from data such as in table 3.3. The result is what is called a Lorenz curve, which is represented by the curved line in figure 3.4.[58] The further the curve is from the diagonal line, the more income inequality there is.

Although this graph was quite an advancement in showing income inequality in its entirety, it was still awkward. It was simply too difficult to compare many nations on the basis of looking at numerous Lorenz curves. Italian economist Corrado Gini proposed that a single ratio be used instead. It divides the area of the curve which departs from the line of perfect equality (shaded in figure 3.4) by the entire possible area (represented by the triangle ABC). The degree of income inequality could then be summed into one number and populations easily compared. Calculating household Gini ratios using the most recent data from the World Bank and International Labour Office yields the figures in column two of table 3.3.[59]

The figures indicate a Gini ratio of .3359 for the United States and one of .3002 for Switzerland (the wealthiest among all nations by GNP per person). The lower the ratio, the less income inequality. On this basis, the United States has more income inequality than most European countries. Yet we are a shade more equal than our neighbor to the north (the Canadian Gini is .3376) and dramatically more equal than Mexico (.5155). Overall, the United States is among the top third of countries that are most egalitarian in distribution of income. Lest we slip into complacency, it should also be noted that our poorest 20 percent of households gets the lowest percent of income among all core countries. Our Gini ratio is still 26 percent above the world's lowest score.

Also obvious are the large differences in Gini scores by world position. Core countries have an average of .32, compared to .42 for the semi-periphery and .48 for the periphery. Such large differences are also

FIGURE 3.4: Lorenz Curve (U.S. Family Income in 1987)

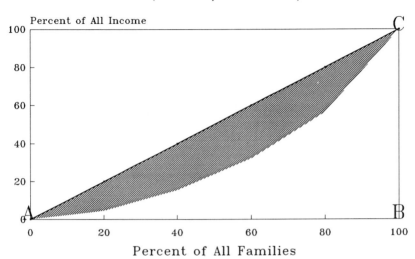

Percent of All Income

Source: U.S. Bureau of the Census, *Current Population Reports,* Series P–60, no. 161, Table 4.

statistically significant. Once again, using an indicator that captures the entire spectrum of income inequality, the conclusion is inescapable. LDCs suffer in both absolute and relative income deprivation when compared to core industrial countries. LDCs are not only poor in terms of absolute income, but *the poorest parts of their populations are relatively worse off* than the poor in more wealthy nations.

The Gini ratio does have a few weaknesses as a measure of income inequality.[60] Yet this seems inevitable with any figure that tries to show a complex process with one number. The Dow-Jones Industrial Average, although widely used and almost religiously followed, is only a composite of a few selected stocks among the many traded on the New York Stock Exchange. At times it has also been criticized for not being representative of activity on the exchange because of its makeup. Yet it continues to provide a useful function for analysts. So too, does the Gini ratio. This technique is the oldest and most reliable of income inequality measurements. It has now been in use for three-quarters of a century. Its utility also depends greatly on how we wish to use the Gini ratio. In an analysis comparing Gini with seven different income inequality measurements, the choice of measure did not really matter in looking at the factors we wish to pursue in this book.[61] Other studies show that the Gini ratio is an ideal way to measure income change within the middle class, which is of great concern to us when we look at trends in the United States.[62]

In the end, income inequality has both absolute and relative dimensions. Both aspects are looked at within this book, since the picture we get of income inequality can shift somewhat depending upon what perspective we use. This does not mean that there will always be disagreement. It is already plain that poor countries are cursed with both absolute and relative income deprivation. Yet there are times throughout the book when the distinction will become more important. Core countries tend to be high on absolute measures such as GNP per person. They are also low on relative measures such as Gini, the proportion of income going to the top 10 percent of households, and so on. This is very true among American states. Wealthy states as ranked by mean family income also tend to have low Gini ratios. The difference is important and must be kept in mind in looking at income inequality.

A Case Analysis of Absolute versus Relative Income Inequality: The Economic "Miracle" of Brazil

There is no shortage of studies done which examines the impact of development upon Third World countries. This is very true in looking at individual nations (the case study approach). Although longitudinal data that is measured over a long period of time does not exist for nearly all countries, there are some shreds of evidence on trends in the Third World.[63] Looking at figures kept over the past ninety years, for example, shows that the growth in Mexico's relative income inequality has shown no sign of finally turning around. Its poorest 40 percent of families have not shown any material improvement since the Revolution of 1910. Meanwhile, while the richest fifth of Mexican families received ten times as much income as the poorest fifth in 1950, this ratio had risen to 20-to-1 by 1977. By this year, Mexico's distribution of income was among the most uneven in the world, but it was to get even worse. In the period of five short years (1982–87), the share of Gross Domestic Product going to wages and salaries declined from 37.2 percent to 24.9 percent.[64]

This painful slide was largely a result of IMF restructuring, which was planned in collusion with Mexican business elites. Within the six years of the de la Madrid regime (1982 to 1988), real wages fell by one-half while debt-service payments Mexico had to pay its creditors rose to nearly two-thirds of the national budget. The inflation rate rose to nearly 25 percent a year in Mexico, while it has had to import over one-half of its basic grains in recent years. What this means is that people are starving! Between 1981 and 1988, the personal consumption of rice, beans, and corn was cut nearly in half. All of this occurred against the backdrop of nominal "success" as Mexico managed to increase its industrial exports by 130 percent in six years. This is supposed to lead to more money, according to IMF wisdom, but what profits were generated also left the country in a massive capital flight. Mexico is actually worse off than before its restructuring, and now has a government which was forced to resort to massive voter fraud in order to stay in power.[65]

The case of Mexico underscores the lack of any meaningful connection between development and help for the suffering majority of citizens within a country. Yet it is especially with Brazil that we can gain an even sharper idea about the dynamics between absolute and relative income inequality. This nation's performance since 1960 as a country brimming with growth earned it accolades such as "the miracle economy." Between 1960–81, the Brazilian economy racked-up large income per person growth at an annual rate of 5 percent year after year. For a few years in the late 1960s and early 1970s, average annual growth was approximately 10 percent. Even after the first shock of oil price increases during 1973–74, it managed to achieve healthy industrial and agricultural growth rates. Much of its economic plan was based upon import substitution. In an effort to free itself from oil imports, Brazil introduced a massive sugar cane industry which produces alcohol fuel. It has also built up its industry as well as agribusiness (soybeans) to increase exports. Gigantic internal projects meant to stimulate economic growth have also been mounted, such as development in the Amazon.[66] Much evidence also shows that promoting exports over industries catering to a domestic market and/or substitutes for imports actually produces more employment in Brazil.[67] In this manner, more income is also redistributed downward to the poor by providing unskilled jobs. Thus, Brazil is a fertile testing ground to look at the relationship between real economic growth and relative income inequality.

Did the majority of Brazil's population share in the run-up of wealth and economic growth during these two decades? In terms of absolute income, the answer is a resounding "maybe." Despite high initial income inequality, Brazil's own census figures for 1960 and 1970 show that all income groups had very large increases in real income. Each 10 percent (decile) of households had nearly 50 percent growth over the decade.[68] Persons within the bottom 10 percent, 20 percent, and 30 percent brackets also showed the same degree of increase as persons in the top decile brackets of 70 percent to 100 percent. It was the middle classes that showed slightly smaller increases of real income, averaging about 35 percent over the decade. Yet Professor José Camargo, a Brazilian economist, disputes this interpretation. If persons who have not earned any income (e.g., those unable to find jobs) are included for both the officially designated "poor" and "non-poor" groups, a sharply different picture emerges. The relative income gap between poor and non-poor persons actually increased in 1960–70 by 44 percent![69]

Noneconomic indicators of poverty and social well-being are less equivocal and show great progress during the 1970–80 period. Literacy rates increased, as did school enrollment percentages. Piped water and sewer connections went up dramatically. Households with electricity climbed from 48 percent to 67 percent. By 1980, over half of all households had a refrigerator and/or a TV, three-fourths had a radio, and nearly one-fourth owned a car.[70]

The growth statistics are quite breathtaking up until 1980. Yet the expansionist economic policies followed by the military junta which ruled Brazil from 1964 to 1985 ultimately led to disaster. Import substitution only worked in a few select industries such as iron and steel. For aluminum, fertilizers, and petrochemicals, real imports have continued to grow, as they have for capital goods. The crucial area of oil substitution, which makes Brazil highly vulnerable to world price flux, showed no change at all during the 1970s.[71] To finance further growth at continued high levels, Brazil was willing to add even more external debt to fuel its booming economy. Credit subsidies and incentives were heavily used to favor export industries, while higher taxes to pay for the growth were avoided like the plague. Such debt increases came to about 28 percent per year between 1973 and 1978.[72] As the ensuing world recession developed, Brazil's export performance slowed. It became more and more difficult to pay off the mountain of debt it had accumulated from international banks. By 1982 Brazil was forced into an austerity program dictated by the IMF. The result to its economy goes beyond the usual pain of decline, however, ending in an annual rate of inflation for 1988 of 942 percent!

Some scholars argue that because of its vast size and richly endowed resources, Brazil is in more of a position to be independent of the world system. It may have an ability, if we were to regard it as a semi-periphery state with *some* inherent power, of weathering the periodic storms sweeping through the world economy. Sociologist Peter Evans points out that it is too simplistic to think of emerging industrial powers in terms of the old Dependency school, operating only at the whim of core countries.[73] Rather, in some countries like Brazil there is frequently a triple alliance that forms between the state government, large native capitalist interests, and multinational corporations from core countries eager to invest within LDCs. The state acts to mediate the alliance in such a way as to encourage multinational investment. At times it may combine with large local firms or now and then it may choose to set up its own enterprises in conjunction with foreign firms. The point to his detailed analysis of Brazilian industry is that this nation is not at all powerless in the worldwide economic pecking-order. The government will insist that certain conditions must be set before multinationals are allowed to come in and set up shop. Many of these strings involve coalitions with the state and/

or local capital, import restrictions, quotas for the hiring of Brazilian labor or contracting, and so on.

Yet the bottom line to the triple alliance still leaves Brazil under the thumb of countries in the core. The success of such industrial growth ultimately lies with the willingness of multinationals to invest, international bankers to make huge loans, and core countries to consume exports from Brazil. The government of Brazil and its largest firms may wrangle among themselves in the quest for greater accumulation and profit, but they must ultimately satisfy foreign investors with enough sugar coating on their deals. Since this can threaten the profit margin of Brazilian big business and the state, they always respond by squeezing the wages of workers:

> Whether products were developed locally or abroad by multinationals or local firms, they were developed in response to perceived opportunities for profits, which given the skew of Brazilian income distribution, is hardly synonymous with the satisfaction of needs. . . . The maintenance of the delicate balance among the three partners militates against any possibility of dealing seriously with questions of income distribution, even if members of the elite express support for income distribution in principle. . . . Nothing indicates the divergence between the benefits expected from industrialization and the actual results better than the changes in Brazilian income distribution between 1960 and 1970. In a decade during which the production of television sets tripled and the top 5 percent of the population almost doubled their average income, the 80 million on the bottom remained stagnated at incomes averaging below $200 a year. . . . The rate of infant mortality in Sao Paulo, one of the most modern and heavily industrialized cities in the world, was 84 per 1,000 live births in 1969, about a third higher than the rates for the entire nation of Argentina. The rate for Recife, the largest and most advanced city in the northeast, was 263.5 per 1000 in 1971, about 60 percent higher than the rate for the rural population of Chad, which was the highest national rate recorded by the United Nations. Even more discouraging is the fact that Recife's rate of infant mortality is apparently no lower than it was a generation ago.[74]

In other words, Brazil as a nation may remain strong despite economic penetration by foreign firms. Perhaps some of its sectors will even be better off and "more developed" as a result of continued investment from the outside. A few of its corporate elites may also benefit greatly from such growth. Yet the vast majority of its citizens still remain in abject poverty. An ever escalating GNP per capita has no meaning to hungry children in the favellas overlooking Rio or the rural poor in the northeast section of this country. Yet even within the affluent major cities of the southeast—such as Sao Paulo and Rio de Janeiro—there is a major question whether Brazil as a nation is better off from having followed the golden path of development. Sao Paulo is Brazil's richest city, where most of this nation's manufacturing is concentrated. Local jobs here pay relatively high wages. Yet after the "miracle" had started pumping out industrial products for export, infant mortality had actually increased from the already high level of 80 deaths per 1,000 live births. Even in rich Sao Paulo, one-third of households lacked running water while 60 percent had no sewer connections during the 1970s.[75] Despite the healthy growth in manufacturing exports, the proportion of the labor force in the informal sector (24 percent) has not budged between 1969 and 1983.[76] The informal sector is made up of people doing anything to survive, who do not hold regular jobs which earn a wage. In Rio they are the street vendors selling T-shirts, drugs, sex, a gamut of personal services, and the like. Since unemployment nearly doubled in the same period, this means that jobs in the formal sector have slid by 5 percent as well. At the bottom line, export growth has not created enough jobs to even make a dent in bettering the distribution of income.

In Berkeley economist Albert Fishlow's opinion, the state definitely dropped the ball.[77] By mindlessly chasing growth through unwise borrowing, the government failed to introduce needed change to its economy in order to maintain its health. When the crunch came, as it always must to those drowning in a sea of red ink, the common people had to pay the price for the final reckoning. Ironically, this led to the downfall of the military junta and the return of civilian government in Brazil—which was to be the only ray of sunshine to this debt calamity.

On a relative basis there is much poverty. Within Brazil, between 1960 and 1980 the richest 10 percent increased their share of income from 40 percent to 48 percent. At the same time, the share of income received by the lowest 80 percent actually fell. The richest one-fifth of all households in the United States averages twelve times the income of the poorest fifth. The same ratio in Brazil is 33-to-1.[78] The Gini ratio of income inequality actually *increased* from .52 in 1960 to .565 in 1970 to .590 in 1980 among the economically active population.[79] During the 1960–70 decade, the upper 3.2 percent of the population enlarged its share of Brazil's total income from 27 percent to 32 percent. The increase in real income during the same time period did not reduce the percent of those under the poverty line. The absolute gap of real income instead widened by 25 percent between the poor and non-poor during these 10 years.[80]

Wherever one looks, economic inequality in Brazil has increased sharply during the past three decades of development. Helga Hoffman, an analyst at the United Nations, reports that income of individuals, income of the economically active population, and family income all became more unequal during the 1960s. This growth of inequality slowed somewhat during the 1970s (even slightly reversing for families, who were forced to put children to work).[81] But by 1980 the income share of the poorest half of Brazil's population had actually gone down from 15.6 percent to 13.4 percent while the richest 10 percent of the population laid claim to one-half of all income within the country. Industrial concentration, already massive, actually went up during the same decade. The top one-half of one percent of firms now accounts for one-half of all total sales in the country, while the top 3 percent of firms accounts for 70 percent of all industrial capital.

As business firms were growing larger and ever richer, an economic nosedive took place at the same time for the Brazilian working class. Professor José Camargo of the Department of Economics, Catholic University of Rio de Janeiro, presents evidence that this slide in wages was deliberately planned:

> The period 1964–1974 was one of strong political repression. After the military coup of March 1964, unions were dissolved and strikes repressed by the military force and, as a result, the position of the workers was drastically weakened. Unable to press their demands, the workers had no choice but to accept the wage adjustment imposed by the government. On the other hand, government priority was to reduce the rate of inflation and a wage squeeze was a powerful instrument by which to attain this objective. . . . As a direct consequence of this policy, those wages whose adjustments followed the formula grew at rates much lower than the inflation rates. The real wage declined sharply. . . . There is a decline of 20 percent for the real minimum wage between 1964 and 1971. . . . In 1978 it was still 14 percent lower than in 1963.[82]

There were other costs to the rule by military junta as well. As is true whenever the military dominates a country, funds for defense tripled in the 1963–73 period. Jan Knippers Black details many cases of jailing, killing, torture, and disappearance of politicians, scientists, professors, educators, artists, and others who dared oppose the new order.[83] In her book *United States Penetration of Brazil,* she presents evidence of U.S. complicity through military channels in the 1964 coup which brought the Brazilian army to power. Her analysis also tracks multinational corporations within Brazil and their role in bringing about the downfall of this nation's constitutionally elected democratic government. There was much to lose in the eyes of these corporations! The rake-off for U.S. firms in Brazil has been astronomical in comparison to other countries. In 1969, for example, many U.S. businesses recorded the following high profit levels in their Brazilian subsidiaries: Exxon (15.7 percent), Johnson

& Johnson (16 percent), GM and RCA (20 percent), Squibb (20.5 percent), Union Carbide (21.8 percent), GE (22.6 percent), Goodyear and Atlantic Richfield (23 percent), Texaco (28 percent), Xerox (64 percent).[84] After the coup, U.S. dollars gushed into Brazil in the form of government aid and new business startups—climbing 71 percent during the 1960s alone.

The major result, according to Black and other scholars, has been denationalization of Brazil's most profitable industries. Lavish concessions flowed to U.S. firms from the generals, which included full repatriation of corporate profits to the core, much lower taxes, more favorable bank credits, etc. While foreign firms could borrow money at 7–8 percent, Brazilian domestic firms had to pay as much as 48 percent. Most of them went belly-up within a few years or were devoured in a piranha-like fashion by the very same multinationals that were being so unfairly subsidized by the junta. In this manner, foreign capital came to control 70 percent of the 679 largest firms within Brazil by 1970. From the coup through 1976, Brazil had received more U.S. economic and military aid than any other Latin American country. Given the high profit levels and the very favorable multinational investment climate that Brazil offers, this is not surprising.

A more insidious result in addition to the bleeding of capital from Brazil has been the destruction of anything uniquely native to its own culture. Deep penetration has been economic, but it has also been strong in social, cultural, political, and military channels. Brazil has come to resemble a chameleon, taking on the hues and colors of the nations which it hosts through their corporate subsidiaries. Jan Black provides an eloquent quote by former Brazilian congressman Marcio Moreira Alves that distills the essence of resentment such institutional domination causes in the people who are forced to live under the strong shadow of U.S. penetration:

> Everything we consume in our daily lives betrays a foreign presence. We are bandaged at birth by Johnson & Johnson. We survive on Nestle or Gloria Milk. We dress in synthetic clothes produced by French, British, or American firms. Our teeth are kept clean by Colgate toothpaste and Tek brushes. We wash with Lever Brothers and Palmolive soaps, shave with Williams and Gillette. Resting in the sun we drink Coca-Cola—and now even the largest producer of *cachaca,* the white rum national drink, is owned by Coca-Cola. We ride Otis elevators, drive Volkswagens and Fords and ship our goods on Mercedes-Benz trucks fueled by Esso and Shell, our rubber is Pirelli, we talk with Ericsson telephones, communicate through Siemens telex, type on Olivetti machines and receive IBM-processed bills. We eat out of American and Canadian

made cans packed by Armour, Swift, and Wilson. The Beatles' beat comes out of Philips radios, and we dance to RCA records. Our General Electric TV sets are connected to ITT satellites. We can rely on old Bayer for aspirin, or, if trouble develops, on Squibb for antibiotics. From the comfortable Goodyear mattresses of our American hospital beds we can look through Saint-Gobain windows on gardens tended by Japanese lawnmowers. If we die (say, from lung cancer puffed from British or American cigarettes) we may finally have a chance of entering into our 94 percent share of the economy—graveyards are owned by the Santa Casas de Misericordia, an old Brazilian institution. But the family must pay the electricity bills to Canadian Light and Power—with money manufactured by Thomas de la Rue or by the American Bank Note Company.[85]

Dependency scholars predict that income inequality cannot help but grow in Brazil and other countries like it.[86] This will always be true wherever there is industrial development and growth in a modern sector going on next door to traditional, poor sectors such as subsistence agriculture. The contrast in Brazil is quite vivid between Rio de Janeiro and Sao Paulo versus its Northeast region. Large gaps of both absolute and relative income remain between Brazil's states as well as marked urban and rural contrasts.

Most growth advocates point out that real income will nonetheless advance for most people. They argue that for a relatively affluent LDC such as Brazil, the increase in real absolute income can amount to a tidy sum. Even if this were true, however, we must never forget that we are dealing with incredibly low incomes at the bottom of the Brazilian income hierarchy. During the economic boom period of the early 1970s, one expert estimated that it would take twenty to thirty years of growth at current rates to raise the poorest 10% of the population up to an annual $100 per person income![87] Even during the high growth period of the late 1970s, 40 percent of Brazil's export earnings had to be spent on servicing its foreign debt.[88] This was before Brazil, along with other periphery countries, ran into serious trouble during the early 1980s because of the second oil price increase and world recession.

In order to pay off its massive debt, Brazil submitted to an IMF austerity program in 1983. This led to further cuts in domestic spending. As usual, the poor and workers were the first to suffer. Although complete statistics will not be available until Brazil's 1990 census has been taken, the first estimates are very bleak. The downturn in its economy is severe! Within the 1980–83 period, industrial production declined 11 percent and capital goods production slipped by 45 percent. Projections indicate that at best, Brazil will be unable to resume a growth rate in its Gross Domestic Production (GDP) greater than its population growth until 1989. Even at that point, its GDP will be 19 percent lower than in 1980. Within four years (1980–84), Brazil's standard of living declined 17 percent—while it is projected to be 20 percent less in 1989 than in 1980.[89] Put bluntly, Brazil's economy has ended up in the gutter!

Very recent statistics are now available to help us assess the grim reality of this decline. The government of Brazil gathers yearly data on its economy by means of cross-sectional surveys. These surveys show virtually no change in the degree of income inequality occurring in the country up through September of 1987, despite a rebound from the 1982–83 recession.[90] Although it is now plain that income inequality has finally stopped growing at astronomical rates, it is still at an all-time high and shows no sign of reversing.

In the meantime, many experts continue to attest to the loss of real income and an increase in grinding poverty among the masses. Since 1980 the poor have born the brunt of austerity measures. It is by now very likely that even the paltry gains in absolute income eked out during the 1960s and 1970s will have been lost during the 1980s. Although the government has set a minimum wage, this has done nothing to help stave off the slip in Brazil's living standard. Yet it does serve as a stark yardstick of how bad the situation really is. Data for 1983–85 show the minimum wage to be one-fifth to one-seventh the amount needed to cover a family's basic needs. This was at a time when only 10 percent of the work force earned the equivalent of five minimum wages. Put differently, by 1986 nearly two-thirds of the Brazilian population was at a level between misery and extreme poverty. The purchasing power of a minimum salary had declined by 50 percent.[91] The current situation is not fair nor is it just. This is especially true when we realize that productivity has quadrupled in Brazil since 1940. It is cruel to expect others to undergo such want and deprivation while being this hardworking and industrious.

It is very likely that even more "doom and gloom" lies waiting in the future for Brazil. Because of the decline in prices of its exports and the increase of interest payments on its mountain of debt—the vital force of the country's economy is being bled off. By mid-1988, Brazil owed $118 billion—a full 10 percent of all Third World debt. When the military took power in 1964, Brazil owed $3.5 billion. By the time it stepped down in 1985, over $100 billion of external debt had accumulated. Thus, in a period of two decades, debt owed to foreign banks increased twenty-nine-fold while per capita income went up by only 130 percent.[92] Paying off this huge debt has made Brazil the world's largest capital exporter after Japan. It has also caused endless turmoil and bickering among political and economic elites within its own borders. The acrimony has stopped any coherent, workable plan from emerging despite the return of democracy. Instead, a variety of economic policies have alternated between expansion and contraction in the 1980s. Such a "stop and go" mentality has virtually destroyed stability and the credibility needed for the economy to work normally.

Brazil does need to grow at an explosive pace just to stay even. This is because population continues to multiply at a much faster pace than the growth of jobs. The poor in Brazil have a rate of natural increase three times that of the rich. Over time, the fact that women in poor Brazilian families have an average of 7.6 children compared to 3.3 children for high-income women can mean only one thing. The larger absolute and relative numbers of needy persons will increasingly twist the maldistribution of income in Brazil. Income inequality in this country will thus be even more grotesque by the year 2000.[93] According to projections, the ranks of the poor and deprived will swell larger even if the miracle growth rates briefly evident in the 1970s were to stage an unlikely comeback:

> Models that simulate the rate of growth of the formal sector find that, even when the overall economy grows at a rate of 7 percent a year, the rate of increase in formal-sector employment is only around 1.6 percent (or less). Since the rate of increase in labor supply is much larger (2.4 percent a year), the findings suggest that, if present trends continue, the formal sector will never fully absorb new additions to the labor force. Analyses of population growth by level of household income indicate that the poor are at a particular disadvantage. Estimates for 1980 show that the poorer sectors of the Brazilian population experience rates of natural increase on the order of about 3 percent per year. The relatively low rate of job creation in the formal sector and the high rate of increase in labor supply (especially among the poor) mean that, without a fundamental change in the structure of Brazil's economy, the proportion of poorly paid workers will increase even with high rates of economic growth.[94]

Desperation and the Fight to Stay Alive: The Human Cost of Income Inequality in Brazil

To personally find out more about the impact that such gross inequality has upon its people, my wife and I recently visited Brazil. It was an opportunity to meet with economists, scholars, and government officials who graciously donated their time and services to my study. By interviewing Brazilians closely connected with the development of their nation, it was possible to get firsthand opinions about whether their country was dominated by foreign interests. Almost every expert said "no" to this question. The intellectuals we talked with were unanimous in their view that Brazil was powerful enough in its own right to resist or

manage corporate domination from abroad. Nationalism in Brazil is
rampant, extending far beyond the fanaticism of its soccer fans. One
authority proudly told me that his nation had managed to build the
world's first and only Apple Macintosh computer clone. Ironically, although he felt foreign powers were relatively weak in Brazil, he said in
the next breath that the government had yielded to pressure from Apple
Computers and had decided not to sell the clones.

Brazilian economists have a touching faith in growth-oriented policies, even if these procedures have brought them so much distress today.
One official jokingly told me that "Brazil was doomed to grow." We
could see he was pleased with the prospect. The general message from
all economists was that although Brazil had serious problems, it would
once again surge forth among the world's economies with explosive
growth. In my opinion, this is a tenuous assumption. It is accepted on
good faith that free markets will reign supreme long into the future. The
reality seems to point toward the other extreme. Many contemporary
economists believe a once-unified world economy will split into at least
three trading-blocs (Europe, North America, Japan/Asia). Tariffs and
trade barriers will prevail in the future, as exports dry up.[95]

But whether this scenario is accurate or not really begs the question. By focusing on growth, Brazilian officials have turned the spotlight
off the enormous inequities that are so painfully obvious in their country.
The implicit view is that growth will take care of poverty more or less
automatically. As real income goes up, the need to be concerned about
unfair income distribution will go down. (Perhaps as foreigners not used
to the country, my wife and I saw things that Brazilians may have long
taken for granted. Luxury hotels line Avenue Atlantica aside Copacabana
Beach in Rio de Janeiro, "glamour capital of the world." Outside their
doors, literally only a few feet away, is the most dire poverty I have ever
encountered in my life. Homeless families live on mattresses on the side-
walk or beneath highway viaducts. Beggars accost tourists wherever
they go. Returning to our room one morning at 2:00 A.M., we counted
nearly a dozen prostitutes on one corner of a single block.)

These are the seamier sides of life without money, of being forced
to do anything to feed yourself. If I were asked to describe Rio in one
sentence, it would be "Two blocks of Paris along the beach with Ethiopia
surrounding it." In most areas, the city of Rio de Janeiro is only four to
six blocks wide before steep hills are encountered. On these hills are the
favellas, slums where the poorest of the poor live. Two totally different
classes exist side-by-side and the streets of Rio reflect this. Graffiti is
scrawled everywhere, even on the churches. Rich Brazilians live in con-
dominiums along Ipanema Beach or one block in; yet they are only three
blocks away from devastating poverty. Armed guards continuously pa-

trol the entrances to these condos, while all ground-floor windows have iron bars or steel shutters.

It is unsafe to walk in most areas of the city, whether you are a tourist or carioca (native-born to Rio). It is mandatory not to wear a watch, carry a camera, have much money on your person, speak English, or even look as if you do not know where you are going. Tourist books give some warnings to these facts of life for vacationers headed for Rio. Yet the warnings simply cannot convey the reality of the scene, which is akin to entering a war zone. A tourist is continuously watched by many street people, vendors, beggars, taxi drivers, thieves, pick-pockets, pimps, armed police, and assorted persons seeking favors. Nearly all of them are desperately trying to get money in any way possible.

Although we were told it was safe to walk along Avenue Atlantica (Copacabana Beach) at night, where manned police kiosks alternate every few blocks—it proved to be poor advice. One hour after dusk on our third night in Rio, we were jumped by eight favella teenagers on this busy avenue. They jostled and pushed us. As fear and confusion quickly set in, one youth reached for my shirt pocket and ripped it open. Money scattered on the ground, and we were abandoned in the scramble to pick it up. Then the gang melted into the shadows. The attack must have lasted only thirty seconds at the most!

With my shirt in shreds, we returned to the safety of our hotel brimming with anger and a sense of deep violation. This soon gave way to fear, as we began to realize what could have happened aside from the loss of a few dollars. In the remaining week in Rio, fear became our constant companion. A deep wariness of everyone we came in contact with set in. We began to suspect that we may have overreacted, that we were being paranoic. When we started to tell cariocas about our mugging, however, it was as if a dam broke loose. Their own fear would come gushing out. Native Brazilians who had lived all their lives in the city began to tell us about the danger they felt and how unsafe things had become. On our plane ride back, we met a young Brazilian man who had emigrated to New York City eight years before. He said New York was safer than Rio because he could actually walk to work without fear.

One native told us there is at least one murder per night along Copacabana during Carnaval. According to official statistics, this may be an underexaggeration. While New York City is about the same size as Rio, New York had 1,896 murders during all of 1988. In contrast, Rio suffers from a virtual avalanche of homicide—500 killings in the month of April, 1989, alone![96] Brazilian sociologists are reporting that the violence is increasingly based on social class differences, and that many of the poor are now seeing the killings as an act of social justice. It has become routine to rob and kill the unwary rich who are foolish enough to drive through poor neighborhoods. The slums of Rio bristle with automatic weapons which outgun the police. In many cases it is drug-dealing teenagers who are behind much of the violence; but the angry, resentful, and desperate residents of the favella tend to support the killings. They see the murders as a blow for social justice, as helping to right many of the wrongs inflicted upon them because of the gross income inequality in Brazil. There are now at least 200,000 homeless children living in the streets of Rio, which is akin to pouring gasoline on a fire. Their presence fuels the crisis of robbery, mayhem, and violence as they fight like animals merely to stay alive. Roger Cohen, in a *Wall Street Journal* article, gives us a telling glimpse of just how brutal life can be in the slums of Rio:

> Luiz Pereira da Silva looks out over the slum to the middle-class district of Santa Teresa only a few hundred yards away. Beyond it rises Sugar Loaf mountain, with its cable cars filled with tourists. Below it is the blue of Botafogo Bay and its yacht club, where membership costs several thousands of dollars a year. Luiz Perreira da Silva earns $80 a month as a laborer. He keeps his wife and five children in the one-room mud-and-timber hut he bought seven months ago for about $100. . . . He says the neighborhood is full of drug dealers. "But it's best not to look, best to ignore it," he says. Below his home chickens feed on garbage, and open sewers gurgle down the hillside. A boy is urinating against a wall. Another, standing nearby, has a pistol tucked into his Bermudas. Such children often pour down into the suburban streets to rob rich children on their way to private schools. . . . Some of Rio's homeless children spend their nights beneath the bridges of an expressway that snakes along the glittering shore past beaches, yachts, and luxury apartments. . . . The grassy shoulder of the expressway that whisks commuters past the scantily clad beach crowd to downtown offices has become a dumping ground for corpses. "Killers seem to favor it because they can make a quick getaway," says Military Police Sgt. Alberto Gatti. A corpse found last month was identified as a lawyer's. It lay half-covered by a black plastic garbage bag.[97]

The experiences my wife and I had in Brazil are totally subjective and profoundly emotional, as are those of this journalist. Yet they add conviction to the statistics on poverty and low income already given. A very unfair income distribution, especially in a country that is poor to begin with, is a recipe for disaster. It guarantees the growth of various social pathologies, death, disease, inhumanity, and a smorgasbord of vices. It is cemented through feelings of hopelessness and despair. A tortured anguish sets in when such desperate people are forced to watch rich tourists and cariocas live in what they see as opulence. While the children of the poor go hungry, a few blocks away the children of the rich cavort in Rio's nightclubs.

Things may be getting this desperate in the United States! Income has begun to skew more to the wealthy, while the poor get even less. Chapter 5 shows how the middle class in America is eroding and documents the parallel rise in poverty. With an obvious burgeoning of homelessness, climbing crime rates, and constant media hyping of "lifestyles of the rich and famous"—it can well be asked if the Brazil model has come home to roost in the United States already. The point is certainly worthy of debate, although it is unlikely to be broached on the mainstream television networks owned by conglomerate corporations intent on preserving "the American way of life" for the rich.[98] It is certainly too early to ring a death knell of hopelessness, yet it is time to sound the alarm bell. It is by a stroke of fate that we were not born in the favellas of Rio, a hut in Ethiopia, or a hovel in Bangladesh. The station in life we start at is a given that none of us have control over. We still have some say, however, in how the economic pie is cut in our society. Therein lies hope for the future.

4

MULTINATIONAL CORPORATIONS: INCOME INEQUALITY AND BASIC NEEDS

The evidence which points to large gaps in world income is impossible to deny. In terms of real dollars, poor countries are actually worse off in comparison to industrial countries today than just after World War II ended. As measured by relative wealth, this is also true. Less Developed Countries (LDCs) have witnessed their economic elites grab even more income out of the hands of the poor within the past few decades. How has all this come about? Why is it permitted to continue?

A major reason is that such injustice is sold as "progress" by bankers, corporate heads, state leaders, and others who stand to greatly benefit by development and investment. There is another persuasive reason given from the realm of social science which has been used to justify such obvious deprivations of the poor. In making global comparisons, economist Simon Kuznets noted that most nations tend to follow an inverse U-shaped curve. Countries will typically go from small income inequality at the start to greater inequality as they develop. Growth ends with much more equality during the final stage of evolution.[1] At this point, as the scenario goes, a greatly enriched middle class will share the wealth. Both the poor and the rich will be only small parts of the population.

There are a number of good reasons why we should expect income inequality to get worse within countries as they develop. Real growth is nearly always a result of getting rid of subsistence agriculture. The other route to more wealth is to bring in advanced industry. This growth of good-paying jobs and economic change first takes place within a nation's major cities. Thus, the already yawning chasm between rural and urban incomes becomes still larger. Even within the mega-metropolises of LDCs, an underclass and informal sector is born which serves as a classic "surplus proletariat" to keep wages low for much of the working class population.[2] There emerges a very modern, corporate group of well-educated executives and highly skilled labor who command high wages. Opposed to this well-off minority is a much larger traditional sector of unskilled service workers or low-paid factory assemblers. In this bizarre hodgepodge, it is not unusual to see street vendors barely surviving by selling single cigarettes to pedestrian traffic. Such life and death drama occurs within the shadows of monolithic, modernistic skyscrapers which house the headquarters of the "new economy." Yet this will eventually change, the poor are told, as the economy of their land reaches a blastoff point of self-sustaining, continuous growth. At this point, more education, unions, and productivity will lead to a more equal sharing of the new wealth among all citizens.

The evidence for this rosy picture does seem overwhelming—at least at first glance. Kuznets' idea led to a great deal of research that showed a curved relationship between economic development and income inequality. The first systematic study was done by the International Labour Organization (ILO).[3] Their analysis of fifty-six countries found that as Gross Domestic Product (GDP) per person went up—especially among countries in the $300 to $500 range—income inequality also grew larger. When a fairly high level of income was reached ($2,000 or more)—inequality took a steep nose dive.[4] The findings were the same whether income inequality was measured using Gini ratios or percent of income going to the top 5 percent, top 20 percent, or bottom 20 percent of recipients. Research by the World Bank followed close on the heels of the ILO study. The World Bank verified that LDCs show much greater income inequality than developed nations. Income inequality was much greater among the lowest- and middle-income groups within these sixty-six nations because of their smaller shares of income in comparison to the rich.[5] As GDP per person increased in countries from $250 to $500, the percent of income going to the poorest 40 percent of the population actually goes down from 12 percent to 10 percent. Although this may not appear to involve much money, at close to subsistence levels the difference may mean life or death.

As the base of countries expanded to seventy-one and research became more refined, scholars were able to estimate a turning point of $243 (in 1971 dollars). At this point the Gini ratio peaks for developing countries. Thereafter, as GDP per person increases in countries—income inequality begins to fall.[6] Since the Gini ratio is an average number for the entire population, all segments will not necessarily become more equal at the same rate. The share of the top 5 percent of income actually starts to fall at the $200 level, while the share of the bottom 20 percent does not begin to increase until GDP per head reaches $500. A more recent analysis by the ILO adds support to what seems to be an indestructible

TABLE 4.1   Household Income Distribution by Country Level: Gross
              Domestic Product Per Person

Country GDP Level	Average GDP Per Person	Average Household Gini Ratio	Average Percent Income going to:	
			Lowest 20 Percent	Top 10 Percent
Group 1[a] (Under $500)	$ 292	.4472	5.33	37.33
Group 2[b] ($500–$999)	699	.4513	5.0	37.2
Group 3[c] ($1,000–$1,499)	1,196	.5378	3.1	44.9
Group 4[d] ($1,500–$2,999)	2,226	.4354	4.4	33.9
Group 5[e] ($3,000 and over)	11,505	.3312	6.4	25.1

a. Bangladesh, Zambia, India, Kenya, Sri Lanka, and Indonesia.
b. Philippines, Senegal, Ivory Coast, Thailand, El Salvador, and Egypt.
c. Turkey, Colombia, Mauritius, Peru, and Brazil.
d. Mexico, Costa Rica, Malaysia, Hungary, Argentina, Panama, South Korea, Yugoslavia, and Portugal.
e. Trinidad and Tobago, Spain, Hong Kong, Italy, Australia, Finland, Denmark, W. Germany, Norway, Venezuela, Switzerland, New Zealand, United Kingdom, Netherlands, Ireland, Israel, Belgium, Canada, France, Sweden, Japan, and U.S.A.

Kuznets curve. Gini ratios climbed from an average of .437 for countries with GDPs per person under $200 to .545 ($331–$700). Thereafter Gini scores decline to .487 ($700–$1,650) and bottom out among the developed countries at .381 ($1,651–$4,760).[7] Yet this study used more dated calculations of Gini ratios than desirable, as well as GDP figures for 1971. Table 4.1 contains more recent World Bank figures. These results are also the same as prior studies.

The GDP income levels for countries have been increased somewhat to account for inflation since the 1971 time period. Nonetheless, virtually the same results obtain in 1986 that were uncovered in all prior research. The industrialized, wealthier developed countries found in Group 5—with GDPs per person ranging from $4,000 to $21,000—are more equal in their income distributions than are LDCs. This is true no matter which of the three measurements are used. Core countries have the lowest household Gini score (.3312), lowest percent of income going to the top 10 percent of households (25.1 percent), and highest percent of income going to the poorest 20 percent of households (6.4 percent). The poorest countries with GDPs of under $1,000 per person actually show less inequality than the peak middle group of countries ($1,000 to $1,500 per person). The third group can be equated to developing nations. The differences between core countries in Group 5 and developing countries in Group 3 are both large and significant.[8]

The usual warnings of potential bias in the sample of countries and possible nonrepresentativeness are even more crucial in this instance. One study indicates that the relationship between income per head and income inequality is much less strong among LDCs. This is mostly because of poor quality data in comparison to developed nations.[9] There can also be great instability at where the so-called turning point toward greater income inequality for LDCs is reached. Its size depends upon the number of countries used in the analysis. The amount has ranged in samples from $371 (forty countries) to $468 (sixty countries) to $800 (thirty countries).[10] At least one study involving sixty-seven countries has also raised the question of whether there actually is a turnaround. It instead found a tendency for the income share of the poorest 20 percent to steadily decline in the course of economic development.[11] The twelve nations in Group 3 (inegalitarian "developing" countries) represent countries with GDPs per person in the $1,000 to $1,499 range. This boils down to only five countries: Turkey, Columbia, Mauritius, Peru, and Brazil. Just a few nations, then, are often held up as representative of LDCs around the globe. Because of the low number of nations involved plus the other flaws just mentioned, major questions must remain. Can we regard the five nations in Group 3 (where income distribution data is available) as representative of developing countries without qualifications?[12]

Social and economic reality is very complex. What appears to be true on the surface may not actually exist when all other factors are considered. For instance, a common (and true) statistic is the high linkage between a great many babies and the large presence of storks in given areas. Are we to conclude from these actual facts based upon valid data that storks bring babies? Common sense leads us to search for more realistic answers. The stork and baby example is a good illustration of what is called a "spurious" relationship. Below the surface the correlation falls apart when other variables that can cause fertility are examined. One of the most important factors which tends to encourage large families is living in rural areas. Storks also tend to flourish in rural areas. "Ruralness" therefore turns out to be an important variable causing increased childbearing when all other factors are held equal (e.g., the presence of storks).

The stork illustration provides an extreme example where a variable is shown to be entirely spurious. On the surface storks appear to be causing high birthrates, but in reality storks have nothing to do with fertility. Unfortunately, social and economic life is never this simple. There are a number of forces which contribute to changing income inequality with widely varying impacts. Although questions have been raised about the human capital perspective, it does play a part in lowering income inequality. So does a country's growth in GNP and GDP per capita. So do, however, a number of other factors that are never remotely considered by traditional economists, bankers, financiers, and politicians. Most of these forces are "unmentionables" in the view of economic elites. Yet they have much to do with the reality of power and how money is spread around the world. We come back to a country's position within the Modern World System. A nation's rank is of great importance to sociologists and political scientists, if not to IMF and World Bank officials. What is the effect of this crucial variable? How does it compare to many of the other more conventional economic factors that act to reduce income inequality?

The Rise of Multinational Corporations

World System supporters strongly argue that a nation's economic welfare does not hinge upon its balance of payments, exports, debt owed, type of industry, and so on. The crucial force which sets its income is its location in the global economic pecking order. The main idea of this theory sees periphery countries as forced into never ending subservience. Its root cause is an economic system of world commerce favoring core nations. The power of core nations allows them to dictate the terms of trade. LDCs will always pay more for the manufactured products from the core. Third World countries will get less for raw materials that they sell to the core. The system works very nicely for core countries. If they are the buyers, they get to set the price. If they are the sellers, they get to set the price!

A deal is cut between the leaders of major firms in the core and business elites within the periphery. Its target is always labor within the periphery. This power bloc acts to suppress the cost of wages. While it keeps production costs down, it also brings about more income inequality. Local consumer markets and domestic industries are further eroded due to the presence of foreign multinational firms from core countries. These firms are successful at manipulating weak LDC governments into giving them a variety of gifts. Often these concessions take the form of tax reductions and startup loans. Any desire that periphery countries might have to start their own industries is actively discouraged by foreign multinationals. It is these core firms who would then have to compete for native capital and local markets. In the end, the core firms wish to keep alive the import dependency within these countries for their own products. As a result, independent local growth stagnates or declines in LDCs even while core multinationals open new factories in these countries. Nearly all major business and trade in the periphery is largely controlled by rules laid down through foreign corporate policy.

A hint at what frequently takes place in developing countries can be gained from Africa. Within the Ivory Coast, for example, European managers and heads of large corporations earn more than twenty times the salary of Africans. In Swaziland the ratio is about 12-to-1. Nearly three-fourths of all income inequality has been attributed to being white and European within the United Republic of Cameroon.[13] The presence of multinational staff within these foreign countries, then, can distort the local salary structure by a large amount. Wage scales are paid in terms of the core country that serves as corporate headquarters. It is often believed that incoming firms create new jobs and raise the pay scale for laborers by bringing in higher wage scales. Yet this is true only in the short run scheme of things.[14] There is much evidence to show that dominance by multinationals in LDCs is a recipe for financial disaster in the long run.

The simplest definition of a multinational corporation would be a firm that owns and manages economic units in two or more countries. What this means is that direct foreign buyouts and management control take place across foreign boundaries. When the figures are examined, a great variation in size and degree of global spread rapidly becomes apparent. The size of these firms can be huge, but the end result is always the same. The new global corporation is made up of a complex pattern of subsidiaries, branches, and affiliates. This became most apparent as multinationals bought foreign firms that themselves had foreign subsidiaries. Business abroad ends up involving many nations stretching over a wide range of products, services, and manufacturing processes.[15]

These corporations have become very big and represent a wide gamut of interests. Thus, they can no longer be viewed as being necessarily loyal or affiliated with the home country they are headquartered in. An increasingly complex degree of interpenetration between corporations has set in. This is particularly the case in core countries. Antimonopoly laws simply do not apply against foreign companies who decide to align themselves with domestic firms in the same fields. Goodyear Tire and Rubber has cooperated with its French competitor Michelin in the coproduction of synthetic rubber while sharing technology with its Japanese competitor, Bridgestone. While U.S. Steel complained about unfair competition from abroad, it invested in partial ownership of eleven foreign companies operating on five continents. Their foreign buy-up came to include four mining and mineral processing businesses in South Africa. Even as early as 1970, General Electric became the single largest owner of stock in Toshiba electronics. By that year, GE had licensing agreements with over sixty Japanese companies, while Westinghouse had become the principal shareholder of Mitsubishi.[16]

The past growth in size and dominance of the 180 largest U.S. multinationals shows that in 1950 over three fourths operated in six countries or fewer while none owned businesses in twenty or more countries. By 1970, fewer than 7 percent were involved with only six countries but nearly one third owned subsidiaries in twenty or more countries.[17] The growth of American multinational firms worldwide has been astronomical:

> From an accumulated direct investment of only $11.8 billion in 1950, the book value of American direct investment abroad had risen to approximately $234.4 billion by 1984. . . . In 1981, American foreign direct investment was more than two-fifths of the world's total foreign direct investment. . . . The largest fraction of postwar investment went into advanced manufacturing industries (particularly automobiles, chemicals, and electronics) . . . By the early 1970s . . . international production by American multinational corporations had surpassed trade as the main component of America's international economic exchange. Foreign production by the affiliates of U.S. corporations had grown nearly four times as large as American exports. . . . By 1969, the American multinationals alone produced approximately $140 billion worth of goods, more than any national economy except those of the United States and the Soviet Union. Many of America's largest corporations had placed more than half of their total assets abroad, and more than half of their total earnings came from overseas. . . . Although the rate of growth of foreign investment declined by the 1980s, the United States remained heavily dependent on its multinationals for access to foreign markets and for the earnings they produce.[18]

At the start of 1988, U.S. direct investment abroad stood at $309 billion. This was twenty-six times the amount in 1950 and nearly one-third as much as the total in 1984.[19] What this means in reality is that nearly three-fourths of the manufacturing cost for an IBM PC computer is spent overseas. Over 27 percent goes to branch plants of American multinationals while nearly half is spent in direct buying from foreign firms (46 percent).[20] The manufacturing of Ford's highly successful Escort involves parts which are assembled in sixteen countries on three continents. Seven General Motors and two Chrysler plants were opened between 1978 and 1982 along the northern border of Mexico. Direct foreign investment by U.S. firms increased sixteen times in 1950–80, but the rate of increase for American GDP was only half as much.

By 1970, about three-fourths of total U.S. exports and over one half of all imports were transactions between the domestic and foreign subsidiaries of the same U.S. multinational firms.[21] A survey of the 200 largest U.S. multinationals has shown them earning one third of their revenues through off-shore subsidiaries.[22] This amount can vary somewhat from one firm to another, but it is always large. Table 4.2 contains the most recent data[23] for the forty largest American multinational corporations, ranked by absolute amount of foreign profit earned in 1987. Even to qualify for the top 100, a firm had to earn over $1 billion per year from foreign sources. Even such "Americanized" corporations as McDonald's have increased their sales by foreign expansion, climbing from 23 percent to 30 percent in just four years. Thirteen U.S. corporations earn over one half of all their revenues from overseas sales. Among them are: Exxon (75 percent), Pan Am (68 percent), Gillette (63 percent), Mobil (61 percent), Colgate-Palmolive (56 percent), Dow Chemical (56 percent), Coca-Cola (55 percent), and IBM (54 percent). Coca-Cola, of course, has long prided itself in advertising its product as a forerunner of U.S. presence overseas. It has become the international icon of Americanism abroad.

We have seen that much of the rise of American multinationals has been due to the unscathed position of the United States after World War II. Having the dollar as the medium of exchange also helped to fuel U.S. expansion in other lands. There are many added factors, however, which led to the voracious growth of overseas corporations. These had less to do with our enviable position and more to do with the nature of free market capitalism. To begin with, revolutionary developments in communication, travel, and computer technology created a new and unique possibility. For the first time ever, separate parts of actual production could be easily linked around the globe. Information has now been more centralized while control is less concentrated. Exotic systems—such as Satellite Business Systems owned by IBM, Comsat, and Aetna Life Insurance—are used only by corporations. Such sophisticated communication hardware allows firms to effectively bypass any dependence on governmental agencies. Jet travel and electronic media which allow contact to be made in an instant have smashed barriers to world commerce.

Among other reasons has been the explosive growth of manufacturing technology and the stampede it created in the rapid development of products. Core countries have long been involved in the costly process of research. This is needed to create and develop new products for the market. During the initial stage of development, corporations enjoy a monopoly over these new technologies which is used to raise their profits. Over time, the new inventions and manufacturing technology spread to other countries. Rising trade barriers and the growth of foreign competition make it necessary to locate production in foreign lands. Saturation of the core market occurs. A search to locate and expand new

TABLE 4.2   Revenue and Assets of the Forty Largest U.S. Multinational Corporations: 1987

Company	Foreign Revenue (millions of dollars)	Foreign Revenue as Percent of Total	Foreign Assets as Percent of Total
Exxon	$57,375	75.1%	51.0%
Mobil	31,633	60.5	48.9
IBM	29,280	54.0	54.1
General Motors	24,091	23.7	23.4
Ford Motor	23,955	32.8	39.4
Texaco	17,120	49.8	31.1
Citicorp	13,314	48.4	45.1
EI du Pont	11,651	38.2	27.5
Dow Chemical	7,431	55.6	49.0
Chevron Oil	5,905	22.7	20.2
Proctor and Gamble	5,524	32.5	28.1
Eastman Kodak	5,265	39.6	34.7
Chase Manhattan	5,021	46.7	37.6
ITT	4,891	25.0	14.8
Xerox	4,852	32.1	24.3
United Technologies	4,713	27.4	32.8
Phillip Morris	4,544	20.4	19.7
Amoco	4,400	21.5	23.1
Digital Equipment	4,373	46.6	36.7
Unisys	4,237	43.6	28.8
Coca Cola	4,185	54.7	26.0
RJR Nabisco	4,045	25.7	26.4
Goodyear	3,997	40.4	34.6
Hewlett Packard	3,968	49.0	29.7
American Intl Group	3,875	34.4	38.9
Johnson & Johnson	3,845	48.0	45.0
Tenneco	3,834	25.9	25.1
General Electric	3,799	9.4	15.5
Minn. Mining & Mfg	3,616	38.3	30.6
JP Morgan	3,590	52.5	51.8
American Express	3,525	19.8	20.5
Sears, Roebuck	3,180	6.6	3.0
Colgate-Palmolive	3,161	56.0	45.0
Bankers Trust New York	3,156	55.4	53.4
NCR	3,081	54.6	42.4
BankAmerica	3,051	31.3	31.4
FW Woolworth	3,037	42.6	44.4
Motorola	2,937	43.8	31.0
American Brands	2,835	47.0	24.1
Monsanto	2,756	36.1	25.1

markets assumes more importance as the product becomes common-
place at home. Since many global firms dominate markets with only a
few others (oligopoly), their competitors also tend to locate branches and
subsidiaries in countries where one company pioneers. Expansion in
given countries then tends to resemble a "follow the leader" mentality as
each firm tries to stabilize and protect its share of profits. Production is
by now standardized to the point where manufacturing can be done anywhere, often resulting in the location of plants where costs are cheapest.

Location of plants in LDCs by corporations may also be caused by
threats from periphery governments to erect trade barriers to imports
from core countries. As part of the cost of doing business in some of
these lands, firms have been forced to guarantee that large portions of
assembly and manufacturing will be kept in the host country. This is a
way to preserve jobs and to protect the economy. Avoidance of trade
tariffs and protected markets in the host country can also have a lot to do
with the decision of a firm to open a branch in a given nation.

Much expansion of transnational firms can also be laid at the feet
of new types of financial groups. A "stateless capital" has been created
by the flood of dollars abroad (Eurocurrency). This is now being made
available to fund risky mergers or questionable development schemes
that traditional and more conservative lending agencies have refused to
bankroll.[24] Yet more stable banks have not been immune to adventuristic
projects in the Third World as well. Banks have also entered into races
with each other for the profits that can be made from expansion loans.
Huge consortia of banks made up of members from many different
countries evolved in the 1970s and 1980s to amass the gigantic sums
needed by the multinationals.[25] In short, a global banking network was
created with almost no constraints. No protective shields exist to prevent
harm to nations or individuals doing business with these cartels. Capital
now moves from nation to nation at a blink of an eyelash—or more
accurately put, the click of a computer key. Frequently, in this high-level
game of financial lending, LDCs who seek development funds actually
find themselves in competition for scarce capital with multinational firms
also intent on growth through merger. In 1981, for example, the
amounts borrowed by economic actors (in billions of dollars) in descending order were: Mexico (11.3), Brazil (6.8), Mobil Oil (6.0), Gulf Oil
(6.0), Argentina (5.6), Texaco (5.5), Marathon Oil (5.0), DuPont (4.0),
Seagrams (3.9), Venezuela (3.6), South Korea (3.2), Cities Service (3.0),
Allied Corporation (3.0), Conoco (3.0), Panama (2.7), etc.[26]

U.S. military and economic policy has been used to greatly encourage the overseas expansion of multinationals as well. The foreign
presence of American firms is seen both as a demonstration and alternative development model to communist and nonaligned LDCs. Some-

times this has led to the use of more covert and rather ugly activities in the host country:

> Whatever their manifest military purposes, American troops, military advisors, offshore cruising naval vessels, strategic long-range bombers, and, eventually, long-range ballistic missiles all helped at least indirectly to extend American interests abroad. During these years, the U.S. government made commitments to a whole network of antidemocratic dictatorships, whose leaders seemed dedicated, along with keeping themselves in power locally, to promoting the entry of American business enterprise into their economies. In this context, many of America's new Third World allies—South Korea, Taiwan, Brazil, and Argentina—courted U.S. firms by offering terms that were unbelievably tempting, especially low wages and prohibitions on free union activity. The modern equivalent of U.S. gunboats—much more subtle covert intelligence operations and secret funding of military and paramilitary operations—protected these regimes from internal dissent and external attack, while U.S. diplomats averted their eyes from the official government terrorist campaigns to crush free trade unions and, for that matter, free democratic popular elections of any kind.[27]

Economists Barry Bluestone and Bennett Harrison see a variety of other ways which have been used to push American corporate foreign investment.[28] U.S. tax and tariff policies clearly fed such an expansion of firms abroad. American corporations can deduct the full dollar value of all of their foreign income taxes against the domestic taxes they owe here. The normal way to deduct costs of doing business is from earned revenue. These taxes also do not have to be paid in the United States until the profit from foreign branches actually comes into our country. Rather than repatriate, firms have simply used profits from their subsidiaries for further foreign expansion in a steamroller effect. "Transfer pricing" also makes foreign expansion quite lucrative. This is the practice of overpricing products made by American companies which are then sold to their own foreign subsidiaries. This reduces the profits of the subsidiaries, and thus the taxes due on them in the United States. The opposite pattern is also used for host countries with high tax rates, who then overcharge their parent U.S. company. According to some estimates, the bottom line to all these incentives results in a real tax rate of 5 percent on foreign earnings. Lastly, subsidies for foreign expansion are available through cuts in tariffs. The slashes are made by calculating import value only on a portion of manufacturing costs. This allows U.S. firms to ship components abroad for assembly in LDCs where wage labor is cheap. The goods are then imported back to our country. The tariffs due are

.only for the "value-added" from the foreign subsidiary. The list of in-dustries deeply involved in this process is a compendium of products that once came from the American industrial heartland. The import roster includes autos, stereos, televisions, computer chips—even capital goods such as machinery used in textile manufacturing.

Cheap labor and low wages may be the major reason so many firms have gone the multinational route. Much of this "out-sourcing" has been to Japan, West Germany, Canada, Mexico, Malaysia, Singapore, the Philippines, Korea, Taiwan, Hong Kong, and Haiti (in descending or-der). Nearly all countries involved are LDCs which have actively sought the entry of American, Japanese, and European corporations. The avowed goal is always an effort to jumpstart their economies. They see the entry of such firms as a means to improve wages and provide jobs. They believe this will enlarge their modern sector and improve overall standards of living. Most of the newly industrialized economies, for ex-ample, have created "Export Processing Zones" (EPZs). These are areas specifically set aside by the host country to build new branch plants for multinational firms. The zones typically include state-of-the-art infra-structure (seaports, roads, airports, generating plants, etc.). They also allow companies that locate within them large cuts or a complete holiday from taxes; weak or nonexistent pollution controls; and a docile, non-unionized labor force. The first such zone was established near Shannon Airport in Ireland in 1967. By 1980 there were more than eighty such zones in the Third World.[29] In Mexico, this approach is called the Border Industrialization Program or the *maquiladora* plan. A 12.5 mile strip along its northern border has been set up to help U.S. firms who are looking for cheap labor in a virtual tax- and tariff-free environment. Seventy-two American plants set up shop within the first two years of its inception in 1969, but by 1974 the number had risen to 655.[30] By the end of 1987, General Motors had twenty-three plants operating inside of Mexico, mostly within the *maquiladora* region. Ford's Hermosillo plant, which contains state-of-the-art production equipment, has just been com-pleted.[31]

The Hermosillo plant also highlights an entirely separate problem on the part of core firms. They fret over escaping high technology, which eventually erodes their business competitiveness. Yet little doubt exists that "99 percent of all inputs in these assembly plants are imported, mak-ing them little more than sweatshops exploiting cheap labor."[32] The worldwide gaps in typical manufacturing wage levels have made global expansion a sure thing due to all of the conditions listed above. Chief executives of transnational firms, salivating after greater and greater prof-its, have not hesitated to pull up stakes. They are eager and willing to move entire plants anywhere the job can be done more cheaply, as long as there is a stable political environment. In 1982, while the average hourly wage of U.S. workers in manufacturing was just short of $12, it stood at $2.43 in Brazil, $1.97 in Mexico, $1.77 in Singapore, $1.57 in Taiwan, $1.22 in South Korea, and 21 cents in Sri Lanka![33] In 1987, the hourly wage of auto workers was highest in West Germany ($21.38), followed closely by the United States (20.53).[34] A major gap develops between these two nations and the third highest paid labor market in Belgium ($16.59), followed by core nations (in descending order) all within the $15 to $13 range (Sweden, Canada, Japan, Netherlands, Denmark, France, Italy). At the bottom of the list, to no one's surprise, are Taiwan ($2.99) and South Korea ($2.13). Corporations have not ignored the huge profits in such subsistence level wages.

Nor have these trends been constrained only to blue-collar assembly work. The "global factory" is now being joined by the "global office" as firms again take every opportunity to exploit cheaper wage scales abroad. It was once argued that service and office jobs would be created to take the place of manufacturing jobs that had been lost to foreign countries. Today the signs indicate that global corporations make every conceivable effort to shave labor costs to the bone. This is true even for allegedly sacrosanct white collar jobs which have been viewed as "safe." New York Life Insurance has set up a claims-processing center in rural Ireland, where there is a large pool of educated young people who need jobs. They are willing to work for wages lower than those in the United States. In the operation, claims are sent directly to a post office box at Kennedy International Airport in New York City. They are flown to Ireland each day, processed, and then sent back via a leased transatlantic line to the company's mainframe computer in New Jersey. From there, the claim is settled almost immediately by simply issuing a check to the beneficiary.[35] Another firm (Saztec International) employs three hundred people at a data entry branch which has been operating in the Philippines for nearly ten years. Four years ago American Airlines moved most of its keyboard entry processing to Barbados and the Dominican Republic. Its spinoff company, Caribbean Data Services, employs over 1,000 workers at a wage scale starkly lower than that prevailing in the United States.

U.S. multinationals are not the only villains in this drama of labor exploitation, especially in view of what has happened in the past decade. Japanese and European firms have become much more active in foreign expansion. This is true both within core countries such as the United States and also within LDCs. Although Japan still accounts for only 7 percent of total world direct foreign investment, it has strongly increased its overseas presence. During the 1980s, it reinvested the explosion of profits from its large trade surpluses. Much of the buying has been for manufacturing plants, businesses, and real estate within the United States. It has also spent vast amounts of money in developing countries, however, and in particular the Pacific Basin. Although Americans are in the habit of considering South Korea as one of the nation's pet economic development projects, Japan is the largest direct investor in this country. It also owns the majority of foreign firms in Thailand, Malaysia, Indonesia, and Iran.[36]

Between 1986 and 1987, total Japanese business investment in Asia more than doubled, rising to nearly $5 billion per year.[37] With more than three thousand Japanese companies operating in the Pacific, Japanese growth shows no signs of slowing down. In Thailand alone, 77 percent of incoming foreign investment funding stems from the Land of the Rising Sun. This translates to the startup of one company per day. The "Four Tigers" of South Korea, Singapore, Hong Kong, and Taiwan credit Japanese investment as a major reason for their success. At the same time, Japan has now surpassed the United States as the foremost trading partner in East Asia. China, South Korea, Indonesia, Thailand, Malaysia, and Singapore imported more from Japan in 1986 than from any other country.

Lest there be any lingering doubt that Japan has become the economic king of the hill, at least in the Far East, this nation has now become the largest provider of development assistance to most of Asia. Over two-thirds of its foreign aid went to Asian nations in 1987, which totalled $3.5 billion. Recently, Japan has agreed to pledge $30 billion worth of public and private funds to developing countries. The first part of this development assistance will funnel $2 billion to the World Bank, $3 billion through the IMF, and an additional $2.6 billion to organizations such as the Asian Development Fund. A second level of spending amounts to $20 billion, which is to be disbursed by the end of 1990. By that year, Japan's Official Development Assistance will exceed $7.6 billion annually. By 1986, Japan had become the second largest provider of Official Development Assistance in the world. Yet it still had not toppled the United States as the primary source of assistance funds.[38]

Much of the reason for Japanese expansion is also due to a search for wages lower than those existing within its own country. The major point is that the expansion of multinationals stems from only a handful of advanced core countries and shows no sign of ending. In fact, there is every indication that the trend toward opening branch plants in LDCs is likely to go up in the future as the "global office" movement gains momentum. Completing the circle of expansion, ironically, are such successful newly industrial countries as South Korea that are also looking for opportunities to raise their own world presence.

It is the developing global work force that is the very center of the new world economy. The economies of core nations are the nexus which mainly administer, finance, and develop business deals. Branch plants are then set up to manufacture goods in peripheral countries for export to the world market. At the pinnacle of the new coterie marching forth from developed core countries is the multinational corporation. These firms, above all else, have provided the vehicle which was needed to achieve the new supranational economy. Within only one year (1981), total worldwide foreign direct investment came to one-half trillion dollars. In just five years (1979–84), almost one-quarter of a trillion dollars was invested overseas by U.S. firms alone. During the last decade, while corporations invested within America's borders at the rate of 12 percent a year, the comparable rate of foreign expansion by U.S. firms was 19 percent—over one and a half times as much.[39] The magnitude and extent of multinational corporate dominance upon LDCs is bound to be very pervasive—whether for good or evil.

Multinational Penetration and Income Inequality: Do Periphery Countries Benefit?

The search for lower wages on the part of multinationals has been described as "exploitation of labor" by many critics, especially union members within core countries. Yet it is only fair to ask whether these nations actually do benefit from the presence of subsidiaries. Transnational firms are among the first to claim that they help the host countries they enter by introducing jobs. They say their plants work to greatly raise the local wage scale. Spinoff business demand opens up new opportunities for local firms to feed into the needs of their branch plants. Thus, how can scholars and critics from either developing or core countries really be skeptical about whether this expansion is good for nations that are so obviously poor to begin with? It would seem that for a host country to question the benefits of multinational activity in their country reeks of ingratitude. It bites the hand that feeds them.

There are defenders of multinationals who claim that their expansion is mankind's salvation. They feel such firms have a Midas-like ability to bring riches to all lands they touch. Such firms always seem to bring the latest technology, modernity, economic growth, and a better life to LDCs. Some believe they are the hope of peace in the future. Many point out that these firms have a large number of cross-cutting allegiances. They are thus likely to exert pressure on nations to settle their differences without war. At the least, they increase efficiency and lower production costs by locating plants in areas closest to resources and markets. Multinationals are frequently portrayed as evil, all-powerful manipulators of weaker, victimized nations. Yet this may be furthest from the truth! There has been seizure of corporate property by LDC governments. Revolutions and nationalistic movements with hostile overtones do take place in the real world. Many host countries now insist, as a condition of entry, that these firms must manufacture a certain percent of a product's worth within their borders. Tax privileges for multinationals have been harmfully altered or revoked once expensive plants are built. Domestic industries are frequently protected from the ravages of imports from core countries. Some multinationals report considerable local pressure to share the latest productive technology. This can allow industries in the host country to acquire knowledge and techniques that core firms have spent a great deal of money for in their own research and development. Hence, the agreement to open shop in some countries can end up cutting the throats of transnationals by stealing their competitive edge.[40]

Most of the claims that the results of multinational rule are either beneficent or benign are open to question. These assertions cannot be answered here for lack of time and space. We *can* ask, however, whether the presence of such firms in LDCs actually does cause economic growth—and for whom. The view that real income tends to increase because branch plants are set up in these lands is debatable. It may actually enrich a select few, who it seems are always the economic/political/ military ruling oligarchy. Yet it fails to benefit the masses, who are instead thrown into desperate poverty.

This becomes clear when we speak to the very basic human need of getting enough to eat. Frances Moore Lappé and Joseph Collins point out that export-driven development plans in Third World countries have gone hand in hand with worsening hunger and outright starvation.[41] Brazil again provides a good example. Its attempt to boost agribusiness exports led it to win second place among world agricultural exporters. Ironically, as food and soybeans have been shipped abroad in ever greater amounts, the percent of Brazilians who feel the pangs of hunger also grew. Those who are undernourished went from one-third to two-thirds of the entire population within the space of two decades. While beef exports from Central America have increased six-fold within the past twenty years, nearly three-fourths of Salvadoran infants are underfed. While export earnings from Mexico increased twelvefold between 1970 and 1980, the portion of imports devoted to food went down from 12 percent to 9 percent. The authors report that such huge multinationals as Dole and Del Monte virtually abandoned Hawaii as a source of canned pineapple production because fieldworkers had successfully organized. They had managed to raise their minimum wage to $3.25 an hour. After pulling up stakes, these firms relocated in the Philippines where labor was at a more acceptable level of $1 a day! These below-subsistence wages are damaging to workers who are also now exposed to harmful pesticides. More land that was once used to grow food for local peasants is removed from production. Many reclaimed acres have often been forcefully taken from the poor, who are beaten and occasionally killed. At the same time, the Philippine government has offered land-lease inducements to foreign agribusiness monoliths at $18 per acre in order to attract their business.

Fully 85 percent of the profit from exports ends up in the hands of multinationals, bankers, traders, distributors, and various stockholders rather than staying in the host country. World prices for food and mineral commodities have fallen steadily, recently reaching their worst level ever in comparison to costs of imported manufactured goods. Real commodity prices at the end of 1987 were one-third below the average for prices in the 1980–84 period.[42] Since prices have deteriorated so badly, *many LDCs are now punished for their success.* A large number of Third World countries have ended up efficiently exporting more while in actuality getting less money in return. Much of this is due to the fact that certain multinational firms within the world market have a monopoly which permits them to set prices. Such corporations often start price wars among LDC nations competing for multinational purchasing dollars. In the end, according to the founders of the Institute for Food and Development Policy (Food First), we cannot assume that exports are the answer. It is a very real question whether world trade can generate and distribute enough income to alleviate hunger and poverty:

> Simply put, third world exporters find themselves in a buyer's market. They lack bargaining power. Over half of the countries in the third world obtain more than 50 percent of their export earnings from just one or two crops or minerals. When prices fall, many countries have no alternative source of foreign exchange earnings; they cannot hold out for better prices. In fact, they feel even more compelled to step up exports. . . . Of course, this response undercuts prices still further. . . . In most third world societies, the poor are hurt by export-oriented agriculture:
>
> - It allows local economic elites to ignore the poverty all around them that limits the buying power of local people. By exporting to buyers in higher paying markets abroad, they can profit anyway.
> - It provides incentive to both local and foreign elites to increase their dominion over third world agriculture and fuels their determination to resist economic and social reforms that might shift production away from exports.
> - It mandates subsistence wages and miserable working conditions. Third world countries compete effectively in international markets

only by crushing labor organizing and exploiting workers, especially women and children.

- It throws the poor majority in third world countries into competition with foreign consumers for the products of their own land, thus making local staple foods more scarce and more costly.[43]

Although mainly sympathetic to multinationals, Theodore Moran points out that it is the very firms who share only a few competitors (oligopoly) that are most likely to locate in foreign lands. This allows them to dictate prices, set wages, and keep down operating costs with impunity in the host country.[44] Moreover, research has shown that these firms do not typically bring in much outside capital. When setting up shop in foreign lands, they instead eat up local money through LDC loans and other concessions used to attract them. By such means, they may end up completely dominating the economy of the host country. This explains the origin of the term "banana republic." The concept notes the role of economic supremacy being played by such firms as the United Fruit Company in Central America. The end result can create a small labor elite while driving the bulk of workers into the ranks of the unemployed. At the same time, profits are siphoned off from the host country for repatriation to core firms. Evidence has shown an intrenched habit of foreign firms is to avoid purchasing inputs from host country sources. Such buying could generate the startup of local industry and cause economic growth. Yet multinationals, to no one's surprise, continue to buy goods from their own branches in other lands.

Multinationals have often run behind-the-scene schemes in LDCs to enrich their corporate coffers. They encourage projects in Third World countries that are unneeded, or that have dubious and harmful effects. Westinghouse reportedly paid a relative of Ferdinand Marcos nearly $80 million in bribes to get the Philippine government to build the Bataan Nuclear Power Plant. This is in spite of its location near a volcano and several earthquake faults. Although the plant was mothballed by Aquino when she assumed office, the Philippine people are still paying off the $2.2 billion debt used to pay for this boondoggle. The payback includes an enormous interest payment which alone amounts to one-half million dollars a day.[45] A United Nations study proves that the presence of multinational firms aggravates the balance-of-payments problem for Third World countries. Profits earned through the trade generated among the branch plants is more than offset by the borrowing of LDCs for money needed to keep these firms in their countries.[46]

The evidence cited to prove or disprove any harmful effects by multinationals upon LDCs has been largely taken from single case studies of particular countries. Such studies can be useful in highlighting the problems of particular poor nations. Yet they may not be at all typical or representative of the majority of LDCs. What is needed in the end is research addressing the impact of core firms upon the economic well-being of host countries in the periphery. As many nations as possible should be included in such a study. A large sample tends to increase accuracy. Only then can we decide whether money spent by the firms of core countries for foreign expansion is actually of some help to the majority of LDCs.

The first comprehensive effort to answer this question came only a decade ago. In what is called a "meta-analysis," Bornschier, Chase-Dunn, and Rubinson looked at all prior studies. They pointed out that the effects of investment upon income inequality were of the same two kinds we are examining in this book. Both absolute income as measured by Gross National Product (GNP) or Gross Domestic Product (GDP) per person and relative income inequality (often Gini ratios) are affected.[47] The authors found that among all five of the earlier research studies, greater investment caused more relative inequality. Contradictory evidence was found on whether investment caused absolute income to go up. The reason for the disagreement lay with how investment was measured. If it is measured by the current inflow of foreign capital (either through International Monetary Fund loans, other foreign aid, or multinational expansion), it causes an immediate period of economic growth in GNP per person. Looking at the stock owned by foreign firms as opposed to total stock in a country gives a dramatically different picture that is also more long range. The end result of investment dependence as measured in this way works as a drag on economic growth. This occurs despite a short initial burst in immediate GNP per person.

To test this in more detail, the authors performed a new analysis of seventy-six less-developed countries. Their analysis used both money flow and stock ownership to measure investment dependence. Their new study found that both factors work to change real income within LDCs, but again in opposite directions. Ownership of local businesses by foreign capital (stocks) was most important in reducing the growth in GNP per person within these countries. It was more powerful than was the inflow of foreign investment, which does tend to increase average GNP somewhat. Thus, the net effect of foreign investment in LDCs is negative. Poor nations lose more money than they gain. *The effect of foreign investment was even worse among the wealthier LDCs* than among the poorest. This surprising finding is because poor LDCs are typically engaged in extractive exports—such as coffee, sugar, bananas, and minerals. The richer LDCs are frequently involved with more manufacturing. Part of the reason why multinationals' lower real income may thus be due to the makeup of their industry.

A study looking at fifty-six nonsocialist nations by core, periphery, or semi-periphery status also looked at economic development and relative income inequality.[48] At first blush it appears that as development progresses, the share of money going to the richest quintile declines but so does the amount going to the poorest 20 percent. The biggest winner is the middle class in LDCs, which rang up large increases in its share of income. An initial glance thus seems to show that development leads to less income inequality. Yet another view is seen when a nation's strength vis-a-vis other countries is measured by the size of its debt as a percentage of GDP. Income inequality skyrockets when debt goes up. Being plugged into the world market means that a nation's relative income inequality will climb as a result. This is true for LDCs who have either huge exports or massive imports (as a percentage of GDP). The portion of income going to the poorest 20 percent of persons also went down as the role of importing and/or exporting went up. The results conclusively show that a growth in economic development had no major effect in reducing income inequality for nations. It was being tied in with the export market, having high levels of imports, and/or owing huge amounts of debt that proved most responsible for greater income inequality. Any good effects from economic development largely vanished when these factors were strong.

The thrust of these major studies was to seriously weaken the argument that free market economic forces help make everyone more wealthy. The challenge did not go unanswered. One critic pointed out that Modern World System research forgot to use other important variables that have an effect upon GNP per person. High population growth rates in LDCs work to drive more people into poverty. Poor nations simply cannot make enough to feed and clothe their rapidly growing numbers. Population size can affect efficiency. Large economic enterprises—such as steel production—are more expensive in smaller countries than in larger ones where a possible internal market may exist.[49] Among seventy-two Third World countries, it was found that savings were an important part of growth in GNP per capita. In fact, by adding size of population in the analysis, the effect of foreign stock ownership upon slower GNP per person growth actually disappears. Other skeptics have claimed that high rates of military participation tend to equalize income inequality as well. The degree of democracy within countries is a variable that can greatly affect equalization of income. Electorates have become angry with blatant unfairness and literally voted their leaders out of office.

In a study that included these factors, a curve was found much like that predicted by Kuznets.[50] Using several different income inequality measurements (Gini, top 20 percent, low 20 percent), it was found that development was strongly related to more equality. This was true over and above the effect of trade, dominance by foreign firms, and the like. Military participation and the strong role of democracy in nations also played major roles in reducing inequality. On the whole, little or no support was found which showed that relative inequality went up because of dependence on external markets.

Edward Muller sees Canada as an example which refutes the dependency/World System perspective. Of all nations, Canada is one of the most highly penetrated by transnational corporations. Yet it ranks as one of the most economically equal countries in the world. The great bulk of multinational penetration (mostly from the United States) did not occur until after World War II. This growth has failed to produce any increase in the distribution of income inequality.[51] Muller goes on to fault earlier findings that show negative effects of foreign firms by questioning the adequacy of the data used in these studies. He objects to including Yugoslavia since it is a communist country outside the pale of free market influence. After making other corrections to the data, he found that neither penetration by multinational firms nor amount of debt acts to increase inequality, as measured by the percent of income going to the top 20 percent of recipients.

The debate between scholars has been sharp and often rancorous. Yet what much of the fight boils down to is which factors should be looked at as a cause of later income inequality. In the search to throw out spurious variables—such as the false effect of storks in our fertility example—close attention must be paid to the theory behind it all. We ask what influences are expected to cause change in absolute or relative income on the basis of the ideas we have before we do the study. This is particularly crucial since nearly all of the studies on inequality use multiple regression. In order to be valid, there should be only one more variable for every ten nations in the sample.[52] In studies with seventy nations, therefore, only about seven variables could be used. Since the size of samples where income inequality data is available is quite small, we cannot control for everything at once. It is simply impossible to make all other factors equal while looking at the impact of multinationals upon income inequality within nations.

Given these constraints, Bornschier and Chase-Dunn to their credit have attempted to correct the flaws in their early work by a more careful recent research effort.[53] Again echoing their fear of multinational dominance, the authors point out that fully one half of all world trade today passes between such firms. The free market is completely avoided. Transnational firms now have a major influence on foreign trade and in determining who does what, both within the core and in the periphery. This is very true for the "new dependency" which is created by locating new manufacturing plants in LDCs to exploit cheap labor. It is in contrast to the classical dependency of LDCs who export only a few agricultural products such as sugar, coffee, minerals, etc. When firms enter countries in the periphery by opening new industrial facilities, there is an initial growth spurt. Yet long-range economic stagnation, unemployment, and increasing poverty all come in the end for the majority of the population. Evidence from their study shows that this new form of dependency has become more important during the 1970s and 1980s among LDCs.

In their review of thirty-nine previous studies, the authors once again find that when measures such as foreign flow of investment into LDCs are used to measure penetration, the results nearly always indicate an immediate increase in real income.[54] Yet again using the better way to measure penetration (stock ownership by foreign firms), the authors find that corporate dominance by core firms led to a great decline in growth of GNP per capita between 1965 and 1977 for 103 countries. This is true even when other variables are held constant. Table 4.3 includes their multinational penetration scores of countries arranged by World System position.

It may not be obvious from the table where much of the multinational penetration is actually occurring. Figure 4.1 indicates that globally, South America seems to take top honors in degree of dominance by firms. This is indeed true, with nearly 55 percent of its countries scoring in the top-third of penetration (figure 4.4). North America (figure 4.5) comes close to this level as well, with a comparable figure of 50 percent in the high range. The United States is the only nation in the region with a low penetration score (Central America is highly penetrated). The thirty-six countries in Africa (figure 4.2) show almost 40 percent of all nations to be highly dominated by such firms, although nearly a third score in the low end of penetration as well. Europe and Asia (figure 4.3) are regions with comparatively low penetration. Both areas show only about one-sixth of their nations as being highly dominated by foreign corporations. Nearly two-thirds of Asian but only one-third of European countries fall into the low-dominance realm. It is clear that countries particularly vulnerable to dominance by foreign firms have been in the Western Hemisphere within Latin America.

Multinational penetration becomes more important going from the core (39.8) to the semi-periphery (42.0) to the periphery (60.0). This is not surprising given the findings in the last chapter and the tendency for LDCs to actually encourage these firms to locate within their boundaries. The crucial question is still whether their presence is actually good or bad for the host country. Since the impact of multinational entry may vary depending upon how developed a country is to begin with, core and periphery nations have been separately analyzed.

Using the latest World Bank data available (1986), countries were examined using development and inequality variables found important in earlier studies. The multinational penetration score has been deliberately measured at an earlier time (1967) to estimate what effect it had

TABLE 4.3   Multinational Penetration of Countries by Position within Modern World System: 1967

Core	Semi-Periphery	Periphery	
Australia (101)	Argentina (61.4)	Afghanistan (3.3)	Laos (NA)
Austria (23.8)	Bulgaria (NA)	Albania (NA)	Liberia (103)
Belgium (52.2)	Burma (1.3)	Algeria (77.5)	Libya (104)
Canada (104.0)	Cuba (NA)	Benin (21.1)	Madagascar (31.8)
Denmark (72.1)	Cyprus (NA)	Bolivia (60.5)	Mali (5.0)
France (30.1)	E. Germany (NA)	Brazil (67.1)	Malta (NA)
Greece (27.8)	Finland (10.9)	Burkina Faso (14.0)	Mauritania (102)
Italy (31.6)	Hungary (NA)	Burundi (22.8)	Mexico (43.5)
Japan (3.1)	India (6.6)	Cameroon (60.6)	Mongolia (NA)
Luxembourg (NA)	Iran (44.5)	Cent. Afri. Rep. (48.9)	Morocco (25.5)
Netherlands (40.0)	Ireland (102)	Chad (17.3)	Nepal (3.9)
Norway (24.3)	Israel (26.5)	Chile (101)	New Zealand (64.8)
Sweden (18.9)	Jordan (21.9)	China (NA)	Nicaragua (58.0)
Switzerland (36.8)	Kenya (34.4)	Colombia (52.1)	Niger (20.7)
U.K. (64.8)	Lebanon (NA)	Congo (NA)	Nigeria (58.5)
U.S.A. (18.0)	Malaysia (100)	Costa Rica (94.1)	Panama (105)
W. Germany (27.7)	Pakistan (21.6)	Czechoslovakia (NA)	Paraguay (29.0)
Yugoslavia (0)	Peru (78.8)	Dominican Rep. (61.2)	Poland (NA)
Average = 39.8	Philippines (38.9)	Ecuador (26.0)	Rwanda (22.4)
	Portugal (53.6)	Egypt (3.9)	Saudi Arabia (102)
	Rumania (0)	El Salvador (42.4)	Senegal (90.1)
	S. Africa (101)	Ethiopia (10.2)	Sierra Leone (85.5)
	S. Korea (5.9)	Gabon (NA)	Somalia (18.0)
	Spain (36.4)	Ghana (55.4)	Sudan (7.8)
	Sri Lanka (42.8)	Guatemala (51.8)	Syria (9.9)
	Turkey (11.5)	Guinea (83.0)	Taiwan (NA)
	Uruguay (21.0)	Haiti (46.2)	Thailand (13.7)
	U.S.S.R. (NA)	Honduras (101)	Togo (60.9)
	Venezuela (103)	Iceland (NA)	Trinidad and Tobago (105)
	Average = 42.0	Indonesia (7.3)	Tunisia (48.6)
		Iraq (31.9)	Uganda (14.4)
		Ivory Coast (85.5)	Vietnam (NA)
		Jamaica (104)	Yemen (NA)
		Kampuchea (NA)	Zaire (60.0)
		Kuwait (NA)	

(NA = Not Available)   Average = 60.0

FIGURE 4.1: Global Multinational Penetration

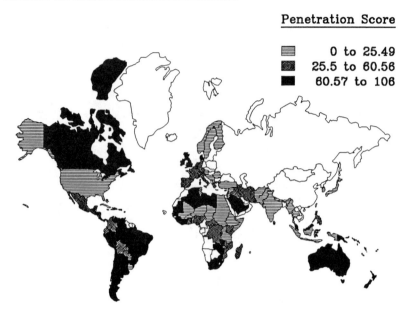

FIGURE 4.2: Multinational Penetration in Africa

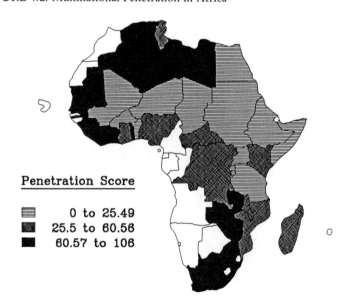

FIGURE 4.3: Multinational Penetration in Europe and Asia

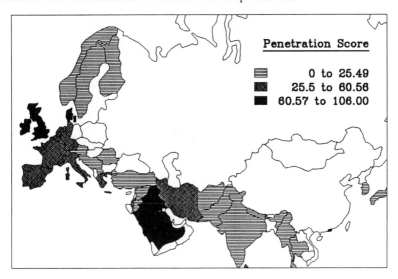

FIGURE 4.4: Multinational Penetration in South America

FIGURE 4.5: Multinational Penetration in North America

Penetration Score

▤	0 to 25.49
■	25.50 to 60.56
■	60.57 to 106.00

upon later growth in GNP. Table 4.4 shows virtually no difference among nations either in the core or semi-periphery in terms of absolute income. The GNP levels per person are about equal between countries regardless of how dominated they are by multinational firms. This is not true among the periphery nations! Here there are much higher incomes among countries where the presence of multinational firms is also high. If we went no further, it would be easy to conclude on this basis that multinationals cause higher income among LDCs. Such an opinion seems strengthened by the greater export activity going on in nations where multinationals locate. It appears that especially within LDCs, high penetration leads to an export-driven economy. Also, the flow of investment dollars from abroad is much greater among Third World countries dominated by foreign firms.

All of this is supposed to lead to more money for the population, according to the free market advocates. This view would be a gross mistake! We need only look at annual growth rates in GNP between 1965 and 1986. While a high degree of dominance by firms leads to higher growth rates in core countries, the exact opposite is true for LDCs.

Within the periphery (and especially within the semi-periphery), penetration goes hand-in-hand with slower economic growth rates.

Another important mark of the healthiness and financial independence of an economy is its gross domestic investment. Gross domestic investment for the most part taps spending for fixed assets within an economy, such as machinery, new factories, a buildup of inventories, and so on. It is the degree to which a nation invests in itself. Not surprisingly, the capacity for Third World countries to do so has been cut severely because of the worldwide recession since 1980. The effect of multinational entry serves to aggravate the problem quite a bit for the Third World while it actually proves to be an advantage within core countries. Another frequently used indicator of economic robustness is the increase in energy consumption. This tries to measure how modern and industrial a particular nation has become. Again, the figures indicate much less growth among countries dominated by multinationals. This is true regardless of world position, but is especially severe among LDCs.

Debt and Multinational Dominance

What about the growth in debt claimed by Susan George and other critics of the Development model? It is alleged that the presence of foreign firms actually works to erect a mountain of debt for poor persons within the Third World while benefiting only a select few. Much of the debt is claimed to originate because corporations eat up scarce local capital. This is done either directly through loans or in the form of "inducements" such as forgone taxes, repressed wages, and the like. This in turn prevents local industry from forming, further retarding economic growth. The World Bank again provides the most recent data on debt structure within LDCs, although the same data for core countries is unfortunately lacking.[55]

Whichever indicator one uses, entry of multinationals is highly associated with greater debt within Third World countries. Among all periphery countries highly dominated by these firms, an average long-term outstanding debt exists that is as large as three-fourths of their GNPs. The same figure for LDCs with low penetration is only about one-half. The percent of GNP actually devoted to paying back these debts is again much higher among LDCs that are dominated by multinationals. In comparison to the lesser dominated periphery, the ratio is almost 2-to-1. The debt per person was more than twice as high where multinationals are dominant. Even official development assistance as a percentage of GNP is largely quashed by multinational presence, both within the periphery and semi-periphery.

The only information remotely comparable to the data on debt

TABLE 4.4   Differences among Development Variables by Penetration and World System Position: 1986

Economic Indicator	Core Countries		Semi-Periphery Countries		Periphery Countries	
	Low Penetration	High Penetration	Low Penetration	High Penetration	Low Penetration	High Penetration
GNP Per Person, 1986 (GNP)	$11,158	$11,348	$2,481	$2,480	$550 ★	$1,528 ★
Household Gini Score (HHGINI)	.314	.331	.417	.451	.430 ★	.502
Average Percent of Growth in GNP Per Person, 1965–86 (GROWGNP)	2.7	2.1	2.9 ★	1.5	1.3	1.0
Average Percentage Growth in Gross Domestic Investment, 1980–86 (GDI)	1.4	2.4	−1.9	−7.2	−1.9	−4.0
Gross Domestic Investment as Percentage of GDP, 1986 (GDIOFGDP)	23.7 ★	19.8	20.4	19.1	17.5	17.8
Exports as Percentage of GDP, 1986 (XPORTGDP)	28.0	34.0	25.0	32.7	15.8 ★	27.5
Total Energy Consumed Per Person in Kilograms of Oil, 1986 (SIZE)	252,431	117,404	35,595	30,307	8,572	8,704

Variable						
Average Percent of Growth in Energy Consumption, 1980–86 (NRGYGROW)	1.4 ★	.7	3.3	2.5	4.4 ★	1.3
Flow of Foreign Direct Investment, 1973 (FDI)	55.7	91.6	31.3	64.4	41.1 ★	102.5
Total Debt as Percent of GNP, 1986 (DEBTGNP)	NA	NA	49.6	59.7	52.4 ★	75.8
Debt Service as Percent of GNP, 1986 (DEBTSERV)	NA	NA	5.7	6.8	3.6 ★	6.3
Total Debt per Person, 1986 (DEBTPRSN)	NA	NA	$ 1,510	$487	$309 ★	$799
Development Assistance as Percent of GNP, 1986 (ASISTPCT)	NA	NA	4.0 ★	.5	9.6 ★	5.8
Balance of Payments Per Person, 1986 (AVBOP86)	$97	–$275	$25	–$27	–$22	–$43
Domestic Savings as Percentage of GNP, 1986 (SAVEGDP)	24.3 ★	20.4	16.7	22.1	9.4 ★	15.3
Number of Countries in Group	12	5	15	7	25	29

★ = Differences between pairs significant at .10

NA = Not available

structure which allows us to compare LDCs with the core is balance of
payments per person. This takes into account the value of goods exported versus the expense of products imported, plus money transferred
because of profits and investment. Again, a massive bleeding of funds is
evident wherever multinationals fester, whether in advanced countries or
among the poorest of nations. What is equally appalling is that the percentage of average GNP needed to pay off this outflow is about the same
for core countries (− 2.4 percent) as it is for the periphery nations (− 2.8
percent) that are dominated by foreign firms.

Debt and development variables have been broken down into an
even more refined analysis within the Third World (table 4.5). Nations
were split on the basis of median GNP at $730 into "richer" and "poorer"
LDCs. When this is done, the effect of multinational dominance is seen
as even more damaging. Penetration by foreign firms is sharply associated with debt among the poorest of Third World countries. Other
large differences also exist which point to stagnation of economic
growth. On most of these variables, the poorest of LDCs are much
worse off than the richer Third World countries where multinational
presence is strong.

Thus, there is clear evidence to indicate that multinational investment carries with it some heavy burdens for Third World countries. This
is especially true among the poorest of nations. *Penetration by foreign multinational corporations reduces the average growth of income per person.* All of
this happens despite high inflows of foreign direct investment, high rates
of saving, previous level of economic development, high exports, and a
large domestic market. Bornschier and Chase-Dunn found less GNP
growth to be especially true among larger LDCs with populations over
1.5 million people and among the wealthier Third World nations with
average GNPs above $400. Penetration did not have an effect among the
rich, core countries. Yet it was highly negative for the eighty-eight LDCs
within their study. Their findings do point to some important effects of
traditional free market variables. Among them are such things as inflow
of investments, exports, and domestic market size. Yet in the end, penetration by foreign firms emerges as the single most important cause
which slashes absolute income among LDCs.

Figures used in the Bornschier and Chase-Dunn study were updated with World Bank data for 1986. A regression analysis using
slightly different procedures was run to estimate the importance of all
variables in contributing to economic growth (see table 1A in the appendix). For the most part, the findings support their earlier conclusion that
dominance by firms weighs down economic growth. While dominance
has no great effect in the core, such penetration is the most important of
all economic factors in lowering economic growth among semi-

TABLE 4.5   Differences among Development Variables by Penetration Within Rich and Poor Periphery Nations: 1986

Economic Indicator	Poorest (Under $730)			Richest ($730 and Over)		
	Low Penetration		High Penetration	Low Penetration		High Penetration
GNP Per Person, 1986 (GNP)	$264	★	$468	$1,140	★	$2,953
Average Percent of Growth in GNP Per Person, 1965–86 (GROWGNP)	.54		−.08	2.9		2.4
Average Percent of Growth in Gross Domestic Investment, 1980–86 (GDI)	−3.1		−5.7	−2.7		−1.7
Gross Domestic Investment as Percent of GDP, 1986 (GDIOFGDP)	15.4		15.5	20.3		22.1
Exports as Percent of GDP, 1986 (XPORTGDP)	13.9	★	30.2	19.0	★	32.5
Total Energy Consumed Per Person in Kilograms of Oil, 1986 (SIZE)	2,704		2,234	23,160		14,898
Average Percent of Growth in Energy Consumption, 1980–86 (NRGYGROW)	3.3	★	−.5	4.3		2.6
Flow of Foreign Direct Investment, 1973 (FDI)	39.7	★	105	59.1		90.2
Total Debt as Percent of GNP, 1986 (DEBTGNP)	56.7	★	88.7	50.6		73.0
Debt Service as Percent of GNP, 1986 (DEBTSERV)	3.4	★	5.7	5.2		7.0
Total Debt per Person, 1986 (DEBTPRSN)	$170	★	$499	$625		$1,115
Development Assistance as Percent of GNP, 1986 (ASISTPCT)	12.8		10.8	3.3		2.3
Balance of Payments Per Person, 1986 (AVBOP86)	−$13.2		−$25.9	−$47.5		−$90.6

★ = Differences between pairs significant at .10

periphery countries and the second most crucial factor in nations of the periphery. It is very true that where a particular LDC starts in terms of average GNP will also set the pace for its later economic growth. Wealthier nations have faster growth rates. Exports are quite important for the eighteen semi-periphery countries in pushing economic growth. Exports are not significant, however, among the fifty-four Third World countries in my analysis. This again calls into question International Monetary Fund (IMF) wisdom which dictates that LDCs must compete in a cutthroat world market through exports. While these nations do so, they neglect their internal economic well-being. The data show that gross domestic investment plays a crucial role in promoting growth within a nation—whether in the periphery, semi-periphery, or core. In light of this finding, the U.S. figure of 18.0 percent gross domestic investment as a proportion of total GNP is quite low. It is much less than in other core nations (22.5 percent), in the semi-periphery (20.2 percent), and even in the periphery (19.1 percent). A clear message is evident. The nation that invests in itself gains in the future.

No one has so far tried to look at debt structure and economic development while also taking into account the other variables found important in earlier research. Again, we have colorful and insightful case studies of particular nations, but no overall picture of what really takes place among all nations in the global economy. Debt will obviously have a devastating impact upon nations unable to get fair prices for their products in foreign markets. Yet we have had no idea to date of its importance in comparison to other development factors. Another analysis using regression was run for the semi-periphery and periphery countries using three of the debt variables identified in table 4.4 as important to LDCs. Unfortunately, core countries had to be dropped from the analysis because such information has not been included in the World Bank's data set or its *World Development Report*.

Nonetheless, the figures from table 2A in the appendix are quite enlightening. When debt variables are added in with economic development factors, penetration remains a dangerous force which threatens a nation's economic well-being. The degree of long-term outstanding debt is a major cause of economic stagnation in its own right among LDCs. Both penetration and debt carry equal weight in stopping the economic growth so important to the world's poorest countries. From the evidence it is plain that greater "development assistance" or having more multinational branch plants open up within their borders is the last thing these nations need. Self-investment for poor nations seems most predictive of success. Their economies actually do have a chance to flourish without the usual IMF austerity ropes which tie them down to a vicious circle of debt. Gross domestic investment in their lands is possible if no foreign firms are draining off profits to headquarters within the core.

Bornschier and Chase-Dunn use the experiences of Brazil and South Korea to show that manufacturing holds no answers for poor nations if it is done via the entry of multinationals. Both nations have been absorbed with efforts to build industry during the past few decades. Both have met success. The major difference between the two nations is seen in the degree of corporate penetration. In 1967 the average penetration score for all nations was 48.6. Brazil had a fairly high score of 67.1 while South Korea had a score of 5.9—one of the lowest in the world. At that time, both countries began serious expansion of their manufacturing base. Brazil chose to receive massive doses of foreign capital and multinational investment. South Korea used the resources it had at home. During the 1968–73 period, both countries recorded high annual rates of per person GNP growth (8–9 percent). The upward paths of these two nations began to unravel, however, after the world recession set in around 1979. Brazil's growth faltered badly while South Korea's went on to break new ground. The fact that foreign penetration is eleven times greater in Brazil than in South Korea also acted to increase relative income inequality as well as to retard absolute income growth:

> The differences in the industrial development model employed by Brazil and South Korea are not related only to aggregate economic growth. Despite similarities with regard to their authoritarian and repressive political regimes, there are other considerable differences. The poorest 80 percent of South Korea's income recipients had a share in total income of 57 percent (1971), whereas the same group had only 37 percent of national income in Brazil (1970). Already by 1975 observers reported that Brazil's wage freeze policy had led to stagnating domestic markets for consumer goods because effective demand was weak. In contrast to this, the standard of living of the masses has improved in South Korea due to substantial wage increases. . . . Furthermore, Brazil shows a considerable and increasing balance of payments deficit after years of pronounced import substitution, whereas South Korea's balance of payments has nearly equilibrated in recent years. Moreover, total foreign debt is comparatively low in the case of South Korea . . . whereas it amounted to the then astronomical figure of $46 billion in the case of Brazil.[56]

Looking at all nations together reveals no difference in the type of penetration by multinationals. It matters little whether foreign firms dominate mining, agriculture, or industry. The effect upon the host country is always the same. GNP growth rates stagnate or fall in comparison to lands who have been spared the penetration. In the end, it is wise for poor nations to ignore the urgings from such core institutions as the IMF and World Bank. The path to greater income does not lie only with more industry and exports. This is clearly an impossibility for LDCs if they came under the influence of the core. Such dominance may take place either through inordinate bank loans and/or the opening of branch plants by core firms. The effect is always the same in the end. The meager sums that do exist in poor nations end up in the coffers of foreign firms or the mega-banks of core countries.

Relative Income Inequality and Multinational Dominance

Relative income inequality has been neglected so far because of our focus on economic growth and real income levels. Here again, however, fourteen of the fifteen studies done through 1985 agree that the penetration of foreign dollars always yields a more poorly shared income distribution in LDCs. The one exception was the study talked about before which used percentage of the population in the military. When this is redone using more reliable country data and by correctly measuring penetration, the finding vanishes. The figures from table 4.4 indicate that relative income inequality goes up wherever foreign firms come to dominate. Their impact is even greater in the poorest of countries. Yet penetration by firms does not change economic growth in core countries at all!

What this means is that it may be possible for core firms to essentially cross-breed with one another without increasing the degree of income inequality. This seems to be the case with the United States and Canada, or the United States and Japan. Yet *the absence of penetration causing inequality can happen only within advanced industrial countries.* Exactly the opposite happens when multinationals locate within the boundaries of Third World countries. The main force in the increase of inequality is prevention of unions and strong efforts to keep wages very low in the labor force. All of these "attractions" are set up by accommodative Third World elites at the behest of their resident foreign firms.

A clear test by Bornschier and Chase-Dunn using seventy-two countries revealed that the Kuznets curve was simply false in its prediction of inequality. This curve does show higher income inequality among nations in the middle of successful transitions in their economic development. Yet the inequality curve disappears among LDCs when multinational penetration is included in the equation. In fact, by adding a nation's position within the World System, the effect of the Kuznets curve within core countries even flattens out. What this means is that relative income inequality is not reduced as GNP per person goes up in the fourteen developed, industrial countries of the world.[57]

Production for foreign markets goes hand-in-hand with penetration by foreign firms. It is thus no surprise that an increase in exports will not lead to less relative income inequality either.[58] Exports increased from 19.9 percent to 25.1 percent between 1960 to 1975 among forty-six nations. Yet, there were no declines in Gini ratios in either core or periphery countries. In fact, more exports actually led to greater income inequality within LDCs (although not in core countries). When exports are held constant, the curve between absolute income and relative income inequality disappears. In other words, it is not necessary for a country midway in the path of economic development to suffer from even more relative income inequality. Yet to avoid this pitfall, LDCs must forego the IMF plan of export expansion being held out to them as their salvation. Poor countries can avoid the national debt and extravagant borrowing that this path entails. To do so, they must keep away from the perview of international banking. They must also beware the price fixing so easily set by monopolistic transnational firms.

A reanalysis using the most recent information was again run with much the same result. The forces found most predictive of relative inequality in earlier research were used. In particular, multinational penetration and GNP per capita in 1986 (to measure the Kuznets curve) were employed. Average balance of payments in 1986 was used to tap the effect of debt in both advanced and Third World countries. This is less satisfactory as a direct measurement of debt for LDCs, so total debt as a percent of GNP was also used among periphery countries (table A3 in the appendix). The results show that the most important variable to drive up income inequality within Third World countries is still multinational penetration. Its impact is six times greater than debt! Surprisingly, debt has an effect opposite than expected within LDCs. As total debt increases, relative income inequality falls. The impact of debt, however, remains rather weak.

The Kuznets curve does operate at a smaller level within LDCs. Yet it is not as important in raising inequality as the presence of multinationals. Within core countries there is once again nearly a complete absence of the curve. Inequality does not grow as advanced industrial countries pass through a "middle range" of income. Surprisingly, even here the dominance of multinationals works to increase relative income inequality. Its force, however, is only half of what its strength is among periphery nations. Not surprisingly, the more negative the balance of payments is within core nations—the more income becomes unequal. Among core nations, the United States ranks fourth worst among seventeen nations on average balance of payments in 1986 (− $586 per person). Predictably, West Germany ($613), Switzerland ($696), and Japan ($706) are at the other polar extreme on this vital sign of economic health.

On the basis of their findings, Bornschier and Chase-Dunn are very sure that inequality will not go down in LDCs simply because it has in some core nations. My analysis, which both replicates and goes beyond their original study, also strongly agrees with what they have found. At the same time, far more attention needs to be given to national debt in future inequality studies. These factors are central in works put out by Food First, the Institute for Policy Studies, and the Transnational Institute.[59] The amount of debt owed by LDCs affects the very survival of the world's poor people.

By now, it is painfully obvious that the economic misfortunes of Third World citizens are bound up with the financial fortunes of those in the First World. Most of this occurs mainly by means of multinational dominance. This is because all nations are part of a world economic system that both causes and perpetuates income inequality. There may be some growth for all countries in this system. Yet it is always true that if a few rich nations gain in the core—many poor nations will lose in the periphery. Multinational entry leads to more relative income inequality while it cuts real GNP growth. The deadly web of multinational impact is mostly spun within the Third World. A plan which therefore relies on growth in export industry, led by foreign firms that seek to set up shop in a poor country, courts ultimate disaster. In the end, the life-and-death needs of the bulk of the population will not be met by this strategy. It is even more likely to backfire. Its effect often yields a worsening of living standards, deterioration in wages, mounting debt, underemployment, ill-health, and even starvation.

Meeting Basic Human Needs in Poor Nations

Can the argument that living standards will improve as a country develops be a Trojan horse? Is there more to the story than just worry over the size of income shares? Most of us by now would agree that countries cannot be judged solely on the basis of their annual GNP growth rate. We know all too well that much of the supposed good effect of modernization does not "trickle down" to the bulk of the masses. Side by side with futuristic skyscrapers, natives often exist and barely survive in the most primitive poverty within LDCs. Even if no major new shuffling of income shares has taken place within LDCs, however, some feel that living standards will automatically get better. This is because of the development of a modern sector. Many argue that meeting basic human needs is bound to improve as more income flows into an industrializing society because of its increased exports and participation in world trade patterns. Following economic rules laid down by core nations, then, will guarantee enough food to eat. Basic literacy will improve as foreign firms demand a more educated workforce. It is possible that partial modernization may give large portions of the population many benefits even if they do not receive higher real income. Much attention has been devoted to widespread improvements in health through the introduction of easily-imported, cheap Western medicine into Third World countries. For example, after World War II the death rate in Ceylon was cut in half during one year simply by spraying the island with the insecticide DDT. This virtually killed off malaria overnight. And so the arguments go.

While there is some disagreement as to what basic human needs are, evidence indicates that measures which simply add a large number of indicators together are weak.[60] Yet even using a combination of infant mortality, life expectancy, and basic literacy shows large gaps to exist between rich and poor.[61] The higher the average GNP per person in a country, the higher is its quality of life. This is also true when each of the separate components is considered by itself. Richer countries have higher literacy rates and life expectancies, while also showing much lower infant death rates.

What other factors may be operating to improve or lessen the delivery of basic needs? Who benefits and who does not? What other forces, aside from a high GNP per person, may be operating to increase or decrease quality of life? As we have seen, penetration in poorer countries by multinational firms has had much to do with retarding real economic growth. It also drives up the gaps in relative income. Because of this, we might also reasonably suspect that penetration may lower standards of living to the point of threatening basic survival. Also, does a position in the periphery within the modern World System always lead to lower quality of life? Is this still true if GNP and penetration are the same? In the end, it is not enough to look only at economic performance. Within a nation, in many cases, there are major population segments that do not benefit regardless of how high the GNP may climb. The large number of homeless within the United States serves as a sobering reminder of this point.

A new study by Bruce London and Bruce Williams looks at how dependency acts upon the provision of basic human needs within eighty-six LDCs.[62] A nation's GNP per person was the most predictive of all factors that work to meet basic human needs. Using the penetration scores in table 4.3, the authors found that *multinational corporate dominance reduces the provision for human needs within the Third World.* This is true when money inflow, gross domestic investment, and initial GNP per person are high to begin with in these nations. The results were the same for every human need they looked at! Corporate dominance lowers the amount of calories eaten daily by persons. Foreign firms also reduce the amount spent on welfare benefits within countries. Multinational entry

cuts the average length of life as well. Lastly, multinational presence tends
to raise infant mortality and the lack of physicians in LDC populations.

Nonetheless, a more valid test of market forces versus World System variables was not present in this study. It left out the all-important
effect of debt, exports, growth of GNP, and World System position.
Some attention must also be given to the effect of relative income gaps
as well as absolute income (GNP per person). We do know for a fact that
relative income inequality is itself a cause of meeting or preventing the
satisfaction of basic human needs. This is true for such basics as death
rates and population per physician.[63] The impact of income inequality
can be seen in table 4.6. Nations have been split into high and low inequality on the basis of the median for household Gini scores. Looking
at six very crucial human needs, it is easily seen that low income inequality goes with higher levels of well-being. Nations with low income inequality spend a higher share of their GNP on welfare. They have a
higher percent enrolled in school and a larger daily calorie supply for
each person. More equal nations also have a higher expectation of life at
birth. Egalitarian countries are also marked by much lower infant mortality rates and population-to-physician ratios. The reverse holds true for
countries with high income inequality. Such nations are plagued by short
life, infant death, and a less bountiful supply of food. There are fewer
doctors for more people and lower numbers in school. The amount of
money these nations spend as a portion of their GNP on housing, welfare, and social security is miniscule.

These drab statistics are very real in their impact. They can come
down to sheer survival in some countries. Tables A4 and A5 in the appendix give added weight to the view that many ill effects follow a
growth of income inequality. Economic development does not guarantee
a better life for the world's poor in Third World nations. Where a nation
starts the race in meeting basic needs for its population has much to do
with the outcome. Being more affluent is by far the most important predictor of meeting basic human needs. Remember that getting high levels
of income among the world's nations, however, stems from their global
economic position to begin with. The vulnerability that LDCs have to
multinational dominance drives the last nail in the coffin. The mix of
world position and penetration is the second most important force in
keeping basic human needs from being met. The more a country is penetrated by multinationals and the further away it is from the core, the
less able a country is to guarantee the survival of its population. LDCs
with high multinational domination have much higher numbers of
people per physician. These LDCs are also plagued by lower portions
going to school, not enough food to eat, and a lower percent of GNP
spent on welfare, housing, and social security.

TABLE 4.6   Comparison of Provision for Basic Human Needs by Degree
            of Household Income Inequality: 1986

Basic Human Need Indicator	Low Household Gini Ratio		High Household Gini Ratio
Percent of GNP Spent on Housing, Welfare, Social Security	12.2	★	3.0
Life Expectancy at Birth (years)	73.5	★	64.2
Number of Persons per Physician	1,052	★	4,047
Percentage of Age Group Enrolled in Secondary Education	83.6	★	47.8
Infant Deaths per 1,000 Live Births	17.4	★	56.8
Daily Calorie Supply Per Person	3,181	★	2,660
Sample Size =	24		25

★ = Significant at .01 level

There is some good effect evident from market forces in table A4 of the appendix. A large export market is weakly tied in with more school attendance and higher spending on welfare. Infant mortality also goes down. Yet, the positive effect of this free market force all but vanishes in table A5 when relative income inequality takes the place of our debt measure. Balance-of-payments was dropped since it did not show much impact upon meeting basic needs. When this is done, greater income inequality clearly lowers school attendance and increases infant mortality. Some weak effects remain from market forces, especially growth in GNP per person. Yet we need to keep in mind that such growth tends to be blocked within LDCs by multinational penetration to begin with.

In summary, neoconservative, traditional axioms of free market theory have been preached and promulgated by such core agencies as the IMF and World Bank. Yet following these axioms has had almost no positive effect for the great majority of poor nations. On the basis of case histories and quantitative studies involving large numbers of countries, we can be sure that it is suicidal for countries in the periphery to seek their fortune through economic development. This is true, at any rate, for economic growth as it is thought of and practiced within today's minority of rich industrial nations. What has worked for core countries in the past has no relevance for underdeveloped economies in today's world. LDCs are primarily dominated and penetrated by these power centers to begin with.

The agents of doom launched by core nations—huge and omniscient multinational corporations—occupy and dominate the hinterland much like the Roman Legions of a past era. Such economic dominance is more subtle and less visible than military occupation. Yet the effect of economic dominance is no less pervasive. Financially, it saddles the people of the Third World with ruinous debt that can never be paid back. The World System acts at the same time to impose hidden taxes to pay for the very agents of LDC repression—the multinationals themselves. The poor of host countries are forced to continue laboring for less-than-subsistence wage levels. This demand to do without is imposed upon the poor by their own ruling elites to feed the ravenous demand for profit. Foreign firms must above all have the mouths of their branch plants succored. The very economic growth hoped for by many of these nations is prevented when multinationals set up subsidiaries. Investment capital is bled off, preventing local businesses from starting up or surviving. Profits are sent back to the core. Rich nations help to maintain military dictatorships within LDCs in order to keep justifiably enraged populations from revolting. The political and military fine points of protecting core multinational investments abroad have been vividly told in great detail elsewhere.[64] The means have nearly always been terrorism, intimidation, repression, torture, and outright warfare by Third World governments against their own people. The very latest evidence of multinational penetration shows an unmistakable pattern. When foreign corporations enter a country, an increased likelihood of its citizens suffering from political violence is the end result.[65]

Among the more obvious and easily measured "benefits" of the multinational menace in the Third World are the privileges of less medical care; shortened educational opportunity; and paltry sums spent upon welfare, housing, and social security. As a reward for their third-class citizenship in the world economy and global workforce, the poor in LDCs get even less to eat—which eventually ends in hunger and starvation. Their babies die of malnutrition. All the while they are treated to the spectacle of their affluent ruling elites rubbing shoulders with visiting corporate and banking leaders from "advanced" Western nations. These rich elites unanimously praise the miracles brought by economic growth and the new global workforce. Yet decline has set in among LDCs as a result. Relative income inequality has grown at a rampaging pace within their societies. The end result has been discontent, violence, brutal domination—and total revolution in some cases.

There is an obvious moral dimension to these colorless statistics. Most Americans have no idea about the ill-effects that the corporations of our nation inflict upon poor countries. It is hard to see the forces behind the great availability, cheaper prices, and endless products in our consumer-oriented, pock-malled society. In a "shop 'till you drop" mentality, little thought is given to where the goodies have come from, who produced them, and at what price in human suffering such products have been bought from the Third World. Heedless to the wounds we give the rest of the world, Americans have been content to believe our government and our corporations have brought only good to poor countries.

A few who realize the harm done by the world economy agree that the supposed benefits to poor nations may not be all that tangible. Yet one might argue that even if the Third World loses—we gain. In a hardnosed, practical manner, core nations may have been lucky to undergo early development and dominance. Yet will we now squander our economic inheritance gained by the pluck and hard work of our forefathers? Although it is a pity that these countries are destined to never-ending poverty by impersonal market forces, is it our fault? Although multinational domination is hard upon people in poor nations, does it not at least increase the economic well-being of those in the advanced core countries? Experts claim that the global economy benefits the average American. We no longer have to do the dirty work of manufacturing, which has led to work injuries, pollution of the environment, and depletion of resources. Since many other countries now do this job for us, we can concentrate on cleaner, more lucrative areas such as the information industry. Most Americans will be better off because of greater purchasing power. This is literally due to cheap foreign goods. Higher U.S. income is made possible from corporate profits returned to our country as stock dividends.

There seems to be no end to such rationalizations! In the next chapter, which looks at U.S. income inequality, we will see that most of these enrichment assertions are false. Rather than benefiting from the suffering prevalent in the Third World, most Americans have been on a downward slide of real income. This has taken place while a small minority of our population has been able to enjoy even more opulence. Like those in the Third World, the majority of U.S. citizens have also caught the disease of failing economic health. Not only has real income slid, relative income inequality has also become worse. The cause for most of this decline has its locus in the rise of the global economy as well. Its effect has been to take money away from lower- and middle-income persons while thrusting even more into the hands of the very wealthy.

5

APPLE PIE AND ECONOMIC PIE: THE AMERICAN PATH TO A SMALLER SLICE

At the end of World War II, American dominance of the global economy was clearly beyond dispute. Although the war had cost our nation many lives and casualties, while it depleted local natural resources, the wartime economy had left the United States in hyperdrive. Our industrial capacity had been raised to a dizzying height of efficiency and volume. In steel production, for example, only the United States had undamaged plants to meet sharply renewed demand as the world went about rebuilding its bombed-out cities and factories. By 1950, American companies were making 45 percent of the world's steel.[1] The war had also firmly yanked the United States out of its prolonged depression of the 1930s. Fully one-third of the nation's Gross National Product (GNP) was generated by federal spending during the war. The rapid speedup of using technological break-throughs was another unrecognized byproduct of the war. Over 82 percent of the major inventions and discoveries came from the United States in the decade of 1940–50.[2] The effect was to leave our country in a strong position to maintain its economic supremacy for many decades to come.

All this was translated to boom times and good times for American citizens, at least for a quarter of a century. Between the end of the war and 1973, the average weekly earnings of forty-year-old men grew by nearly 3 percent per year. This was after the effect of inflation is subtracted out. In the two terms of office held by Dwight Eisenhower (1952–60), real family income increased by nearly one-third.[3] During the period from 1945 to 1970 the standard of living of the average American worker climbed into the stratosphere. This was true for all wages, whether they were paid by the hour, week, or year.[4] Relative income inequality also went down. The economic pie got larger. Magically, every worker's piece of it did also.

The minority of workers with earnings below the poverty level wènt down during this same period. The New Deal of the Depression had introduced some welfare measures and Social Security. Yet it was especially during the 1950s and 1960s that the social "safety net" for workers was solidified and legitimized. Unemployment and health insurance became the norm, together with sick leave and liberal vacations. Nearly all of these costs were paid by employers, whose profits were setting records. It was a time of hope, of great confidence in the future. After living through the pain of financial depression and the horrors of war, America had finally seemed to achieve its salvation and just reward. Parents looked forward to the future. They were confident that their children would be rewarded even more than they in what seemed an endless cornucopia of consumer goods.

"Mourning" in America

Despite the signs of economic deterioration discussed in previous chapters, there are still with us many apologists of unflinching optimism. They continue to argue even today that it is once again "morning in America." The incredible growth in wealth and affluence that was the earmark for decades after World War II remains undiminished in the eyes of a few. Most such claims, however, are politically motivated. For example, during the election of 1988 George Bush sought to ride into the Presidency on the coat-tails of the Reagan legacy of economic "growth." Bush was fond of pointing out that during the past five years of the Reagan presidency, 17 million new, well-paying jobs had been created in America. Although this assertion is open to fierce challenge and will be discussed later, there were significant goals attained by the White House during the 1980s. When Reagan assumed office, the annual inflation rate was well over 10 percent, conditions in financial markets were chaotic, and short-term interest rates were higher than at any time since the Civil War.[5] It was true that the Federal Reserve drove the prime rate up to an incredible 21 percent in the early 1980s. This also acted to give the nation its sharpest recession since the Great Depression of the 1930s. Yet the end result in the eyes of George Bush was to save thousands of dollars of mortgage interest costs for later home buyers as the rates went down soon after. During the 1981–87 period, the share of a typical family income that went to an average-priced house slid from 40 percent to 31 percent.[6]

Yet when the slide of real income is taken into account, this alleged gain is illusory. Over the 1975–85 period, median prices for first homes rose 125 percent while the average income of married couples aged 25 to 29 who were renters rose only 80 percent. What this means is that fewer couples today can even qualify for mortgages. In 1975, three-fourths of married couples aged twenty-five to thirty-five met the criteria for an 80 percent mortgage. By 1985 the figure was below one half of their number.[7] Younger couples are simply being priced out of the housing market. Even if mortgage rates go down, the waning of real income for young adults has put the basic American dream of owning a home beyond their means.

Election year politics also saw a claim that average real family income (after subtracting the impact of inflation) went up 7.5 percent from 1981 to 1987. This assertion, however, is made on a shaky premise. Some economists believe the Consumer Price Index (CPI) overstates the effect of inflation on purchasing power since the CPI includes the cost of current housing and mortgage interest rates. These experts maintain that this cost affects only a few first-time home buyers and not the majority of people who already own their own homes. If this factor is deleted, then it can be shown that all income groups—from the poorest fifth to the richest fifth—actually had increasing real income during the Reagan years. Some groups did better than others. The elderly over 65 years old increased their real income by nearly 19 percent, well-educated women by 20 percent, and the richest fifth of income groups by 13 percent.[8] Predictably, the poorest-fifth income group saw the least rise of real income—a paltry 1.5 percent over eight years. This comes to about two tenths of one percent per year, and *only after the figures are fudged* in such a way as to exclude the basic costs of shelter that we all need.

This type of arithmetic is very dubious! It seems that some experts are more than eager to start tinkering with such basic indexes as the CPI when it fails to give them the figures they want. When the measurements are left alone, a markedly different picture begins to emerge. The true relative and absolute income of Americans will be examined shortly. For now, it also needs to be pointed out that another way to manipulate statistics into a more rosy picture is simply not to comment on the embarrassing data. None of the Bush campaign's economic advisors brought up how well America was doing in reducing its trade deficit, its budget deficit, its consumer debt, or its corporate debt load. The true impact of these unmentionables has yet to be felt by most Americans, although it must be in the end. Even economist William Niskanen, a former member of Reagan's Council of Economic Advisers, likens these deficits to smoking. While it may be enjoyable in the short run, it will kill us in the long run.[9]

The Decline of American Affluence

The silence in the 1988 presidential campaign regarding America's long-term economic skid was deafening! Yet the signs can no longer be ignored. Perhaps the drop of America from its top position as the most vital economy of the global marketplace was inevitable. Luck and good fortune had left our nation with no damage to its plants after World War II, but this did not last as our allies and previous enemies rebuilt their industrial might. By using the latest and most technologically advanced machines, many industries in Japan and West Germany became dangerously competitive with U.S. business from the day they went on line. Also, the entire postwar American strategy was to rebuild these economies to stimulate free trade and contain communism. Their success was part of the plan. Yet as these countries and a variety of other European and less-developed countries (LDCs) built up their industries, the weakness of older, more vulnerable U.S. plants was painfully obvious. This becomes very apparent in looking at the world's largest firms. In 1956, forty-two of the top fifty were American. By 1980 this number had dropped to only twenty-three.[10]

Other nations began to produce the same goods that the United States did. Thus, a greater variety of goods at more competitive prices was the result. In an era of free trade, this meant that Americans could buy from foreign sources goods that were cheaper (and of higher quality) than those made in the United States. Figure 5.1 vividly reflects the rise in imports to the United States as a proportion of the value of American-made goods.[11] By 1986 Americans were buying $45 worth of imports for every $100 worth of goods made here. At the end of World War II, the ratio was less than $10. Translating such data into more immediate terms, this has meant great losses in jobs. Plant closings went up in the United States as foreign competition rose for America's purchasing dollar. Decline ensued in one industry after another. While imported steel was only 2 percent of the American market during the 1950s, it is 20 percent today. In 1960, America made three-fourths of all the world's cars. Today we account for only one-fourth of global automobile production. During the mid-1980s, the high-tech semiconductor industry lost $2 billion while 25,000 employees were laid off in the computer industry.[12]

Fully three-fourths of American goods must now face competition from foreign sources. We have not met this challenge with good grace. The very nature of our trade has shifted more toward the profile of a Third World country as we increasingly export food, raw materials, lumber, and unprocessed goods. A crucial sign of the relative advancement of a nation is its ability to produce its own capital goods, if not export them. Capital goods are those products used to make other goods—such as machine tools, construction equipment, plant presses, robots, etc. Again, U.S. decline is unmistakable. In just ten short years (1975–84), imports of machine tools rose from less than 10 percent to

FIGURE 5.1: U.S. Imports (as a percent of manufacturing GNP)

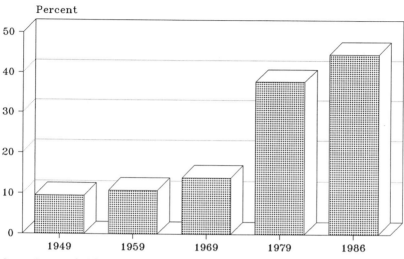

Source: Data graphed from Harrison and Bluestone, *Great U-Turn* (N.Y.: Basic Books), pp. 8–9.

almost 42 percent.[13] While there was $5 worth of capital goods sent abroad in 1965 for every $1 worth imported to the United States, this figure had become dead even by the end of 1986.[14] In a like manner, some of our most advanced industries—such as semiconductors, computer chips, consumer electronics, and the like—have all found more fertile ground on foreign shores. While the Japanese and European Economic Community (EEC) continue to erode our high-technology base of world sales, the battle for the middle ground of manufactured goods has already been lost.

Our abrupt skid as an economic powerhouse is very obvious when yearly trade deficits are looked at. Figure 5.2 dramatically illustrates the trend. Since the end of WWII to about 1970 the United States continuously exported more than it imported in dollar terms. Trade deficits first appear in 1971. Yet in hindsight they were relatively benign, hovering at around $30 billion per year until 1982. Directly as a result of disasterous Reaganomic policies, our deficit climbed to $67.1 billion in 1983, $112.5 in 1984, $124.4 in 1985, $156 billion in 1986, and $170 billion in 1987. Only in 1988 did the trade deficit finally begin to sink, to a "smaller" gap of $137 billion.[15] Much of this was due to a severely deflated dollar, which had lost a third of its value over the year. Most experts are very worried because the deficit did not shrink even more; they see the stubbornness of its staying power as ample proof that America has lost its competitive edge. In sum, our country has been bled of nearly a trillion

FIGURE 5.2: U.S. Trade Deficit (billions of dollars)

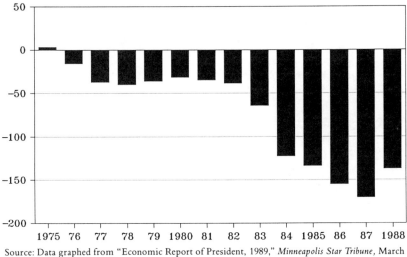

Source: Data graphed from "Economic Report of President, 1989," *Minneapolis Star Tribune,* March 1, 1989.

dollars since the deficits began. Over 85 percent of this took place after Reagan came into office. Our imports were at an all-time high in 1987 while our exports have withered on the vine. We must earn money, like any other nation, by selling our goods to the world. The buying spree can thus only go on so long before our pockets are empty. Many would argue that this has been the case for quite some time, and that we have been coasting on our past global dominance.

Much of the decline in exports and the explosion in the trade deficit can be traced to an unwillingness or inability on the part of American industry to invest in itself. While most industrial countries were forced to upgrade, rebuild, and modernize after 1945, our physical plants remained relatively unchanged. Excess money was used to build new factories in other countries. While this decision need not affect a corporation's profit sheet, it does reduce the competitive stance of our country. During the first half of the 1980s, average annual investment was one-third less than in the previous three decades. Today, Japan spends nearly 50 percent more and Germany about one-third more (as a percentage of GNP) on research and development than the United States.

The latest data from a National Science Foundation survey looked at the performance of America's 200 leading industrial companies (which account for 90 percent of all corporate research and development spending).[16] After removing inflation, the data show that these firms have not increased R & D spending between 1985–87, although they had been raising such spending by 5.8 percent each year between 1975–85 in real dollars. The study faults leveraged buyouts as the major culprit, but the end result is the same whatever the cause—layoffs of scientists, engineers, and researchers at a time when the economy can least afford it. The long-term health of the economy is under attack from this brain drain due to games of jeopardy being played on Wall Street.

Another major avenue of investment is the willingness a society has to educate and train its own people. Even here we are falling behind. About 40 percent of German college students graduate with degrees in science and engineering, while less than 10 percent of American college students do. There were actually *fewer* Ph.D.s awarded in these fields in the United States in 1985 than in 1970.[17] At the same time, given our sharp turn toward "paper entrepreneurialism," the proportion and number of business majors and MBAs has risen dramatically over the past decade. Although we now have more paper shufflers and dealmakers than needed, there is a severe shortage of workers in creative and innovative areas.

One telling sign of this erosion is the shift in technology transfer. American media, politicians, and corporate officials are quick to claim that the real action in the global marketplace is at the high-technology end of the trade spectrum. We are told that America never needs to worry because of our great lead in science. Yet our dominance is in jeopardy even here. Nearly twice as many patents are granted to foreigners than to U.S. firms or individuals. Our greatest technological competitors have been out-producing us with innovations and inventions since the mid 1960s (Germany) and mid 1970s (Japan).[18]

The most recent and dramatic example of our technological tumble lies with high-definition television (HDTV). Unfortunately, while Japanese consumers are saving for their first sets, most Americans have not even heard of it. The new technology will give 1,125 lines of definition compared to the current standard of 525. The result will be clarity similar to movie films we see projected in theaters. Both Europe (spending $250 million on research alone) and Japan are feverishly working with well-developed projects and a number of consortia to bring this new technology on line by 1990. Although HDTV is to be the next generation of television, with an estimated $50 billion in sales potential, the United States has no company which is even attempting to develop it.[19]

The stakes are colossal! The high-technology spinoffs from HDTV involve telecommunications, computer graphics, semiconductors, medical diagnostic equipment, and military operations. Concerned with the failure of American electronic firms to enter the competitive arena, the Defense Department has started its own plans to develop HDTV. It is hoped that this move will finally stimulate American industry to at least try to keep up with other industrial countries in the field of electronics. There are now some belated signs that American industry is finally beginning to respond; yet a concrete plan is far from being put into play. A consortium of thirty-six U.S. electronics companies through the American Electronics Association is asking Congress for a relaxation of antitrust legislation so they can cooperatively work on HDTV. The group also wants $150 million in federal grants over three years plus an additional $300 million in federally guaranteed loans for startup costs.[20] So far, the Commerce Department has been quite cool toward the money request. Even if funds are quickly found for the new venture, it may be too late. Since Japan has already spent $700 million to develop the needed hardware, it will no doubt have the leading edge with this future technology.[21]

With many countries making products only the United States and a few other countries manufactured just a short time ago, the fight over relatively dwindling markets has become cut-throat. Given our failure to invest in modernization, our penchant to borrow and spend beyond our means, and our lack of support for product development through research—it should come as no surprise that American productivity has suffered massive declines. Productivity is measured as the total value of output in the economy divided by the number of hours worked. In the 1948–65 period American productivity rose 3.2 percent per year, with the increases slipping to 2.4 percent in the 1965–73 period and 1.1% in the 1974–78 period. Productivity actually dipped to an average − .8 percent for 1979 and 1980. Although it was to briefly spurt up again in 1983 because of a stupendous military spending spree, it quickly slid lower again in the next few years and was in the red once more by 1986. The effect of this loss is registered directly in take-home pay. A 1.0 percent decline in productivity typically yields a 2 percent growth in the proportion of low-paid workers.[22] Most important, however, is our failure to compete with established industrial powers that pay similar wages. Comparing the United States to ten other industrial countries on productivity in the 1973–79 period shows us to be only one country away from the cellar. (The United Kingdom is in the unenviable last position.)[23]

The short-lived spurt in productivity in the mid-80s was mainly due to a huge increase in defense expenditures. Rather than viewing this as a cause of productivity growth—even in the short run—military spending is akin to hauling water with a hole in the bucket. The United States has long been a heavy spender for military hardware, justifying these gargantuan wartime levies as a necessary cost in the fight to contain communism. Increasing the military budget was a particularly important goal for the Reagan Presidency. With almost no opposition, his conservative coalition managed to drive up the budget for the Department of Defense to an unheard of level. As shown previously, spending for defense more than doubled between 1980 and 1987, growing at a rate three-and-a-half times the real growth rate of GNP. Despite some claims, *military spending retards the economy* rather than speeding up growth:

> But now a major reassessment of the benefits spun off from military driven research and development is underway. . . . More and more analysts ranging across the ideological spectrum are raising doubts about the long-term benefits of military research and development. . . . Massive defense spending actually *harms* high technology by creating bottlenecks in production, encouraging inefficiency, and diverting human and capital resources away from pressing social problems. . . . Moreover, preoccupied with their contracts with the Pentagon, "American small aircraft manufacturers, including Beech, Cessna, and Piper, have failed to invest in the technology necessary to develop an aircraft that can compete effectively in the fast-growing commuter airline market. Defense technology has become so exotic that its transferability is increasingly limited even in the aircraft industry, our premier source of export earnings. Hence, America's commuter airlines are turning to Canadian, French, and Brazilian firms to fill their needs." (Stowsky 1986)[24]

Although defense spending does increase employment somewhat, it demands large amounts of capital to do so because of the skilled labor, expensive raw materials, and technical staff needed to build sophisticated weapons. Thus, although 21,000 jobs are created for every $1 billion spent on guided missiles, the same amount spent on education would yield 71,000 jobs.[25] One estimate shows that decreasing military spending by $35 billion and reallocating this money to programs for housing, transportation, and education to rebuild America's economy would create 250,000 new jobs.[26] We now also know, for example, that for each $100 spent on the military, there is $16.30 less spending for consumer durable goods (e.g., cars, appliances), $11 less for producer durable goods (e.g., factories, machines, business equipment), and $11.40 less for homes.[27]

The real damage is done to the economy at large. This is particularly true since the military drains off any future ability our country may have to function and compete in the global economy. The evidence that has been gathered on this topic is compelling and of one voice. The more a nation spends on its military, the lower its investment, productivity, and civilian research and development (R&D) tends to be. We actually spend more in the United States on "defense" than we do on private domestic investment. By assigning a greater priority to the military,

FIGURE 5.3: Military Drain on Investment

Investment as Percent of GDP, 1986

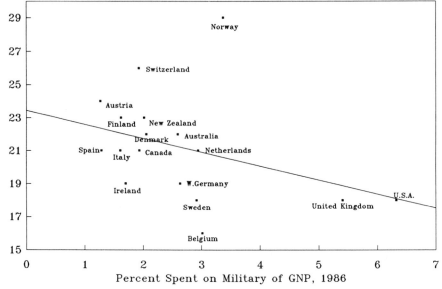

Percent Spent on Military of GNP, 1986

Source: Calculated from data in *World Development Report 1988.*

more than one-third of our scientists, engineers, and R&D money is shunted away from civilian and commercial needs.[28] To put it bluntly, the United States has been outperformed in economic terms by just about all industrial countries because of our higher military spending. Figure 5.3 chronicles the dismal performance of the United States in sapping its own economic strength to feed the voracious appetite of its generals and Pentagon brass.[29]

Nearly all of the record military buildup, it will be remembered, was done without any increase in taxes. Quite the opposite! A large-scale tax cut was instituted exactly at a time when military spending shot through the roof. The large holes that would have resulted in the ceiling plaster of our federal budget had to be patched up. America borrowed enormous amounts from abroad to stem the tide of red ink. Massive growth in the national debt was a direct result of giving too much to the military.

The data which shows the extent of this run up in debt has already been presented. Perhaps not enough has been said about its ultimate effect. America has been unable to earn money abroad by selling its own goods. Yet we insist upon buying more from other countries than we can afford. To attract more funds from Newly Industrialized Countries

(NICs), Japan, and other nations awash with new trade surpluses, U.S. interest rates were raised. This made our country a haven for investment by foreign powers. Other countries began to spend the money we have needed to invest in ourselves. In the early 1960s less than 3 percent of the direct foreign investment of other industrial countries was in the United States, but this had risen to one-fourth by 1978.[30] As an example, to pay our $100 billion trade deficit in 1985, foreigners bought $20 billion in U.S. real estate and business firms, $26 billion in U.S. Treasury notes, and $80 billion in corporate stocks and bonds.[31] Unfortunately, this means foreigners get the profits—just as our multinationals were able to drain money from LDCs in the 1950s and 1960s. America, it seems, is in danger of becoming the victim of its own parasitical game.

How much of a run has there been on the store? The figures are very bad. By the end of 1988, the foreign claim on U.S. assets was $1.5 trillion, which reflects a tripling since 1980. Full or majority ownership of U.S. companies by foreign firms had also increased three-fold, growing from $83 billion in 1980 to $262 billion seven years later. Such direct investment includes the creation of jobs like Toyota's new factory in Kentucky, but fully 84 percent of the money influx in this category has gone to buy up existing U.S. firms.[32] Typically, large staff reductions accompany most takeovers through mergers or buyouts. It is worrisome to witness the growth of foreign control over U.S. jobs and the loss of profits that would have normally gone to American firms in the past. What may be even more dangerous is that only 17 percent of foreign penetration is in a fixed, concrete form. Most foreign holdings of U.S. securities are highly liquid, such as U.S. bonds, portfolio stocks, cash bank accounts, and the like. The money can be gone overnight—in the click of the proverbial computer key. In a word, foreign interests may now have the power to destabilize the U.S. economy or make things much worse in a time of financial crisis.

Is the crisis already here? The answer is given in the evolving scandal surrounding the insolvency of the savings-and-loan industry. Much of the precarious situation for this industry is due to deregulation, which allowed questionable loans to be made in a shaky pyramid of debt. Estimates vary as to how much the bailout will ultimately cost to guarantee deposits in many of these failing banks. Some projections are as high as $500 billion. The failures should not be that surprising in the face of the huge volatility in domestic and international economic markets. According to figures compiled by the Federal Deposit Insurance Corporation (FDIC), banks failed in the 1980s at a rate comparable to that of the Great Depression. Whereas an average of only ten banks per year failed in 1943–81, 138 failed in 1986. The record rate of 184 failures was set in 1987.[33]

All of these economic indicators come together in giving America a loud and clear message. Our nation's financial well-being is at stake. There is a common denominator in one trend after another—that of decline. Yet in looking only at macro or structural trends with global dimensions and national repercussions, it becomes easy to dismiss the very real pain that this decline has had on people. A percentage slide in productivity, a bank failure in Texas, or national deficits that approach numbers none of us can truly comprehend may prevent us from seeing how we are affected on a daily basis. Because of the workings of the global economy and the machinations of economic elites directing American multinational corporations, however, the financial security of most Americans has plummeted. The direct consequences have been increasing poverty, declines in real income for most people, and an explosion in relative income inequality.

The Growth of Poverty

Given such a deterioration in postwar trends together with more than eight years of "voodoo economics," it should come as no surprise that poverty has been increasing within the United States for quite some time. In an era of unfettered corporate growth, grandiose mergers, and speculative mania on the world's stock markets, not much is heard about how the other half lives. Unfortunately, the poor are still with us! Their ranks have become swelled both relatively and in absolute numbers.

The U.S. Census Bureau gathers yearly statistics on the extent of poverty, a very important indicator of financial well-being. It classifies people as under poverty if their money income is below a certain threshold. The level of poverty is newly revised each year to account for inflation. It is calculated from the Department of Agriculture's economy food plan estimating what it costs to feed a typical family. Since this is about one-third of the budget of a poor family, the cost of the market basket is multiplied by three to obtain the poverty cutoff points. These thresholds will vary somewhat depending upon a family's characteristics. Obviously, a larger family has more mouths to feed and thus needs more money. The elderly need less because their food consumption normally goes down as they age. In 1987, the poverty thresholds varied from a low of $5,447 (one person living alone who is over sixty-five years old) to $23,105 (a family of nine or more persons). For the average family of four persons, the guidelines assign them to poverty status if they received less than $11,611 of income a year. This would mean, of course, that a comparable family receiving $12,000 would not be "poor." Former President Reagan believed these eligibility cutoffs were too high since they allowed social assistance programs to serve persons other than the "truly needy." Most experts are of the opposite opinion. The nearly unanimous feeling is that the way poverty is defined by the government is way too low to be realistic in identifying those who are greatly deprived.[34]

The statistics on poverty are not all negative. Much depends on what your analysis starts with, since data have been gathered since 1959. Tracking the poverty line from this date shows a huge decrease in both the number and percent of poor, at least until 1973. Persons under poverty went down from 39.5 million to just under 23 million in this fifteen-year period, whereas the rate was actually cut in half (going from 22.4 percent to 11.1 percent). Since huge sums had been spent for the War on Poverty as well as the war in Vietnam, both of which helped to keep people working, this should not be too surprising. The decline also took place at the end of American hegemony, before it had become evident that the U.S. economy was faltering. In essence, manufacturing jobs were still relatively available and higher paying. It is more than a coincidence that the upturn in poverty started in the same year that the real wage of American workers started its skid.

Figure 5.4 traces another unmistakable rise in poverty, peaking in 1983 just at the end of the very severe 1982 economic recession. While both the number and percent of poor persons declined a few years later, in 1987 there were still nearly 33 million people who were living under poverty in the United States. In this year, the poor comprised more than one out of every eight people. There has been a slight decline in poverty since 1983. Yet there is no reason to celebrate. To begin with, the figures are based only upon the Current Population Survey (CPS) of 60,000 households. They do not represent a complete count of people, such as we get every ten years with the Census of Population. Although the source for error is small, the Census Bureau itself admits that in comparing rates since 1983, "the year to year changes in these figures have not necessarily been statistically significant."[35]

What is more central is the increase in poverty America has witnessed since 1978. The peak in the percent of poor persons in 1983 was the worst in nearly a quarter of a century. A rate this high had not been seen since 1965. It is now a little less than in 1983, but our number of poor people is still equal to the number in 1965. Put differently, the number of poor people went up by one-third between 1978 and 1987, a rate three times the rate of growth for the population. William O'Hare of the Population Reference Bureau points out that these 35 million poor people exceed the population of all but twenty-three countries in the world—including Argentina, Canada, and Austria. More ominously, he notes that the depth of poverty increased dramatically in only five short years. *Between 1978 and 1983 the number of the "poorest" families under poverty grew 46 percent* (families with annual incomes under $5,000 went

FIGURE 5.4: U.S. Poverty Rates by Race (percent of all persons under poverty)

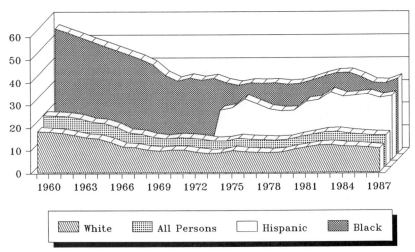

Source: U.S. Bureau of the Census, *Current Population Reports*, P–60, no. 161, March 1988.

from 3.9 percent to 5.7 percent of all families).[36] The median income of all poor families in 1983 dollars had actually fallen in this time period from $5,507 to $4,225! This occurred at the same time as a major dismantling of the social safety net was taking place in the country. As a result, there was actually less help available to aid the indigent when it was needed the most.

The brunt of poverty actually falls on some people more than others, as can be seen in figure 5.4. We have long known that blacks suffer under poverty at much higher rates than whites. In 1987, fully one of every three blacks was poor. This is a rate three times higher than for whites. The black poverty rate also seems to be carved in stone, showing very little change since 1968.[37] More than one of every four Hispanics is also poor. Yet their rate tends to display more volatility than do black rates. Both minority groups show a slight worsening in poverty rates during the 1980–87 period, while the white rate has shown a steady improvement (less poverty) in the past five years.

Residence makes a difference as well. A common reality of big-city life always seems to include extremes of wealth and poverty, which is evident in the official statistics. Almost one in five of central-city residents in metropolitan areas are poor. Yet only 8.5 percent of those outside the central city are poor. For the most part, these are suburbanites. In 1987, the South continued to consistently register greater levels of poverty (16.1 percent) than the Northeast (11 percent), Midwest (12.7 percent), or West (12.6 percent). This pattern is clearly illustrated in figure 5.5, which maps the poverty level among families.[38] The South appears as a solid block of poverty, with the lowest proportion of poor families among states in the upper Midwest and Great Plains.

Contrary to their impoverishment in the 1960s and 1970s, the elderly are no longer heavily represented among the poor. This is one of the few bright spots among the dismal figures documenting a nearly universal rise in poverty. Because Social Security was indexed in the late 1960s to automatically increase payments as an offset to inflation, the proportion of elderly living under poverty is today only one-third of the rate that it was three decades ago. Although their rate is slightly greater than for persons eighteen to sixty-four years old (10.8 percent), it is a vast improvement over the past.

The same cannot be said for just about any other group. We need only consider age once again. There has been a very large growth of children living under poverty. Together with the elderly, children make up over half of the nation's poor. More than one in five children were living under poverty in 1987. The number of poor children has grown by one-half from the all-time low set in 1969. Children have always shown higher rates than the general level. In 1959, their rate was 4.5 percentage points higher than the average rate of all persons. By 1987 this had risen to 7.1 percentage points—well over half that of the original

FIGURE 5.5: Percent of Families Living Under Poverty, 1979

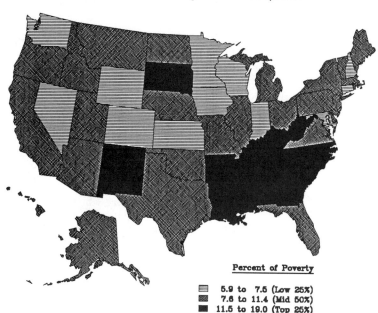

Percent of Poverty

≡ 5.9 to 7.5 (Low 25%)
▨ 7.6 to 11.4 (Mid 50%)
■ 11.5 to 19.0 (Top 25%)

gap. A Congressional study voices concern over this sharp rise, while also identifying a few major sources for this dramatic increase.[39] The study's researchers point out that the reason why nearly half of poor children are forced into poverty is because hours of work have been reduced for one or more parents. Only one-fifth of poor children have been driven into poverty due to the rise in households headed by females.

A recent Urban Institute study has also compared the U.S. poverty rate among children to that of seven other industrial countries, with some shocking results.[40] America has a higher proportion of children living in poverty than any other country in the study (Australia, Canada, West Germany, Norway, Sweden, Switzerland, and the United Kingdom). Excluding second place Australia, the U.S. rate is 60 percent higher than the next lowest rate of the United Kingdom. With respect to the severity of this poverty, the United States also has the worst record. We are first among these nations in the proportion of children who are in families with incomes 25 percent below the official poverty cutoff (about one in every ten children). Again, with the exception of Australia, comparable rates in other industrial countries hover between 2 and 3 percent!

Partly to blame for the sharp rise of children in poverty has been the systematic attack upon social welfare programs that went on during the 1980s. One of the most widely publicized and infamous was the decision by Reagan officials to recategorize ketchup from a condiment to a vegetable in the federal school lunch program. This helped them pinch a few more pennies from the budget while depriving poor children of badly needed nutrition. There have been ongoing slashes in the benefits paid for Aid to Families with Dependent Children (AFDC) as well as cuts in other basic welfare programs. A major cause in the rise of poverty among children has been the reduction in AFDC benefits paid to single mothers of these children. Between 1976–82 the average monthly federal payment dropped from $400 to $303 after the effect of inflation was subtracted (real dollars).[41] On the whole, the average real dollar AFDC benefit level for a family of four without any other income fell by nearly one-third between 1972 and 1988.[42] Much of the new poverty now emerging has hit the poorest of the poor! For example, *in 1972 every single state paid some AFDC benefits to families with wages under 50 percent of the poverty line; by 1988 this was true of only thirty states!* In 1988, if a single mother with two children had worked fulltime at the minimum wage, she would have earned $7,071. This wage would put her family at a level 25 percent below the poverty line. In 1976 for nearly all states, this family would have been raised above the poverty line after AFDC and food stamps had been added in; but by 1988, this was true for only ten states. In just over a decade (1976–1988), the real disposable income of families such as these had declined by one-fifth.[43]

The harshness of these changes becomes evident in a recently released Congressional Budget Office study of how poverty changed in the United States between 1979 and 1987. If it is measured only by income, the 8 percent increase in the proportion of poor persons is barely perceptible. Critics have argued, however, that the poor are actually better off because of transfer programs and in-kind assistance such as food stamps. When these are added in, the "real" poverty rate in 1979 is 9.9 percent versus an unadjusted rate of 19.1 percent. Yet mostly due to the sharp erosion of benefits during the 1980s, by 1987 the "real" poverty rate had climbed to 12.6 percent of all persons. This is an increase in the poverty rate of 41 percent in just under a decade. Principally *as a result of the Reagan war on welfare, nearly 9 million more persons were pushed into poverty.* The researchers conclude that almost half of this shift was due to ripping apart the social safety net, while one-fourth resulted from sheer population growth and another one-sixth came from a slide of job income.[44]

Since the social safety net has been shredded, it is not surprising that the number of homeless has been on the rise in the United States as well:

> In recent years, destitute men and women have become an increasingly common sight in parks, downtowns and suburbs. Their growing numbers, constant visibility and costly needs have pushed homelessness to the forefront of issues confronting local, state, and federal officials. "A lot of people thought the homeless thing was a short-term phenomenon," says Democratic Rep. Bruce F. Vento of Minnesota, the sponsor of a permanent housing plan introduced in the House in January. "What is becoming evident is it is becoming a permanent issue."[45]

Estimating the number of people within this category of dire need is difficult, but not impossible. Expert opinion puts their number between 560,000 and 680,000.[46] Of these, nearly one-fourth are in families (mostly headed by women). Recalling some of the worst scenes in Dickens novels to describe modern-day America still cannot do justice to this calamity. There are 100,000 children without a permanent roof over their heads in our country today!

Research by psychiatrist Ellen Bassuck found that homeless preschoolers are much worse off than children in low-income families with permanent shelter.[47] She has documented that over one half of these children have one or more developmental deficiencies, compared to 16 percent of children who have homes. As for the adults in this group, one in five admit to having been hospitalized for mental problems while one-half express or show signs of severe depression. The median incomes for homeless single people ($64 a month) and homeless families ($300) fall far below 50 percent of the poverty cutoff. Well over one-third of the homeless eat only one meal a day or less, while only a fourth get three meals a day! If you recall, former President Reagan stated just before leaving office that the homeless are without shelter because that is their "choice." Yet it appears from all of the data gathered so far that their numbers have become swollen for a combination of reasons. In some cases homelessness may be primarily the result of de-institutionalization of people incapable of caring for themselves (another example of the rapidly evaporating social safety net). For families it is without doubt a sign that the economic status of the poor is declining.[48]

Despite the growing evidence of desperate poverty, frequent attacks on the poor have continued. They are blamed for their lack of income, as if they are somehow defective. They are shamed for needing help. "Welfare queens" are said to retire into luxury by having children in order to live off the taxpayer. Irresponsible, promiscuous teenagers with raging hormones and not enough will power to "just say no" are accused of swelling welfare rosters when they get pregnant. Enough of a trend exists to perpetuate some of these stereotypes. For instance, there has been an undeniable rise in single-parent families due to the ever-growing number of divorces. In 1987, one in every five families with children under age eighteen was headed by a woman with no husband present. This was well over the proportion in 1959.

We also know that the creation of female-headed families has a great effect in casting these women and their children into poverty. Of all the poor families in the United States, one of every two is headed by a woman with no husband present. Yet there is little support for the stereotype that the mothers of these children are lazy and uncaring about whether they work. In 1987, 47 percent of poor family householders worked, compared to 81 percent of non-poor-family households.[49] The labor force participation rate of poor women is high, considering they have children and no other adult to help with childcare. The majority of people who enter the AFDC program stay in it for less than three years. There is no correlation between states with higher AFDC payments and higher rates of poverty among children. Nor is there any evidence that such welfare benefit levels encourage out-of-wedlock births.[50] Although there is a moderate effect of welfare benefits increasing divorce, the findings are not very consistent.[51] For that matter, while the number of single parent families rose 42 percent in the 1975–85 period, the number of families receiving AFDC has stayed at about 3.5 million since 1975.[52]

According to one estimate, welfare at most can account for only one-seventh of the 1960–75 growth in single mothers.[53]

The attack on welfare programs in the 1980s was often disguised racism. It was built upon the false assumption that the real cause of poverty is due to indiscriminate promiscuity of black women. While single black women with children form a relatively larger portion of poor families, blacks as a whole are more likely to be poor. What many analysts have also failed to note is the dramatic rise of poverty and low income among white males in the United States. Females are still more likely than males to be poor, due to many of the factors discussed above. But within the 1978–83 period, for example, the proportion of poor males grew at a rate nearly triple that of poor females![54] Michael Harrington argues that much of the rise is due to the "new poverty" among young workers.[55] It may affect especially males, who no longer can find and keep high paying industrial jobs that were once abundant. This assertion is in line with the previous deindustrialization argument which states that the erosion of good, well-paying jobs in favor of more part-time, low-wage service jobs has left a large hole in the typical American's pocketbook.

Many analysts, whether conservative or liberal, now seem to focus on the idea that poverty hinges upon how well our economy does. There has been a position emerging that anti-poverty programs and the social safety net have less to do with economic well-being than does continued growth in the economy. Common sense would seem to support such an argument, since a thriving economy would tend to drive up wages and employment levels. Yet, there is a need for caution before embracing the idea that we can "grow our way out of poverty (debt)." Such an argument is the same as the one used to justify development in the Third World. Economic growth did not work to benefit the masses in most LDC countries. Nor is there any reason to believe that boom times will necessarily lead to less poverty in the United States. In a study looking at whether economic growth works to reduce poverty, it was found that *increased real income was NOT associated with any decline in poverty.*[56] The authors found that "secular economic growth" (such as technological improvements, increasing productivity, etc.) was important in the 1950s and 1960s. Yet its impact had dropped to almost nothing by the 1970s and 1980s. During this time period, growing gaps in the income inequality distribution became a major force in rising poverty.[57]

There is much greater consensus around the need for full employment as an effective way to wean people away from poverty. Cyclical business changes—with associated unemployment and employee layoffs—are a major cause of poverty. In a recent and thorough review of all U.S. poverty research, Isabel Sawhill finds that "slack labor markets and poverty tend to go hand in hand."[58] If any factor emerges as the most robust in raising or lowering poverty, it is unemployment. A fall in the demand for labor may not result in outright layoffs as much as more part-time work and/or reduced hours. The effect is the same. All have the result of whittling away at family income. More to the point, a downturn in the economy is not spread evenly over all income groups. The well-off are more insulated and may even benefit from their investments earning higher interest rates. The working heads of poor families, however, suffer relative income losses three times those of middle-income families.[59]

Recognizing the importance of business cycles does not mean, however, that social support programs are unneeded when employment levels are high. Nor should they be cut any further. On the contrary, we will shortly see that there has been a large-scale real income erosion for most people in the United States. This has led to growing income inequality, which in turn causes more poverty. In the face of this reality, the safety net should be increased! Despite today's temporary low unemployment (5.5 percent in much of 1988), U.S. rates have been much higher for most of the past two decades. Our unemployment rate averaged 4.8 percent in 1960–69, 6.2 percent in 1970–79, and 7.7 percent in 1980–87.[60] The majority of economists are certain that the United States is headed for a major recession within the next year or two.[61] When this occurs, unemployment will rocket up. Poverty will then rapidly rise once again—perhaps to a new high.

The point worth emphasizing in all of the debate about what factors are important in reducing poverty is that a growing mean or per capita income will not help the poor! When the economy is booming, the well-to-do benefit the most. On the downside, however, the poor are impoverished even more. Macroeconomic policies are important in helping the poor, therefore, but only to the extent they encourage full employment.

A closely related debate took place in the 1980s involving those who have such touching faith in growth. In their rush to pay tribute to a laissez faire doctrine, pro-capitalist conservatives have alleged that the war on poverty was a failure. For example, critics such as Charles Murray have accused social programs of creating welfare dependency, of encouraging the poor to remain so because of benefits, and of failure to eradicate poverty.[62] Some empirical evidence claims to show a U-shaped curve between welfare spending and the percent under poverty.[63] It has been asserted that benefits can actually rise to the point where they are attractive to people, who then choose to stay on welfare rather than work. A recent re-analysis of what is now called the "Laffer Curve" indicates that this is a false relationship.[64] Instead, the tendency is in the direction we would expect. Poverty did decline in the 1960s as welfare spending rose. The proportion of poor people increased in the late 1970s and early 1980s when benefits leveled off and then went down. Part of the error in the early research was in using per capita income as a predictor of poverty. This is a gross average masking other factors such as recessions. Other miscalculations in the early research stemmed from looking only at federal spending (not state or local), using spending per person of the entire U.S. population rather than those who actually received the aid, and ignoring in-kind benefits (e.g., food stamps).

Sawhill's thorough review of the literature also yields no support for the idea that welfare *causes* poverty.[65] She notes that the safety net has worked admirably in some places (especially for the elderly, but also in medical assistance and compensatory education programs such as Headstart). In her summary of the research, the inescapable conclusion is that poverty would have been much higher were it not for the existence of income transfer programs. Despite all such governmental efforts, she sees continued poverty as stemming from past high unemployment and failure of average real income to grow within the past twenty years.

It *is* proper to question the effectiveness of any government program. In the end, however, this should also include the various "wealthfare" programs that benefit the rich. One good example would be the cut in the capital gains tax being pushed by George Bush, which would serve to benefit only the well-to-do. The exorbitant scale of Pentagon budget levels should be looked at as well. One can argue that by draining money needed for productive investment in our nation, such prolific spending serves to perpetuate poverty while increasing income inequality. Above all, the very welfare programs that conservatives are so fond of attacking, whether relatively effective or not, would largely be unneeded if more humane decisions by the private sector were set into play. The health of the United States economy together with the jobs, income level, and poverty rates it produces—is dependent upon the behavior of huge corporations. Unfortunately, these decisions have led to moving plants and jobs abroad or into low-wage areas of our country. Their ultimate effect has been to reduce income as a whole in addition to driving up poverty rates.

The Decline in Wages

In an attempt to convince the American electorate that our country has been enjoying an unprecedented economic boom, George Bush often bragged during the 1988 Presidential campaign about the continuing increase in per capita income. The figures, oft-cited by supporters of Reaganomics as evidence that their economic policies have been working, are certainly true. In 1987, per capita income stood at an all-time high of $12,290, which was over 16 percent greater in real dollars than 1982. Per capita income is calculated by dividing total money income by the entire population. In essence, there was more money available in a theoretical sense for each man, woman, and child in the United States in 1987 than ever before.

Yet there is reason to be entirely skeptical about accepting these figures as "proof" that America has been enjoying economic growth and prosperity. Per capita income is a measure that is similar to mean GNP per person, so often used to show how development policies have worked in LDCs. As seen in previous chapters, real GNP per person can increase in the Third World without necessarily benefitting the masses. The same can be said of the United States with regard to per capita income. The increase in per capita income is a single, gross average that hides a large-scale decline of real income for most Americans. While real average income has been largely stagnant or slipping since 1973 for most workers, some people at the top of the pay spectrum are definitely making more money. The real explanation lies with a larger dose of income inequality. What has been happening in the United States over the past few decades is a very fast rise of income for top businessmen, chief executive officers, and stockholders—coupled with a serious dip for blue-collar, retail, and service workers. When persons at the richer end of the income distribution receive ever greater amounts of money, they will pull per capita income up even while median income remains basically unchanged. This rise is shown in higher per capita income, but it has not filtered down to most Americans.

To begin to make sense of what has been happening to the income picture in the past two decades, it is important to distinguish between wages, earnings, and income as defined in government statistics. Wages reflect the amount paid to production and nonmanagement workers in the private sector (excluding farm and government workers). Wages also do not reflect the earnings of professionals, business managers, and others who draw a salary. Nonetheless, wages are paid to 80 percent of all those employed. Whether wages grow or decline will thus have a major impact upon the economic well-being of most Americans. Earnings data cover wages, but also salaries and income from self-employment. Income figures cover an even wider gamut of sources—such as wages, salaries, government transfer payments (AFDC, Social Security, etc.), savings and bond interest, rental income, child support, alimony, pensions, etc. In short, income includes just about all the sources we are required to report on our income tax forms. By looking at all three data

FIGURE 5.6: Weekly Industry Earnings (constant 1977 dollars)

Source: Data graphed from *Economic Report of the President, 1989*, p. 359.

sources, we can see which groups in our economy are surging ahead and who is being left behind:

> Since wages are falling and many government transfer payments (for example, welfare benefits) have not kept pace with inflation, much of the divergence between real wages and personal income must be a result of higher salaries for managers and professional workers, increased dividend and interest payments, and higher property income. Such forms of income are mainly concentrated among upper income individuals. The growth in various forms of non-wage income thus helps to explain why the distribution of income in the United States is growing more unequal.[66]

To begin with, since reaching its peak in 1972–73 real average weekly earnings have fallen by over 18 percent through November of 1988.[67] A graphic illustration of this can be seen in Figure 5.6, which traces the performance of average weekly earnings paid in the United States since the end of World War II. The Bureau of Labor Statistics (BLS), which collects and monitors such data, has converted the earnings into constant 1977 dollars to remove the effect of inflation and permit a fair comparison to earlier years.[68] The facts speak for themselves. The average American worker is worse off today than twenty years ago. In terms of real earnings, today's typical worker earns about the same pay as workers in 1961!

FIGURE 5.7: Average Weekly Earnings by Industry (constant 1977 dollars)

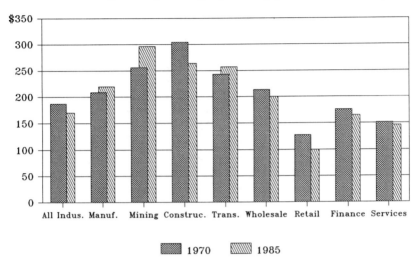

Source: U.S. Bureau of the Census, *Statistical Abstract, 1987.*

The picture gets worse. The decline in wages has been fairly wide-spread, although some sectors have managed to stay even or even inch ahead slightly. Figure 5.7 tracks the performance of real average weekly earnings (in constant 1977 dollars) by private industry groups between 1970 and 1985.[69] Although the figures show general decline for all earnings recipients as a whole, some workers were able to eke out a few gains. Those jobs in the service sector—which are supposed to be the highlight of our emerging high-tech, information-age economy—display serious erosion. To the extent we lose manufacturing jobs in industry and substitute service jobs, we can expect a greater skid in wages for the future.

In 1987 constant dollars, all males fifteen years old and over received a median income of $17,552 in that year—compared to $8,101 for females. Full-time, year-round workers of both sexes were paid considerably more in 1987: $26,722 for men and $17,504 for women. These figures show continuing income inequality for women in our society. Full-time male workers still receive over 50 percent more income than full-time female workers. While this fact is deplorable, there is a silver lining to the cloud. Real income for women has shown a tireless climb. Median real income for all women has grown larger and larger over the years, increasing by 13 percent between 1973 and 1987.

By contrast, income for all males fifteen years old and over has been steadily getting smaller. The real loss of income was not just limited to one occupational spectrum—although we will see that manufacturing jobs were hardest hit. The slide in wages for white males was evident across a wide range of jobs. Many of these, even including such professional employment areas as the law, business management, engineering, etc. have been widely regarded as erosion proof. Table 5.1 reveals this notion to be false. In nearly every occupation, whether white or blue collar, professional, or service category, white males have taken serious cuts in their pay between 1969 and 1979.

In 1973, median male income in constant 1987 dollars was $20,603. By 1987 this had shrunk to $17,752—or minus 14 percent. The loss in real dollars of $2,851 may not have seemed very large over fifteen years. It comes to about $190 dollars per year. Yet this same rate of dollar loss when applied to LDCs would have supported over one-quarter of a bil-

TABLE 5.1 Mean Earnings of White Men by Occupation: 1969–79

	Mean Earnings (1984 Dollars)		Percent Change
	1969	1979	
All White Males	$19,619	$19,307	−1.6%
Professional and Managerial			
Executives, Administrators, Managers	35,845	33,770	−5.8
Management-Related Occupations	29,470	28,174	−4.4
Engineers & Natural Scientists	34,833	30,530	−12.4
Doctors, Dentists, etc.	68,306	70,507	3.2
Teachers (all levels)	25,032	28,368	13.3
Lawyers and Judges	55,734	52,574	−5.7
Miscellaneous Professionals (Ministers, Social Workers, etc.)	23,422	19,909	−15.0
Other White-Collar Workers			
Health Aides, Technicians	20,736	16,989	−18.1
Technicians other than Health	23,880	22,616	−5.3
Sales-Related Occupations	24,529	24,003	−2.1
Administrative Support	18,306	17,821	−2.6
Blue-Collar Workers			
Craftsmen and Precision Workers	21,012	20,760	−1.2
Machine Operators	17,884	17,729	−.9
Transport Equipment Operators	18,538	19,449	4.9
Handlers, Laborers, etc.	10,836	11,349	4.7
Service Workers			
Protective Service Workers	19,897	17,888	−10.1
Food, Building, Childcare, Restaurant, and Personal Services	10,257	9,429	−9.1
Armed Forces	12,451	13,193	6.0

Source: Frank Levy, *Dollars and Dreams:* 128–9.

FIGURE 5.8: Median Income by Sex (constant 1987 dollars)

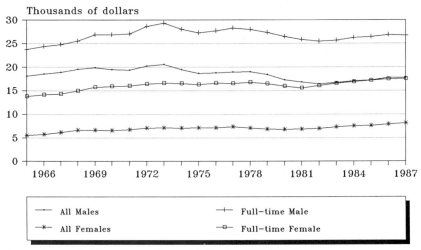

Source: Data graphed from *Economic Report of the President, 1989*, Table B–30.

lion people in nine of the world's poorest countries for each of the past fifteen years! Perhaps there was no outcry because the change was so gradual and because inflation made it seem as if wages were actually going up. Yet the decline is very persistent and long term, spanning Democratic and Republican Presidencies alike. It has continued to grow ever larger and been stubbornly resistant to any change. In the end it highlights the fact that the forces pushing American wages down may be difficult or impossible to remove.

No doubt there was some cushion to the fall. Many of these men are married to women whose take-home pay did go up. Although females gained only $950 in real median income during the fifteen years ($63 per year), more women are working now than ever before. Within fifteen short years, the presence of married couples with children and two full-time workers in the paid labor force nearly doubled. Their proportion climbed from 14 percent in 1970 to 26 percent in 1986.[70]

There has been a real loss of earnings for the majority of American workers in the past fifteen years, therefore, after the disguising effects of inflation are removed. What has happened to the pay packet of the American worker relative to the global economy? We hear much of labor unrest around the world—strikes in the dockyards of Poland, agitation in South Korea, street riots among many Latin American countries—where economic deterioration is clearly a reality. The fairest comparison would be to look at wages comparing the United States to other industrial countries. The Bureau of Labor Statistics has conveniently indexed starting pay at 100 in 1977 U.S. dollars for seven industrial countries to make just such a comparison.[71] Figure 5.9 shows wages increased within all countries. All levels should have gone up in this eleven-year period since inflation has not been removed. Yet it is the *rate of climb* that is the most astounding. The hourly compensation for manufacturing workers more than doubled in all other countries and almost tripled in Japan. Even the United Kingdom, which generally registers dismal economic performance in most measures, easily out-distanced America.

There has been an even sharper erosion in the U.S. payscale compared to other countries just within the past few years. Much of this has been caused by devaluation of the dollar on global currency markets. The dollar lost a third of its value within a year. In U.S. dollars, 1985 average hourly pay for U.S. production workers at $12.96 was well ahead of all other industrial countries. It was twice as high as Britain ($6.19) and Japan ($6.47), well ahead of Italy ($7.40) and France ($7.52), and comfortably ahead of second place West Germany ($9.56). America had slipped to fifth place only three years later. By 1988, West Germany led the wage scale pack at $20.19 per hour, followed by Italy ($14.77), France ($14.03), and Japan ($13.80). The United States remained ahead of Britain alone ($13.62 versus $11.06), but even here the gap is likely to be reversed given our weak rate of increase (79 percent in the United Kingdom compared to 5 percent in the United States). While in 1985 West Germany had a pay rate about three-fourths that of the United States, in 1988 the United States had a pay rate only two-thirds that of West Germany.[72] Rarely in the economic history of nations has the table turned so quickly!

Harrison and Bluestone report compelling figures from their analysis of Current Population Survey (CPS) data going back to 1963.[73] After removing the effects of business expansions and recessions, the researchers report that between 1975–1986 inequality in earnings increased by 18 percent for all workers. Nearly two-thirds of this inequality could be laid at the feet of less pay per hour. Only one-third was due to the fact that some employees were working fewer hours (which may in itself have been less a result of personal choice than the lack of full-time jobs).

Many analysts have claimed that much of this growth in earnings inequality is really caused by the huge influx of women into the labor market (who have always been paid less). The rest can be blamed on the gigantic postwar baby boom invading the labor market all at once, which has also driven wages down because of over-supply. These types of explanations often border on rationalization. The implication is that after such trends run their course, things will get back to normal and every-

FIGURE 5.9

A. Index of Hourly Manufacturing Pay (100 = U.S. 1977 dollars)

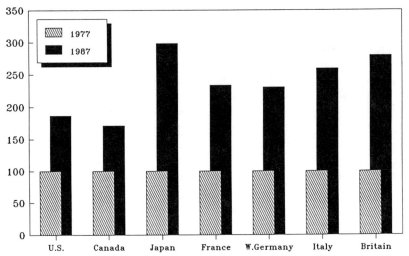

Source: Data graphed from *Economic Report of the President, 1989*, Table B–110.

B. Hourly Pay of Production Workers (U.S. 1988 dollars)

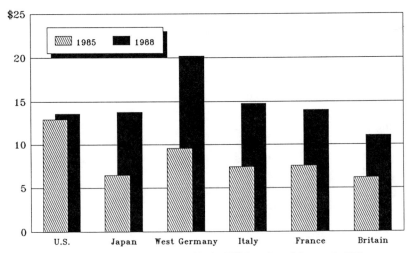

Source: Bureau of Labor Statistics, as reported in the *Wall Street Journal*, January 9, 1989.

thing will again be fine. The connotation is that once jobs are found for all the baby boomers and/or women who would have stayed home in an earlier epoch, pay rates will bounce back.

Such demographic factors actually do affect earnings to some degree and should not be completely dismissed. Frank Levy has estimated what happens to the real income of males (as a proxy for earnings) as they age, comparing the results to prior epochs. In 1949, an average forty-year-old man increased his real income by 34 percent during the ten years it took to reach age fifty. During the 1960s a similar passage for a man going from age forty to fifty produced a 29 percent rise in real income. But a man who turned forty in 1973 actually earned 14 percent less in constant dollars by the time he turned fifty in 1983! Put differently, a young man who left his parents' home in 1973 now earns 25 percent less (rather than 15 percent more) than his father had earned in 1973.[74] Yet Levy in the end also sees a combination of cyclical and structural changes in the U.S. economy as partly responsible for changing earnings as well.

The truth is that the decline in pay has taken place for just about every group (although it has hit younger people and white males harder). When looking at the impact of demographic variables alone, Harrison and Bluestone found:

> The baby boom and the growth in the number of female workers have had no *significant impact whatsoever* on the increase in inequality of wages. Indeed, men's and women's wages actually converged slightly in this period—owing more to declines in the average wage of males than to increases in the wages of women. The wages of white women and women of color are now almost indistinguishable. Put another way, all of the increase in inequality since 1975 must have occurred *within* age, race, and sex groups, not among them. Inequality is growing among whites as well as nonwhites, among the old as well as the young, and among women as well as men.[75]

Most of our discussion has so far been limited to looking at the wage performance within large industrial groups—such as comparing production workers from one country to those of another, or the manufacturing wage level between 1973 and the present. Although a very real decline is evident here, there has been another trend of massive proportions taking place in the United States. Up to now, deindustrialization has been alluded to only in passing. Yet this is one of the most significant economic factors to occur in the United States within the last few decades.

The decline in manufacturing jobs has been going on for quite some time now, as well as a parallel increase in service employment. Service workers are found in a wide variety of occupations and industries, but are concentrated in wholesale and retail trade.[76] By occupation, sales clerks, secretaries, bartenders, computer data processors, advertising agents, janitors, waiters, beauticians, and a host of other workers are included who are not directly involved in manufacturing a tangible product. Service industries made up over half of all hours of employment in 1947, a figure that had risen to nearly three-fourths by 1984.[77] The real crisis started to develop in 1981 when the expansion of jobs in goods production not only halted but began to get smaller.[78] Manufacturing jobs count for a lot! In November of 1988 the average weekly earnings of people in industry stood at $424, compared to $186 in retail trade. Not all service workers are poorly paid (for example, government employees), but on the whole most of the growth in service jobs has been in such areas as fast food or janitorial services. While such low-paying jobs have been on the rise, the top-paying blue-collar jobs in heavy industry have been disappearing.

Lester Thurow believes that intense international competition has been one of the major causes at the bottom of American decline. He gives, as an example, the $170 billion trade deficit in 1987. This can be brought into better focus when we realize it takes one million full-time U.S. employees to produce $42 billion worth of goods. Thus, the trade deficit in just this one year was akin to squeezing more than four million workers out of manufacturing and forcing them to take other jobs. Thurow presents evidence to show that *manufacturing jobs are more highly paid AND have a more equal distribution of pay* in comparison to service jobs. Given these facts, then, the decline in manufacturing must always lead to more inequality in the distribution of earnings:

> In addition to paying higher wages, the exporting and import-competing industries generated a more equal distribution of earnings. In 1983, 41 percent of the entire work force worked at jobs that paid less than $12,500 per year, whereas only 31 percent of the workers in exporting industries and 30 percent of those in industries competing with imports held such jobs. Furthermore, whereas 56 percent of the total work force earned from $12,500 to $50,000 per year, 66 percent of the workers in exporting industries and 67 percent of those in the industries competing with imports were at this level. . . . The meaning of these statistics is that when exports fall and imports rise to create a trade deficit, the distribution of earnings moves toward inequality. Jobs are lost in both exporting and import-competing industries and are replaced by jobs with lower, more unequal earnings in the rest of the economy. This factor is the principal

reason for the observed decline in earnings of males. The industries that have been hit hardest by international competition—automobiles, steel and machine tools—are precisely the ones that have provided a large number of upper-middle-income male jobs.[79]

Thus, erosion of wages is mostly due to the shift in the industrial mix going on within our country. Harrison and Bluestone estimate at least a fifth of the overall inequality in wages since 1978 has been caused by the disappearance of manufacturing jobs.[80] Without a doubt, this has been a major reason that real wages of men have been in a virtual free fall. The rise of low-income earners among men has also not been due to the baby boom effect, education/job experience, or the unemployment rate.[81] In their earlier report to Congress, Bluestone and Harrison pointed out that while only one in four new jobs taken by white men in 1973–79 were low wage, this had risen to 97 percent by the 1979–84 period![82] In the latter period, the industrial Midwest had lost a million middle- and high-wage jobs but only gained 900,000 new low-wage jobs. Since the number of jobs around the entire country in manufacturing actually went down, there were no new jobs to calculate whether any improvement had taken place in this sector.

In their analysis of CPS data, Harrison and Bluestone divided jobs into low-, middle-, and high-wage groups by first looking at the prevailing wages in 1973. This was America's best year for earnings, a level which has not been duplicated since. Their research arbitrarily cast jobs with earnings at one-half the median wage as "low-wage." "High-wage" jobs were defined as being at twice the median wage in 1973, since the earnings distribution is skewed so far toward high incomes. Revising these figures to 1986 dollars as well as other years along the way allowed them to do a time series comparison. Lastly, figures were converted to reflect year-round, full-time pay. In 1986, low-wage jobs were those paying less than $11,103 while high-wage jobs were those paying $44,413 or more.[83]

The researchers then compared the types of new jobs created within three time periods, with highly instructive results. The 1963–73 period could be described as our golden days when growth and increasing pay were the norm. In the 1973–79 period there were several severe disruptions to the economy, including two OPEC oil embargoes, fierce inflation, and the costs of the Vietnam war coming home to roost. Nonetheless, momentum in the American economy still carried us further. By the 1979–86 period, however, the rust had finally started to show on the body of the American economy. Table 5.2 compares growth in low-wage and high-wage new jobs for the three time periods. Separately analyzed are a number of categories (such as sex, age, race, location, type of industry, etc.) which have been popular as competing explanations for our wage decline. None of them can serve to justify why the decline has taken place. Put differently, a slide is evident for all age, sex, race, region, and industrial groups!

There was a 10 percent decline in low-paying jobs between 1963 to 1973, while one-third of all new jobs created in 1979–86 were low-paid. At the opposite extreme, the golden years saw nearly one in four (22.2 percent) new jobs created at a high pay scale, compared to only 14 percent in the latest period. For group after group the figures nearly always say the same thing. The proportion of low-paying new jobs is on the rise. The only exception is for the middle-age group and the New England/Northeast regions to some degree. Yet even here there is a large erosion of jobs at the top of the pay scale. The figures are also consistent with Harrison and Bluestone's major point. The changes in our economy are producing a polarized income picture. High-wage jobs have been increasing for most groups at the same time low-wage jobs are being spawned in record numbers (although not nearly by as much). The proportion of new jobs at the high end of the pay scale has doubled between the 1973–1979 and 1979–86 periods (6.2 percent versus 13.9 percent). The proportions in the top end also doubled for men, women, the South, and in services. They have more than tripled for whites, and for those in the Northeast and New England regions. In the end:

> The polarization of jobs is becoming increasingly universal, no matter what the color of workers' skin, their sex, their age, or for that matter, the industry within which they work. . . . Consider, for example, the position of men—historically the most privileged group in the workforce. . . . The proportion of net new employment that paid middle-level earnings to male workers—between $11,000 and $44,000 a year—has literally crashed, from nearly 78 percent between 1963 and 1973 to only 26 percent in the period ending in 1986. This is polarization with a vengeance. . . . Tragically, low-wage employment rose sharply among workers of color beginning around 1979 after more than a decade-and-a-half of improvement. Indeed, virtually all of the improvement experienced by black, Hispanic, and Asian workers between 1973 and 1979 disappeared in the 1980s. Younger workers were also hard hit after 1979. Almost three-fifths of the net new YRFT [year-round full-time] employment that went to workers under the age of thirty-five since then has paid less than $11,000 a year. . . . Not unexpectedly, the condition of the old industrial Midwest is the most extreme. It leads the nation in generating new low-wage jobs. What new employment has been created is *all* in the extremes of the distribution of wages—and fully 96 percent is in the bottom. There are no new jobs in the middle stratum

TABLE 5.2   Percentage of Net Growth in Low- and High-Wage Jobs by
             Selected Characteristics: 1963–86

Selected Characteristics	Percentage Net Growth in Jobs		
	1963–73	1973–79	1979–86
All Workers			
Low-Wage	−9.8	19.2	36.0
Middle-Wage	87.6	74.6	50.1
High-Wage	22.2	6.2	13.9
Men			
Low-Wage	−17.2	17.9	46.9
High-Wage	39.4	12.9	27.1
Women			
Low-Wage	−1.0	19.8	29.4
High-Wage	1.5	2.8	5.7
Whites			
Low-Wage	−8.9	22.2	35.1
High-Wage	25.6	5.8	15.7
Nonwhites			
Low-Wage	−14.6	1.4	39.0
High-Wage	4.7	8.3	8.1
Age 20–34 Years			
Low-Wage	0.6	19.4	57.6
High-Wage	8.2	0.6	7.0
Age 35–54 Years			
Low-Wage	−36.1	23.4	17.9
High-Wage	54.8	12.6	16.4
Northeast			
Low-Wage	−29.6	38.5	24.7
High-Wage	41.2	−8.4	23.9
Midwest			
Low-Wage	−5.2	16.5	96.0
High-Wage	23.8	2.7	8.8
South			
Low-Wage	−13.2	16.2	33.7
High-Wage	15.2	7.5	13.5
West			
Low-Wage	5.1	16.4	29.8
High-Wage	19.2	12.2	10.1
New England			
Low-Wage	−70.7	29.6	16.6
High-Wage	52.8	3.8	21.6
Manufacturing			
Low-Wage	−9.0	4.1	No New Jobs!
High-Wage	27.1	24.9	
Services			
Low-Wage	−4.8	23.2	33.0
High-Wage	15.9	4.6	11.8

Source: Harrison & Bluestone, *The Great U-Turn*, Table A-2.

at all! Deindustrialization, more prevalent in the Midwest than any-where else, is plainly taking its toll. As well-paying manufacturing jobs disappear, new employment is almost entirely in the poorly paid jobs in the service sector, with a handful of new workers at the top. . . . Those workers traditionally most favored in the U.S. labor market—whites, men, and workers in the high-wage Midwest—are joining the low-wage segment in record numbers.[84]

Support is widespread for the view that real wages have slid lower. They have become more unequal in a relative sense as well. Leann Tigges has looked at the absolute earnings decline in an attempt to isolate the major cause. Comparing data from the 1960 and 1980 Census Bureau public use samples, she was able to trace what has happened to earnings over twenty years. Through multivariate regression analysis, the effect of sex, education, race, service versus manufacturing jobs, and employ-ment in core versus periphery industrial sectors were compared. There was every reason to believe that demographic factors could have driven down earnings, since the labor force was less white, more female, and younger in 1980 compared to 1960. Yet during the same time there was a massive shift away from manufacturing toward services, which could also cause a slide. The regressions effectively hold all of these variables constant simultaneously. Although there has been more earnings decline for younger males, deterioration was also apparent for older men as well.[85] The decline in earnings, then, cannot be laid at the feet of the huge influx of baby boomers into the labor force. Yet, decline in the core ver-sus the periphery of industry also was apparent. Although the association between working in service jobs and receiving low pay did not get worse, it did not get better either. It remained a very important factor in the slide toward lower earnings. Much of the erosion within core indus-tries was because of the increasing negative influence of service work in this sector.[86] Tigges also found no evidence that the increase in profes-sional, technical, and managerial jobs over the past twenty years acted to increase earnings. Completing the circle of bad news was the finding that the impact of education upon earnings actually went down.

Analysts are prone to argue that differences in findings are caused by different techniques and methods used in separate studies. Yet, the amount of agreement documenting a continued deterioration of earnings has reached a crescendo. A recent RAND report concludes that even using ten different measurements of earnings inequality, and examining total earnings versus wage and salary income combined, yields the same general conclusion.[87] This report describes a period of stable earnings inequality from 1967 to 1980 being replaced by growing relative earnings inequality in 1980 to 1986. Inequality grew even for full-time year-round workers, as it did for all age and sex groups. The labor force entrance of younger workers was not primarily responsible for more inequality. Nor was the influx of more women into the labor force a cause.[88] Finally, although the increase in service industry served to drive up earnings inequality, it would have grown much larger even without this shift away from manufacturing.

Flight from the Social Wage: "The South Shall Rise Again"

One argument raised by a variety of researchers is that the growth of relative income inequality and decline in absolute earnings is associated with regional shifts within the United States.[89] In a nutshell, it is asserted that American corporations simply folded up their tents from northern, frostbelt states during the past few decades. Their goal was to avoid high pay scales and cantankerous unions. Rather than submit to what some executives see as "inflated wages," business policy has instead been geared toward relocating in the South and West. Many states in these regions have right-to-work laws which make it difficult to unionize and to strike.

There is much truth to this view. For example, critics claim that in addition to fleeing high northern wages, business has been actively avoiding the social wage that has typically gone with the pay package as well. Corporations and individual workers have been paying taxes for community amenities, social services, education, welfare benefits, and the like all along. These forms of the social wage are much more evident within northern states than in the South, as figure 5.10 shows. Here the states have simply been divided into three equal groups on four different social characteristics. It is clear that unions are much more dominant in northern states, along with larger welfare payments, higher taxes, and more spending per student on education. All of this plus other social services translates to a higher cost of doing business. In the eyes of corporate accountants geared to the bottom line, this is a major sin. Rather than pay for such a social infrastructure, firms have instead opted to move abroad or at least to the South and West for what they deem a "better business climate." Within poorer regions of the country, companies can pay lower wages that may still be higher than the local scale.

It has definitely been in the Sunbelt—whether in the deep South or in the Southwest—that more jobs have been created. Jobs have disappeared quickly from the Northeast and industrial Midwest at the same time. Just looking at one ratio—jobs lost divided by jobs created in the 1969–76 period—shows the Sunbelt to have been a big winner in competition for earnings (figure 5.11). The map also shows just how desperately the South still could use higher yearly earnings. Even in 1985 this

FIGURE 5.10

A. Percent of Labor Force in Unions, 1980

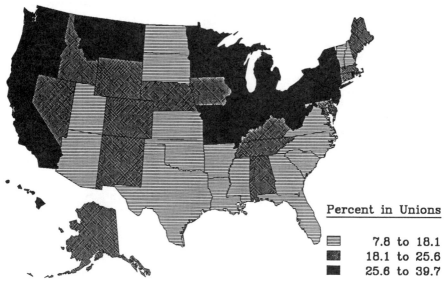

Percent in Unions

▦	7.8 to 18.1
▨	18.1 to 25.6
■	25.6 to 39.7

Source: *Statistical Abstract 1987*, p. 408.

B. Effective Business Tax Rate, 1975

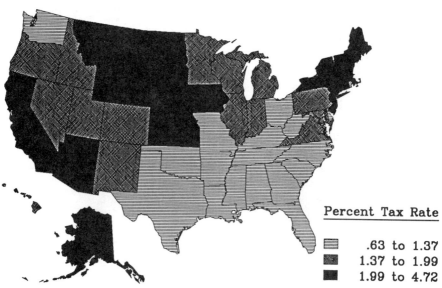

Percent Tax Rate

▦	.63 to 1.37
▨	1.37 to 1.99
■	1.99 to 4.72

Source: *Deindustrialization of America*, p. 186.

C. Average AFDC Monthly Payment, 1984

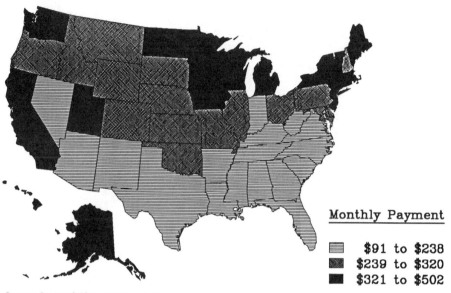

Monthly Payment

$91 to $238
$239 to $320
$321 to $502

Source: *Statistical Abstract 1987,* p. 365.

D. Per Capita Expenditure on Education, 1980

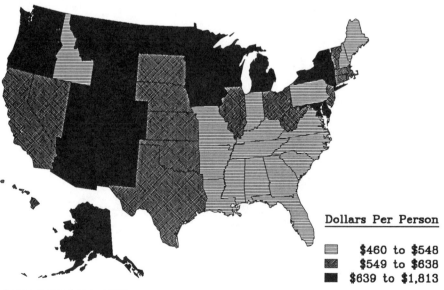

Dollars Per Person

$460 to $548
$549 to $638
$639 to $1,813

Source: *Statistical Abstract 1982.*

FIGURE 5.11

A. Ratio of Jobs Lost to Jobs Created, 1969–76

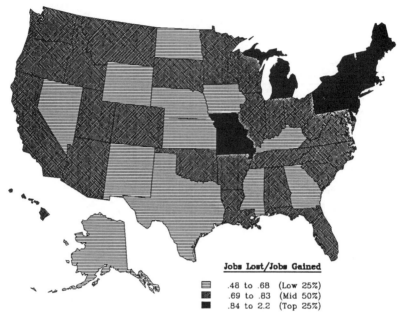

Jobs Lost/Jobs Gained

.48 to .68 (Low 25%)
.69 to .83 (Mid 50%)
.84 to 2.2 (Top 25%)

Source: *Deindustrialization of America*, pp. 266–9.

B. Average Yearly Earnings, 1985

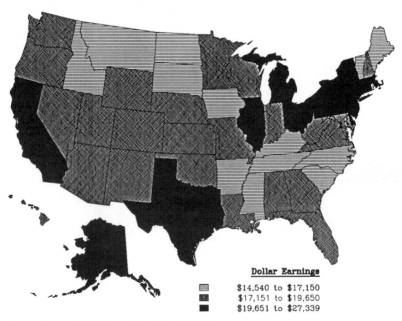

Dollar Earnings

$14,540 to $17,150
$17,151 to $19,650
$19,651 to $27,339

Source: Congressional Research Service, #87-377 E.

region continued to have a greater proportion of its states in the bottom quartile of earnings compared to other areas. The South Atlantic states (Florida, Georgia, South Carolina, North Carolina, Virginia, West Virginia, Maryland, District of Columbia, and Delaware) displayed the lowest earnings of any region—at 85 percent of the U.S. average.

On the other hand, the change in earnings between 1979 and 1985 heavily underlines a related trend. The East North-Central Census region (made up of Michigan, Wisconsin, Illinois, Indiana, and Ohio—our industrial heartland) dropped from first place to third in average earnings. It had only a 34.2 percent increase in earnings over six years, the smallest of all regions. Although manufacturing jobs posted average wage gains well above other types of jobs, there was a hidden cost to the victory. The increase was largely made possible by cutting back on jobs or moving them out of the North. Within just six years, work in manufacturing had fallen 8.2 percent around the country. The loss came to 1.8 million jobs.[90]

Not only has the number of job openings been on the upswing for the South, wages have also been going up relative to the older industrial states of the North. Figure 5.12 shows very large percentage increases in weekly manufacturing earnings over the past decade in the South and West relative to the Midwest and Northeast. There are other ways of looking at the figures, however, which may take some of the gloom away for the industrial heartland. Despite decades of deindustrialization and the vanishing of jobs, conditions remain better with respect to manufacturing earnings in the North. Northern states still had higher average weekly manufacturing earnings in 1988 than in the South, while their absolute dollar raises have been higher in the past decade as well. Much of this is no doubt due to the fact that northern salaries started at much higher rates than in the South. Thus, even with smaller percentage raises many of the increases tend to be larger than in the South.

There is little room for cheer in most of the data. The decline in manufacturing has been most prevalent in the northern states and is directly related to the failure of American corporations to invest in themselves and to compete in the world market. To begin with, the manufacturing sector of the United States has been very concentrated in only nine states, seven of which are in what is now called—by way of summing up this decline—the "rust belt." The states of New York, New Jersey, Pennsylvania, Ohio, Michigan, Illinois, and Indiana together with California and Texas each accounted for over $20 billion of manufacturing in 1977:

> Many U.S. export markets shrank from 1962 to 1979 by more than one-half. The declines are especially severe and important from an

FIGURE 5.12

A. Average Weekly Manufacturing Earnings, 1988

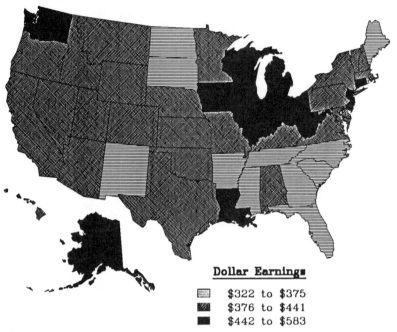

Dollar Earnings

▤ $322 to $375
▧ $376 to $441
■ $442 to $583

Source: BLS *Employment and Earnings,* 1988.

B. Increase in Weekly Manufacturing Earnings, 1979–88

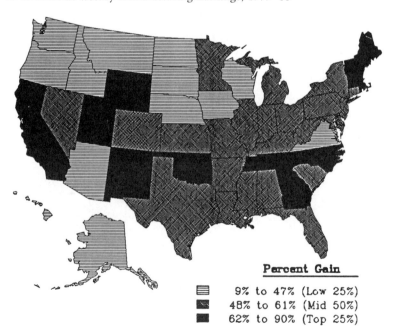

Percent Gain

▤ 9% to 47% (Low 25%)
▦ 48% to 61% (Mid 50%)
■ 62% to 90% (Top 25%)

Source: BLS *Employment and Earnings,* 1979, 1988.

employment perspective in motor vehicles, chemicals, and agricultural machinery. Altogether, American industries lost 23 percent of their share of world markets in the 1970s. These losses are all the more important in that they came at a time when the U.S. dollar depreciated by about 40 percent. This should have made American exports cheaper and foreign imports more expensive.[91]

At the same time, business responded by fleeing the North and in many cases our nation as well. When they did stop and rebuild on this side of the Rio Grande, it was nearly always because of the cheaper wage structure of the South. Many experts believe it was the decentralization of manufacturing production which led to the economic revitalization of the South. Yet, there was less financial benefit in wages than would have occurred if these industries had stayed in the North. One in three jobs within manufacturing in the South was below the national average for all production workers.[92] A quick glance at the map in figure 5.12 tells the whole story. Most of the production work within the South in 1988 was still being done at wages below the prevailing national norm. Despite the fact that many of these new jobs are in recently built factories within high-technology industries, the pay level is quite low. The appeal of this regional periphery made up of the South and Southwest stems from the same concerns that led U.S. corporations abroad—greater profit! The low wages, hostility toward unions, minute sums spent on social services, and cheaper energy costs translate into greater dollars for corporations leaving their old northern homes in the industrial core. Were it not for the attractiveness of the South, the national erosion of wages and real earnings would have been even worse as plants relocated to Mexico, Thailand, or wherever a compliant workforce could be bought at the cheapest rate.

The War with Labor

One of the primary causes for the continuing decline in wages and earnings, according to Bennett Harrison and Barry Bluestone, is the relentless war being waged on labor by American business.[93] The drop in the ability of the United States to compete in trade around the globe meant that profits went down for American corporations. As a response to the drop in profitability, American firms had a choice to make. A need existed to retool factories and invest in the most up-to-date technology money could buy. In this way, goods could be made more cheaply through a better, more efficient production process. According to free market forces, firms would be able to sell more goods because their products could be made more cheaply with higher quality.

Unfortunately, another avenue was also available to protect and even enhance profitability. This strategy was to sidestep the need for large investment in new capital goods. The plan was to simply slash pay. Wages could be and were attacked on a broad front using a variety of means. By simply moving factories to the South or out of the country, firms pressured unions in the old northern industrial core to agree to wage rollbacks or two-tier wage contracts. Two-tier contracts simply protect the benefits of older workers. The union agrees with management that new workers who are hired will be forced to take much lower pay while doing the same job. The popularity of such contracts seemed to explode over night. Almost one in ten labor contracts negotiated in 1985 involved a two-tier wage system—up from virtually zero in 1980. Not surprisingly, the two-tier system is more common in nonmanufacturing contracts where unions are weaker (17 percent), where government deregulation has taken place (35 percent in the airline industry), where profits in the firms are low, where intense competition exists from foreign imports, and in areas where strong shifts in consumer demand take place (one third of wholesale and retail trade now involves two-tier agreements).[94]

Another means to reduce labor costs and thus raise profit is to convert full-time work into part-time labor. In this way, various added costs such as health plans, pensions, and higher rates of pay can be avoided. The use of temporary worker agencies such as Kelly Services and Manpower, Inc. grew twice as fast as our nation's GNP in 1970–84:

> Contingent labor—leased and temporary workers, involuntary part-timers, employees of subcontractors, and homeworkers—grew from 8 million in 1980 to 18 million by 1985. That number is nearly 17 percent of the total work force. If those whom the BLS [Bureau of Labor Statistics] considers to be "voluntary" part-time workers are added to the count, fully a quarter of the 1985 labor force could be considered contingent employees. . . . In slack periods, employers are less concerned with developing promotional ladders to keep their most prized employees and more interested in finding cheap and efficient ways of reducing the number of workers at the first sign of a downturn in sales. The use of contingent labor provides them with just such a mechanism. . . . The stagnation of real wages since the early 1970s also means that more and more families *need* whatever work their members can find, however "contingent." . . . Practically 100 percent of the net additional part-time jobs created in the United States since the late 1970s are held by people who would have preferred full-time jobs but could not find any. . . . That is, we should look to the behavior of employers and not employees to explain the growth in part-time jobs.[95]

One of the results steming from the active hostility employers have directed toward unions is a decline in their membership. As unions have been forced into wage concessions and two-tiered contracts by the threat of closed factories, they have become less effective. To the degree unions are less effective, fewer workers want to join them. Included in the arsenal of weapons companies have used to weaken or destroy unions has been out-sourcing orders abroad or into southern plants that were previously done by a unionized work force. Campaigns to decertify unions have also been slick, well-orchestrated affairs that have met with some success. Even bankruptcy laws have been used to abrogate prior wage agreements reached with unions. When these strategies are considered together with growth in traditionally non-unionized service jobs and movement to right-to-work states, it is not surprising that membership in unions has declined. In 1975, union members made up almost 29 percent of all those employed, but this had reached a postwar low of 18 percent by 1985.[96]

Harrison and Bluestone conclude that earnings inequality in the American labor force increased by a full 18 percent between 1975 and 1986.[97] This occurred even after the effects of inflation and downturns in the business cycle were removed. About one-third of this growth toward greater inequality was due to more part-time work. The other two-thirds stemmed from a growing polarization in wages and earnings, mostly because high-paying jobs were eliminated in the face of a more competitive global market. Looking only at the growth of inequality in earnings and ignoring the trend toward part-time work, the authors found that one fifth of wage inequality was the result of the shift away from manufacturing jobs and into the service area. The rest they believe is due to *internal cutting of wages within occupations and industries.* Much of this was done with rollbacks, concessions, tiered contracts, elimination of high-wage jobs, paying less for newly created jobs, not replacing workers lost through attrition, forcing early retirements of top-paid staff, reducing or eliminating fringe benefits, refusing cost-of-living (COLA) raises, moving to a lower wage section of the country, etc. Just about every conceivable means was used to force wages lower in order to keep the profit margins up. Since earnings are the major portion of income for most of us, it will come as no surprise that mounting evidence points to a full-blown crisis for the American family as well.

The Decline of Income

The United States has largely failed to hold its own in the global economy. Our goods are overpriced and of shoddy quality. They come from antique plants made by a work force using outdated technology. Because of these factors together with record U.S. interest rates and an over-valued dollar during most of the 1980s, our ability to export to the rest of the world has abruptly dropped. Severe trade deficits have been the inevitable result. They have literally turned the United States completely around. We have been humbled in the eyes of the world, going from the largest creditor nation to the largest debtor nation within five short years! The mounting trade gaps have left our nation in hock to other advanced industrial countries such as Japan, West Germany, and even Great Britain. These countries have come to own more and more factories, bonds, trea-sury notes, stock portfolios, and real estate in the United States. In 1980, U.S. assets abroad totalled $607 billion compared to $501 billion of for-eign assets in our country. By 1984 these figures were nearly dead even at $896 billion versus $893 billion—but by 1987 there was nearly one-third more foreign assets invested in the United States than there was American investment in other lands.[98] Much of the profit from these endeavors, of course, is repatriated elsewhere and does not stay in the United States to percolate into our parched economy. The money that does stay may be reinvested, but again this serves ultimately to transfer funds out of our country in the form of dividends, profits, and interest to foreign shores.

As our competitors have invested in new factories with the latest and most efficient production techniques, we have slashed our R & D funds to the bone. Instead, an expanding pot of money has been gifted to the military for esoteric projects with no commercial value. Not sur-prisingly, productivity of the American work force has also taken a nose-dive. Without the watering that any growing, healthy economy needs—the fruit of profit has withered on the vine. To meet the decline in profit and the drop in real money return, all actors in this drama of decline borrowed more money. National debt exploded, as did corporate and personal debt.

With the nation awash in red ink, conservative politicians and busi-ness spokesmen responded to the crisis by attacking "welfare free-loaders" and "overpaid union drones" rather than by dealing with the root cause of the crisis. The immediate impact was a drastic cut in the real income benefits of welfare and anti-poverty programs. This in turn led to a growth in the poor and homeless populations. What is less rec-ognized is the long-term loss of earnings that has taken place in America. This slide has reduced the real wages of just about everyone in the labor force, regardless of race, sex, age, industry, or region of the country. Some have been more hard hit than others in the 1980s, such as white males and workers in our core industrial region. Manufacturing jobs lit-erally disappeared. Unions were forced to accept humiliating losses, which led to a subsequent drop in membership as well. The pay of manufacturing workers has stopped rising and now lags far behind the wage scale in other industrial countries. It is true there has been job growth in the United States, but a large portion of this has been in service work with significantly lower pay. Quite simply, there have been fewer good-paying jobs being created in the 1980s than in the 1960s and 1970s.

It should then come as no surprise that the real income of most Americans has gone down since the peak was reached in 1973. Figure 5.8 documented a long-term decline for males since that date, with only a slight gain for women during the same period. A few things need to be said before the data is analyzed in more detail. How we perceive the figures can depend very much upon the time frame we use. It is possible to look at the same data and have one analyst label it a "crisis" while another would see some "significant improvement." For example, the Census Bureau reports that "Since 1982, real median family income has increased by 11.8 percent."[99] This statement is undeniably true. The fact is also true, however, that until 1987 our median family income ($30,853) was lower in every single year than the high it reached in 1973 at $30,820 (in 1987 dollars). It had actually gone down by over 10 percent to $27,591 between 1973 and 1982. Figure 5.13 traces the history of median family income since 1947.[100] It documents huge growth of real family income during the 1950s and 1960s. By the early 1970s, the climb had petered out. Real income, after taking out the effects of the up and down wave action, has declined since 1973. There has been some improvement in the past few years, as well there should after an uninterrupted seven year economic expansion. Yet on the whole there were two long-term dips of real family income between 1973 and 1987. Despite minor growth in absolute dollars in the past few years, *it was not until 1987 that median family income finally climbed back to what it was in 1973!*

The bottom graph in figure 5.13 shows two important trends. There is a long-term gap in median incomes between white families versus black and Hispanic families in the United States. It seems as if these deprivations are cast in concrete. No improvement appears for minority families. No hopeful sign exists that might point to some closing of the income gap over the past fifteen years. For that matter, real family income is getting worse for all families—regardless of minority status. On average, white families have lost $267 since 1973, but Hispanic families lost approximately $1,500; and black families saw $331 vanish during this time period. Not only have minorities lost greater absolute dollar amounts, but their percentage declines have been much heavier as well since they start from a much lower base in comparison to white families.

If one were to summarize the history of family income in the United States, it would be sharp real growth in the 1950s and 1960s followed by sputtering decline since 1973. While there has been real "in-

FIGURE 5.13

A. Median Income of Families (constant 1986 dollars)

Source: Data graphed from U.S. Bureau of the Census, *Current Population Reports 1987*, Series P–60, no. 159, Table 11.

B. Median Family Income By Race (constant 1986 dollars)

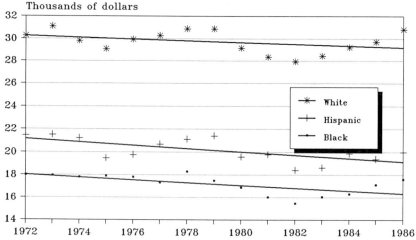

Source: Data graphed from U.S. Bureau of the Census, *Current Population Reports 1987*, Series P–60, no. 159, Table 11.

crease" since 1982, it should be remembered that this year saw the worst economic recession since the Depression in the 1930s. In a word, *anything* would look good in comparison to this base year. Put another way, it took fourteen long years before the U.S. economy could muster up enough energy to get back to the real prevailing median family income of 1973. To do so, our nation had to run record trade and budget deficits while drowning in unsustainable debt.

How long can this go on? We cannot run a tab indefinitely with our major creditors. Economists also agree that we are long overdue for a recession and the return of inflation. When this occurs, unemployment is a predictable offshoot—with automatic spurts in poverty and lowered family income. On the whole, there is good reason to suspect that an even sharper drop of real income will occur within the next few years which may run well into the 1990s.

A future downturn is sure to happen, since all of the elements are so firmly in place. Yet even without another recession, the slight rise of real income over the past few years has not been felt by all groups in American society. In 1987, white families had an income 78 percent larger than black families (in constant dollars)—while in 1970 this ratio was a "smaller" 63 percent. The 1987 black median family income of $18,098 was still lower than their peak year of 1978 ($18,952).[101] By gender, there has been a minute improvement of female income in our society from 1973 to 1986, but this increase is more than offset by a large decline of male income. Looking only at median family income also hides another pothole in the American economy. The number of earners in families has been going up. The reason is not hard to fathom. In an attempt to stay abreast of loss in real income, wives in husband-wife households have entered the labor force in record numbers. It will come as no surprise that if more persons work in a family—including children who are also going to school—real median income will rise accordingly. Again, in 1987 median family income went up by nearly 60 percent going from a one-earner family ($23,192) to a two-earner family ($36,990). Income more than doubles between a one-earner and three-earner family ($46,961).

There is inherently nothing wrong with more family members choosing to work—if it is a choice. Many women have greatly benefited from their increased labor force participation. It may have made more egalitarian relationships with men a reality, as women won their own financial freedom. There are other benefits to work that are harder to measure but do exist, such as pride in craftsmanship, intrinsic satisfaction, job-related friendships, service to humanity, and the like. Working wives have also removed the traditional burden which held men completely responsible for the financial well-being of the family. To wit, there are many positives connected to wives who work—to themselves, to their families and husbands, and to society in general. Given the decline in real income, however, especially for males and for young adults—there is some doubt that the major reasons why dual-earner families have increased are really "voluntary." Of all families, only 18 percent of wives worked in 1949 compared to 40 percent in 1984:

> During the 1960s labor force participation grew moderately among women of all ages, but during the 1970s it exploded particularly among women in the traditional child-raising years (aged 25 to 34). Among these women, about half worked in 1973. By 1983 the proportion exceeded two-thirds. In total, white women's labor force participation increased faster over 1973–83 than it had over the previous twenty-six years.[102]

One simulation shows that family income inequality among married-couple families increased by 8.6 percent between 1968 and 1984, but that it would have increased 50 percent more (by 12.1 percent) if married women had not worked.[103] In a recent, exhaustive review of previous studies, Judith Treas points to a major consensus in the research. Working wives have been an equalizing force on the income of husband-wife families. This has been especially important because of the cutbacks in social welfare benefits and the drastic fall in the earnings of younger males. In short, "Besides blunting overall inequality, women's greater workforce involvement has also worked to smooth out income disparities between age groups, between generations, and even over the life cycle."[104]

Table 5.3 illustrates the decline in both absolute and relative terms of real family income between 1973 and 1987, in today's dollars.[105] If we were to rank all 65 million families along a continuum of income, we could divide them into equal fifths going from low to high (a very common division in income analysis). The poorest fifth of all American families has gone through a shocking experience. On the face of it, the drop in real income of $683 does not appear very large, but this is about a 7.5 percent decline of income for a segment of our people that is impoverished to begin with. At the other end of the scale, the richest fifth of American families saw a gain of about 19 percent in real income during the past fourteen years. The average family income for this category climbed from $60,120 (in 1987 dollars) to $71,490—a real income gain of over $11,000!

It is no wonder, then, that a minority of persons in our society have been supporters of Reaganomics. They are obviously better off now than

TABLE 5.3   Change in Real Income for Richest and Poorest Families:
1973–1987 (constant 1987 dollars)

| Year | All Families in: | | Dollar Gap |
	Poorest Fifth	Richest Fifth	
1987	$8,411	$79,901	$71,490
1973	$9,094	$69,214	$60,120
14 Year Difference:			
Real Dollars	−683	+10,687	+11,370
Percent Change	−7.5	+15.4	+18.9

Source: Calculated from *Current Population Reports,* Series P-60, no. 161, Tables 3–4; P-60, no. 159, Table 12.

during the 1970s. Yet the shadow looming over this rosy scenario is the equally blatant loss in real income among our poorest families. There has been an undeniable bipolarization taking place. Had the economic pie been growing since 1973, the fact that the poorest fifth of families received less in percentage terms would not have mattered as much. On the average, however, the trend has been to lower real income since 1973 for the country as a whole. This decrease has taken its toll on those least able to afford it. On the other hand, the major exception to this slide has been the richest families, who have actually seen their incomes go up. The implications for the future are ominous if these trends continue without letup. Given time, it is possible for the unrelenting deprivation of the Brazil model to emerge with all of its malevolent force within the United States.

The statistics are even worse for families with children. This group contains a growing proportion of female-headed families. In 1970, just over 11 percent of families with children were headed by single mothers. By 1986 this proportion had nearly doubled to twenty percent. More often than not, there are no earners in such families (60 percent of all female-headed families) as opposed to one (57 percent) or two earners (26 percent) in husband-wife families.[106] Coupled with the real dollar decline in AFDC and other welfare benefits over the past decade, we should not be surprised if actual income has gone down even more severely for this group. By definition, it excludes older families without children. Some of these are empty-nesters who are retired but who are now getting pensions and inflation-adjusted social security benefits. Other families not included are younger with no children. Although young adults are not doing as well via real income, the wife is nearly always working full-time at this stage in the family cycle.

A Congressional report issued in 1985 looked at the income experience of families with children from 1968 through 1984.[107] In constant

1984 dollars, the richest 20 percent of families received $52,731 (about 10 percent more than in 1968). The poorest 20 percent lost over 37 percent of their real income—plunging from $9,343 in 1968 to a new depth of $5,877 by 1984. Most of this loss (56 percent) took place in the five years from 1980 to 1985 rather than in the twelve years before the nation was exposed to trickle-down economics. The findings of this study held even when income was adjusted for need, which controls for changes in size of the families over time. Most important, however, was the vitality these two different groups had in rebounding from the effects of recession. While both groups lost real income during the severe 1982 recession (26 percent for the poorest fifth, 5 percent for the richest fifth), the top group quickly recovered while the lowest 40 percent still had incomes significantly below what they had before the recession (and much further below their 1973 levels).

Jumping Ginis: The Surge in Relative Income Inequality

With the growing gaps of real income among and within such a wide variety of groups (e.g., age, gender, industry, race), we can safely predict that relative income inequality has been on the rise in America as well. If anything, the statistics are even more unanimous on this point. The Gini score for the distribution of family income declined from .376 in 1947 to .348 in 1967—a drop in inequality of 7.5 percent in twenty years. Although this was not an incredibly large amount, at least the trend was toward more equality at the very moment that real income was increasing for nearly everyone. Since 1968, however, relative income inequality has again gone up rather steadily, rising 12.6 percent to a post-World War II record Gini score of .392 in 1986. Inequality is greater today than at any time in the past forty years. While it increased by less than 5 percent between 1968 and 1979, between 1980 and 1986 it rose an additional 7.5 percent as well. Figure 5.14 illustrates this climb of income inequality for families of all races since 1966. It also shows a startling reversal in the percent of income going to the richest 5 percent as opposed to the poorest 40 percent of families. By 1982, for the first time in twenty-five years, the share of national income going to the wealthiest 5 percent of families was actually greater than the bottom 40 percent. It kept widening at a blazing speed after this point through 1986. Put differently, if income were divided in a totally equal manner, the *top 5 percent was getting three-and-one-half times more* than it normally would while *the bottom 40 percent was getting over three times less* than what would be expected!

In a study tracing income inequality from 1967 to 1984, Blackburn and Bloom have also seen Gini ratios increasing steadily for all persons and for families. In addition, the researchers examined the changing size

FIGURE 5.14

A. Family Income Gini Scores: 1966–86

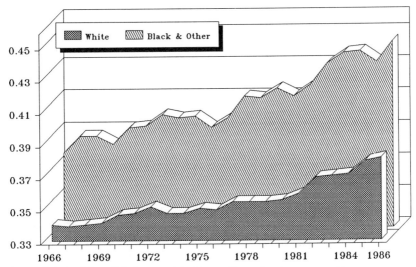

Source: Calculated from U.S. Bureau of the Census, *Current Population Reports 1987,* Series P–60, no. 159, Table 12.

B. Shares of Family Income: 1960–1986 (poorest 40% and richest 5%)

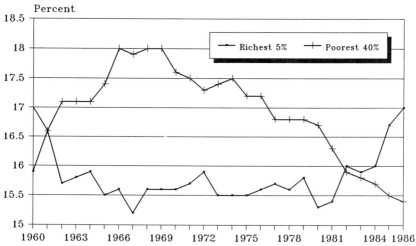

Source: Graphed from U.S. Bureau of the Census, *Current Population Reports 1987,* Series P–60, no. 159, Table 12.

of actual income classes. Rather than using quintiles, Blackburn and Bloom believe a different way to categorize income classes is more sensitive to change. They define lower class as income less than or equal to 60 percent of median income, lower-middle class as income above 60 percent of the median up to the actual median, middle class as income above the median up to 160 percent of the median, upper-middle class as above 160 percent but less than or equal to 225 percent of the median, and upper class as income above 225 percent of median income. By these criteria, the upper class has gone up by one-half of its original proportion over the eighteen years of this study, taking 8.3 percent of all family income in 1967 but 13 percent in 1984.[108] On the whole, Blackburn and Bloom see the increasing proportion of women who work as being of some importance in reducing inequality for husband-wife families, but having almost no general impact for all families. The researchers also conclude that there has been a drop of nearly 16 percent in the number of middle-class families between 1969 and 1983.[109] Even combining the three middle-class groups (upper-middle, middle, and lower-middle) fails to hide the decline. In 1969, these three groups made up 71 percent of all families—but were only 65 percent of all families in 1983.

When we look at quintiles, the full extent of the change seems to be understated because more of the instability is at the far ends of the income distribution (bottom and top 5 percent) rather than within the much broader 20 percentile range. Nonetheless, even here a growing amount of income dispersion at the extremes is also evident. To get a clear picture, we can compare the family income pie shared by each of the quintiles in 1973 and 1987. The share of the bottom quintile became worse, going from 5.5 percent of all family income to 4.6 percent. The top 20 percent of families received more income in 1987 (43.7 percent) than in 1973 (41.1 percent). For that matter, the richest fifth of families set a postwar record of getting the most income while the slice for the poorest fifth has not been this small since 1950. A similar pattern is true for the richest 5 percent of families as well (16.9 percent), which has not seen a slice this big since 1952. The share of the richest 5 percent was actually 9 percent more in 1987 than in 1973, while the share of the poorest quintile was 16 percent less than in 1973. Literally, then, any way the income pie is sliced points to the rich getting more and the poor getting less within the past fifteen years.

The flood of greater relative inequality is more evident in families with children, which contain the poorer female-headed households. A Congressional study computed quintiles for families with children, starkly illustrating the slide for poor families at the same time rich families became more affluent.[110] Figure 5.15 highlights the differences between 1968 and 1984. The graph is not able to show the steady slide year

FIGURE 5.15: Share of Income by Quintile (families with children)

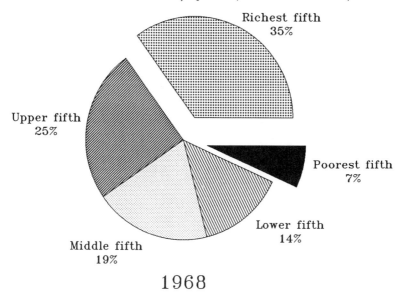

1968

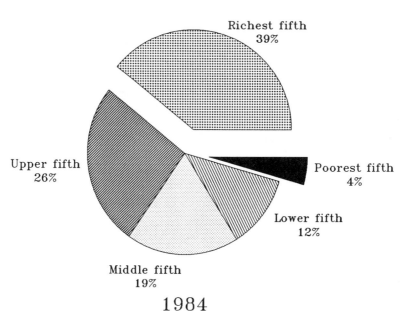

1984

Source: Graphed from Kenneth Cahill, Congressional Research Service, Report 85–1017 EPW (1985).

after year for the poorest quintile, however, which is evident in the original data. This group lost over one-third of its income during the seventeen-year time period, while the richest fifth of families with children garnered 12 percent more income in 1984 than in 1973.

The newest data for families with children show that the pace of income loss has accelerated in recent years to even worse levels. A just-released Congressional study controls for the shift toward smaller families that has taken place over time. It shows the proportion of family income going to the poorest fifth as declining by nearly one-third between 1973 and 1987. In contrast, the richest fifth increased its relative income by 10 percent.[111] Two-thirds of this relative income erosion happened between 1979 and 1987 for the poorest fifth, while 92 percent of the increase for the richest fifth took place during the 1980s.

Figure 5.16 gives us a vivid picture of what has been taking place among families with children. Both absolute and relative incomes have changed dramatically. Again, over $8,000 of the more than $10,000 gained in real dollars by the richest fifth of families with children came into their pockets during the Reagan era. The poorest fifth lost $2,834 real dollars over this fourteen-year period. Yet almost two-thirds of the income loss happened in the 1980s!

By now it is plain that however we chose to measure income inequality, whether in relative terms or absolute dollars, it has gone up by a large amount in the past decade and a half. Yet there are some experts who believe this deterioration of real income is mostly due to changes in demographic factors. Frank Levy, for example, in his book *Dollars and Dreams* does a good job of stressing the impact that a number of such changes have upon income inequality.[112] While family income has gone down in real terms, Levy points out that family size has also been reduced over the years (especially due to lower fertility). Today there are more persons living alone than at any time since the end of World War II. More women, particularly wives, are working than ever before. The shift toward female-headed families has also had a major impact upon family income, since these units are much more prone to poverty and hardship. They are also heavy recipients of government transfer programs and more likely to have no earners, which affects the family income picture. Levy points out that the proportion of families with no one working nearly tripled in the 1957–84 period (increasing from 5.4 percent to 15.1 percent). To account for these changes, he "adjusts" the income figures away from the Census definition to add in the value of transfer benefits (such as food stamps, Medicare, employer health insurance, etc.) while subtracting for taxes paid. In his view, the tax structure takes a bigger bite out of higher income families so that inequality is artificially increased by not looking at post-tax income. Once all of these

FIGURE 5.16

A. Change of Income Shares: 1973–87 (families with children)

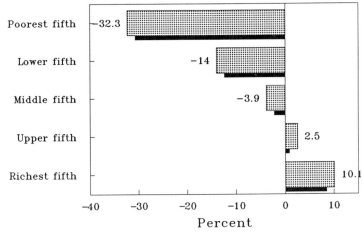

Source: Graphed from U.S. House of Representatives, Ways and Means Committee, *Background Material and Data,* March 15, 1989, pp. 984–85.

B. Change in Real Income: 1973–87 (families with children)

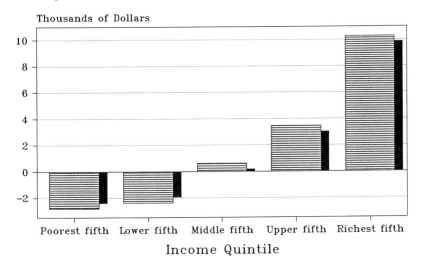

Source: Graphed from U.S. House of Representatives, Ways and Means Committee, *Background Material and Data,* March 15, 1989, pp. 984–85.

adjustment factors are built into the data, it can be shown that family income was more equally shared in 1984 than in 1949. In essence, the poorest fifth actually received a slightly higher proportion of income while the richest fifth of families ended up with slightly less income.[113]

There are a number of reasons to challenge any conclusion that income inequality is actually less today than previously. To begin with, Levy compares almost all of his current (1984) income data to 1949. This was at a time when sharp inequality existed, before the long term decline to 1973—at which point inequality started increasing again. I would argue that the relevant comparison should run from 1973 to the present. Otherwise we ignore the very large increase of real income and decline in relative inequality during the 1950s and 1960s. In a word, the U-shaped history of postwar inequality is made invisible. In the one table where he gives another date, it becomes apparent that between 1979–84 the poorest fifth of families lost income and the richest fifth gained income—despite all of these adjustments to the data![114]

More to the point, however, is the alleged need for such adjustments. It is certainly true that changes in the family structure have cushioned the loss of income since 1973. Yet this speaks volumes about the skid in real income, rather than how we all might be better off because more wives work now than ever before. No one disputes the beneficial impact of wives who work. In a recent review of the nine studies that address the impact of working wives, it was found that all agree upon one basic point: working wives equalize income (at least among whites). The strongest finding is that income inequality would have increased at an even greater rate if wives had not entered the labor force in such record numbers:

> There is a growing sentiment that the wife's paycheck is what enables many families to maintain a toehold on the middle rungs of the income ladder. . . . To sum up, the economic prospects of young men deteriorated at a time when young women commanded higher wages than ever. Labor force participation by married women undoubtedly permitted young families to achieve middle-class consumption standards that would have been impossible on one paycheck alone. The trade-off was that families lost some of their inflexibility to field additional earners, should the main bread-winner become unemployed.[115]

There is also strong evidence that income inequality would have been worse were it not for increasing welfare and transfer payments during the 1960s and early 1970s—at least for families headed by women and unrelated persons of either sex.[116] Rather than seeing such trends as benign, however, they may also be viewed as proof that the decline of income has touched just about every one of us. It is equally valid to see many of these demographic shifts as being caused by the scaling-down of real income—thus masking the true savagery of the decline—rather than interpreting them as trends that hide more equality. The decline in fertility and average family size is a good example. This has allowed families to partially escape the full brunt of declining real income. Yet the fall in fertility is likely due to the slide in real income, rather than a fall of fertility causing a rise in real income. This is a classic example of the chicken or the egg dilemma. My guess would be that there is less "choice" behind declining family size and later marriages as the financial well-being of families has waned. People react to adversity and bad fortune. If the cost of living rises and/or real income goes down, they will act in ways to protect themselves. One way would be literally to cut back on the mouths to feed or perhaps not to get married at all. In this sense, it is questionable to suggest that smaller families result in higher relative or per capita income when they may in actuality be caused by a drop of real income.

The same may be said of the increasing role welfare payments have played in the distribution of family income. Some authorities argue that in-kind benefits such as food stamps hide what would be a larger income among the poor. Yet, is it not more appropriate to ask why there has been such a sharp need for these benefits in the first place? The number collecting such benefits may expand because the ability of low-income families to survive has become more difficult. In a stagnant or declining economy, many husbands among the poor simply cannot find work. One means of coping might then become separation, divorce, or ruse to produce the eligibility of female-headed households needed to collect most benefits.

There is an unstated premise underlying the argument that welfare benefits to the poor actually "increase" their real income. The implication is that the system is generous and compassionate in taking care of these unfortunates. In fact, it is so generous that we should perhaps cease to think of the poverty-stricken as "really that poor." By the same token, no one asks why the system has failed to provide the means for poor families to support themselves, why decent paying jobs are becoming more scarce, why recessions are more frequent and severe, and why earnings have been cut so severely in industry after industry from one occupation to another.

Lastly, these "adjustments" have been made, we are told, to more fairly estimate the true income of families. Why is it that in-kind benefits such as employer health-insurance or the dollar value of food-stamps have been factored in as adjustments, but not capital gains? While the former benefit lower- and middle-income families, adding capital gains to family income would skew the distribution incredibly. Such large amounts of money accrue almost exclusively to rich families and without a doubt would show income inequality to be much worse than current government statistics. One current government report even uses an adjustment that removes the cost of home mortgages, reasoning that the record rates in the 1980s drove the consumer price inflators up above "normal." [117] The feeling was that since this affected only a few first-time home buyers, mortgage rates should not be used. We can only imagine what a baby-boomer family looking for their first house would think of this reasoning!

In the end, it seems obvious that certain values tend to guide what may or may not be used to "improve" the data. Politics may at times be lurking behind the scenes as well. For instance, on the whole it seems such adjustments have so far ended up fudging the data in favor of underestimating the true degree of income inequality. In view of indisputable evidence pointing to declining income and a sharp growth of inequality using undoctored data, it may not be surprising that some analysts have become eager to introduce new adjustments. In the absence of compelling reasons to do otherwise, however, it seems more fair and objective to leave the data as is. By using the official statistics, it is impossible to deny that a decline of real income and growing inequality have ravaged our land.

Economist Katherine Bradbury offers a clear description of the enormous scope involved with this slide of real income. [118] Her study controls for most of the factors that could possibly confuse the reasons why such a loss developed in the first place. She defines a family income of $20,000 to $49,999 as middle class—or nearly half of all families. Comparing family incomes to 1973 (in 1984 dollars) shows an increase of 13 percent in low-income families (below $20,000). A corresponding decrease of about 10 percent occurred in the middle class while nearly 5 percent was added to the proportion in the upper class ($50,000 and above) in this eleven-year period.

Critics have cautioned that such a slide is worse than it appears since there has been such a decrease in the nuclear family. Real income has steadily increased for unrelated individuals. Singles now make up a larger portion of our population with income. Adding this group in with families and recalculating the proportions, however, does not change the significance of the findings. The middle class still declines by 11 percent, while the lower class grows by 12 percent. The upper class does shrink, however, by a small 2 percent. Smaller family size, the baby boom, population shifts to the South, more working wives, and greater numbers of female-headed households all affect real family income as well. The strength of their impact was calculated by Bradbury. In a word, the effect

TABLE 5.4   Demographic Contributions to Income Shifts: 1973–84

	Change in Percentage of Families with Middle-Class Income (percentage points)	Change in Median Family Income (Percent)
Total Change	−5.1	−7.3
Estimated change due to shifts in:		
Family size	−0.3	−1.5
Region	−0.2	−0.5
Age of head	+0.3	+0.4
Family type	−1.4	−2.9
Labor force status of spouse	+1.2	+3.8
Sum excluding labor force status of spouse	−1.6	−4.5
Sum	−0.4	−0.7
Changes to be explained by other factors	−4.7	−6.6

Source: Katherine Bradbury, "The Shrinking Middle Class." Table 3.

of these demographic variables in causing the income decline was very small. *Cuts of income resulted within all of these groups!*

Surprisingly, the effect of the baby boom was opposite from what many would expect. The baby boom actually drove up family income slightly, mainly because this cohort is now entering middle age (thirty-five to forty-four years old, a time when income peaks). Very young families under age twenty-five, where income is lowest, have actually gone down in proportion by over one-third. Thus, although real income went down for every family whose head was under sixty-five years old—the fact that so many boomers were surging all at once into middle age and peak income actually neutralized the effect of age.

Yet these changes do have some impact upon a declining middle class and loss of real family income. Table 5.4 shows the overall effect of these separate variables as estimated by Bradbury. When taken alone, many of these exhibit strong effects. Looking at family income, for example, shows that nearly one-third of the impact of demographic variables is due to the increase in female-headed families while one-sixth is caused by smaller families. Yet 42 percent of all of the demographic effect—which resulted in *higher* family income—can be attributed to working wives. The major effect is that these variables tend to cancel one another out. Of all the loss that occurred in family income between 1973 and 1984, only 10 percent can be explained by shifts in demographic

characteristics. Fully nine-tenths of the decline in real family income cannot be explained by any of these factors. Bradbury surmises that much
of the decline may be due to wounds suffered in our industrial heartland
as manufacturing jobs have vanished, but does not examine this factor
directly.

To sum up, the great majority of research in the 1980s has continuously pointed to one fact that is impossible to deny. Real income has
dwindled in America at the very time that relative inequality has sky-
rocketed. Using a variety of techniques and definitions, most studies
agree that poverty is once again haunting the land as the proportion of
poor families grows relentlessly larger. There is also basic agreement that
the rich have grown even more wealthy, at least since the early 1970s.
There is less agreement about the reasons for the slide in the financial
well-being of most Americans. Debate has centered upon shifts in basic
demographic characteristics, such as more working wives, the youth and
size of the baby boom, more female-headed families, regional shifts, and
the like. While the importance of these factors taken one by one is an
undeniable fact, when considered together they tend to neutralize one
another. The root causes of the decline are not easy to see, and argument
continues to swirl between different viewpoints.

Although the general effect of demographic variables as a whole is
weak, there is still no direct proof that large-scale economic changes are
behind the decline as well. There is plenty of evidence regarding the
association, however, between declining income, growing relative inequality, and the gutting of our industrial infrastructure. America has
literally undergone a transformation in its basic mode of production.
Manufacturing is rapidly disappearing while service work is on the rise.
Whole regions such as the Midwest have suffered long-term decline as a
result of this shift. Yet the economy as a whole has also suffered. We have
witnessed mounting personal, corporate, and governmental debt. A gap-
ing trade deficit refuses to go away. Losses in productivity preceded a
slash in wages. Cutbacks on R & D and a decline in new plant investment
have robbed future generations of income. All the while, mergers, buyouts, and outright purchase of U.S. businesses and property by foreign
powers continue to erode our nation's capacity to generate income for its
citizens. Scurrilous defense budgets dumped into an endless vacuum have
sucked away the very lifeblood of America's economy, rather than provide the security that was promised.

In a word, there is a great deal of face-validity to the argument that
the decline of America in the global economy has been at the root of
income loss and growing inequality. In the next chapter, we will examine
some of these economic and demographic factors as they effect income
locally within the United States. There is a rich history of research into

the variation of income inequality between regions, states, and smaller localities that is worth exploring. By looking at such forces on a more local level, we may be able to get a better view of the interaction of shifts in global and national forces upon income inequality. We will also see clear evidence of a very wide spectrum of inequality within the United States. It seems an axiom of life that as some fail, others will prosper. Perhaps because of such sharp geographic variation, at least part of the general impact of America's slip toward financial mediocrity may have remained hidden.

6

SUNSET IN THE SUNBELT: HOW GEOGRAPHIC VARIATION HIDES INCOME INEQUALITY

There are many sections and communities in the United States that suffer from low income. Other areas are cursed with high relative inequality. Although all Americans are aware that income inequality exists within our country, we persist in viewing our society as middle class. While much of our population is well off or at least financially comfortable, there are pockets of poverty which remain effectively hidden from the mainstream. Many of them are in the rural South. Surprisingly, however, even such areas of affluence and high culture as New York, Atlanta, Dallas, Miami, Los Angeles, and San Francisco are host to virulent inequality. These metropolitan counties plus other areas in the United States adding up to 41 million people have a household income Gini ratio greater than that of India. The income inequality that we tend to see as a problem of the Third World is just as much a part of our culture as those of less-developed countries (LDCs)—at least on a relative basis. Put in a slightly different context, the 41 million Americans subjected to the same monstrously high income inequality as India are separately greater than the populations of other nations with inequality just as high: Sri Lanka, Portugal, Argentina, Trinidad, Costa Rica, Venezuela, Malaysia, Senegal, Columbia, Zambia, Kenya, the Ivory Coast, Peru, and Panama. Taking all the countries in the world where income data exist, nearly 70 percent of their population (numbering 1.7 billion) live under less inequality. In the end, income inequality is not just a Third World problem!

In the past few decades Americans have also experienced a tremendous caldron of economic shifts going on between and within a variety of geographic boundaries. Such changes can be seen as partially hiding the average decline of absolute income taking place within the country since 1973. The growth of relative inequality is also easily masked when some sections of the nation have become obviously more affluent. Nonetheless, by looking at smaller units—such as regions, states, and counties within the United States—we can see uneven economic development. As with other countries around the world, an attempt has been made in this chapter to piece together the causes which increase or decrease both absolute and relative income inequality for various regions within the United States.

Any analysis of regional differences must bow in the direction of historical forces and geographic specializations. Because of early settlement, the northeast seaboard came into early dominance within the country. Emerging at the same time was a southern economy geared toward cotton growers with large plantations using slaves. The West soon became the breadbasket for the nation, while manufacturing took root in the Northeast. Industry in this region was first thrust into world competition by needs arising in the Civil War.

Above all, the dramatic rise in the economic fortune of southern states is one of most significant trends in this century. The South has long been an underdeveloped region in comparison to other parts of the United States. It was particularly devastated by the Civil War. Because the South was treated as an occupied country by an unfriendly, hostile foe—it was impossible for this region to develop in the last century. A combination of internal factors in this area, which are discussed below, also stopped any major increase in the South's industrial base. But this region's successful climb out of an economic swamp first became evident in the 1930s. New Deal programs and the spread of the defense industry were major prods to development and expansion. Retirement of relatively wealthy northerners to states such as Florida helped to disperse income. The huge out-migration of poor southern blacks to northern industrial cities drained some poverty from the South as well. The South has been this century's Horatio Alger story of regional economics. Since the end of World War II, and especially beginning in the 1970s, the region has experienced an explosion of growth.

Whistling *Dixie* to *Auld Lang Syne:*
The South Grows Richer as the North Declines

One of the rallying cries heard long after the Civil War in the South was that it would one day rise again. It would re-emerge from the calamity and defeat of the war to challenge Yankee supremacy. Few believed this would be in terms of renewed military battle, but there were many embittered souls in the South who longed for a day of reckoning. They hoped a time of retribution would arrive some day in the future. Many southerners have celebrated the decline of the North with joyful glee. They see the consequences as doubly sweet. Income in the North has stagnated or gone down as manufacturing jobs have virtually disap-

TABLE 6.1   Personal Per Capita Income in Regions as a Percent of the U.S.
Average: 1840–1980

Region	1840	1880	1920	1960	1980
United States	100%	100%	100%	100%	100%
Northeast	135	141	132	114	105
North Central	68	98	100	101	100
South	76	51	62	80	86
West	—	190	122	105	103

Source: John Agnew, *The United States in the World Economy*, p. 92.
Northeast Region: Maine, Vermont, New Hampshire, Massachusetts, Rhode Island, Connecticut,
New York, Pennsylvania, New Jersey.
North Central Region: Wisconsin, Illinois, Michigan, Indiana, Ohio, Iowa, Kansas, Minnesota,
Missouri, Nebraska, North Dakota, South Dakota.
South Region: Delaware, Maryland, District of Columbia, Virginia, West Virginia, Kentucky,
Tennessee, Arkansas, Louisiana, Mississippi, Alabama, Georgia, Florida, South Carolina,
North Carolina, Texas, Oklahoma
West Region: Idaho, Montana, Utah, Colorado, Wyoming, Washington, Oregon, California,
Nevada, Arizona, New Mexico, Alaska, Hawaii.

peared. At the same time, there has been a large-scale upsurge of manufacturing, business relocation, and industrial investment taking place in
the South. One consequence has been more jobs, many of which would
have stayed in the North twenty years ago. As a result of the greater
availability of jobs—often at higher pay than was thought possible by
locals in terms of their recent past—income has gone up in the South.

The movement toward greater equality of income between our
country's geographic regions can be easily seen in table 6.1. By looking
at personal per capita income as a percent of the average for the country
as a whole, two related tendencies leap out. The dominance of the
Northeast as an economic core has dwindled in the past 150 years while
the resurgence of the South in this century has been obvious. While in
1840 per capita income in the Northeast was 135 percent of the nation's
average, this had gradually lessened to 105 percent by 1980. The effect of
the Civil War on the South is easily seen in the data, but after the turn of
the century this region started its long but steady climb out of America's
economic basement. In 1900 the South had a per capita income only one-
half that of the United States as a whole; yet this had gradually increased
to 86 percent by the time of our last Census of Population in 1980. Lastly,
the effect of the Gold Rush, railroad expansion, and land giveaways
through the Homestead Act can be seen in the West, which saw a dramatic loss of per capita income set in before the turn of the century.
Much of this decline in per capita income may also have been due to a
huge influx of poor people seeking their fortunes. Many chose to follow
the popular adage of a century ago: "Go west, young man, go west!."

Despite the gradual growth, just after World War II the South was

still far below the nation's average income level. Frank Levy has converted regional median family income figures existing in 1949 into 1984
dollars.[1] At that time, the far west states of Washington, Oregon, California, and Nevada had the highest family income at $15,416. The Great
Lakes manufacturing core states of Wisconsin, Illinois, Michigan, Indiana, and Ohio were not far behind, however, at $14,997 per family. This
was still much above the national average of $14,100—but the southeast-
ern region was still over a third less than this at $8,856. These twelve
states, forming a tier running from Virginia down to Florida through
Arkansas and Louisiana, have long been poor kin to the rest of the country. Figure 6.1 divides the United States into the four regions used by the
Census Bureau. From the map of median family income earned in 1979,
the South obviously still has relatively more states in the lowest income
quartile than the other three regions. Although per capita income figures
are gross averages and stand accused of many weaknesses, they are the
only up-to-date figures we have by states until the 1990 Census is taken.
Measuring increases in per capita income over the last four years shows
healthy growth for southern states. For an allegedly declining core, the
Northeast displays amazing vigor in money growth! Even the Great
Lakes manufacturing states show at least average income growth in comparison to the plains states and the Southwest. The slow growth in the
plains and southwestern states, which are quite dependent upon energy
and mineral products, is due to the steep drop in the price of oil within
the past few years.

The latest median family income figures by region, which cover
1987, show that the South is the only region continuing to gain income
(2.0 percent in real income gain over the previous year).[2] Median family
income now stands at $28,250 in this region. Southern family income is
still less than the Northeast ($33,940), Midwest ($30,990), and the West
($32,030). Yet the South is now within 92 percent of the median family
income for the whole country ($30,853), which is the closest it has been
to absolute parity in its entire history. If the strength of this trend continues, the South will finally pull even with the rest of the nation by the
dawn of the next century.

A more complete picture of increases in absolute income can be
seen in table 6.2. Median family income does remain lower in the South,
but the growth over the 1970s for this area has been much greater than
in other regions. The seventeen states of the South had an average increase in median family income of over 120 percent in the 1969 to 1979
period. This pace was much higher than the Northeast (98 percent), and
comfortably ahead of the Midwest (113 percent) and the West (114 percent). Trends in the 1980s—discussed below—may not bode so well for
the South. Also, although the growth of income in this region continues

FIGURE 6.1

A. Median Family Income, 1979

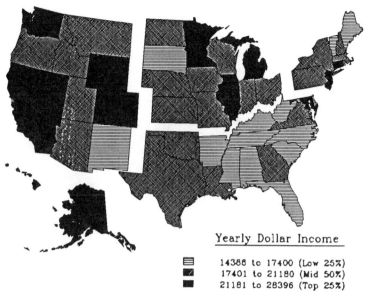

Yearly Dollar Income

14388 to 17400 (Low 25%)
17401 to 21180 (Mid 50%)
21181 to 28396 (Top 25%)

Source: 1980 Census of Population PC 80–1–c.

B. Percent Change in Per Capita Income, 1984–87

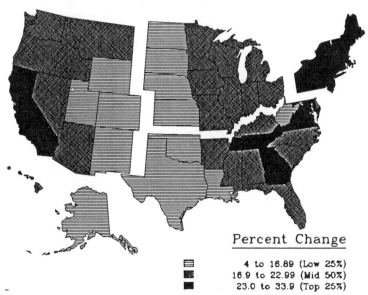

Percent Change

4 to 16.89 (Low 25%)
16.9 to 22.99 (Mid 50%)
23.0 to 33.9 (Top 25%)

Source: 1989 House Ways and Means, pp. 1069–70.

to be well ahead of the rest of the country in percentage terms—this is only one side of the proverbial coin. It is obvious that southern states start from a much lower income base, so that the same amount of dollar increase in this region would yield a higher percentage increase than in the North. This is exactly what happens in the data. Between 1969 and 1979 families gained more in absolute income in the West ($11,097), the Midwest ($10,611) and even the Northeast ($9,909) in comparison to the South ($9,732). As with LDCs in comparison to core industrial countries, because such absolute dollar differences are so great to begin with—closing the income gap in real dollars is harder to do than the percentage increase figures seem to indicate.

Nonetheless, change for the South is in the right direction. And in the end, southern growth has been spectacular:

> For example, gross regional product nearly doubled between 1960 and 1975, while industrial output more than doubled. Between 1970 and 1976 fast-growing Texas added more nonfarm jobs than Michigan, Illinois, Ohio, and Massachusetts combined. In 1976 the industrial output of Texas alone exceeded that of Australia. Between 1970 and 1977 per capita income increased at a national average of 71 percent, while Arkansans and Mississippians saw their personal incomes rise by 86 and 83 percent, respectively. These states had traditionally been the South's slowest growing, and any significant increase would appear dramatic when considered on a percentage basis. Still, even in more economically advanced Florida, per capita incomes grew by 69 percent during this period as compared to only 58 percent improvement in New York. . . . By the 1970s the region was attracting approximately half of the nation's total annual foreign industrial investments.[3]

Southern banks were soon bulging at their seams with a new torrent of cash. Asset growth in the largest five southern banks grew six times faster than the five largest U.S. banks between 1977 and 1987.[4] By 1983, the South had overtaken the North in terms of commercial bank deposits—having the largest amount among the four regions. In both absolute and relative terms, therefore, the south's deficit of investment capital has mostly disappeared. Although southern banks continue to be conservative, preferring to allow loans for regional expansion to originate in northern banks, southern banks are definitely in a position to encourage their own investment should the need arise.

In order to understand the internal dynamics of the economic changes happening across the South today, we need to know a little about the area's history. This region was once host to a plantation economy based upon slavery and gross income inequality. The interests of a small

TABLE 6.2   Median Family Income and Percent Change Between 1969–79
            by States and Regions

	Median Family Income			
Region and States	1969	1979	Rank	Percent Change
Northeast				
Maine	$ 8,205	$16,167	(49)	97.0%
Vermont	8,928	17,205	(41)	92.7
New Hampshire	9,682	19,723	(25)	103.7
Massachusetts	10,833	21,166	(14)	95.4
Rhode Island	9,733	19,448	(28)	99.8
Connecticut	11,808	23,149	(2)	96.0
New York	10,609	20,180	(19)	90.2
Pennsylvania	9,554	19,995	(24)	109.3
New Jersey	11,403	22,906	(4)	100.9
Unweighted average of all states	$10,084	$19,993		98.3%
North Central				
Ohio	$10,309	$20,909	(16)	102.8%
Indiana	9,966	20,535	(18)	106.1
Michigan	11,029	22,107	(8)	100.4
Illinois	10,957	22,746	(6)	107.6
Wisconsin	10,065	20,915	(15)	107.8
Minnesota	9,928	21,185	(13)	113.4
Iowa	9,016	20,052	(20)	122.4
Missouri	8,908	18,784	(32)	110.9
Kansas	8,690	19,707	(26)	126.8
Nebraska	8,562	19,122	(29)	123.3
South Dakota	7,490	15,993	(50)	113.5
North Dakota	7,836	18,023	(35)	130.0
Unweighted average of all states	$ 9,396	$20,007		112.9%
South				
Delaware	$10,209	$20,817	(17)	103.9%
Maryland	11,057	23,112	(3)	109.0
District of Columbia	9,576	19,099	(30)	99.4
Virginia	9,044	20,018	(23)	121.3
West Virginia	7,414	17,308	(39)	133.5
Kentucky	7,439	16,444	(47)	121.1
Tennessee	7,446	16,564	(46)	122.5
Arkansas	6,271	14,641	(45)	133.5
Louisiana	7,527	18,088	(34)	140.3
Mississippi	6,068	14,591	(51)	140.5
Alabama	7,263	16,347	(48)	125.1
Georgia	8,165	17,414	(38)	113.3
Florida	8,261	17,280	(40)	109.2
South Carolina	7,620	16,978	(42)	122.8
North Carolina	7,770	16,792	(44)	116.1

TABLE 6.2   (*Continued*)

Region and States	Median Family Income			
	1969	1979	Rank	Percent Change
Oklahoma	7,720	17,668	(36)	128.9
Texas	8,486	19,618	(27)	131.2
Unweighted average of all states	$ 8,079	$17,811		120.5%
West				
Montana	$ 8,509	$18,413	(33)	116.4%
Idaho	8,380	17,492	(37)	108.7
Wyoming	8,944	22,430	(7)	150.8
Colorado	9,552	21,279	(12)	122.8
Utah	9,320	20,024	(22)	114.8
Nevada	10,687	21,311	(11)	99.4
New Mexico	7,845	16,928	(43)	115.8
Arizona	9,185	19,017	(31)	107.0
Washington	10,404	21,696	(9)	108.5
Oregon	9,487	20,027	(21)	111.1
California	10,729	21,537	(10)	100.7
Hawaii	11,552	22,750	(5)	96.9
Alaska	12,441	28,395	(1)	128.2
Unweighted average of all states	$ 9,772	$20,869		113.6%

Source: *1980 Census of Population*, vol. 1, Chapter C (PC-80-1-C)

planter aristocracy were constantly at odds with both poor whites and blacks held in bondage. Matters did not improve after the Civil War. Although slaves were now legally "free," they were kept in a position of subservience and dire poverty through Jim Crow laws, denial of the ballot through poll taxes or literacy tests, violence, lynchings, and any other means that worked.[5] Poor whites, although not much better off economically, at least were less likely to be the victims of brutal physical intimidation and attack. Yet they were also held back through dependency on agriculture in an area of poor soil. A share-cropping system had emerged in the South that operated on rules similar to serfdom in medieval Europe. Few were lucky enough to own land directly. Even fewer could farm much of the land, which was marginal. Too much concentration upon only a small number of cash crops, such as tobacco or cotton, also took a predictable toll. As market economies have a habit of doing, prices would tend to fluctuate wildly. At best, this led to insecurity. More often than not, however, another unavoidable result was financial ruin. It was hard to pay creditors when crops were largely worthless. Frequent bankruptcies would end in the loss of farms. The land more often than not reverted to a few large land-owners, some of whom were remnants of the plantation aristocracy.

Thus, the South was a largely agrarian society with only sparse manufacturing well into the twentieth century. What little industry did flourish in the region was connected with textile and clothing manufacture, which was also associated with low wages and unstable prices. In a word, the southern economy was similar to what we would call an LDC on the international scene. The South functioned as a periphery region for a more wealthy core located in the North. The Yankee aristocracy was made up of big business tycoons who had made their wealth in heavy industries such as steel, railroading, shipping, petroleum refining, and the like. It was this circle and its northern economic interests that placed the South in a "most favored" colony status that was to last a century after the Civil War. Although almost all industrial development, economic growth, and financial advancement took place in the North— there were still some "trickle down" benefits for the lagging, economically dependent South.[6]

The South had to be content with the leftovers from the feast of northern economic expansion. It could do so because there were always a few industries and factories which were nearly obsolete, operating on the fringe of profit. While such companies could not survive in the high-wage mecca of the North, they did rather nicely south of the Mason-Dixon line. Low production costs, especially bottom-of-the-barrel wages, kept some firms from going under. This dismal fact of life also guaranteed a slow but steady growth of industry in the South, as weaker core firms were spun off to this region. By doing so, northern interests were also served by keeping expenses down while southern spinoffs operated as feeders to the more lucrative, profitable companies in the core.

It was especially after the Civil War that the manufacturing belt around the Great Lakes was formed, linked to the newly emergent railroad empires of the Northeast. This formed an American economic core which was to remain dominant at least through the 1950s. Regional growth rates and geographic specializations were set by the core, which demanded massive raw materials from the hinterland. These resources were made over by industry and exported both abroad and back to the periphery as finished goods. John Agnew gives a concise account of the shifting fortunes of America's regions:

> The North constituted a core, but the periphery was not united. Rather, it consisted of a West into which vast investments were placed . . . and a South which was drained of its resources rather than developed through investment. After the Civil War, the South

sank into a tributary condition as the most backward section of the national economy. . . . The South had lost a war and paid the penalty by becoming dependent on the North and by missing out on the western bonanza. . . . National income during the period from the Civil War until the 1890s was systematically redistributed from the periphery to the core. In particular, the South helped pay for northern industrialization either through higher prices for domestic goods or through duties on imported products. The export of southern cotton underwrote northern economic expansion rather like collective agriculture was later to underwrite Soviet industrial expansion. Economic subordination of the South . . . [was needed] . . . for American overseas expansion.[7]

Regional and historical conditions thus play a large role even today in the amount of income we end up taking home in our paychecks. Original settlement patterns, ethnic groupings, racial barriers, regional specializations, natural resources, the fruits of war, outright domination by economic giants, and like factors all enter into the formula which can fix a region's income level. Yet there is still room for local forces to work as well. At least within the South, there has also been a large degree of influence by native elites which has slowed the region's economic development. There has long been a conservative bias operating in southern banks, for example, which acts to favor a powerful landowning class. Interest rates were kept high and industry was at times actively discouraged from entering. The fear was that wages would be raised if many firms were to compete for labor.[8]

The companies that were allowed to come in had to pass an anti-union, low-wage litmus test given by local economic elites. This gate-keeping function persists even today! Major local resistance is often aroused when a unionized plant with good paying jobs wants to set up shop. The Phillip Morris Tobacco Company was frozen out of Greenville, South Carolina, because its new plant and its 2,500 workers would be *unionized*. Mazda Motor Company was actively discouraged from building its new plant in the Greenville/Spartanburg area for the same reason—even though three thousand direct jobs and another three thousand support jobs would have been created in their new auto factory:

> Some business leaders feared that it would upset the existing wage scale and force the multitude of textile and apparel manufacturers in the area to raise their wages. After Mazda ultimately chose the Michigan location, in part because of the highly skilled (and unionized) workforce in that state, the Spartanburg County Development Association cheered the decision in its monthly newsletter by noting: "It is our considered view that the Mazda plant would have had

a long-term chilling effect on Spartanburg's orderly industrial
growth. An auto plant, employing over 3,000 card-carrying, hymn-
singing members of the UAW [United Auto Workers] would, in our
opinion, bring to an abrupt halt future desirable industrial prospects."[9]

It *is* with the question of wages that the major clue to these large
regional income inequality differences can be found. The South has long
prided itself on being a safe place for business, where wages are low,
taxes are almost nonexistent, and the institutional climate is hostile to
unions. The norm of low wages grew out of the slavery-ridden plantation system which in turn gave way to sharecropping after the Civil War.
Low pay was built upon racism and chronic poverty, so that workers
were desperate for whatever little income could be gained from an economically barren system. This deprivation acted to attract the very industries that were seeking out low-wage workers. Thus, the system was
to perpetuate itself in a vicious circle. Some northern core industries first
started relocating in the South to take advantage of submarginal wages
by the late 1800s. New England textile firms went to the rural areas of
North Carolina, South Carolina, and Georgia at the turn of the century
in search of cheap labor.

This pattern was to repeat itself endlessly throughout the twentieth
century, especially peaking during the 1970s and 1980s. Southern politicians and community spokesmen have actively and aggressively sought
to attract industries to locate in their hometowns. As they have competed
with one another and especially with northern states, southerners have
repeatedly sold business firms on their "superior" location by stressing a
favorable business climate. The package making up a favorable business
climate always contains the same items: cheaper wages, no unions, low
taxes, abundant raw materials, fewer energy costs, growing consumer
markets, tax holidays, a free or subsidized infrastructure (roads, schools,
utility hookups, etc.). Yet it is especially the low wages that are continually mentioned:

> The salesmen have included southern governors, state development
> boards, local chambers of commerce, and assorted industrial front
> men. All have sung the virtues of southern industrial development
> to U.S. and foreign investors. In a world guided by business max-
> ims, where profit is the guiding principle to social and economic
> life, southern boosters found that their product, the South, sold best
> when it was packaged as a place where labor was abundant and
> cheap, where unions were not welcome, and where local commu-
> nities were willing to offer a large variety of financial inducements
> to attract new industry. A measure of the success (whether real or

imagined) of this public relations program has been the highly publicized population explosion in the Sunbelt states. The decade of the
1970s was truly one of romanticizing the wonders of southern
growth and development.[10]

The Bloom Is Off the Magnolia Blossom

Because of this stress on low wages, then, the South has ended up attracting the very industries and jobs that are unwilling or unable to pay decent
wages. While there has been sharp job growth, the rise of income has
not been as rapid. For one thing, although job growth has been higher
than in the North, manufacturing jobs actually increased at a slower rate
than population growth in the South.[11] More job growth actually occurred in low-end service work located in major cities, just as in the rest
of the country. The South has also been most attractive to industries at
the end of their product development stage, when all innovation, creativity, and technological breakthroughs have long since been wrung out of
the manufacturing process. In such nongrowth to declining types of industries, long and stable production runs are needed with minimal costs.
At this point, cheap labor becomes a major factor in keeping profits
alive. It is branch plants of this kind which lead some critics to view the
South as an economic periphery, working to serve the interests of core
conglomerate corporations located in the North. The same charge has
been leveled at such high-wage nations as Japan, who have actively
sought the cheaper pay scale here than at home.[12]

The prevailing footprint of plant relocations and startups in the
South proves this point. William Falk and Thomas Lyson have looked at
changes in all southern counties between 1970 and 1980, concluding that
30 percent of all growth in manufacturing jobs took place in nonmetropolitan areas where the pay scale was at its absolute lowest.[13] Most of
these jobs were from branch plants of northern corporations. Although
urban and metropolitan counties have gained many more jobs, they tend
to be in service and high-technology industries that pay more than in the
nonunionized rural hinterland among poor blacks, where corporate control is at its absolute maximum. In the rural South, two-thirds of all new
jobs are manual in nature. This area has been described as a stagnant
backwater of the American economy. Few of these jobs are what we
would normally describe as "good"—but are more a part of the secondary labor market (janitors, food service workers, factory assemblers,
etc.). Most manufacturing has been limited to low-end production.
Thirty-five percent of the manufacturing workforce in southern rural
counties, for example, is in textile and clothing firms. Such industries
have a stunted opportunity structure for workers. The great majority of

employees are at the unskilled, blue-collar level. Their pay reflects this reality! Even in urban areas, the authors conclude that many of the new jobs are in poor-wage, low-skill service work.

Yet, because poverty and deprivation have existed for so long in the South, especially in rural areas and particularly among Blacks, the labor force has been even more than docile and undemanding. Poor southerners have flocked to apply for jobs that pay much more than what the people were used to, but much less than what comparable workers were making in unionized, northern factories. In a word, the South's poor were grateful for these jobs:

> Even in the Sunbelt era southern workers continued to respond to the neopaternalism of anti-union employers such as Nissan Motors. Although one United Auto Workers leader told *Newsweek* that Nissan's desire to hire "hard working country people" really amounted to an attempt to employ "peasants," the company's guarantees of lifetime employment, its efforts to involve employees in management decisions, and its recreational and fitness programs drew 100,000 applications for 2,600 jobs at its Smyrna, Tennessee, plant. Union officials were perplexed at the attitude of one Nissan worker who insisted: "If the company treats the workers well . . . there's nothing a union can offer." Such assertions were particularly confounding in light of the fact that this worker could have earned a starting wage that was $2.50 per hour higher if he had been employed in a unionized automobile plant in the North.[14]

What this means, in the end, is progress with a small "p"! There has been undeniable improvement. The South is better off in terms of higher income, economic growth, and in closing what seems an ageless gap of income with other regions in the United States. But critics point out that the gains have been nothing in comparison to what they could have been if the South had not been so hostile to organizing workers. It is riddled with so much dire poverty that *the belief that any job is a good job is still unchallenged.* Because of what amounts to an institutional addiction to low wages, the South of the 1980s has remained the nation's number one economic problem.[15] Industrial development not only failed to generate large-scale prosperity, but it has left a large number of southerners trapped in poverty. In 1980, Texas was the only state in this region with a per capita income above the national average. Over 44 percent of the nation's poor lived in the South, while Mississippi and Kentucky had lost $200 between 1960–80 in constant dollars of their already below-normal per capita income. During this period, Arkansas, the Carolinas, and Georgia also saw declining per capita income. James Cobb concludes from his analysis of the southern economy that without doubt this region's nonunion climate helped to depress wages.[16] For example, as of 1980 North Carolina was the South's most industrialized state but the nation's least unionized (7 percent of the workforce). One result is that its workers are the most poorly paid in the United States, at 74 percent of the national hourly wage. Despite (or because of) North Carolina's self-proclaimed industrial "progress," the average hourly manufacturing wage paid in the state fell from $1.05 below the national average in 1972 to $1.90 below the norm by 1980.

Conditions are better in the cities. Analysis reveals urban and metropolitan areas picked up the great bulk of good, high-paying jobs in the 1970–80 period. In fact, southern cities such as Atlanta, Miami, Houston and Dallas are often referred to as "the Jewels in the Crown"—locations where growth and opportunity beckon to all. These giant metropolitan areas acted as magnets to attract high-technology industry and expanding business during the past two decades. The growth rate of southern metropolitan areas (nearly 2 percent per year in 1970–80) was twice that of metro population increase in the nation as a whole.[17] Yet there was a down side to such glitter and hoopla as well. Heavy in-migration from poor rural areas, especially among impoverished blacks, drove up income disparities within these cities while overloading the limited social services that did exist. Atlanta soon became known as the "homicide capital" of the Deep South, but was challenged for this title by Houston with its own murder rate two-thirds higher than New York City.[18] John Agnew has offered a vignette of Houston that is anything but flattering: no zoning regulations, a huge poor population, America's largest concentration of illegal migrant workers from Mexico (excluding California), depletion of the city's water table, heavy traffic congestion, high air pollution, abysmal education, and high unemployment (20 percent) in an area that is supposed to have abundant jobs.[19] Miami has become the drug smuggling capital of the United States, offering a Swiss-type banking haven for capital flight and laundered money coming from Latin America. All the while, racial tensions and conflict are higher here than in any other American city. With the fall in the price of oil, Dallas and Houston are now among the five worst real estate markets in the country.[20] Millions of square feet of recently completed office buildings go unoccupied in their downtowns, as well as entire developments of subdivisions, townhomes, and condos.

In a word, the sheen is off the golden egg of southern industrialization. A variety of developments in the 1980s have combined to challenge the wisdom of unrestrained economic growth at any price. To begin with, the southern economy remains heavily dependent upon the investment of others—whether wealthy multinationals from Japan or northern core firms who may decide to keep going further south—into

Mexico or other LDCs. Commentators on the southern growth cycle now agree this region is no longer insulated from the problems of northern wage earners. Despite lower pay, many firms are relocating out of the South into the Third World. Southern textile industries, for example, still suffer from an exposure to intense foreign competition. Although some domestic protection exists, it has not been enough to stem the tide of business out-migration.

The precarious nature of southern development is evident in its almost complete reliance on northern bank loans and investment funding.[21] The hand that giveth can taketh away! Gary Green notes that these investors have increasingly chosen to flee our country in search of even cheaper wages, resulting in deindustrialization within the South as well.[22] More than 750,000 jobs were lost in the textile industry alone in just the past decade. The businesses that do stay must automate and reduce their reliance on paid workers to stay competitive with imports, which again serves to slash the work force. Lastly, external financing acts to drain profits away from the South back into the North or to Japan. These funds, if resulting from native investment, could be used for even more regional expansion. Although there has been dramatic growth of investment within the South, and a sharp rise in the amount in southern commercial bank deposits, Green reports that *the rate of commercial loans has not even kept pace with population growth in this region.*

A number of other conditions exist which leave the South more exposed to economic collapse than other regions. The area is overloaded with military installations and bases. By the 1970s the defense industry was the largest single employer in many southern states. In that decade, southern states held nine of the top twenty-one spots in dependency upon total employment related to defense spending.[23] When the Pentagon budgets are finally cut, as they must be if we are to remain economically viable as a nation, the South will bleed the most. Military spending is only one of six pillars to the strength holding up the roof of the southern economy, although it is an important one.[24] Overreliance on low wages may ultimately backfire as multinationals pull out in search of greener pastures in LDCs. Real estate values have already taken a dive as in-migration to the South slowed (mostly due to an economic spurt in the Northeast). Energy as an economic pillar crumbled during the 1980s as the price of oil scraped bottom. Although this helped the rest of the nation, it aggravated conditions in petroleum-producing states. By the fall of 1986, Texas had registered a $6 billion budget deficit—the largest of any state in U.S. history—while Louisiana and Oklahoma were losing $50 million in tax revenues for every one dollar drop in the price of oil.[25] The spreading farm crisis has moved out of the Midwest to enfold southern agriculture as well. Income from agriculture has been smothered by a long-term slide in world food prices, driven up in the short-term by severe drought in recent years. Lastly, many believe the confidence put into high-technology industrial growth as a panacea for economic ills is grossly misplaced. Critics challenge whether there have been any meaningful financial benefits for those southerners who assemble electronic parts. They continue to be paid at marginal levels.

Definite clouds have loomed over the horizon in the Sunbelt. In Georgia, manufacturing output, construction, and employment have recently declined while vital services and the trade sector remain flat. In North Carolina, hours worked per week by industrial employees dipped while Louisiana has entered its second year of negative economic growth. The gross regional product for the entire southeastern division sank by 42 percent last year! In this twelve-state region, all leading economic indicators are flat, with almost no growth in the region. The South has now become the slowest growing region in the country in retail sales.[26]

The Grand Canyon of Income Inequality: Gaps of Income Within Regions and Between Counties

One of the major results of market systems that everyone agrees upon— whether Marxist, capitalist, economic nationalist or World System advocate—is that the process of development is uneven. In our discussion of the Third World as it ties in with wealthy industrial countries, it was obvious that major differences between poor countries exist. In this sense, the model of core/semi-periphery/periphery seemed to fit best with what has actually been taking place in the world economy. The dependency that LDCs had upon core investment could be seen in their penetration by multinational corporations. As a result of this development, income inequality rose as elites were enriched while labor was forced to work at subsistence wages to keep production costs low.

The parallels with the South are obvious. Applying the core/periphery model to this region seems fitting. Gary Green, for example, presents detailed evidence that most finance capital for industrialization in the South came from northern banks in the core.[27] William Falk and Thomas Lyson prove beyond doubt that southern development seems to have literally bypassed rural areas, especially where large numbers of blacks live.[28] Falk and Lyson admit that cities in the South have reaped greater benefits from the influx of northern or foreign firms; but even within metropolitan areas, greater income inequality has been an unfailing byproduct of development (especially minorities versus whites).

Quite some time ago Nobel-winning economist Gunnar Myrdal argued that the process of development is by its very nature unstable.[29]

It spawns conflicting forces as investment gushes into underdeveloped regions. *Spread effects* are forces which act to make the poorer region better off. Examples include the introduction of advanced production technology, creation of a small cadre of skilled workers, greater profits for local business elites, a larger market for regional products, etc. *Backwash effects* make the poor region worse off. Because of superior technology and financing in the rich core, for example, the periphery has no chance to build its own industrial base to compete with the core's giant corporations. The periphery can become locked into a subordinate status where locals are forced to work for core branch plants, but at much lower wages than in the core. Profits are drained away from the periphery, also quashing any chance at independent local development in the region. The rich region can thus become even more wealthy while the poor region suffers further economic setbacks.

What makes Myrdal's theory different from modern World Systems theory is that it at least holds forth the possibility that a backward region may possibly win as it goes through development. It is possible that this could be taking place in the South as the real income of the region increases. The drama has yet to play itself out. What is more certain, however, is that backwash effects do result in any area that goes through modernization. Uneven regional development can rob the income of some groups—which then sink further into the mire of poverty. This has been especially true of the South. In a review of industrial migration to this region, David Smith found that city slums and rural poverty remained largely untouched—again most markedly among blacks.[30]

Recent research shows that the rural South, when judged on a variety of measures of social well-being, is the most ill-equipped region of the country.[31] It is the highest of any region on:

1. The number of banks who quit financing farm loans;
2. The percentage of farmers who went out of business or declared bankruptcy;
3. The number of farmers with delinquent Farmers Home Administration loans;
4. Dependency on off-farm employment to make ends meet;
5. Counties with chronic low income (92 percent of all U.S. counties in this group are in the South);
6. Poverty levels (21 percent of rural southerners live below the poverty line—a proportion recently growing larger);
7. Low levels of educational attainment (nearly all of the nation's 489 counties with the lowest proportion of high school graduates are in the South);

8. Rates of functional illiteracy (difficulty in basic reading and writing comprehension).

It is becoming more apparent that the development strategy built upon low wages in the South has backfired. Low-wage manufacturing jobs were supposed to yield to high technology once industries were firmly established. Instead, multinational branch plants are being relocated to LDCs. Over one half of the 1.5 million jobs lost in the South between 1979 to 1984 were in manufacturing.[32] The counties with the fastest rates of employment growth are also those with the lowest percentages of workers in manufacturing. This is especially serious for the rural South, where employees are just as dependent upon manufacturing as workers in the industrial heartland of the Midwest.[33] The rural South is completely helpless to compete for topnotch industry that does remain in the United States, since these businesses demand an educated work force with highly developed technical skills.

On the basis of these economic forces alone, then, we could expect huge regional differences on income to emerge and persist within the United States. To the extent that the South remains a periphery to a northern core, income will be low and show all of the gross inequities that are so obvious within the Third World. There are social and cultural conditions which feed into this inequality, however, that are not directly economic but are very important all the same. As a result of the slave plantation heritage in the South, there is more conservativism in the region which may have led to union hostility. There is certainly more racism. Within the rural South, two out of every five black men are without jobs, cannot find a full-time job, or cannot earn enough money to raise themselves above the poverty line.[34] There is a continuing, strong degree of employment discrimination directed against blacks in the rural South, which works to impoverish them even further. This is not surprising given the evidence of much higher levels of racial prejudice and discrimination here than in the North.[35] And in the South, the higher the proportion of blacks in a locale—the stronger is the discrimination. Even today there are large numbers of rural blacks concentrated in many southern counties. We can thus expect major income differences between areas within this region if only due to race.

Because of pronounced cultural differences, region has an important impact upon the level of income in its own right. Stuart Holland in his book on the interplay between regions and economics argues at great length that income differences between areas are due to more than just the normal functioning of market forces.[36] Among other important variables that he highlights are slavery, federal protectionism, and regional specialization of products difficult to duplicate elsewhere (such as sugar, cotton, and tobacco). Support for this view was found in a study of 180,000 men after their army enlistments had expired.[37] In comparison to human capital variables, such as education and work experience, about one-sixth of earnings differences are due to what region the worker was employed in.

The importance that region has upon income differences begins to become more apparent when we look at U.S. counties. All 3,186 counties were ranked by median family income in 1979. Current data by counties will unfortunately not be available until several years after the 1990 Census of Population. Although more recent per capita income figures are available, they do not directly reflect the spread of economic well-being as well as the family income figures do. Per capita data is analogous to a gross or crude average that could hide true deprivation in families because of the presence of a few super-rich persons—especially at the smaller county level. Moreover, analysts frequently focus upon families because their average income has relevancy to several others in the unit. Although there will also undoubtedly be some dramatic changes for a few counties in the 1990 Census, the general rankings of the great majority of counties will be relatively unchanged.

Table 6.3 lists the *300 poorest counties* in the United States, which is about 10 percent of all counties. A brief glimpse at this list reveals that almost all of these are in the South. Most are also rural. A glance at table 6.4 shows that with a few major exceptions (Alaska), a great number of the *300 richest counties* are suburban counties of major metropolitan areas, nearly all of which are in the North. All U.S. counties were arbitrarily divided into the highest quartile (25 percent) for rich counties, the middle 50 percent to comprise middle-income counties, and the lowest quartile of family income to designate poor counties. In 1979 the poorest fourth of counties had a median family income of less than $14,322 while the richest quartile showed a median family income of $18,906 or more.

The profile of these counties is quite instructive. For instance, the poorest quartile of counties again shows a heavy regional bias toward the South. This section of the country has 1424 counties, or 45 percent of all U.S. counties. Yet the South has over two-thirds of the 782 poorest counties. In short, it has over 50 percent more poor counties than would be expected on the basis of the normal proportional representation in each region. Table 6.5 shows the breakdown of these counties by the four regions. The percentage of poor, middle, and rich counties are listed along side of the percent change from what should be expected on the basis of normal regional representation. All regions outside the South are heavily underrepresented on poor counties. At the other extreme, the South has a −46 percent gap of rich counties while all other regions are over-represented by these counties. It is very clear that the Northeast and

TABLE 6.3   Median Family Income of Poorest 300 U.S. Counties: 1979

Rank	County	Income	Rank	County	Income
1	Owsley, KY	$ 7,170	49	Wheeler, GA	$10,330
2	Tunica, MS	7,685	50	Sierra, NM	10,350
3	Hancock, TN	7,830	51	Shannon, MO	10,362
4	Clinton, KY	8,312	52	Hale, AL	10,368
5	Mora, NM	8,608	53	Conejos, CO	10,377
6	Starr, TX	8,627	54	East Carroll, LA	10,388
7	McCreary, KY	8,746	55	Presidio, TX	10,394
8	Castilla, CO	8,803	56	Knox, KY	10,425
9	Jackson, KY	8,823	57	Tensas, LA	10,447
10	Holmes, MS	8,898	58	Chicot, AR	10,453
11	Clay, KY	8,901	59	Metcalfe, KY	10,515
12	Lee, AR	8,988	60	Miner, SD	10,522
13	Morgan, KY	9,114	61	Guadalupe, NM	10,532
14	Searcy, AR	9,301	62	Monroe, KY	10,546
15	Tallahatchie, MS	9,317	63	La Salle, TX	10,563
16	Newton, AR	9,356	64	Boyd, NE	10,565
17	Sharkey, MS	9,406	65	Bullock, AL	10,623
18	Fentress, TN	9,438	66	Maverick, TX	10,623
19	Jefferson, MS	9,442	67	Scott, AR	10,666
20	Casey, KY	9,447	68	Taliaferro, GA	10,668
21	Buffalo, SD	9,500	69	Ozark, MO	10,671
22	Lee, KY	9,506	70	Real, TX	10,674
23	Wayne, KY	9,612	71	Wilcox, AL	10,679
24	Wolfe, KY	9,669	72	Madison, LA	10,679
25	Zavala, TX	9,728	73	Grant, ND	10,696
26	Sanborn, SD	9,759	74	Claiborne, TN	10,705
27	Lowndes, AL	9,766	75	Magoffin, KY	10,721
28	Clay, GA	9,842	76	Prairie, MT	10,724
29	Quitman, GA	9,855	77	Leslie, KY	10,728
30	Stone, AR	9,861	78	Pushmataha, OK	10,730
31	Hickory, MO	9,863	79	McPherson, SD	10,752
32	Ripley, MO	9,865	80	Dickens, TX	10,769
33	Green, AL	9,917	81	Carson, SD	10,786
34	Johnston, OK	9,930	82	Breathitt, KY	10,796
35	Cumberland, KY	9,944	83	West Carroll, LA	10,807
36	Stewart, GA	9,973	84	Todd, SD	10,833
37	Perry, AL	9,983	85	San Miguel, NM	10,841
38	Wayne, MO	9,983	86	Douglas, SD	10,857
39	Oregon, MO	9,986	87	Fulton, AR	10,862
40	Ziebach, SD	10,000	88	Phillips, AR	10,874
41	Pickett, TN	10,107	89	Wilkinson, MS	10,891
42	Shannon, SD	10,208	90	Noxubee, MS	10,892
43	Rockcastle, KY	10,288	91	Atoka, OK	10,898
44	Quitman, MS	10,301	92	Dixie, FL	10,920
45	Clay, TN	10,301	93	Elliott, KY	10,961
46	Humphreys, MS	10,307	94	Menifee, KY	10,971
47	Russell, KY	10,310	95	Douglas, MO	10,975
48	Union, GA	10,327	96	Swain, NC	10,982

TABLE 6.3   (*Continued*)

Rank	County	Income	Rank	County	Income
97	Towns, GA	$11,004	145	Saguache, CO	$11,485
98	Kemper, MS	11,006	146	Latimer, OK	11,489
99	Franklin, FL	11,018	147	Bennett, SD	11,497
100	Crenshaw, AL	11,021	148	Lawrence, KY	11,500
101	Screven, GA	11,022	149	Hart, KY	11,509
102	Carter, MO	11,032	150	Covington, MS	11,514
103	Hyde, NC	11,053	151	Zapata, TX	11,523
104	Johnson, TN	11,058	152	Menard, TX	11,531
105	Woodruff, AR	11,060	153	Edwards, TX	11,554
106	Madison, NC	11,072	154	Luna, NM	11,555
107	Montgomery, AR	11,131	155	Faulk, SD	11,583
108	Clay, AR	11,167	156	Bath, KY	11,584
109	Leake, MS	11,190	157	Kidder, ND	11,586
110	Mellette, SD	11,191	158	Calhoun, WV	11,594
111	Coal, OK	11,202	159	Brooks, GA	11,596
112	Hudspeth, TX	11,204	160	Lawrence, AR	11,608
113	Lake, MI	11,210	161	Howell, MO	11,624
114	Gregory, SD	11,213	162	Issaquena, MS	11,625
115	Bolivar, MS	11,216	163	Hanson, SD	11,630
116	Campbell, SD	11,229	164	Bollinger, MO	11,637
117	Tattnall, GA	11,250	165	Dallas, MO	11,639
118	Clay, WV	11,259	166	Sunflower, MS	11,639
119	Jenkins, GA	11,262	167	Lake, TN	11,641
120	Cherokee, NC	11,274	168	Webster, WV	11,646
121	Lewis, KY	11,279	169	Panola, MS	11,660
122	Adair, OK	11,287	170	Kalawao, HI	11,667
123	Sharp, AR	11,292	171	Attala, MS	11,669
124	Atkinson, GA	11,294	172	Okfuskee, OK	11,679
125	Dimmit, TX	11,301	173	Motley, TX	11,695
126	Izard, AR	11,316	174	Rio Arriba, NM	11,699
127	Coahoma, MS	11,326	175	Keweenaw, MI	11,705
128	Marion, AR	11,332	176	Wright, MO	11,719
129	Pemiscot, MO	11,355	177	Logan, AR	11,737
130	Choctaw, MS	11,360	178	Randolph, GA	11,748
131	Adair, KY	11,361	179	Owyhee, ID	11,748
132	Jeff Davis, TX	11,365	180	Jackson, TN	11,752
133	St. Helena, LA	11,370	181	Jefferson, FL	11,761
134	Kenedy, TX	11,384	182	Webster, GA	11,762
135	Hancock, GA	11,400	183	Lafayette, AR	11,769
136	Scott, TN	11,403	184	McIntosh, GA	11,788
137	Monroe, AR	11,416	185	Charles Mix, SD	11,812
138	Glades, FL	11,427	186	St. Francis, AR	11,814
139	Edmonson, KY	11,441	187	Whitley, KY	11,823
140	Willacy, TX	11,443	188	Telfair, GA	11,825
141	Macon, AL	11,454	189	Grundy, TN	11,827
142	Hughes, OK	11,464	190	Montgomery, MS	11,831
143	Haywood, TN	11,474	191	Ashe, NC	11,835
144	Kinney, TX	11,483	192	Carroll, MS	11,854

TABLE 6.3   (*Continued*)

Rank	County	Income	Rank	County	Income
193	Yancey, NC	$11,855	240	De Baca, NM	$12,052
194	Bertie, NC	11,861	241	Liberty, GA	12,055
195	Apache, AZ	11,872	242	Sioux, ND	12,057
196	Amite, MS	11,873	243	Calhoun, MS	12,059
197	Overton, TN	11,876	244	Green, KY	12,069
198	Allendale, SC	11,878	245	Braxton, WV	12,072
199	Conecuh, AL	11,880	246	New Madrid, MO	12,078
200	Prairie, AR	11,882	247	Campbell, TN	12,079
201	Catron, NM	11,884	248	Blaine, NE	12,083
202	Lincoln, KY	11,891	249	Hidalgo, TX	12,083
203	Brooks, TX	11,893	250	Knott, KY	12,085
204	Crowley, CO	11,894	251	Taos, NM	12,089
205	Madison, FL	11,895	252	Putnam, MO	12,096
206	Clay, NC	11,896	253	McIntosh, OK	12,100
207	Worth, MO	11,901	254	Grainger, TN	12,104
208	Haskell, OK	11,902	255	Sumter, AL	12,106
209	Red River, TX	11,902	256	Yazoo, MS	12,109
210	Delaware, OK	11,903	257	Banner, NE	12,109
211	Candler, GA	11,908	258	Wheeler, OR	12,109
212	Tippah, MS	11,908	259	Richland, LA	12,112
213	Bell, KY	11,913	260	Jasper, MS	12,114
214	Madison, AR	11,928	261	Pawnee, NE	12,130
215	Macon, GA	11,928	262	Northampton, VA	12,131
216	Cocke, TN	11,933	263	Iron, WI	12,138
217	Franklin, LA	11,937	264	Washington, FL	12,140
218	Jefferson, GA	11,939	265	Union, TN	12,142
219	Hamlin, SD	11,939	266	Gilmer, WV	12,147
220	Barbour, AL	11,952	267	Hand, SD	12,150
221	Greeley, NE	11,962	268	Roberts, SD	12,155
222	Fannin, GA	11,969	269	Robertson, KY	12,160
223	Torrance, NM	11,978	270	Madison, MO	12,163
224	Choctaw, OK	11,984	271	Lee, VA	12,174
225	Avoyelles, LA	11,987	272	Leflore, MS	12,177
226	Montmorency, MI	11,995	273	Roosevelt, NM	12,178
227	St. Clair, MO	11,995	274	McDonald, MO	12,181
228	Gilchrist, FL	11,999	275	Webb, TX	12,181
229	Dewey, SD	12,000	276	Morgan, MO	12,186
230	Clark, SD	12,003	277	Northampton, NC	12,190
231	Deuel, SD	12,004	278	Van Buren, AR	12,194
232	Warren, NC	12,008	279	Montgomery, GA	12,199
233	Texas, MO	12,011	280	Irwin, GA	12,202
234	Logan, ND	12,018	281	Harmon, OK	12,203
235	Cedar, MO	12,030	282	Washington, ME	12,210
236	Dunklin, MO	12,033	283	Frio, TX	12,211
237	Marion, GA	12,040	284	Tyrrell, NC	12,216
238	Holmes, FL	12,051	285	Bledsoe, TN	12,218
239	Polk, AR	12,052	286	Socorro, NM	12,219

TABLE 6.3   (*Continued*)

Rank	County	Income	Rank	County	Income
287	McIntosh, ND	$12,220	294	Van Buren, TN	$12,258
288	Marshall, OK	12,230	295	Pulaski, IL	12,266
289	Wheeler, NE	12,237	296	Scotland, MO	12,266
290	Copiah, MS	12,239	297	Ogemaw, MI	12,270
291	Bamberg, SC	12,241	298	Edmunds, SD	12,272
292	Evans, GA	12,246	299	Val Verde, TX	12,274
293	Sherman, NE	12,251	300	Choctaw, AL	12,277

TABLE 6.4   Median Family Income of Richest 300 U.S. Counties: 1979

Rank	County	Income	Rank	County	Income
1	Bristol Bay, AK	$40,236	34	Fort Bend, TX	$27,179
2	Juneau Borough, AK	35,786	35	Arapahoe, CO	26,945
3	Montgomery, MD	33,702	36	Fayette, GA	26,939
4	Fairfax, VA	33,173	37	Fairbanks North Star, AK	26,927
5	Sitka, AK	32,732	38	Hamilton, IN	26,778
6	North Slope, AK	32,113	39	Macomb, MI	26,666
7	Valdez-Cordova, AK	31,799	40	Loudoun, VA	26,660
8	Ketchikan Gateway, AK	30,992	41	Santa Clara, CA	26,659
9	Falls Church City, VA	30,817	42	Hunterdon, NJ	26,618
10	Anchorage Borough, AK	30,730	43	Jefferson, CO	26,617
11	Du Page, IL	30,430	44	Fairfield, CT	26,598
12	Howard, MD	30,328	45	Prince William, VA	26,533
13	Los Alamos, NM	30,307	46	Contra Costa, CA	26,510
14	Douglas, CO	30,154	47	Manassas City, VA	26,510
15	Marin, CA	29,721	48	Kendall, IL	26,509
16	Morris, NJ	29,283	49	Collin, TX	26,406
17	Fairfax City, VA	29,244	50	Livingston, MI	26,339
18	Somerset, NJ	29,172	51	Porter, IN	26,334
19	Oakland, MI	28,803	52	Putnam, NY	26,305
20	Arlington, VA	28,771	53	Dakota, MN	26,230
21	Nassau, NY	28,444	54	Geauga, OH	26,136
22	Kodiak Island, AK	28,351	55	Washington, MN	26,059
23	Rockland, NY	28,243	56	Sweetwater, WY	26,038
24	Johnson, KS	28,153	57	Matanuska-Susitna, AK	25,999
25	Lake, IL	28,045	58	Orange, CA	25,918
26	Wrangell-Petersburg, AK	27,981	59	Montgomery, PA	25,803
27	Ozaukee, WI	27,766	60	Chesterfield, VA	25,753
28	Waukesha, WI	27,648	61	Charles, MD	25,747
29	Bergen, NJ	27,517	62	Will, IL	25,740
30	Campbell, WY	27,479	63	Rockwall, TX	25,734
31	Kenai Peninsula, AK	27,378	64	Natrona, WY	25,693
32	San Mateo, CA	27,279	65	Summit, CO	25,667
33	Westchester, NY	27,278	66	McHenry, IL	25,655

TABLE 6.4   (*Continued*)

Rank	County	Income	Rank	County	Income
67	Middlesex, NJ	$25,603	115	Racine, WI	$23,836
68	Poquoson City, VA	25,595	116	Calvert, MD	23,831
69	Chester, PA	25,533	117	Scott, IA	23,812
70	Prince George's, MD	25,525	118	Lake, CO	23,758
71	Alexandria City, VA	25,496	119	Genesee, MI	23,717
72	Benton, WA	25,472	120	Boulder, CO	23,705
73	Pitkin, CO	25,469	121	Hancock, WV	23,703
74	Washtenaw, MI	25,465	122	Skagway-Yaku-Angoon,	23,693
75	Norfolk, MA	25,434		AK	
76	King, WA	25,333	123	Warrick, IN	23,685
77	Brazoria, TX	25,302	124	Tazewell, IL	23,627
78	Union, NJ	25,266	125	Williamson, TN	23,617
79	St. Louis, MO	25,265	126	Ventura, CA	23,602
80	Platte, MO	25,151	127	Midland, MI	23,598
81	Hennepin, MN	25,133	128	Clay, MO	23,585
82	Kane, IL	25,046	129	Clackamas, OR	23,572
83	Anoka, MN	24,885	130	Harford, MD	23,565
84	Washington, OR	24,819	131	Honolulu, HI	23,554
85	Routt, CO	24,809	132	Colonial Heights City, VA	23,539
86	Hendricks, IN	24,788	133	Sussex, NJ	23,530
87	Anne Arundel, MD	24,771	134	Eagle, CO	23,523
88	Lake, OH	24,661	135	Olmsted, MN	23,505
89	Medina, OH	24,619	136	Prince of Wales, AK	23,472
90	Carbon, WY	24,596	137	Haines Borough, AK	23,413
91	Eaton, MI	24,574	138	Washoe, NV	23,394
92	Scott, MN	24,557	139	Williamsburg City, VA	23,373
93	Monmouth, NJ	24,526	140	Clinton, MI	23,368
94	Montgomery, TX	24,442	141	Carroll, MD	23,340
95	Baltimore, MD	24,413	142	Hartford, CT	23,320
96	Bucks, PA	24,402	143	Woodford, IL	23,282
97	Gwinnett, GA	24,327	144	Monroe, MI	23,281
98	Harris, TX	24,322	145	Ramsey, MN	23,267
99	Uinta, WY	24,287	146	Hanover, VA	23,261
100	Monroe, NY	24,256	147	Burlington, NJ	23,251
101	Grundy, IL	24,235	148	St. Charles, LA	23,223
102	Midland, TX	24,232	149	Linn, IA	23,194
103	Randall, TX	24,229	150	Rock Island, IL	23,188
104	Suffolk, NY	24,194	151	Clear Creek, CO	23,181
105	St. Charles, MO	24,167	152	McLean, IL	23,165
106	Hancock, IN	24,119	153	Kenosha, WI	23,161
107	Converse, WY	24,055	154	De Kalb, GA	23,136
108	Middlesex, MA	24,039	155	Dutchess, NY	23,123
109	Tolland, CT	24,028	156	Carver, MN	23,112
110	Denton, TX	23,999	157	Delaware, PA	23,103
111	Washington, WI	23,962	158	Middlesex, CT	23,090
112	Lake, IN	23,961	159	Snohomish, WA	23,084
113	Cobb, GA	23,853	160	Rio Blanco, CO	23,081
114	Richmond, NY	23,842	161	Cook, IL	23,077

TABLE 6.4   (*Continued*)

Rank	County	Income	Rank	County	Income
162	Moffat, CO	$23,068	210	Brooke, WV	$22,182
163	Dane, WI	23,024	211	Erie, OH	22,161
164	Winnebago, IL	22,992	212	Allen, IN	22,160
165	Lapeer, MI	22,984	213	Boone, KY	22,158
166	De Kalb, IL	22,972	214	Wayne, MI	22,134
167	Mercer, NJ	22,972	215	Fremont, WY	22,126
168	Stafford, VA	22,927	216	Boone, IN	22,125
169	Johnson, IN	22,911	217	Saginaw, MI	22,125
170	Peoria, IL	22,877	218	Warren, OH	22,086
171	Galveston, TX	22,871	219	Cumberland, PA	22,076
172	Alameda, CA	22,863	220	Cuyahoga, OH	22,071
173	Putnam, IL	22,829	221	Trumbull, OH	22,066
174	Monroe, IL	22,801	222	Sangamon, IL	22,063
175	Whiteside, IL	22,788	223	Ottawa, MI	22,058
176	New Castle, DE	22,704	224	Bay, MI	22,034
177	Green, OH	22,697	225	Carbon, UT	22,030
178	Henrico, VA	22,685	226	Burleigh, ND	22,026
179	Boone, IL	22,681	227	Howard, IN	22,015
180	Oldham, KY	22,676	228	Wake, NC	21,977
181	Greenlee, AZ	22,661	229	Lake, MN	21,959
182	Washington, OK	22,649	230	James City, VA	21,959
183	Frederick, MD	22,639	231	Milwaukee, WI	21,958
184	York, VA	22,630	232	Davis, UT	21,948
185	Morgan, UT	22,618	233	Livingston, IL	21,946
186	Canadian, OK	22,604	234	Ingham, MI	21,921
187	Maui, HI	22,579	235	Jefferson, LA	21,920
188	Roanoke, VA	22,570	236	Lehigh, PA	21,906
189	Polk, IA	22,512	237	Garfield, CO	21,902
190	Nantucket, MA	22,489	238	Carson City, NV	21,883
191	Dubuque, IA	22,484	239	Gloucester, NJ	21,882
192	Lorain, OH	22,475	240	St. Croix, WI	21,878
193	Napa, CA	22,426	241	St. Tammany, LA	21,870
194	Butler, OH	22,417	242	Dallas, TX	21,870
195	Douglas, NV	22,412	243	Gilpin, CO	21,849
196	Orange, TX	22,404	244	Outagamie, WI	21,835
197	Rockdale, GA	22,378	245	Rock, WI	21,822
198	Litchfield, CT	22,339	246	Defiance, OH	21,821
199	Wood, OH	22,327	247	St. John the Baptist, LA	21,818
200	Chambers, TX	22,316	248	Virginia Beach City, VA	21,809
201	Black Hawk, IA	22,310	249	Williamson, TX	21,797
202	Johnson, IA	22,294	250	East Baton Rouge, LA	21,754
203	Ochiltree, TX	22,281	251	Cass, ND	21,738
204	Billings, ND	22,241	252	Shiawassee, MI	21,737
205	Warren, IA	22,239	253	La Salle, IL	21,730
206	Beaver, PA	22,239	254	Macon, IL	21,726
207	Calumet, WI	22,227	255	Clermont, OH	21,726
208	Kalamazoo, MI	22,211	256	Bartholomew, IN	21,707
209	Delaware, OH	22,202	257	Henry, IL	21,698

TABLE 6.4   (*Continued*)

Rank	County	Income	Rank	County	Income
258	Cole, MO	$21,698	280	Morgan, IN	$21,552
259	Weston, WY	21,698	281	Piatt, IL	21,551
260	Hamilton, OH	21,693	282	Lee, IL	21,533
261	Platte, WY	21,693	283	Kent, MI	21,530
262	Story, IA	21,679	284	Cowlitz, WA	21,526
263	New Haven, CT	21,668	285	Sheboygan, WI	21,525
264	Placer, CA	21,662	286	Jefferson, TX	21,523
265	Essex, MA	21,660	287	Lucas, OH	21,519
266	Clayton, GA	21,652	288	La Porte, IN	21,505
267	Sheridan, WY	21,652	289	Emery, UT	21,501
268	Allegheny, PA	21,643	290	Clark, WA	21,484
269	Santa Barbara, CA	21,630	291	Hillsborough, NH	21,483
270	Douglas, NE	21,629	292	Lafayette, LA	21,472
271	Brown, WI	21,622	293	Hemphill, TX	21,469
272	Summit, OH	21,617	294	Jefferson, OH	21,458
273	Solano, CA	21,606	295	Kitsap, WA	21,456
274	Sedgwick, KS	21,584	296	Madison, IL	21,419
275	Ogle, IL	21,583	297	Cleveland, OK	21,414
276	Menard, IL	21,580	298	Warren, NJ	21,412
277	Tarrant, TX	21,577	299	Summit, UT	21,410
278	Ascension, LA	21,572	300	Cass, MO	21,401
279	Sarpy, NE	21,569			

the West are especially fortunate, having a relative absence of poor counties but an abundance of counties in the top quartile of family income.

All of the counties have been mapped for each state by median family income (Appendix B). The map key is geared to the U.S. distribution as a whole. It is thus easy to see how the counties in each state compare with the national norm. By skimming through these figures, it is apparent that most states have at least a few rich counties, regardless of what section of the country they might be in. Yet the highest income counties continue to appear most often in the Northeast, Midwest, and West while the low-income counties concentrate in southern states.

The average median family income of all U.S. counties in 1979 stood at $16,796. Among counties in each region, the Northeast led the pack with an average of $18,941 compared to the West's $18,266 and a North Central average of $17,432. The difference from the southern average of $15,544 (which is well below the norm) is dramatic. In essence, going by counties alone the average median family income of northeast counties is nearly 22 percent above those of southern counties. Although select areas in the South may be doing better, the large number of poor counties in this region pull down the average by quite a bit. An analysis of variance on the data also shows that *the differences between regions are* much greater than the differences on median family income between the counties within each region. In other words, each region is fairly homogeneous within itself. Counties in the South are fairly equal in being of low income. Counties in the other regions are fairly similar in being of higher income. The big difference continues to be found between a uniformly low-income South versus the other three more affluent regions of the country. This finding continues to dramatize the deep sectional differences of income in the United States. Southern incomes remain lower than elsewhere in the nation. Perhaps progress has been made by a few states or few counties in the South. Yet the majority of the counties in this region are saddled with low to middle income in comparison to counties outside of the region.

Poor counties also tend to be nonmetropolitan. Almost 97 percent of poor counties are located outside of any metropolitan area, while 77 percent of all U.S. counties are nonmetropolitan.[38] On the other hand, rich counties tend to be situated in a metropolitan complex—although usually on the suburban county fringe of a lower-income central-city county. Well over half of all rich counties are metropolitan—a proportion 140 percent greater than would be expected if rich counties were distributed simply in proportion to their normal metro/non-metro percentages.

Table 6.6 contains the mean averages for a number of different variables which help us identify what other forces might be operating to increase or decrease family income within these counties. In a study of earnings for both black and white males between the ages of thirty-five

TABLE 6.5   Regional Location of Counties by Family Income: 1979

	Region				
Income Category	Northeast	North Central	South	West	Total Number
Percent Poor	.9	23.5	68.3	7.3	
Percent Different from					782
Expected by Region	−667.0	−69.9	50.4	−91.8	
Percent Middle	7.5	34.2	44.6	13.7	
Percent Different from					1566
Expected by Region	8.7	1.8	−1.8	−2.1	
Percent Rich	11.7	42.6	24.4	21.3	
Percent Different from					788
Expected by Region	69.6	26.8	−46.3	52.1	
Total Counties In Region	217	1055	1424	440	

TABLE 6.6   Mean Values of Selected Characteristics, County Income
             Groups: 1980

Characteristic	County Income Group		
	Poor	Middle Income	Rich
Percent Urban	19.0%	34.0%	58.0%
Percent Black	14.5	7.4	4.9
Percent High School Graduates	48.5	59.5	69.8
Percent of Households Headed by Female	9.5	8.0	7.9
Percent Employed	92.2	93.3	94.0
Percent Employed in Manufacturing	20.8	20.5	21.5
Percent of Labor Force that is Female	39.6	40.0	40.7
Percent of Population on Rural Farms	12.5	10.1	4.9

and fifty-four, it was found that some of these factors had an important impact upon take-home pay.[39] Human capital variables such as education can have a positive effect upon income, but regional differences together with race were found to have a major influence upon earnings. This was especially pronounced between metropolitan and other counties, and for areas where blacks were heavily concentrated.

Huge differences exist between rich and poor counties on degree of urbanization, which again highlights the association between ruralness and low income.[40] The urbanization rate is three times higher in rich counties than in poor counties. The same is true with the percent of residents who are black, but this time the direction is reversed. Poor counties have three times the proportion of blacks as do rich counties. Surprisingly, there is no evident schism in unemployment between poor and rich counties. Nor are there any marked gaps in the percent of the labor force employed in manufacturing. Again, however, existing differences may be masked by regional effects. While manufacturing jobs in the North may be associated with high-income counties, evidence already cited suggests that the reverse case actually holds true in the rural South. Thus, the effect could appear to be cancelled out if region is not held constant.

Other factors associated with the South come together to make differences even sharper. The rural dimension in combination with high proportions of blacks has a lethal effect upon economic well-being in counties. In a study of 778 nonmetropolitan southern counties, it was found that employment in manufacturing was a significant negative predictor of median family income—as were percent black, percent rural, unemployment, and distance from a metropolitan area.[41] One study has found that nearly two-thirds of counties where there are large numbers of farms owned by blacks are in the Persistent Low Income (PLI) category.[42] Counties in this category are frozen in poverty. They have been consistently ranked in the bottom quintile of all nonmetropolitan U.S. counties in the past 30 years on the basis of per capita income. Of the 130 counties in the study cited, there was no instance where median black income was higher than median white income. In most of these remote, poor, poverty-plagued counties—white income was generally twice that of blacks. The average size of farms owned by blacks in this area is anywhere from one-third to one-half the size of all southern farms. Poverty is much greater among the black rural-farm population, while education is at a dismally low level in comparison to rural whites in the region.

The only positive finding to these studies is that even in such rural southern counties, education is sharply related to higher median family income. This at least raises the idea that improvement might be possible, but the lack of education in this area can only be described as appalling. Louis Swanson, in a review of the painful human cost to the low income of the rural South, speaks movingly of the inability this area has shown in its futile effort to eradicate ignorance and illiteracy. The result of such a chronic lack of education translates into dead-end job skills. In this periphery hinterland, even if there were an employment structure that offered job opportunities, rural southerners would be unable to take advantage of openings that involved higher-level skills. Since the jobs are not there to begin with, the question is moot. Rural southerners' poor incomes, which according to the evidence are driven even lower by manufacturing plants in failing industries such as textiles, translate into poverty. In 1979, over one-third of all nonmetropolitan black families had incomes below poverty (56% of black female-headed families). Swanson calls this "suffering" on a massive scale, which is hard to disagree with. Grinding, constant poverty devastates self-esteem. It gives rise to fear and despair, depression and worry, family stress and violence. Yet it has even deadlier effects:

> Once again America is backsliding with regard to nutritional status. Numerous studies . . . have consistently found that poverty is directly linked to malnutrition as well as a host of other health risks. . . . The rural poor are over 65 percent more likely to con-

sume diets which are inadequate for multiple essential nutrients. The rural poor were more than twice as likely as were the U.S. nonpoor to experience severe levels of dietary inadequacy. Of the various regions, the southern poor were consistently in the worst categories. . . . The South was found to be the region in which the rural poor had the highest prevalence of biochemical deficiencies. . . . The rural poor were almost three times as likely to be growth-stunted as were children from nonpoor families. The South was considered to be the most affected region. Consistent with dietary and biochemical findings, the southern rural poor exhibited the highest prevalence of low height-for-age. . . . The worst is saved for last—infant mortality and low birth weight. . . . The findings suggest [they are] considerably higher in rural poor counties than the rest of the nation. While the national infant mortality has declined and then leveled off in recent years, the rate has actually increased in rural poor counties. Data for low birth weights points to a similar disparity. . . . A characteristic of southern rural poverty is hunger, malnutrition, and higher than average levels of infant mortality. This is one dimension of the human suffering that is part of the rural South in crisis.[43]

As with our previous analysis of income levels in the Third World, it is easy for confusion to set in when so many factors are associated with low or high income levels. Once more, it is possible to sort out many of the forces which act to raise or lower median family income in U.S. counties by using multiple regression. It was believed that some variables within the South would have more impact than outside this region. In particular, given stronger racism in the South plus less income payoff of manufacturing jobs in this region, race was expected to have a greater negative effect upon income here than in the non-South. The association between manufacturing jobs and higher income was also expected to be weaker, nonexistent, or perhaps even reversed. Thus, separate regression runs were made for all U.S. counties, nonsouthern counties, and southern counties. Percent of the population that is black when used alone is weak as a predictive variable. It does not reflect the greater likelihood of discrimination that results from a larger proportion of blacks who concentrate in a given area. To tap this dimension, counties were simply divided into low and high by race on the basis of the proportion of their population which is black. Nationally, 11.8 percent of our population is Black. Counties with a black population less than or equal to this percent were designated as low on race while other counties were ranked as high. Table A6 in Appendix A lists the results.

We have attempted once again to sort out the storks from the babies. In other words, how does each variable work to raise or lower the economic well-being of families in U.S. counties? What are their impacts—taken alone or as a group—upon median family income? To begin with, eleven predictive variables were used in the equations based upon our discussion and the results of previous research. For all U.S. counties, *region* (South/non-South) was expected to heavily influence median family income, as was whether a county was part of a *metropolitan area* or not and what percentage of its population was *urban*. The percent of a county's population living on *farms* is less a geographic factor, however, than a labor force indicator. In addition to a variety of southern studies, Frank Levy identifies the shift away from the farm (notorious for low incomes) to manufacturing jobs in northern cities as one of the most important contributors to rising income within our century.[44] In this movement, low-paid jobs in agriculture disappeared through mechanization, but gains tended to be positive. Manufacturing and service jobs in urban areas actually paid more in real earnings, even after the higher cost of city living was subtracted. This effect was measured by *percent of labor force employed in manufacturing*. Education, as measured by the *percent completing high school*, has faithfully been associated with higher income. The crucial effect of *race*, already discussed, was expected to depress family income—as was the *percent of female-headed households* (associated with low family income and poverty in the last chapter). The *percent of labor force that is female* was believed to help raise family income, since it was also found in the last chapter to decrease absolute income inequality. Lastly, prior research has found *percent employed* leading to higher real income, while a high *percent of elderly persons* works to depress income.

Of all of the variables used in the analysis, the impact of percent of the labor force who are female was the only one in the opposite direction to what was expected. The higher the proportion of women in the labor force, the lower the median family income. Rather than promising higher family income, then, counties with high female employment were more likely to be associated with lower income. This is almost wholly due to need: low income within families compels women to work. Industrial and gender bias also plays a part. Women continue to be discriminated against on the payroll. They have consistently earned less than men in comparable jobs with the same levels of experience. Different analyses have also focused upon the use of women as a marginal labor force to keep worker demands for higher wages at a minimum. It is not surprising, therefore, that counties with high proportions of women in the labor force tend to have lower median family incomes. It is also not hard to imagine what might have happened if women did not work in these low-income counties. Were it not for their presence in the labor force, a large number of families would not have been able to find the money needed to keep afloat.

All other variables were also statistically significant, but in the expected direction. Surprisingly, the weakest variable in predicting lower median family income was race! By contrast, the strongest predictor of family income was the percent who had completed high school. Education carried ten times the weight that race did in determining family income. The next most important variable was the percent of a county's population above retirement age (the more elderly, the smaller median family incomes are). About five times more important than racial composition of the county were full employment, percent of population on farms, percent of labor force in manufacturing, and percent of female-headed households. Percent of labor force that is female proved twice as important as race. About four times more powerful in setting family income than race was the percent of urban residents in a county and whether or not a county was in a metropolitan area (both are associated with higher income). Lastly, regional variables were powerful in determining income. As expected, southern residence produces low income in its own right—apart from the impact of all the other indicators. Southern residence had twice the impact of race in depressing family income.

Whatever the varying importance of these forces, however, all of them taken together can account for over two-thirds of the entire variation in median family income within U.S. counties. Their importance in fixing a family's income is beyond dispute. The finding that manufacturing continues to play a positive factor in raising family income provides fresh ammunition to critics who charge that deindustrialization is working against the welfare of most Americans. It also adds credence to the fact that development in the United States has been uneven—and that severe income deprivation continues to exist for southern families in comparison to those outside of this region.

The comparison of southern versus nonsouthern counties also conveys a few major differences. Surprisingly, a higher concentration of blacks in a county is associated with lower family income only in the North. It is not a statistically significant factor in predicting income within the South. This does not mean that racism is nonexistent in the South, but that other factors are much more important in determining family income. Among them are education and percent employed (twice the weight it carries in northern counties). Although the direction of the relationship between manufacturing and higher income was the same in all regions, it was much stronger outside of the South. Given all of the findings to this point, it is not surprising that industrial jobs carry more pay in northern climes. The negative impact due to unemployment and the percent of women in the labor force is much stronger in the South as well. This may again be more a reflection of a marginal, easily exploited labor force as well as the lack of other employment options.[45]

Relative Income Inequality:
Where the Grass Is Greener

David Smith recently wrote an entertaining and informative book describing inequality for a variety of important social variables.[46] Sharp differences among geographic areas tend to exist along many lines of inequality. Yet a very surprising but persistent trend emerged in his data comparing American states. He found that relatively rich states—as measured by per capita income—are not necessarily at the top with respect to indicators of less social pathology (violent crimes, rates of venereal disease, narcotics addiction, illiteracy, etc.). In essence, these are common problems that surface in big cities. As we have seen, areas where urban and/or metropolitan populations dominate also tend to have much higher family incomes. One point Smith makes is especially worth repeating: higher absolute income will not necessarily translate into a better life. The extremes of affluence may bring their own problems of social pathology—such as divorce, alcoholism, higher levels of stress-induced illnesses, and the like. Although poor states are nearly always high on social pathologies, rich states are not necessarily low on these indicators either.

Again, much will depend upon how income is shared. With reference to the Third World, it was apparent that a high Gross National Product (GNP) per capita did not necessarily translate into meeting basic human needs in less developed countries. This is also true of states and counties within America. It is possible that areas with high levels of absolute income may display a large number of social blights such as crime. A variety of vices will tend to flourish wherever income is poorly and unfairly shared. This is especially so when the contrast between the extremely wealthy and the desperately poor is blatant to begin with.

It is therefore crucial to look at relative income inequality in comparing regions in the U.S. It is possible that states or counties that are modest or even poor with respect to absolute family income will fare much better than richer areas when relative income inequality is examined. Also, can we say with impunity that a rich area is well-off if high income is not shared very equally among its people? Popular films such as *Down and Out in Beverly Hills* have vividly contrasted the very rich with the destitute and homeless. The reality of such a caricature can be found in any major city within the United States. The lives of bag ladies, panhandlers, vagrants, drifters, grate-dwellers, and the like collide daily with the wealthy in cities such as New York. Contact may be only momentary as the affluent gaze upon the poor while being whisked away in their limousines, but the glimpses have staying power for both groups. These images add credence to one viewpoint in particular. What good is a high level of income for a community if it is held only by a few persons?

The development argument sold as a panacea for LDC economic woes has been used to rationalize regional variation within the United States as well. The idea has been popular that less developed states will pass through an inverted U-shape experience as income growth sets in. As applied here at home, the usual scenario predicts that a rural, low-income farm state will have a fairly equal distribution of income. As such areas "develop" and grow—usually via the salvation of industry relocation with its associated high-technology and service jobs—real income goes up but relative income gets more skewed and uneven. Finally, as development reaches its ultimate stage, high incomes will be shared more equally among the population. Once past the threshold stage of development, then, everyone benefits with higher income.

On the surface, there is much support for this view. The South has been going through a modernization and development sequence since the end of World War II. As real income has gone up for this region, relative income inequality has dropped. Table 6.7 compares the four separate regions of the country by state on family income Gini ratios, calculated using the same techniques as in earlier works.[47] There has been a definite coming together of relative income inequality between the four regions. In 1949, the South had the highest degree of inequality with a Gini ratio of .4488, which was nearly 22 percent greater than the most equal region of the Northeast. By 1979, the gap had closed to about 10 percent. Although the South still displayed greater inequality, it was not that far removed from the Northeast. More importantly, the South saw a 15 percent decline in its relative income inequality take place in these thirty years while the Gini ratio in the Northeast only declined by 6 percent. Clearly, the sharing of family income within the South is becoming more equal at the same time that absolute income has been going up.

With the move toward growing income inequality taking place within the nation as a whole, the trend toward equality in the South may not continue at such a rapid pace. Perhaps new dimensions of inequality will arise to replace the old patterns. Although the Northeast has been the most egalitarian with respect to family income, inequality actually increased within this region between 1969 and 1979. After income in 1989 is measured by the 1990 Census of Population, it is possible that other regions will join this counter-trend to reflect the return of greater

TABLE 6.7   Gini Scores of Family Income Inequality by State and Region: 1949–1979

State	Gini Scores			
	1979 (Rank)	1969	1959	1949
Northeast				
Maine	.3336 (6)	.3368	.3412	.3843
Vermont	.3404 (9)	.3441	.3579	.3844
New Hampshire	.3218 (2)	.3239	.3301	.3636
Massachusetts	.3454 (16)	.3309	.3401	.3566
Rhode Island	.3442 (14)	.3407	.3444	.3584
Connecticut	.3488 (21)	.3268	.3488	.3664
New York	.3777 (40)	.3594	.3667	.3859
Pennsylvania	.3412 (10)	.3386	.3528	.3554
New Jersey	.3501 (24)	.3335	.3423	.3611
Unweighted Average	.3448	.3372	.3471	.3685
North Central				
Ohio	.3352 (7)	.3311	.3490	.3587
Indiana	.3300 (4)	.3288	.3568	.3643
Michigan	.3459 (17)	.3314	.3483	.3509
Illinois	.3498 (23)	.3391	.3604	.3695
Wisconsin	.3310 (5)	.3335	.3506	.3645
Minnesota	.3414 (11)	.3476	.3717	.3758
Iowa	.3618 (34)	.3525	.3800	.3814
Missouri	.3587 (30)	.3710	.4041	.4276
Kansas	.3507 (26)	.3628	.3786	.4127
Nebraska	.3436 (13)	.3603	.3818	.4020
South Dakota	.3577 (28)	.3844	.3970	.4121
North Dakota	.3452 (15)	.3708	.3750	.4134
Unweighted Average	.3459	.3511	.3711	.3846
South				
Delaware	.3572 (27)	.3430	.3799	.4218
Maryland	.3478 (20)	.3447	.3612	.3826
District of Columbia	.4450 (51)	.4250	.3950	.3960
Virginia	.3647 (37)	.3756	.4111	.4260
West Virginia	.3582 (29)	.3770	.4072	.3980
Kentucky	.3840 (46)	.3970	.4400	.4549
Tennessee	.3815 (43)	.3915	.4412	.4605
Arkansas	.3889 (48)	.4057	.4527	.4954
Louisiana	.3997 (50)	.4077	.4363	.4604
Mississippi	.3990 (49)	.4276	.4775	.5363
Alabama	.3830 (44)	.3983	.4390	.4778
Georgia	.3835 (45)	.3873	.4277	.4763
Florida	.3858 (47)	.3932	.4173	.4537
South Carolina	.3635 (36)	.3795	.4336	.4634
North Carolina	.3629 (35)	.3761	.4288	.4455

inequality. Almost half (fifteen of thirty-two) of all nonsouthern states experienced an increase of relative inequality in the past decade. Most of these are in the midwestern industrial belt or states within the money and banking core of the Northeast. By the time the impact of the 1980s becomes evident in the next census, the erosion of equality will undoubtedly be worse. It may not be as evident in the South, however, where only three of the seventeen states saw increasing inequality in the past ten years. Within this region, it seems on the surface as if the Kuznets curve of rapidly falling income inequality is taking place alongside of growth and development.

But before exploring this question fully, we must be made aware of the distance yet to be travelled for the South to emerge as a full and equal partner to other parts of the country. Figure 6.2 maps the states by their Gini scores. A solid tier of black, indicating high inequality, sweeps across the South. With only a few exceptions, this region contains nearly all of the states in the top 25 percent that are most unequal on family

TABLE 6.7   (Continued)

State	Gini Scores			
	1979 (Rank)	1969	1959	1949
South, cont.				
Oklahoma	.3785 (41)	.3873	.4161	.4396
Texas	.3803 (42)	.3832	.4203	.4421
Unweighted Average	.3802	.3882	.4226	.4488
West				
Wyoming	.3163 (1)	.3468	.3457	.3674
Utah	.3295 (3)	.3389	.3300	.3406
Montana	.3403 (8)	.3516	.3527	.3898
Washington	.3426 (12)	.3374	.3408	.3534
Idaho	.3463 (18)	.3548	.3478	.3783
Oregon	.3472 (19)	.3468	.3510	.3669
Nevada	.3496 (22)	.3353	.3478	.3712
Colorado	.3507 (25)	.3538	.3625	.3957
Arizona	.3600 (32)	.3645	.3788	.4192
California	.3718 (38)	.3524	.3594	.3619
New Mexico	.3738 (39)	.3933	.3945	.4437
Alaska	.3598 (31)	NA	NA	NA
Hawaii	.3606 (33)	NA	NA	NA
Unweighted Average	.3499	.3523	.3555	.3807
Total, All U.S. States				
(Unweighted Average)	.3582	.3604	.3808	.4032

NA = Not Available

FIGURE 6.2: Family Income Gini Scores, 1979

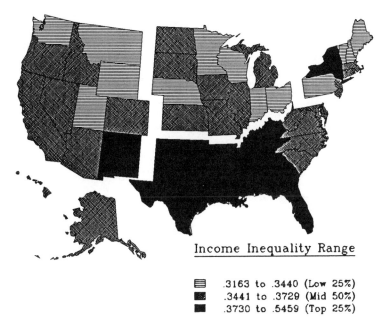

Income Inequality Range

▤	.3163 to .3440 (Low 25%)
▦	.3441 to .3729 (Mid 50%)
■	.3730 to .5459 (Top 25%)

income. Counties were also mapped according to the range of household income inequality for the country as a whole (Appendix C). The one-fourth of U.S. counties most equal had Gini scores of .3617 or less. The most unequal counties had Gini ratios of .3940 or higher, while the remaining 50 percent of counties were cast in the middle range of income inequality.

While nearly all states generally have a few counties with high relative income inequality, southern states continue to dominate with the most inequality. Table 6.8 shows the distribution of relative income inequality groups by region. If high inequality counties were distributed equally, each region would have 25 percent of its counties in this category. As with low absolute income, however, the South is burdened with more inequality as well. Nearly 40 percent of its counties have a fairly lopsided income distribution, while only 6 percent of northeastern counties and 12 percent of midwestern counties do. At the other end, where income is more evenly shared in low inequality counties, the South only has 16 percent of its counties in this category while all other regions have over 30 percent that are most egalitarian. Put differently, the South has 56 percent more counties that are highly unequal while it has one-third fewer counties that are more equal than would be expected if all regions were the same.

TABLE 6.8   Regional Location of Counties by Household Income
               Inequality: 1979

Inequality Category	Region				Total Number
	Northeast	North Central	South	West	
Low	40.1%	31.8%	16.4%	30.2%	789
Medium	53.9	56.5	44.5	49.3	1563
High	6.0	11.8	39.1	20.5	784
Counties in Region:					
Number	217	1055	1424	440	
Percent	6.9%	33.6%	45.4%	14.0%	

Once again, we can gain a sharper view of what high and low income inequality areas are like by looking at the top and bottom three
hundred counties ranked by household income Gini scores. Table 6.9
starts at the bottom with the most unequal 10 percent of counties. A
glance at this roster affirms that the very great majority are in the South,
with a sizable number hailing from Texas in particular.

Most counties that are high on inequality are more rural, but there
are significant exceptions. New York County has the fourth highest
household income Gini ratio among all of the nation's counties. Unfortunately, over 1,428,000 people lived in this income-skewed locale in
1980. Although it is home to many wealthy people, we also know it plays
host to a teeming population of derelict, homeless, and deprived persons.
All told, there are over 75 million people in the most unequal 25 percent
of counties—which was one-third of the nation's entire population in
1980. We will see in a moment that unequal counties tend to be less
metropolitan, hence they will have a slight tendency toward smaller
numbers that is offset by a greater trend toward urbanization. Yet all it
takes are a few mega-counties to swell the ranks of the income-deprived
in the bottom three hundred. In California, these include Los Angeles,
San Francisco, Santa Cruz, Yolo (Davis), and Fresno. Around New York
City, high-inequality counties include New York, Essex (Newark), ritzy
Westchester, and Fairfield in Connecticut. Virginia contributes Rich-
mond and Roanoke Cities, while Tennessee adds Shelby (Memphis). Atlanta's Fulton County makes the roster, as does Miami's Dade County
and the West Palm Beach/Boca Raton metropolitan area (Palm Beach).
New Orleans tips in with Orleans county while Texas registers high inequality especially in its southeastern tip of Hidalgo and Cameron counties (McAllen and Brownsville metropolitan areas). In a word, although
this group of top inequality counties seems paltry at only 10 percent of
the total number, 24 million people live within their boundaries. One

TABLE 6.9   Household Income Gini Scores of the 300 Most Unequal
             U.S. Counties: 1979

Rank	County	Gini	Rank	County	Gini
1	Kenedy, TX	.6675	48	Union, NM	.4433
2	Loving, TX	.6453	49	De Kalb, TN	.4428
3	Sherman, TX	.5479	50	Concho, TX	.4422
4	New York, NY	.4925	51	Caldwell, LA	.4420
5	Cattle, TX	.4895	52	Garza, TX	.4411
6	Sharkey, MS	.4894	53	Catahoula, LA	.4409
7	Sterling, TX	.4868	54	Hart, KY	.4395
8	Randolph, GA	.4775	55	Boone, NE	.4393
9	Knox, TX	.4746	56	Alpine, CA	.4392
10	Young, TX	.4746	57	Wilbarger, TX	.4384
11	Issaquena, MS	.4723	58	La Salle, TX	.4378
12	Galax City, VA	.4673	59	Polk, AR	.4367
13	Yukon-Kayukuk, AK	.4673	60	Goochland, VA	.4364
14	Collier, FL	.4659	61	Sumter, AL	.4363
15	Dillingham, AK	.4646	62	Llano, TX	.4362
16	Madison, TX	.4638	63	Comanche, TX	.4361
17	Geneva, AL	.4638	64	Foard, TX	.4359
18	Wheeler, TX	.4623	65	Petroleum, MT	.4358
19	Erath, TX	.4613	66	Aransas, TX	.4357
20	Sutton, TX	.4605	67	Bethel, AK	.4352
21	Willacy, TX	.4598	68	Glasscock, TX	.4351
22	Blanco, TX	.4597	69	Midland, TX	.4350
23	Scott, TN	.4576	70	Motley, TX	.4344
24	Madison, LA	.4555	71	Indian River, FL	.4341
25	Rains, TX	.4553	72	Humphreys, MS	.4338
26	Fulton, GA	.4546	73	Keya Paha, NE	.4338
27	Tillman, OK	.4542	74	Haskell, TX	.4338
28	Jeff Davis, TX	.4538	75	Caddo, LA	.4337
29	Orleans, LA	.4531	76	Essex, NJ	.4334
30	Walker, TX	.4520	77	Banner, NE	.4333
31	Terrell, TX	.4520	78	Cochran, TX	.4328
32	Harmon, OK	.4518	79	Jones, TX	.4324
33	Roger Mills, OK	.4506	80	Webster, GA	.4323
34	Towns, GA	.4498	81	Dade, FL	.4323
35	Aleutian Islands, AK	.4483	82	Hinsdale, CO	.4323
36	Washington, TX	.4480	83	Wahkiakum, WA	.4323
37	Richland, LA	.4475	84	Daviess, MO	.4316
38	Metcalfe, KY	.4470	85	De Soto, LA	.4312
39	Desha, AR	.4466	86	Scotland, MO	.4311
40	Grimes, TX	.4455	87	Custer, OK	.4310
41	East Carroll, LA	.4447	88	Douglas, NV	.4306
42	West Feliciana, LA	.4446	89	Marshall, OK	.4305
43	Tensas, LA	.4443	90	Clark, AR	.4305
44	Taylor, GA	.4439	91	Borden, TX	.4305
45	Colorado, TX	.4439	92	Walthall, MS	.4301
46	Franklin, TX	.4437	93	Freestone, TX	.4296
47	Radford City, VA	.4435	94	Bailey, TX	.4295

TABLE 6.9   (*Continued*)

Rank	County	Gini	Rank	County	Gini
95	Fisher, TX	.4293	142	Summit, UT	.4239
96	Mitchell, TX	.4293	143	Bastrop, TX	.4239
97	Edwards, TX	.4288	144	Palo Pinto, TX	.4238
98	King and Queen, VA	.4286	145	Lumpkin, GA	.4237
99	Barber, KS	.4286	146	Beaufort, SC	.4236
100	Chatauqua, KS	.4285	147	Treutlen, GA	.4236
101	Acadia, LA	.4283	148	Madison, MS	.4235
102	McMullen, TX	.4283	149	Morehouse, LA	.4235
103	Breathitt, KY	.4282	150	Escambia, AL	.4233
104	Alamosa, CO	.4281	151	Dallas, MO	.4232
105	Wayne, GA	.4278	152	Hansford, TX	.4232
106	Jim Hogg, TX	.4277	153	Grundy, TN	.4230
107	Austin, TX	.4275	154	Crosby, TX	.4229
108	Navarro, TX	.4275	155	Hinds, MS	.4229
109	Nome, AK	.4275	156	Madison, NC	.4228
110	Donley, TX	.4274	157	White, GA	.4228
111	Houston, TX	.4274	158	Brooks, TX	.4225
112	Haywood, TN	.4269	159	Nacogdoches, TX	.4224
113	Williamsburg City, VA	.4268	160	Monongalia, WV	.4222
114	Hamilton, TX	.4266	161	Clay, GA	.4220
115	Tunica, MS	.4265	162	Bolivar, MS	.4219
116	Lawrence, KY	.4263	163	Arkansas, AR	.4219
117	Graham, KS	.4263	164	Wheeler, OR	.4218
118	Ouachita, LA	.4263	165	Russell, KS	.4217
119	Throckmorton, TX	.4262	166	Robertson, TX	.4216
120	Martin, TX	.4261	167	Westchester, NY	.4214
121	Leon, TX	.4261	168	Clarke, VA	.4214
122	Evangeline, LA	.4261	169	Howard, MO	.4213
123	Dallas, AR	.4258	170	Bedford, TN	.4213
124	Morgan, WV	.4257	171	Alachua, FL	.4212
125	Sunflower, MS	.4257	172	Washington, MS	.4212
126	Leflore, MS	.4255	173	Arthur, NE	.4212
127	Benton, MO	.4253	174	Tom Green, TX	.4209
128	Refugio, TX	.4253	175	Tate, MS	.4206
129	Coke, TX	.4252	176	Johnson, WY	.4205
130	Kerr, TX	.4250	177	Petersburg City, VA	.4205
131	Candler, GA	.4250	178	Hudspeth, TX	.4205
132	Northumberland, VA	.4249	179	Hall, TX	.4204
133	Palm Beach, FL	.4247	180	Webb, TX	.4204
134	Jackson, SD	.4244	181	Los Angeles, CA	.4204
135	Northampton, NC	.4244	182	Yazoo, MS	.4204
136	McPherson, NE	.4243	183	Cedar, NE	.4204
137	Adams, MS	.4243	184	Livingston, MO	.4203
138	Early, GA	.4241	185	Conecuh, AL	.4203
139	Shackelford, TX	.4239	186	Iberville, LA	.4202
140	Blaine, OK	.4239	187	Jefferson, OK	.4202
141	San Francisco, CA	.4239	188	Winchester City, VA	.4201

TABLE 6.9   (*Continued*)

Rank	County	Gini	Rank	County	Gini
189	Fairfield, CT	.4200	236	Coosa, AL	.4155
190	Foster, ND	.4197	237	Concordia, LA	.4154
191	Pitkin, CO	.4197	238	Chicot, AR	.4154
192	Choctaw, AL	.4197	239	Pontotoc, OK	.4151
193	Anderson, TX	.4196	240	Glascock, GA	.4151
194	Point Coupee, LA	.4196	241	Albermarle, VA	.4150
195	Jefferson, FL	.4196	242	McCulloch, TX	.4148
196	Crockett, TX	.4196	243	Lauderdale, MS	.4148
197	Sebastian, AR	.4195	244	Colusa, CA	.4148
198	Screven, GA	.4192	245	Wood, TX	.4147
199	Woods, OK	.4191	246	Mississippi, MO	.4147
200	Lancaster, VA	.4189	247	Clay, TX	.4147
201	Payne, OK	.4188	248	Sheridan, NE	.4145
202	Marshall, TN	.4187	249	Union, AR	.4145
203	Jim Wells, TX	.4186	250	San Augustine, TX	.4144
204	Monroe, AL	.4184	251	Hampton, SC	.4144
205	Pulaski, KY	.4184	252	Real, TX	.4144
206	Hardeman, TX	.4183	253	Accomack, VA	.4143
207	Alcorn, MS	.4182	254	Dare, NC	.4143
208	Clatsop, OR	.4180	255	Adair, MO	.4143
209	Schleicher, TX	.4179	256	St. Helena, LA	.4142
210	Cherokee, AL	.4177	257	Cameron, TX	.4140
211	Shelby, TX	.4177	258	Phillips, AR	.4140
212	Whitley, KY	.4175	259	Mitchell, IA	.4140
213	Little River, AR	.4174	260	Washington, TN	.4139
214	Harris, GA	.4173	261	Pacific, WA	.4139
215	Collingsworth, TX	.4173	262	Turner, GA	.4138
216	Vermilion, LA	.4172	263	Saline, IL	.4137
217	Briscoe, TX	.4172	264	Santa Cruz, CA	.4137
218	Macon, NC	.4172	265	Nash, NC	.4136
219	Lexington City, VA	.4171	266	Rapides, LA	.4135
220	Hill, TX	.4171	267	Obion, TN	.4135
221	Columbia, AR	.4171	268	Garland, AR	.4134
222	Crawford, MI	.4167	269	Charlottesville City, VA	.4133
223	Kiowa, OK	.4166	270	Natchitoches, LA	.4133
224	Tallahatchie, MS	.4166	271	Glynn, GA	.4132
225	Cherokee, TX	.4165	272	Limestone, TX	.4132
226	Clarke, GA	.4164	273	Monroe, FL	.4132
227	Polk, TX	.4164	274	Howard, IA	.4131
228	Taylor, FL	.4164	275	Gaines, TX	.4131
229	Richmond City, VA	.4163	276	Shelby, TN	.4131
230	Crawford, GA	.4161	277	Claiborne, MS	.4131
231	Copiah, MS	.4159	278	Covington, MS	.4131
232	Talbot, MD	.4159	279	San Saba, TX	.4130
233	Hancock, MS	.4157	280	Quitman, MS	.4130
234	Hidalgo, TX	.4156	281	Beckham, OH	.4130
235	Crisp, GA	.4156	282	Val Verde, TX	.4129

TABLE 6.9   (*Continued*)

Rank	County	Gini	Rank	County	Gini
283	Union, LA	.4129	292	Rockwall, TX	.4123
284	Dewey, OK	.4129	293	Red River, TX	.4122
285	Jackson, IL	.4128	294	Roanaoke City, VA	.4122
286	Jack, TX	.4128	295	Kent, TX	.4121
287	Coahoma, MS	.4128	296	Putnam, FL	.4121
288	Yolo, CA	.4128	297	Orange, NC	.4121
289	Nelson, VA	.4124	298	Fresno, CA	.4120
290	Lubbock, TX	.4124	299	Clarke, AL	.4119
291	Armstrong, TX	.4124	300	West Carrol, LA	.4119

out of every nine persons is exposed to hard-core relative deprivation on a daily basis within the United States.

Not all of the data is dismal. Nearly 19 million persons live within the 300 most egalitarian counties as well (table 6.10). These equal counties also tend to be metropolitan (41 percent) and non-southern. Most of them are smaller, stand-alone metropolitan areas or suburban counties of a larger, more unequal central city county. As an illustration, in Minnesota the counties of Hennepin (Minneapolis) and Ramsey (St. Paul) make up over 1.4 million persons in the Twin Cities metropolitan area. Their household income Gini scores are fairly high at .3943 and .3810 respectively. Yet this is quite typical of central-city metropolitan areas. Also part of the norm in the ecological distribution of income inequality are relatively affluent but highly egalitarian suburban counties in such metropolitan areas. Surrounding the Twin Cities in Minnesota are a number of counties in the most equal three hundred: Anoka (4th), Washington (35th), Dakota (89th), Scott (230th), and Chisago (297th). The central-city counties of Hennepin and Ramsey rank among the richest 300 on median family income as well (81st and 145th). Yet, their egalitarian sister suburbs are even more affluent. Dakota, Washington, Anoka, and Scott all number within the top one hundred counties in the nation on median family income.

This pattern of an affluent central-city county with high inequality surrounded by richer but more egalitarian counties is vividly illustrated by our nation's capital. The District of Columbia has an astronomically high Gini score of .4450—higher than any of the fifty states. Yet surrounding it are a number of counties and cities that are among the lowest three hundred on relative inequality. These counties include Manassas Park City (1st), Prince William County (5th), Manassas City (6th), Fairfax County (40th), Fairfax City (48th), and Falls Church City (108th) in Virginia. In Maryland, the suburban counties of Charles (30th) and Prince George's (75th) are also among America's most equal counties.

TABLE 6.10 Household Income Gini Scores of the 300 Most Equal
U.S. Counties: 1979

Rank	County	Gini	Rank	County	Gini
1	Manassas Park City, VA	.2693	48	Fairfax City, VA	.3219
2	Los Alamos, NM	.2850	49	Moffat, CO	.3219
3	Greenlee, AZ	.2863	50	Carbon, UT	.3222
4	Anoka, MN	.2888	51	Colonial Heights City, VA	.3235
5	Prince William, VA	.2917	52	Stafford, VA	.3237
6	Manassas City, VA	.2988	53	Kalawao, HI	.3238
7	Campbell, WY	.2989	54	Washington, WI	.3240
8	Franklin, ID	.2992	55	Mineral, MT	.3245
9	Sarpy, NE	.2994	56	Clermont, OH	.3250
10	Emery, UT	.3001	57	Porter, IN	.3251
11	Lake, CO	.3013	58	Converse, WY	.3257
12	Chattahoochee, GA	.3037	59	Will, IL	.3261
13	Kendall, IL	.3059	60	Lake, OH	.3262
14	St. Charles, MO	.3064	61	Clinton, MI	.3263
15	Bullitt, KY	.3064	62	Anderson, KY	.3269
16	Buena Vista City, VA	.3074	63	Clayton, GA	.3270
17	Sweetwater, WY	.3091	64	Box Elder, UT	.3272
18	San Juan, CO	.3093	65	Oneida, ID	.3273
19	Uinta, WY	.3100	66	Noble, IN	.3274
20	Brule, SD	.3106	67	Woodford, IL	.3275
21	Hancock, TN	.3108	68	Golden Valley, MT	.3276
22	Chesterfield, VA	.3112	69	Tolland, CT	.3278
23	Owsley, KY	.3115	70	Van Wert, OH	.3283
24	Howard, MD	.3117	71	Jefferson, ID	.3283
25	Davis, UT	.3117	72	Sherman, NE	.3285
26	Jefferson, MO	.3133	73	Bear Lake, ID	.3286
27	Gwinnett, GA	.3133	74	Weston, WY	.3290
28	Tooele, UT	.3143	75	Prince George's, MD	.3291
29	Hendricks, IN	.3147	76	Menominee, WI	.3291
30	Charles, MD	.3151	77	Perry, PA	.3292
31	Bland, VA	.3158	78	Sheridan, ND	.3292
32	Conejos, CO	.3159	79	Hancock, IN	.3292
33	Douglas, SD	.3164	80	Warren, OH	.3294
34	New Kent, VA	.3167	81	Benton, WA	.3295
35	Washington, MN	.3168	82	Lincoln, NC	.3295
36	Robertson, KY	.3174	83	Dawson, MT	.3295
37	Douglas, GA	.3174	84	Randolph, IN	.3297
38	Caribou, ID	.3182	85	Macomb, MI	.3299
39	Medina, OH	.3186	86	Sussex, NJ	.3300
40	Fairfax, VA	.3191	87	Clinton, KY	.3301
41	Sitka, AK	.3192	88	Whitney, IN	.3301
42	Du Page, IL	.3200	89	Dakota, MN	.3305
43	Tyrrell, NC	.3202	90	Clark, ID	.3305
44	Paulding, OH	.3204	91	Livingston, MI	.3306
45	York, VA	.3205	92	De Kalb, IN	.3308
46	Meade, KY	.3215	93	Boone, IL	.3309
47	Adams, CO	.3218	94	Rockdale, GA	.3309

TABLE 6.10   (*Continued*)

Rank	County	Gini	Rank	County	Gini
95	Oliver, ND	.3310	142	Warrick, IN	.3362
96	Eaton, MI	.3311	143	Putnam, NY	.3363
97	Fremont, WY	.3311	144	Lake of the Woods, MN	.3363
98	Morgan, UT	.3311	145	Routt, CO	.3363
99	Martin, IN	.3315	146	Henry, OH	.3365
100	Rio Blanco, CO	.3317	147	De Soto, MS	.3366
101	Seneca, OH	.3317	148	Ottawa, MI	.3366
102	Menifee, KY	.3317	149	Greene, VA	.3366
103	Brazoria, TX	.3318	150	Hughes, SD	.3367
104	Sherburne, MN	.3318	151	Jefferson, CO	.3369
105	Clay, MO	.3319	152	Lemhi, ID	.3369
106	Madison, VA	.3320	153	Park, CO	.3370
107	Platte, WY	.3320	154	Sanborn, SD	.3373
108	Falls Church City, VA	.3320	155	Franklin, AR	.3373
109	Grundy, IL	.3321	156	Orange, TX	.3375
110	Brantley, GA	.3322	157	Johnson, TN	.3376
111	Boone, KY	.3324	158	Carroll, MD	.3376
112	Lake, MN	.3325	159	Putnam, WV	.3376
113	Craig, VA	.3327	160	Madison, MT	.3377
114	Anne Arundel, MD	.3328	161	Piscataquis, ME	.3378
115	Platte, MO	.3329	162	McDowell, NC	.3378
116	Brooke, WV	.3330	163	Prince George, VA	.3379
117	Pickett, TN	.3332	164	Uintah, UT	.3379
118	Harford, MD	.3333	165	Lorain, OH	.3380
119	Cameron, PA	.3334	166	Mercer, ND	.3381
120	Warren, IA	.3335	167	Kearny, KS	.3381
121	Hancock, KY	.3337	168	Monroe, MI	.3384
122	Reagan, TX	.3340	169	Beaver, UT	.3385
123	Fayette, GA	.3342	170	Auglaize, OH	.3386
124	Campbell, SD	.3342	171	Preble, OH	.3387
125	Buffalo, SD	.3343	172	Putnam, OH	.3388
126	Juneau Borough, AK	.3345	173	Fulton, AR	.3388
127	Valley, ID	.3345	174	Lincoln, MT	.3389
128	Mineral, CO	.3345	175	McHenry, IL	.3389
129	Gloucester, NJ	.3348	176	Bonneville, ID	.3392
130	Juab, UT	.3348	177	Dawson, NE	.3392
131	Hyde, SD	.3350	178	Poquoson City, VA	.3392
132	St. Bernard, LA	.3350	179	Bucks, PA	.3393
133	Clearwater, ID	.3350	180	Middlesex, NJ	.3393
134	Morrow, OH	.3352	181	Echols, GA	.3394
135	Carbon, WY	.3353	182	Warren, VA	.3394
136	Waukesha, WI	.3354	183	Shiawassee, MI	.3395
137	Forest, WI	.3355	184	Teton, ID	.3396
138	Calvert, MD	.3355	185	Kane, UT	.3396
139	Carroll, OH	.3359	186	Montgomery, IN	.3397
140	Schuyler, NY	.3359	187	Middlesex, CT	.3397
141	Berkeley, SC	.3362	188	Washington, CO	.3401

TABLE 6.10   (*Continued*)

Rank	County	Gini	Rank	County	Gini
189	Union, FL	.3402	236	Tazewell, IL	.3433
190	Duchesne, UT	.3402	237	Meade, KS	.3434
191	Morris, NJ	.3403	238	Leavenworth, KS	.3434
192	Polk, TN	.3403	239	Grant, NE	.3435
193	Garfield, UT	.3403	240	Swain, NC	.3435
194	Jay, IN	.3404	241	Lapeer, MI	.3435
195	Johnson, IN	.3405	242	Moore, TX	.3436
196	Pecos, TX	.3406	243	Seneca, NY	.3437
197	Gilpin, CO	.3408	244	Morgan, IN	.3437
198	Crow Wing, MN	.3408	245	Greene, OH	.3438
199	Burlington, NJ	.3409	246	Newton, GA	.3438
200	Chesapeake City, VA	.3409	247	Bryan, GA	.3442
201	Minidoka, ID	.3409	248	Clear Creek, CO	.3442
202	Frederick, MD	.3409	249	Lander, NV	.3443
203	Waldo, ME	.3410	250	Jackson, MS	.3445
204	Franklin, PA	.3410	251	Powell, MT	.3445
205	Ste. Genevieve, MO	.3411	252	Defiance, OH	.3445
206	Potter, SD	.3411	253	Burke, ND	.3446
207	Catoosa, GA	.3412	254	Tuscola, MI	.3446
208	Newton, AR	.3412	255	Union, OH	.3447
209	Meade, SD	.3412	256	Hanson, SD	.3447
210	White, IN	.3414	257	Richland, MT	.3447
211	Hooker, NE	.3414	258	Baker, FL	.3448
212	Wyandot, OH	.3415	259	York, ME	.3448
213	Todd, SD	.3416	260	Mellette, SD	.3448
214	Menard, IL	.3417	261	Taliaferro, GA	.3450
215	Saline, AR	.3418	262	Champaign, OH	.3450
216	Calumet, WI	.3418	263	Douglas, CO	.3450
217	Saratoga, NY	.3420	264	Rockland, NY	.3452
218	Sherman, OR	.3420	265	Cobb, GA	.3452
219	Miami, IN	.3421	266	Union, SC	.3453
220	Fremont, ID	.3421	267	Ottowa, OH	.3454
221	Perry, OH	.3421	268	Williams, OH	.3454
222	Mineral, NV	.3421	269	Marquette, MI	.3454
223	Bon Homme, SD	.3422	270	Columbia, PA	.3455
224	Houston, GA	.3422	271	Adams, ND	.3457
225	Fayette, IN	.3422	272	Clark, IN	.3457
226	Livingston, NY	.3423	273	Stokes, NC	.3457
227	Collin, TX	.3423	274	Sandusky, OH	.3458
228	Sagadahoc, ME	.3425	275	Jones, SD	.3458
229	Cass, NE	.3427	276	Griggs, ND	.3458
230	Scott, MN	.3428	277	Winkler, TX	.3458
231	Wayne, NY	.3428	278	Wyoming, NY	.3459
232	Powder River, MT	.3430	279	Otero, NM	.3459
233	Fulton, OH	.3431	280	Chattooga, GA	.3460
234	Spencer, KY	.3431	281	Mora, NM	.3460
235	Oswego, NY	.3431	282	Cumberland, PA	.3461

TABLE 6.10   (*Continued*)

Rank	County	Gini	Rank	County	Gini
283	Cleburne, AL	.3461	292	Custer, SD	.3465
284	Ogle, IL	.3462	293	Carroll, IN	.3465
285	San Juan, UT	.3462	294	Jackson, IN	.3466
286	Beaver, PA	.3462	295	Renville, ND	.3467
287	Lancaster, SC	.3463	296	Amherst, VA	.3467
288	Grand, UT	.3463	297	Chisago, MN	.3468
289	Rockingham, NH	.3463	298	Fallon, MT	.3470
290	Sierra, NM	.3464	299	Clinton, IA	.3471
291	Randolph, NC	.3465	300	Lenawee, MI	.3471

Rounding out the ring of rosy affluence surrounding one of our country's worst ghettos are wealthy Montgomery (3rd), Charles (61st), and Prince George's (70th) counties in Maryland. In Virginia, these elite wealthy areas comprise Fairfax (4th), Arlington (20th), and Prince William (45th) counties together with the cities of Falls Church (9th), Fairfax (17th), Manassas (47th), and Alexandria (71st). Aside from the obvious conclusion that our federal government's bureaucrats and top military brass are nicely paid, the incredible inequality in metropolitan areas is again dramatized.

Many of the same variables associated with high absolute income are connected to relative income inequality as well. A profusion of studies exists that explores the existence of an inverted U-shape curve between development and inequality. Looking at U.S. states, for example, we have known for quite some time that relative income inequality goes up with percent nonwhite, the dominance of farming in a region, percent urban, greater participation of women in the labor force, living in the South, and percent elderly (over sixty-four years old). On the other hand, income inequality falls in states where employment and educational levels are high, where there are large proportions of workers employed in manufacturing, and where income is high.[48] There is copious evidence showing that even within metropolitan areas, higher income is related to lower relative income inequality.[49] We also are now aware that the larger the size of a metropolitan area, the greater will be its degree of relative income inequality.[50]

The staying power of the Kuznets curve is phenomenal. The correlation between development and reduced income inequality has also been found in U.S. Congressional districts and in a large sample of three hundred counties within twelve eastern states.[51] Table 6.11 lists all such variables found to be associated with relative income inequality by county groups. In the past all of these indicators have been strongly predictive of high Gini scores of U.S. states.[52]

The association of these indicators at the county level with relative income inequality continues to be strong. For example, relative income inequality rises with urbanization but falls with the proportion of counties in metropolitan locations (reflecting the suburbanization effect alluded to above). Education as measured by the percent completing high school is associated with lower income inequality, as is percent employed in manufacturing jobs and higher mean household income. Among the factors acting to increase relative household income inequality are the presence of blacks, percent of households headed by females, labor force participation by females (weak), and the percent of a county's population above retirement age.

All of these factors were regressed with household income Gini scores for U.S. counties to find out what weight each would have in predicting relative income inequality. Two "dummy variables" (in the trade idiom of social science) were added to account for the impact of region (0 = South, 1 = non/South) and being part of a Metropolitan Statistical Area (1 = MSA, 0 = non/MSA). To fully test whether the

TABLE 6.11   Mean Values of Selected Characteristics for U.S. Counties By Relative Income Inequality Group: 1980

	County Inequality Group		
Characteristics	High Inequality	Medium Inequality	Low Inequality
Percent Urban	41.1	35.2	33.7
Percent Black	15.1	7.5	4.2
Percent H.S. Graduates	54.9	59.6	63.3
Percent of Households Headed by Female	9.5	8.2	7.4
Percent Employed	93.7	92.9	93.2
Percent Employed in Manufacturing	17.3	21.2	23.7
Percent of Labor Force that is Female	40.5	40.2	39.3
Percent of Population on Rural Farms	8.4	9.9	9.4
Percent of Population over 64 Years	14.2	13.6	11.4
Percent of Counties in Metropolitan Areas	19.6	20.6	32.7
Mean Household Income	$16,711	$16,792	$18,197

development factor was also operating at the county level, both mean household income and mean household income squared for each county were also included as independent predictive variables. In this manner, we can tell whether a Kuznets curve actually does operate for U.S. counties. According to prior findings at larger geographic levels (U.S. states and Congressional Districts), there was a good possibility that development might lead to lower relative income inequality in the long run. The inverted U-shaped curve proposed by Kuznets would predict low inequality among low-income counties, followed by rising relative income inequality as incomes went up in counties. Finally, the process would supposedly end in counties rapidly becoming more equal as they reach the highest level of affluence. As with all prior research, development is measured in the regression formulas as mean income and mean income squared. Table A7 in the appendix contains the results of this analysis.

To begin with, the percent of a county's labor force holding jobs in manufacturing proves to be in a near tie with the presence of the elderly as the strongest predictor of household income inequality. The more manufacturing jobs, the more equal is the distribution of income. This major finding once again says a great deal for those concerned with the negative ramifications of deindustrialization on the American pocketbook. Not only do industrial jobs promote higher income, they reduce income inequality. The beneficial impact of this factor is hard to overestimate. Based upon these findings, we may fear for the survival of the once thriving middle-class American lifestyle. As these jobs disappear, real income goes down and relative income inequality soars.

The age factor is also highly significant. Counties with large proportions of those above retirement age have higher income inequality. *Counties that are already affluent also tend to be much more unequal than counties with lower income.* This directly flies in the face of the inverted-U curve. The Kuznets relationship is not present for all U.S. counties when taken together. There is no significant relationship with mean household income squared in predicting inequality. On the contrary, there is a sharp linear relationship in the opposite direction between affluence and lower inequality that is statistically significant. In short, within American counties, relative income inequality gets worse as household income goes up!

There is more to the story. Region showed a significant and fairly large influence in the expected direction upon relative inequality. All other things being the same, a county in the South is likely to have higher inequality than a county outside of the South. This is about what we would expect. Even if a development curve does not exist in the South, we know the effect of investment is uneven. Most experts agree that not

FIGURE 6.3: County Household Inequality (Bar Chart Shows Inequality in a Curve—It Goes Up, Then Down as Income Rises)

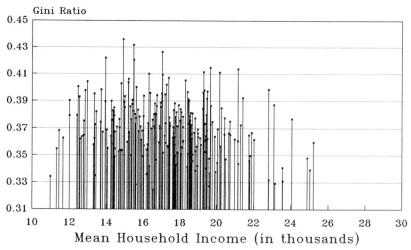

Source: Sample of 235 Non-South Counties: 1979 (five outliers removed)

all segments of a population will necessarily benefit from growth—at least in the beginning of business startups.

What is shocking, however, is that the development curve exists where it is not supposed to and is absent where it would be normally expected! It is not significant in the South. If it were to be, the direction of the relationship would be totally in the opposite direction predicted by Development theory. Yet the association is dominant in nonsouthern counties. In a more affluent region that has supposedly peaked in development and modernization, the Kuznets curve has by far the strongest effect upon inequality. Outside of the South inequality is small in low income counties, increases for middle-income counties, and plunges among high-income counties. A random sample of 240 nonsouthern counties yields a distinct inverted-U curve in the graph of this trend (figure 6.3).

The reasons for the absence of a development curve within the South and its dominance in the North cannot be fully explained by the data. In fact, variation of county income inequality is harder to predict than county income levels. While these variables explain only one-third of the change taking place for inequality, they explain 70 percent of the variation in the absolute income levels of counties. In short, there are still more important predictive variables which await discovery.

However, we can still make a few educated guesses. The very sharp regional differences already described may actually be preventing the curve from emerging in the South. In his original theory, Kuznets explicitly mentioned reactions to growth which lead to reduced inequality—such as successful unionization and political movements to advance the interests of the oppressed. In essence, collective action pursuing enlightened self-interest was supposed to arise after a certain awareness and experience threshold in the population was reached.

With tolerance for low wages and hostility toward unions in the South—even among those who stand to benefit the most—no mass pressure has evolved to engineer needed change. Cobb identifies historical, social, and structural forces operating in the South that have never existed in the North.[53] Among them are deep-seated conservatism and traditionalism that have worked to prevent this region from becoming a carbon copy of the North. The progress forecast for the South never took place as predicted. Many northern commentators assumed that liberalization and enlightenment were the natural offspring of industrialization. As industry relocated in the South and incomes went up, it was felt that the area would develop in a fairly similar manner to what took place in the North. Unions would come, and the greedy corporations would get their comeuppance. Liberal politicians would be elected. Support for a social infrastructure would swell. Racism would wilt away. Relative inequality would erode.

Perhaps all of this may still happen in the South, although Cobb warns us about the great strength of conservatism existing within the region. What also merits some thought, however, is the idea that the old regional core of the Northeast may yet be alive and kicking! John Agnew points out in his study of the United States in the world economy that parts of the old core such as New England have rebounded in the 1980s.[54] Ironically, some of this has to do with the rise of military spending. A portion of the resurgence is also due to heavy foreign investment plus a slower growth in wages than the national norm. High-technology industry with its associated research and development activities, however, remains concentrated in this region. Such capital-intensive industries pay high wages and demand the most skilled workers, so that the income floor has not suddenly dropped out from under this region. It is possible that the type of business formation and expansion outside of the South is exactly the kind which produces a development curve. It is no surprise, given the location of industries in the South dependent upon low wages *and low skills*, that "development" does not create more income equality. The type of business activity in the North, on the other hand, may still encourage a greater sharing of income where high-technology firms are most successful.

These conjectures need to be explored in later research. The point that must be emphasized here is that when development is looked at within U.S. counties, it does not work for the majority. At the state level, where there is an association between high income and low relative inequality, the large gaps between counties are hidden. There are frequently a few monolithic counties that can sway figures for an entire state, hiding many pockets of poverty in outlying areas that do not share the wealth that is so obvious in metropolitan areas. There is indeed a slight positive association between higher household income and lower income inequality for counties. Yet as with our illustration of storks and fertility, we have found that when other factors are looked at—the impact of rising income does not produce less relative inequality. In fact, the reverse happens!

For the large majority of U.S. counties, it is also true that even the spurious association of higher income/lower inequality is not very evident. For example, within southern counties the mean Gini ratio of household income is .391 for the poorest 25 percent of counties and .389 for the middle-income counties. Outside the South, the comparable Gini ratios are .376 and .374 for these income groups. In other words, over three-fourths of U.S. counties show almost no change in inequality as income goes up. This group includes over 87 million people, for whom virtually no relative improvement is shown despite rising household income. These are the people of America's economic periphery, consigned to a stagnant swamp of zero relative growth.

There are also within the United States huge numbers of people that suffer from an income inequality ratio that resembles that of the Third World. India is a good example of this, with a Gini ratio of .4022 for household income. In the United States, a Gini ratio of this size or larger is found in 524 counties, which include 41 million people. We are not used to thinking of ourselves as being in the same league as Asia. Yet with respect to relative income inequality this is certainly true for large numbers of our population. Populous counties within this category include many of those already identified: New York, Westchester, Essex (NJ), Fairfield (CT) in the Northeast; Fulton (Atlanta), Orleans (LA), Shelby (Memphis), Dallas, and Dade, Palm Beach, and Broward (all of Florida) in the South; Denver, Santa Cruz, Fresno, Santa Barbara, San Francisco, and Los Angeles in the West.

The good news, of course, is that America is still a wealthy nation. Relative income inequality here does not have nearly the life-and-death repercussions that it most certainly has in the Third World. Since we start at such a high level of income, most of our poor are much better off than in many other countries of the world. Also, there is room for optimism in the ongoing growth of real income and lessened inequality going on within the South. The time for this region of the country to become an economic equal to the rest of the country is long past due. No one can fault the South for its effort and its partial success as it has tried to engineer its own economic growth. It has even been argued by many critics that were it not for the low wage structure, conservative climate, and hostility toward unions in the South, even more American manufacturing jobs would have been lost to foreign lands.

Yet the South remains vulnerable because of its success! The attraction of this region has been its low wages and anti-unionism. In this era of the global factory, it is getting beaten at its own game of offering the most for the least by desperately poor Third World nations. Thus, the South can no longer compete for industry and is in great danger of losing the marginal factories it does have. Deindustrialization is an even greater threat to the South than it is in the North. We have already seen that a peripheral industrial belt exists in some of the poorest counties within the South, made up of industries at the very end of their product-cycle. And without needed internal resources—such as a well-educated, skilled labor force—it can never hope to gain high-technology firms like those which flourish in the North. In other words, in the smorgasbord of inducements for factory relocation it can offer only a K-Mart line to many corporations that must shop at Saks. It is also true that although progress and growth is obvious in the region—it has left large segments of the underprivileged wholly untouched. Its rural population, and especially blacks, have been forced to continue to do without.

In the final analysis, the low-wage southern strategy may fail. In a way, it is the same as buying a cheap, low-quality car instead of a more expensive one of higher quality. At the start, both may seem to work equally well. Yet over the long run, it may cost more to buy a "cheaper" product than a better one that costs more. Continued durability and long-range reliable performance will in the end yield more in an investment, even if the initial cost is greater. Many decisions by American business firms lend support to this view:

> The belief that investors will seek out pockets of cheap labour in poor regions is not quite consistent with the actual practice of plant location in contemporary America. The South has certainly attracted new industry seeking to economize on labour costs. But the region has not gained much in modern industries such as electronics—high wage, capital-intensive activities—that could make important contributions towards improving the South's income levels, despite the fact that parts of the South appear at first sight to be highly favourable for electronics manufacturing. . . . This is partly

because what matters the most to a modern industrial corporation may be linkages with other related firms, suppliers of components and sources of scientific or technological development which tend to point to a northern or west-coast location. It is also because leading U.S. companies are going multi-*national* rather than multi-regional, locating more investment and employment abroad (e.g. in Europe) than in Appalachia or the deep South. The United States is part of a worldwide economic system.[55]

A common trait has been shown to be repeatedly linked to the trends toward a loss of income and an upswing of inequality. This condition operates alongside of the importance of regional differences, and is crucial to both North and South. The presence of manufacturing jobs remains a crucial part of our economic well-being. This is true whether we are speaking for the U.S. as a whole or for forces operating within each of its regions. The findings consistently emphasize the very great impact that manufacturing has in raising income levels within counties. Median family income levels are highest in locales where manufacturing jobs are abundant. Relative income inequality is strongly predicted by manufacturing employment as well. Where industrial employment exists, income tends to be high and more equally shared.

Within the context of the world economy, the persistence of this finding is shattering. The prognosis for the United States must remain grim if our deindustrialization continues. For every job that is lost in manufacturing to foreign shores or that fails to develop because of investment in new plants abroad, our income shrinks. What little remains is divided in an even more unfair manner than before. We are told that having other countries do the "dirty work" of actually producing things in factories is beneficial to us. It reduces pollution and the drain of resources within our own country while removing boring, strenuous, and/or dangerous jobs. Yet this is more bald assertion than proven, absolute fact. All of the evidence indicates that manufacturing jobs are very desirable. They pay more than the service jobs that are replacing them. Manufacturing employment promotes relative income equality as well. Industrialization is closely connected with a strong middle class and the absence of extreme income inequality. With its disappearance, we may expect many of the social ills to develop that are so typical of impoverished Third World countries. At that point, it will truly be a time of "mourning in America."

We need not be a helpless victim. America is not inexorably doomed to second-rate status. Our income level may not have to fall endlessly into a bottomless pit. We do not necessarily have to become the prey of an all-powerful world economy that destroys jobs, uproots communities, and impoverishes nations. There are a number of strategies that we can pursue as a country, or even as single individuals acting alone, to prevent further income erosion and the spread of inequality. The remaining chapter will consider ways to overcome what perhaps too many of us may see as dark forces beyond our control.

7

DEALING FROM THE TOP OF THE DECK: SOME ALTERNATIVES AND STRATEGIES FOR NEEDED CHANGE

It is plain that huge income inequality persists throughout the world as well as in the United States. At the global level we have seen the gap of real and relative income between nations increase since the end of World War II. This has occurred despite decades of development, international programs promoting growth, massive private investment, and countless plant startups by core multinational corporations in the Third World. While LDCs were promised that the influx of firms from industrial countries would help their economies and enrich their populations, conditions grew worse. Basic human needs were sacrificed. Scarce resources were squandered to attract foreign industries with giveaway tax programs, a costly buildup of infrastructure, and questionable export expansion policies. Authoritarian Third World governments forced a continuation of low wages to keep foreign funds coming in. Promised benefits to workers failed to develop; rather, severe economic decline, depression, suffering, and hunger have worsened during the 1980s in most countries of the periphery. To pay off the mountain of debt which was first urged upon less developed countries (LDCs) by core banks, austerity is now demanded by these very lending institutions. In poor countries of the Third World, this means that already severely deprived people must make do with even less. Income inequality has become worse—the rich are richer, and the poor are poorer!

None of this great transfer of wealth going on from the Third World to wealthy industrial countries has been of benefit to the workers and average citizens of the United States. Within our country real income has declined since 1973, while relative income inequality is now greater than at any time within the past forty years. As the social safety net has been shredded in America, the ranks of the poor have swelled. Homelessness is rampant. A once healthy middle class has become increasingly squeezed to the point where more and more families have descended into

253

the lower class. Baby-boom children now in the workforce have suffered the most dramatic deterioration, with much lower real wages. As a result, they are increasingly locked out of the American Dream—a home of their own. At the same time, the ranks of millionaires and overpaid chief executive officers (CEOs) of major U.S. corporations have swelled. While the firms they head up are increasingly unable to compete in the world market place, they have continued to rain pay increases and opulent stock options upon themselves. In the end, a small minority of Americans has flourished and thrived because of Reaganomic policies and the emergence of the world economy. They are the nation's economic giants who continue to garner huge profits from bloated, nonproductive defense spending. They are the stockholders who have reaped huge dividends from a policy of plant relocation in the periphery—in the South and in Third World lands. America's factories have been gutted of any hope of raising productivity because of shutdowns and refusal of management to retool. High-paying manufacturing jobs have virtually disappeared. The United States has become the victim of deindustrialization.

Only rarely has any widely publicized recognition been given to these harsh facts of life. When the problem is discussed, the tendency is to blame the victim. Americans are accused of being addicted to imports, of being spend-thrift and careless about going into debt, of being lazy and unproductive, of expecting unrealistically high salaries, of not saving enough, of wanting too much. Although there may be some truth to these assertions, the culpability of U.S. multinational business firms and large-scale political policies are conveniently forgotten. There is almost never any connection made by analysts between the emerging world economy, the flight of investment capital from the United States to LDCs, and the slide of income at home. In the never-ending chase for higher profits, wages are relentlessly squeezed. This led to plant relocations where a docile workforce was willing to work for next to nothing. Although the most obvious results could be seen in Third World countries, wages have been steadily pushed down within the United States. More and more women, poor rural farmers, blacks, illegal migrants, and other easily exploited groups are being swept into the domestic labor force. Jobs are often in low-level service work at subsistence pay. Through various antilabor strategies, employers have successfully attacked higher wages by employing part-time workers, relocating to the South, ignoring Green Card restrictions, and the like. There has emerged within America a "peripheralization" of our own labor force.[1] We are poorer because of it.

Not all change has been for the worse. The silver lining has been a consistent increase in the real income of women. Although the median family income of blacks has sunk in the past ten years, a sizable upper-middle class of well-educated minorities now exists in our nation. While the plight of the underclass in urban America is now more urgent, the division between the haves and have-nots in our society is today less purely racial that it has been in the past. If anything, white males have taken the brunt of the loss in real income, especially in the industrial heartland of the Midwest. The South has made steady progress in its uphill climb of real income, while its relative inequality has shrunk in comparison to the rest of the nation. The bedrock of the South's economy is still tenuous because of the low-end industry migrating to the region. Such firms demand low wages. Yet the bottom line has still produced economic growth in the short run.

These shifts have worked to obscure the general, long-term, overall ebbing of income within the United States. Although certain segments and a few regions of our society have financially benefited in the past decade or two, the trend over the last fifteen years has been downward for the average American. Moreover, because of changes in the global economy toward greater efficiency, higher productivity, cut-throat competitiveness, and the flight of U.S. investment capital abroad, the future looks bleak. There does not seem to be any meaningful activity, planning, or policy-making on the domestic front that assures us that the income crisis is being addressed. Instead, the theme appears to be "business as usual." Nonproductive mergers and leveraged buyouts lead to mega-corporations with enormous debt. Such organizations are not suitably positioned to compete effectively in the world market. We have robbed Peter to pay Paul in order to finance this casino-like, runaway expansion. Funds which normally would have gone into R & D and product development have been pointlessly sacrificed to the god of growth. This, together with an overreliance upon military technology, means that the United States has less and less to offer to consumers in the world market place. What we do sell tends to be shoddy and overpriced, a result of U.S. policies that rely on heavy international borrowing, cutbacks in retooling, high interest rates, and trade deficits. America's share of world markets in one industry after another has dropped like a rock.

The implications of income deterioration are ominous. Yet our national economy seems capable only of spawning low-paying jobs in service industries. America continues to undergo explosive growth in violence, drug abuse, crime, illiteracy, and lowered educational attainment. The ghettos now bristle with the latest in sophisticated, automatic weaponry. Nutrition has deteriorated rapidly in parts of the country, while large numbers of people are excluded from minimal health care. The poor, derelicts, bag ladies, assorted petty criminals, and numerous deinstitutionalized, mentally handicapped persons wander our streets without shelter or help. Can there be any doubt about the need to worry? Can we persist in fooling ourselves that all is well in America? Are we really better off than "less developed" countries, which, although perhaps poorer on a per capita basis, at least provide minimal care for their needy?

There is room for anger here as well. We can only hope the awesome growth of the "me-first" attitude and the politics of greed will finally abate in the 1990s. It is unlikely to occur, however, all by itself. Stereotyped notions about the poor need to be challenged. The idea that persons are poor because they are lazy or incompetent or unfit needs to be questioned. Prejudicial notions—for example, that the homeless are out on the streets because they want to be—deserve to be held up to ridicule.

There is a temptation to yield to despair after looking at countless statistics that seem to point to disaster. Global developments and shifts in world markets appear to be far beyond our control. A danger of overexposure to macroeconomic explanations (which may have happened in this book) is to feel overwhelmed: we may believe that we must remain the victims of such all-powerful forces. Since these omnipotent influences are beyond our control, why try to change things? The major actors on the world and national economic stage are, indeed, large and monolithic. Core governments, major corporations, bank consortiums, OPEC, the IMF, and World Bank, to name a few, have all occupied the spotlight at one time or another. If lone individuals seem to make a difference, they are of the stature of the U.S. president, Federal Reserve chairman, CEO of General Motors, and the like. Average citizens seem to be completely out of the picture.

But conditions can change. The situation is not hopeless. First of all, it is important to remember that no trend will go on forever. This thought can help us to at least open the door to positive change. There are also a number of different actions we can take on the individual level that can make a difference. It is possible to prevent the further erosion of real income and the growth of income inequality by supporting a number of different strategies. To simplify the explanation of different goals to pursue in an effort to reduce inequality, I have artificially divided up suggestions for action into global, national, and personal. In reality, all three dimensions interact.

For example, a trendy catch word that became popular as the world market emerged with such clarity in the last decade is "political economy." Myriad articles and books have been published in the past decade with "political economy" as part of their titles. The idea of political economy is that a nation's economy is intimately connected to political forces—and vice versa. A pure market explanation does not recognize the importance and power of government as it affects how the economy works. At best, according to laissez faire arguments, governments should stay out of the business of business. The fact that political leaders do not is widely recognized in most industrial countries today.

In the United States there is no formal recognition of the role of government in the economy, but de facto federal influence on our incomes is very powerful. For example, the 1982 recession was engineered by the painful increase of interest rates. The United States is different from its industrial country brethren, however, in having no overt industrial policy. While this is true, what happens in the economy and even within gigantic multinational firms can be affected by the federal government. We are still a democracy, and as citizens we still have reasonably open access to political influence. Although alone we lack the political influence of Political Action Committees (PACS), many of which continue to be sponsored by corporations, we have a collective force through our votes. Therein lies a major avenue to curbing the damaging extremes of American capitalism. This can be one important strategy in the fight to prevent further income erosion in America while protecting the poor from even more injury. Before getting to specifics, however, a short review of some needed changes at the global level would be helpful.

Global Strategies

The brutal draining of capital from the periphery to core nations must cease if millions of people are to survive. It is utopian to expect multinationals to sell their plants to host countries as long as they yield such spectacular profits. Yet it is still possible to help these countries to keep their heads above water by adopting certain domestic policies. The higher the interest rate in the United States, the more capital flees from LDCs into the United States. We are one of only a few countries (Switzerland, Great Britain) that supply a tax haven for the wealthy elites in more unstable lands. Investments by nonresidents are almost completely free from IRS levies. As a result, fully half of the money lent the largest debtor nations in the 1970s and 1980s flowed right back into American banks and investment houses.[2] Over the same period, interest and management fees paid on these loans were even larger than the capital flight. Because of the run-up in floating interest rates during the 1980s, LDCs were hit with debt obligations they simply could not pay. The profit from these loans has been 50 percent or more per year for the lending institutions. Yet austerity was demanded of Third World countries so they could fork over even more money! According to the *Washington Post,* if interest above ordinary profit rates is treated as a return of principal, U.S. banks have been more than fully paid back.[3] If the U.S. government pursues a tight money policy, interest rates will leap while causing poor nations to be ravaged even more.

Debt forgiveness or in-kind debt reduction for Third World countries should be supported. For the most part, debt has produced a bad recession in Latin America and Africa. The resulting economic decline and austerity have led these nations to cut back on imports, which affected U.S. exports. Healthy economic growth among LDCs is to the advantage of the United States, since they make up many of our best customers. The 1985 Baker Plan, which included incentives to induce private banks to continue lending, has not worked well. Debt remains a serious drain on the world economy. Nicholas Brady, current treasury secretary, is now supporting partial loan forgiveness for nations willing to negotiate individualized concessions. Mexico has entered into a new agreement with the United States partially based upon a new deal, although for now the reduction appears too small to fix Mexico's badly damaged economy. Mexico is also giving up some questionable powers over American multinationals within its borders. In short, any forgiveness may be too little and too late.

The ray of hope is that core countries are beginning a dialogue with the Third World about how to yank them out of their financial quicksand. One strategy that is urgently needed is a debt-for-nature swap. In such agreements, lending institutions via the World Bank and IMF forgive some of the debt if the borrowing country agrees to introduce a particular environmental program. This has involved conservancy of land for national parks and wildlife protection in Bolivia, Ecuador, and the Phillipines. The latest agreement, reached with Costa Rica, is rich with promise and possibilities. This Central American country has swapped $50 million worth of its debt in return for expanding and strengthening its national park system—which already covers 12 percent of its territory.[4] A heritage of bilateral help is growing around these swaps, which greatly increases their impact. Holland bought $33 million in Costa Rican conservation debt bonds to finance reforestation, while Sweden has lent $25 million to complete a dry tropical forest park. Although less than 1 percent of total Third World debt falls under these agreements, their potential is truly exciting.

The best-known effort of this kind, which has yet to bear fruit, involves pressuring Brazil to stop "developing" the Amazon region. The damage to this region has been incalculable as precious rain forests were bull-dozed or burned in the last decade. Such deforestation is often accompanied by the introduction of agriculture. Yet the farms quickly fail because their soil is leached of crop nutrients by torrential tropical rains.

The burn-off of trees or their rotting after being cut releases large amounts of carbon dioxide into the global atmosphere. This, in turn, pushes up the Green House effect one more notch as the world's temperature soars ever higher.[5] Trees are also a major factory for the production of oxygen. Their loss actually removes the air that we breathe. Soil erosion and floods result. Deforestation causes mass extinction of unknown plant, insect, and animal species. Such irretrievably destroyed species could prove beneficial in the manufacture of drugs and chemicals in the future if they were permitted to survive.[6]

The poisoning of our world environment is now unmistakable. Acid rain produced from industrial plants in the United States and elsewhere has mixed with nuclear fallout from accidents such as Chernobyl. The industrial leakage of Union Carbide's Bhopal plant killed and injured thousands in India. The crude oil spill from Exxon's tanker in the straits of Valdez destroyed fish, fowl, and countless miles of pristine shoreline in Alaska. The heavy use of freon has largely contributed to the rapid breakdown of the earth's ozone layer, which promises illhealth, air pollution, and skin cancer in the near future. Debate swirls around whether America's severe drought of 1988 was caused in part by the growing effect of global warming brought on by record air pollution. In that summer of searing high temperatures, swimmers seeking relief from the heat at the beach in New Jersey were treated to AIDs-infected syringes and other hospital waste washing up on shore. Someone had used the ocean as a dumping ground once again!

Since many debts cannot possibly be paid back by LDCs that are essentially bankrupt, debt-for-nature swaps seem like a good deal. (Most of the money was paid back long ago anyway because of exorbitantly high interest rates.) There is some reason to hope that the severe damage inflicted upon Mother Earth by such environmental degradation can be partially healed through these swaps. A promising start has come from the World Bank, which has promised to look at potential environmental damage that could result from any future development loans.[7] Since 1986, Congress has directed U.S. executive directors of multilateral development banks to aim toward four major goals[8]:

1. increasing environmental staffing;
2. involving environment and health officials in development projects;
3. including local nongovernmental and community organizations in planning;
4. giving greater priority to loans with beneficial environmental impacts.

Despite such efforts, there is often fierce resistance from bankers—who fail to recognize the legitimacy of including the costs of negative environmental impact in calculating the bottom line to their loans. Borrowing countries can also be adamant in refusing such swaps. Jose Sarney, as president of Brazil, was shrill in his criticism of the United States' effort to halt the destruction of the Amazon rain forests.[9] According to Sarney, Brazil's patrimony must never be a subject of negotiation with any foreign power. Sarney labels pressures such as these coming from core countries as "ecological imperialism." Thus, issues of nationalism can interfere with negotiations to stop or reduce harmful effects to the environment.

Like the core nations, many countries of the periphery spend too much on the military. Since the end of World War II, the nations of the world have spent about $16 trillion on military activities and materials. In 1986 alone the sum was $825 billion.[10] Since 1960, industrial countries have doubled their outlays in constant dollars, while the Third World has increased its military budget six-fold. Less developed countries cannot afford to spend large amounts on defense, since it stops them from meeting the basic needs of their citizens. For example, the price of one Trident submarine ($1.4 billion) would cover the costs of a worldwide five-year child immunization program that would save a million lives per year.[11] The military buying spree by LDCs has contributed a hefty portion to their total debt. The amount spent on defense between 1977 to 1982 was equal to the Third World debt in 1982, at the onset of the debt crisis. Had these nations not increased their spending for military items from levels existing in the 1960s, they would have been able to pay back two-thirds of all current loans.

LDCs have voluntarily entered the arms race. Yet core countries have also encouraged them to buy esoteric weapons. Such hardware is offered for sale only by the advanced industrial countries. The arms trade is a big business with tremendous built-in profits. Core governments subsidize their own heavy military development costs by selling outmoded equipment to Third World countries. Even so, Third World countries have been able to acquire some of the most sophisticated and deadly weaponry. Although nonproliferation agreements exist between the major powers, they have been helpless to prevent the spread of the latest models in death technology.[12]

The United States has paid for "low-intensity conflict" by such groups as the Contras in Nicaragua or El Salvador's murderous right-wing military junta. Thus, a "need" is generated for even more arms within a variety of periphery nations. Money can be saved over the long run by promoting peace, working to keep conflicts from erupting, helping to settle regional tensions, and the like. The United States should work toward persuading industrial nations to declare an embargo on arms sales to LDCs. A willingness to use UN peace-keeping forces to settle disputes would also save money and reduce the mountain of debt owed by these countries. Costa Rica, one of the most democratic and affluent nations in Central America, completely disbanded its army in the 1950s. They have had no reason to regret the decision since then. Global policies pursued by the major powers and Third World countries to reduce military spending could go a long way to solving the insolvency problems of most LDCs.

Studies by the International Labour Organization (ILO) in Geneva identify a number of strategies that less-well-off nations could follow in reducing the severity of their income inequality.[13] For developing countries, the use of direct taxation on a sliding scale (increasing the size of the tax bites taken from higher incomes) has been effective in keeping inequality lower. The use of tax exemptions to promote development, on the other hand, did not work well, since so much of LDC industry is under monopolies. The ILO also supports a tax on wealth of the richest 2 percent; this wealth is generally held in the form of land and property. Reduced duties on everyday items (food, clothing) plus increased duties on luxury items (gasoline, automobiles) are also recommended. Finally, *increasing public spending to provide free education and health care* (exactly the opposite of IMF austerity mandates) is associated with a large-scale drop in income inequality.

The payoff is substantial for those poor nations who are willing to invest in their own citizens. The International Labour Office is especially clear with regard to subsidies, which can work well if they are targeted toward a low income clientele (small farmers), but tend to fail miserably if they benefit only wealthy industries. A loan subsidy for an agribusiness export firm to pay for an advanced irrigation system will not benefit large numbers within a poor nation. Greater and more equitable changes can come by aiming assistance programs at small landowners and farmers.[14] Finally, the ILO suggests that core lending institutions continue to attach conditions to their loans (as they do now) which would encourage needed LDC changes. By insisting upon progressive direct taxation and higher budgets for social programs (education, health, housing, welfare, agricultural development, etc.), this organization calculates that income inequality could be sliced by 17 percent to 20 percent in most poor nations.

Land reform can be a potent weapon against brimming income inequality. Great progress was made in Taiwan in large part because of changes in the distribution of agricultural land. Reforms included compulsory breakups of large plots and prosecution of landlords who abused their tenant farmers. As a result, the Gini ratio of household income plummeted 41 percent in only eleven years—going from .558 in 1953 to .328 in 1964.[15] Taiwan today is one of the most prosperous countries in the world. Other nations in need of such basic change might be persuaded to embark on redistribution programs as a condition of further development loans. Very sharp inequality in land holdings has been a continuing problem in Latin America. Since most of these countries are so cash dependent upon the United States, IMF, World Bank, and other core lending consortiums, they are also vulnerable to persuasion in an effort to initiate these needed reforms. Debt swaps for such programs may also be part of the answer.

Although some Third World countries are willing to begin reform—realizing it is a major step toward full modernization—the presence of multinational agribusiness firms can sabotage such efforts. In the Phillipines, a genuine effort at land redistribution was sidetracked through compromise and loopholes. Today, about one-third of arable land is planted in export crops, while nutrition levels for Filipinos are appallingly low. Anywhere from 40 percent to 70 percent of peasants are tenant farmers who own no land, but who must pay as much as 75 percent of their harvest to landlords for rent.[16] To begin with, lands owned by multinational agribusiness firms are essentially exempt from the watered-down law. The law permits leasing redistributed land to multinationals, which effectively creates a tenant, laboring class of farm workers. The risks of crop failure are foisted upon the peasants in this manner. Since peasants who receive land also lack access to the credit, technical assistance, and markets that multinationals have, exploitive contracts with them are assured. Del Monte and other gargantuan agribusiness firms are beginning to replace the native landlords of yesterday, although the feudal regime remains intact.

These developments once again underline the need to remain vigilant as reform efforts are mounted. What may appear to be progress can actually be subverted along the way. Yet the success stories of land reform in nations such as Taiwan and South Korea show that such efforts bear fruit. Where it has been effectively used, redistribution of land reduces inequality and pushes up income.

As mentioned in a previous chapter, new money is flowing from Japan to world development. Although Japan will benefit from this assistance, as America did from the Marshall Plan following World War II, LDCs may see some progress as well. Much depends upon what types of projects are funded and whose interests in Third World countries are served. If Japan and the newly industrialized countries elsewhere in Asia are going to put down their hard-earned cash for world development, they will demand and get a much greater say in how it is spent. These agencies will be less and less of an American province in the future.

(None of the strategies put forth by the United States have worked in the past seven years to stem the debt crisis. Any change in the offing from within the World Bank/IMF under a new order promises to be beneficial.)

Finally, less-developed countries can help themselves without looking toward industrial nations for aid. One of the most promising initiatives is south-to-south economic cooperation between LDCs. Walden Bello points out that such regional cooperative schemes can be built on the natural advantages existing in these nations (such as raw materials), with hubs radiating from successfully dynamic industrial centers.[17] He believes Brazil and India in particular are likely candidates for this role, since they have industrial depth, technological expertise, and an untapped reservoir of huge internal markets. Although we are not used to thinking of LDCs as economic power houses, Brazil and India are the ninth and tenth largest noncommunist economies in the world (ahead of Australia, Sweden, and other European countries). Bello points out that in only a decade Brazil has developed a sophisticated computer industry that he expects will go into export hyperdrive in the future. India is now a leader in the export of power-generation equipment, steel mills, and machine tools. The growth of its computer software industry, now at $70 million a year, is at a stupendous 45 percent rate of increase.

Such cooperative economic schemes will not be easy to build, but they are a possibility. We are now seeing a once-divided Europe form a new, united, and formidable European Economic Community that is scheduled to come online by 1992. The reality of this economic region will greatly affect the global marketplace. There is nothing to suggest that LDCs are incapable of arriving at negotiated settlements in a similar manner. Yet a major push toward making such pacts a reality is the result of the misguided policies of industrial nations. Northern countries in the core have continually failed to address issues of central concern to LDCs.

It thus should come as no surprise if we see more movement in this direction in the future. Poor nations are capable of being feisty and independent and should be applauded for being so when it is in their best interests. Certainly the success of the Contradora Peace Plan, agreed upon by all Central American countries despite the persistent opposition of the United States, is a case in point. Nations in this region believed it was in their best interest to negotiate an end to the Nicaragua/Contra armed conflict, irrespective of the wishes of the United States. It is possible that the Third World can repeat such initiatives elsewhere if they can see themselves reaping financial dividends. The presidents of Peru, Columbia, Ecuador, and Venezuela have just announced a major new effort to create a regional economic market among their countries.[18] In the document signed at the end of their summit meeting, the presidents

declared that their four national economies must be integrated in order
to develop. They have called for moves to lower and remove trade barriers between the countries. To do so, they have pledged to work on
reducing bureaucratic red tape, opposition from private business groups,
and political wavering within their countries.

Although World Systems theory goes a long way toward explaining income inequality throughout the world, it tends to present a picture
of periphery nations as permanently locked into a system of perpetual
subservience and dependency with dominant, all-powerful core countries. The "permanency" dimension of this view is open to question.
Change is difficult, especially for countries with few resources, but examples abound of nations that have been able to help themselves—
China, Japan, Taiwan, South Korea, etc. Almost always as a prelude to
their successful increase of real income, however, has been a restructuring
of existing inequality. In the end, nations cannot hope to improve their
position in the world system and successfully compete in a global marketplace without first taking care of business at home. This means caring
for their citizens. It requires meeting their basic needs: far-reaching
health programs; decent education; enough food to ensure a healthy
working population; and the like. If countries are willing to tackle domestic inequality, they will reap economic, cultural, and political dividends in the future.

Domestic Policies

Before outlining what needs to be done in the United States to preserve
our way of life, it is crucial to point out *what we should not do*. Disaster
will result if economic policies similar to those followed in the 1980s are
continued. Our nation can no longer afford business as usual—robbing
the poor to pay the rich. The decline of real income and growth of relative income inequality must be stopped if we are to prevent permanent
damage to our economy.

Nearly everyone believes that changes have to be made, regardless
of his or her political persuasion. Conservatives, however, continue to
blame the victim. Americans are accused of being fat and lazy, of having
grandiose wage expectations, of being unproductive, of spending too
much (especially on imports), and of not saving enough. What we need,
according to some critics, is to get "lean and mean" so we can compete
effectively in the global economy. We need *austerity*! Does this sound familiar?

Advocates of a new austerity for the American public have now set
their sights on middle-class entitlements such as Social Security, since
they have run out of ways to cut welfare and transfer programs. The

fashionable targets of conservative economists are now the allegedly "bloated budgets" connected with Civil Service retirement, farm subsidies, Social Security, and Medicare. The huge runup in defense spending over the past eight years has been conveniently forgotten. Jeff Faux, in a strong critique of the call for austerity at home, points out that the total government outlay for entitlement programs actually dropped from 45.2 percent to 44.1 percent in the 1980–87 period, while military spending rose from 21.6 percent to 27.1 percent.[19] Suggestions have ranged from reducing cost-of-living (COLA) adjustments lower than the inflation rate to raising the age of retirement. The savings from the budget could be used to spur domestic investment. This is akin to the "trickle down" effect that was supposed to have occurred when taxes for the wealthy were slashed. Faux points out, however, that almost 60 percent of the elderly now survive on less than $10,000 a year—most of which comes from Social Security. There is the added benefit of a rapid buildup in the Social Security fund because of the recent overhaul of the system. The intent was to amass money quickly to pay for the retirement of rapidly aging baby boomers. The plan has worked well, yet the money set aside for retirement for those who are also currently paying the added tax is being circled by financial vultures. This represents one area that can be used for future investment. However, even now the "surplus" funds are being used to buy U.S. Treasury notes to subsidize the federal deficit.

It is true that as a nation we are not thrifty; we spend more of our money than we save in comparison to other countries. If we as a nation could save more, money would be available for investment to once again build up our factories and manufacturing base. But Faux points out that the tendency for Americans to go into debt has been forced upon them by the slide in their real income over the past decade and a half. Increases in saving follow an increase in real income, not vice-versa. Although saving by individuals in the United States has fallen, business savings and profits have soared during the 1980s. To this extent, Reaganomics worked. *Yet the corporations chose not to invest in America,* but went to foreign countries to build their new factories. Huge chunks of money were also squandered on ever larger CEO salaries and debt-pyramids to pay for unproductive mergers. Despite all the lucrative business incentives, corporate fixed investment was only 2.4 percent annually under Reagan compared to 6.9 percent under Carter. Faux states that the income transfer from the bottom 90 percent of Americans to the top 10 percent amounted to $129 billion from 1977 to 1988. And the money was frittered away.

Thus, a hands-off policy to promote business expansion will not produce growth. Nor will any policy that forces the American public to save. While some of our debt may have been frivolous, most of it has been forced. We simply do not have extra money to save, even if we are punished through austerity measures in an attempt to force us into doing so. Austerity may, in fact, provoke an unstoppable recession that could swerve into a full-fledged depression. Policies are needed that will put more money into the pockets of average citizens, who will then either save it or stimulate business expansion as they spend it. The record of America's corporate elite in this regard has certainly been poor. The money lavished on corporations during the 1980s has gone up in smoke, while promises of business expansion have not been kept.

This experience should prompt us to oppose the plan of the Bush administration to cut the capital gains tax. The idea behind a cut in the capital gains tax is to "encourage" business to invest in our domestic industries. (This concept is like the idea of cutting taxes for higher income people so they will create more jobs and industries through greater investment.) Without a mechanism for accountability, however, this would be another in a long line of handouts to the very wealthy in our society; it would be equivalent to giving extra recess time to F-students while forcing A-students to stay after school. Why continue to support an idea that has failed so miserably? Why must such a bankrupt notion be allowed to continue? Why should we as a nation allow even more poverty to develop?

Most Americans are unaware of what would take place with a capital gains tax cut. They also continue to be ignorant about who actually benefited from the tax "reforms" that took place in the past decade. The tax cuts passed by the Reagan administration figure heavily in today's federal deficit. One estimate puts the drop in federal revenues at $1.8 trillion over the 1982–90 period.[20] The reality is that the rollback in taxes has damaged the economy. No buildup in infrastructure followed. Instead, our nation went on a military buying spree. Even with a trim in military spending, taxes will have to be increased to stem the tide of red ink.

The 1986 tax cuts were devastating to the poor. A recent Congressional Budget Office (CBO) study shows that the poorest 10 percent of our population will have paid 20 percent more in taxes during 1988 than a decade earlier.[21] The CBO study includes the rise in gasoline, alcohol, and tobacco taxes along with the real rise in state income taxes caused by the cuts in federal social expenditures. The "reforms" have all but destroyed any progressive rates in the tax structure, paring them to only 15 percent and 28 percent. By 1984 the effective corporate tax rate (8.5 percent) was nearly half of what it was a decade earlier (15 percent), while fifty of the top Fortune 500 firms paid no corporate taxes whatsoever. What this all adds up to for the richest 10 percent of America's population is a 16 percent decline in their effective tax burden between 1966 to 1985.[22] Despite the hoopla surrounding the revised 1986 legislation, the new laws are revenue neutral. This means that no new tax money came out of all the change. The Reagan administration tax-cut policies in effect today favor the low-wage service sector over the high-wage manufacturing sector.[23] Given the problems of U.S. heavy industries, these policies are questionable.

Such is the backdrop against which we evaluate the call for a further rollback in the capital gains tax. This is being sold as a means to get the United States back on the productivity track—the revenue saved will be reinvested in new plants and updated technology. The litany is familiar, and the results will be as well. Tax savings failed to be used to buy new plants and equipment in the 1980s. Why should we expect anything different in the 1990s? Under the plan being supported by wealthy interests, the maximum capital gains tax would be 15 percent—down from 34 percent today. Tax expert Joseph Pechman argues that no investment benefit would grow out of such a cut, but that it would be a bonanza for the rich. From his estimates, this would slash $125,000 from the taxes owed for those with incomes of $1 million or more per year.[24] An analysis by the Congressional Joint Committee on Taxation found that 80 percent of the tax benefit of this cut would go to persons who earn over $100,000 per year.[25]

At the top of any agenda to get America back on its economic feet once again should be hefty cuts in the defense budget. Huge military budgets year after year have been largely responsible for the sharp American decline in productivity. It is becoming very apparent as the century draws to a close that a nation's strength can no longer be measured by military hardware and stockpiled arms. It is countries with flourishing export markets—healthy industries manufacturing high-quality products that people want to buy and at a competitive price—that are now receiving respect and deference.

The sheer waste of resources is enormous. Although $1 billion spent for guided missiles creates 21,000 jobs—over 71,000 jobs would result if that same amount were spent on education.[26] The vague communist threat used to justify these gargantuan purchases is actually less dangerous than the havoc caused to the economies of both Russia and America. Until recently, one-seventh of the USSR's resources went to the military—leaving economic growth and technological advancement virtually stagnant for decades.[27] While Russia and the United States were locked in mortal combat slamming shut "windows of vulnerability" and closing alleged missile gaps, Japan quietly walked away with all the marbles. Since Japan spends less than 1 percent of its GNP on defense (while in 1984 the United States and Russia, respectively, spent 7 percent and 14 percent) it could afford to invest in state-of-the-art factories. Within the United States, on the other hand, over \$8.4 trillion were drained off by the military between 1948 and 1984 (in 1984 dollars)— more than the total money value of all human-made wealth in our country.[28] Yet two-thirds of our tangible civilian wealth (which includes factories and machinery, bridges and dams, railroads and airports, etc.) is worn out and needs replacing. It could easily have been renewed were it not for the loss of so much money to the military.

Under Gorbachev's leadership, the Soviet Union has opted out of the escalating arms race. It is now actively demilitarizing much of its economy and would do more if the United States agreed to negotiate parallel cutbacks. Our economy would be healthier if we were to do so, but the defense industry and Pentagon resist. Instead, the United States response to Soviet unilateral arms and force cuts has been to call for even more defense spending. We now want to "modernize" short-range missiles based in West Germany, which has provoked a severe crisis within NATO. The Germans themselves, as well as most other European countries, are opposed to this increase and wish to negotiate in good faith with Mr. Gorbachev. As a nation we seem to be blind to reality, preferring to see a "Red Menace" where one no longer exists. Our allies are shaken by our obsession and dismayed by our go-it-alone attitude in world affairs. Most importantly, they are mystified by our apparent willingness to destroy our own economy:

> In particular, militarism is a central aspect of contemporary American government policy. It provides profits and some jobs, as well as channeling frustrations and insecurities against outside enemies. The *Rambo* phenomenon symptomizes the high level of xenophobia and the continuing love affair with empire that characterizes contemporary America. . . . The justifications for increased American military spending are unclear or fictive except in the contexts of "power projection" and economic stimulation. The sorry saga of Soviet defeat and humiliation in every aspect of its foreign policy since 1948— the loss of China as an ally, the open resistance to Soviet domination in Poland, the defection of Egypt and much of the Arab world, the economic bankruptcy of most of its client states such as Vietnam and Cuba—let alone its own internal woes, offers little justification for the portrayal of the Soviet Union as a successful superpower. Indeed, one can make little sense of the arguments of either Soviet or American leaders except as cynical attempts to hold or recruit allies and provide a defensive screen behind which other imperatives—economic and psychological—are operative.[29]

It was one of the great American heroes of this century that warned our nation against the damaging excesses of the military/industrial complex. Dwight D. Eisenhower, two-term president of the United States and victorious Supreme Allied Commander during World War II, delivered an important message to Americans in his Presidential Farewell Address to the nation in 1960. He told of his fear of the danger from within, of worries that the military needs of our country were overstated as a result of a cozy relationship that had developed between the Pentagon and a powerful defense industry establishment. Each has fed the other's power in an escalating dependency which prevents the real needs of American citizens from being met. President Eisenhower was fond of pointing out that every gun made or warship launched was a theft from those without food and shelter. For the most part, the indefensible waste of defense funds has left the average American a great deal poorer. Its continuation today at past levels of funding reaches beyond reason.

Another strategy open to serious question that the United States is now pursuing relates to an increasingly fashionable "Japan-bashing" mentality. While Japan and other nations erect trade barriers against American imports, they dump their own products at prices subsidized by their governments on America's unprotected shores. The kernel of this argument asserts that *we practice free trade, they don't!* While there is some truth to this charge, it is often overstated and neglects to mention U.S. culpability in these trade imbalances. We are told that the problem can be fixed if we pressure our major trade partners into opening up their borders to American imports. To ensure that they do, Congress passed what is known as the "Super 301" law, which requires that the president start proceedings against trading partners judged to be unfair. Japan, Brazil, and India have been singled out under these proceedings, which threaten to yield more negative than positive consequences. Japan is the major foreign supplier of cash to the United States. If Japan becomes angry or fearful, it could simply stop buying U.S. Treasury notes. This would provoke a crisis of the first magnitude, causing a sharp drop in the U.S. dollar and an abrupt rise in interest rates. A deep recession could follow.

Other negative results could be the formation of an Asian trading bloc dominated by Japan but excluding the United States. Retaliation by our trading partners with their own versions of 301 laws could destroy the global market place, leading to a worldwide recession comparable to that of the 1930s. The Japanese are a people who put great stock in saving face. They are likely to feel unfairly treated as they become targets of U.S. hostility. Japan has already doubled its manufactured imports between 1985 and 1988 in response to earlier U.S criticism.[30] They believe they have done more than enough to respond to charges of unfairness, and that America's trade deficit is of its own making. Japan promises to challenge the 301 law with the ninety-six nation General Agreement on Tariffs and Trade (GATT) organization that oversees free trade in the world. According to Frans Andriessen, the European Community's trade minister, Section 301 runs counter to basic GATT principles and is in clear violation of international trade law.[31] America is behaving much like a dazed boxer who has taken too many hits in the ring. Rather than conserving energy and doing what we need to do to cure the problem, we are wildly flailing about. We are picking fights with our friends rather than facing the painful truth—that it is time to put our house in order.

A number of positive policies can be followed to assure the survival of our country's high level of income. A variety of different avenues need to be followed and promising possibilities pursued to right the listing American economic ship. By starving our manufacturing sector—depriving it of needed technological replenishment—we have dangerously weakened the fiber of American economic strength. Study after study, including the major findings in this book, document the fact that jobs in manufacturing result in higher real income and lower relative inequality. We need to preserve 'industry within our borders and protect our own economic security as individuals to keep America vital and healthy.

In 1987, 4.9 percent of national income was saved, but financing the federal budget deficit left only 1.4 percent left for the nation to use in productive investment. Although the United States had an income of $4.5 trillion, it managed to save only $62 billion. This is similar to a family with a $50,000 yearly income that puts only $700 aside as a rainy-day fund. To make matters worse, had it not been for increased Social Security rates and pension funds of state and local governments, no saving would have occurred at all.[32]

Harrison and Bluestone offer one of the most comprehensive plans available to rebuild and revitalize America.[33] They promote a "revenue-side" goal that aims at boosting productivity, investment, and salaries. Our nation's manufacturing sector needs to be retooled and brought up-to-date to compete effectively with other countries. This would involve the adoption of an explicit industrial policy by the federal government akin to those of our trading partners. A blue ribbon panel report by President Reagan's Commission on Industrial Protectiveness recommends:

1. creation of a national department of science and technology to promote R & D in central areas;
2. more tax credits for companies investing in research and development;

3. ending antitrust barriers so that consortiums of U.S. firms could cooperate in efforts to develop expensive joint products (super-conductors, high definition TV, etc.);

4. initiating a strong export promotion campaign by the president.

Both sunset (declining) and sunrise (growth) industries should be helped. Troubled U.S. industries, such as steel, could be encouraged to build new, more efficient factories through loans with strings attached. These companies should assure the government that they will build new facilities in the United States, which would create more jobs. When cutbacks are imperative, a planned retrenchment could include gradual plant shutdowns, together with retraining and shifting of workers, rather than sudden factory closures that create chaotic emergencies.

The Cuomo Commission Report sets forth a number of different priorities too detailed to review here. Among them is the warning heard in countless other reports on American competitiveness: a nation that does not produce will sooner or later be forced to consume less. Their clarion call is for active and positive government participation in the economy. Without direction and guidance, the United States is a rudderless ship drifting onto the shoals of squandered resources and lowered living standards. State and local government partnerships with corporations are needed, such as state universities helping businesses solve some of their problems. National government policies to promote the development and operation of high-technology industries with promising futures are long overdue:

> Other governments, through incentives and funding, have emphasized producing quality goods efficiently—i.e., "targeted" innovations in process technology. . . . The U.S. ought to do the same. . . . Targeting could take the form of targeted tax credits or a financing facility. . . . Through a new partnership between the private sector and the National Science Foundation, support could be increased for the new technologies needed to make better products. As for tax incentives, we should consider reinstituting an investment tax credit, tailored to encourage investment in new process technology and equipment. This could be part of a program of changes in the tax code to increase competitiveness. Among them would be ways to reorient capital markets toward a longer-term perspective. Without increased "patient capital," investments in technology (whose benefits may not appear in the short run) are less likely to be made.[34]

Although there is a growing chorus of calls for a major effort by the federal government to adopt such policies, there are some hidden dangers to this path as well. One pitfall, alleged by conservatives, is that the government would be cast in the role of picking winners and losers in the economic arena. However, none of the proposals call for an all-or-nothing power in the hands of the presidency or some industrial czar. It would be difficult for the government to pave the way for development in a direction that industry did not want to go. Advocates of industrial policy talk about a *partnership between government and industry.* This entails give and take on both sides.

The danger lies in thinking that this will be enough to protect the further erosion of real income within the United States and to stem the rise of income inequality. Virtually all scholars who have studied our economic slide see a waste of resources caused by the hostility between workers and management. While fault lies with both sides, it is difficult to be sympathetic to American corporations who have enjoyed record profits in the past few decades while dismembering the nation's industries. The money has been there for reinvestment. Labor has been on the defensive for at least ten years. It has seen its power reduced together with cuts in the average wage. All analyses point to one major earmark of Japanese success in reaching a zenith of productivity: there is a close, cooperative, and harmonious relationship between labor and management. The payoff is worker loyalty. The opinions of workers are actively solicited by managers and production supervisors. In return, Japanese wage-earners are willing to go the extra mile for their employers, devoting intense effort to reach new heights of quality and efficiency in their workplace.

There is nothing to prevent a more cooperative relationship from emerging between management and labor in the United States aside from tradition. Indeed, the Japanese are beginning to show us how to do this in plants they operate in the United States. In a typical American manufacturing operation, 40 percent more effort is needed to produce the same amount of products as in a Japanese operation—while twice the number of defects are found in U.S. products.[35] The NUMMI joint venture between Toyota and General Motors in California, which is run by the Japanese, is an excellent case in point. Unheard-of job security and an open-door policy toward labor was instituted in this new plant. As a result, the performance level has nearly matched that of the best factories in Japan. It is an operation where labor has been treated with the respect they deserve. Policies which actively involve real input from line workers, quality circles, solicitation of employee views, and the like increase productivity and quality.

Harrison and Bluestone believe this sort of workplace democracy should reach far beyond simply asking employees to suggest ways to be more efficient on the production line.[36] They suggest labor input on the introduction of new technology, together with decisions about new investments, subcontracting, products, and plant locations. Worker involvement even includes thoughts on design of new products and pricing practices. Corporate heads must realize that management alone cannot come up with all the answers in the ongoing effort to remain competitive. The real answer lies in *help from workers*.

The most recent research which echoes the theme of greater worker involvement is a detailed Massachusetts Institute of Technology (MIT) study on how America can regain its productive edge.[37] This study took a rare bottom-up approach by looking at the economic health of eight different industrial sectors crucial to the vitality of the United States. The prevailing patterns and practices of work, productivitiy, creativity, marketing, and management were evaluated in an effort to come up with concrete answers to the nation's inability to manufacture goods for the world market. Among their findings was that human resources were being neglected. In addition to a more active involvement of workers, the MIT team highlighted the need for public education, sophisticated and formal on-the-job training programs, retraining of employees whose skills are outmoded, and life-long learning programs for all workers.

The lack of basic skills—such as reading and simple arithmetic—has been a severe problem for American businesses seeking a competent workforce. Japanese students are in school twice as many hours per year as American students.[38] This is one reason why American students do so poorly in comparison to students from other industrial countries on standardized tests in mathematics, science, and language skills. In the most recent international study of science achievement, American ten-year-olds placed eighth out of fifteen countries, while thirteen- and seventeen-year-olds did even worse.[39] American students rank far below average on international comparisons in math as well, while three-fourths of U.S. high school graduates lack the basic background for a college engineering course. An estimated 20 percent of the American workforce is functionally illiterate (unable to read newspaper stories, prescription warnings, etc.) compared to less than 1 percent of the Japanese workforce.[40]

To make matters worse, the range of education is much wider in our country than in other industrialized nations. While nearly all Japanese students cluster around the average high achievement scores in their country, American students are scattered over the range of scores. This reflects in part the continued inequality within our education system, especially the inferior learning environment for blacks, Hispanics, and other disadvantaged groups. In addition to language and race barriers, social-class differences are again emerging with a renewed vengeance. Poor high school graduates—without regard to race—were much less likely to attend college in 1987 than in 1975. At the same time, fewer low- and middle-income students attend private universities today than a decade ago.[41] Educational opportunity has been shrinking along with real income in the United States. As a result, a greater gap in living standards will be unavoidable as inequality surges to new heights.

In order for America to be competitive, the skills of its workers must be sharpened. A good beginning would be to raise teacher salaries—which are the lowest among all professions (medicine, law, engineering). Yet, more money for teachers alone will not do the job. A longer school year may be one solution. And students should be expected to perform well on standardized tests as a condition for receiving a diploma. Strict teacher licensure with *periodic testing of classroom personnel* is in order. In a world where American firms must compete in foreign lands for sales, high school students should be required to take at least two years of foreign language before graduating. The foreign language requirement which used to be part of most graduate programs should be reinstituted. More emphasis upon engineering and process development in business courses within universities would restore some of the imbalance created by a glut of MBAs chasing unproductive paper mergers.

In sum, we need an urgent recommitment on the part of the nation toward basic, quality education akin to that which took place after the Sputnik launch in 1957. At that time, there was a major revamping and revision in educational curriculums at all levels which led to more stress on science, math, and languages. America used to be a place famous for its "can do!" attitude. We used to be adept at producing the best goods that money could buy. It is still possible to reclaim such expertise and ability. But to do so we must embrace educational reform. A renewed emphasis on basic skills are a must for survival in the global economy.

The MIT study panel suggested a number of other ways that the United States could improve its competitiveness. Firms must, above all, invest in the long-term, rather than stressing short-term profit. The latter has led to abandonment of markets that are lucrative in the long run (VCRs, computer chips, etc.). Companies need to continually upgrade their manufacturing processes through the latest technology, to embrace flexibility over long-run mass production technology, to customize products for smaller market niches, and to develop new products. Corporations must reorganize to rid themselves of rigid top-heavy management and highly specialized departments. They must maximize productive cooperation within the company while implementing needed feedback and contact with their customers and suppliers. And employees must be given greater responsibility.

No analysis relating the woes of the American economy fails to mention how well the country's best interests could be served by bringing the federal budget deficit back into balance. The interest on this debt alone can stop us from doing what we must to protect our standard of living. The longer it goes on, the more damaging it is to our real income. The funds so badly needed to make us productive again are flowing to foreign banks and lenders, as well as to the ultra-rich within our own country.

The World Policy Institute has come up with a detailed plan for doing just this, while addressing nearly all of the issues discussed in this book.[42] Their program would allocate $215 billion per year in new public investment for the next ten years, while military spending would be reduced $125 billion annually. Among the domestic initiatives funded on a yearly basis would be $44 billion for new investment in civilian R&D, $30 billion for better education, and $22 billion for the modernizing of our infrastructure. Other domestic areas addressed are cleaning up nuclear weapons plant sites and toxic waste dumps, doubling our commitment to build public housing, renewing Head Start and other social programs aimed to help poor children, and increasing law enforcement and prevention programs aimed at drug abuse.

The World Policy Institute is realistic in its call for higher taxes, although careful to prevent the burden from falling on the poor. Rather, the $123 billion in increased tax revenues would stem mostly from a renewal of the progressive tax structure. Those with a greater ability to pay would pay more—which has been the American tradition since well before World War II. Their plan would add two additional tax brackets for high-income taxpayers: 38 percent for families with incomes of $80,000 to $150,000 and 50 percent for those families with incomes over $150,000. Capital gains would be taxed on assets upon inheritance, while financial transfers (to slow down the destructive merger mania) would be taxed at 5 percent. Most importantly, tax loopholes that encourage U.S. corporations to relocate overseas would be removed.

There is much that can still be done to make our tax laws more fair, especially for middle-income and poor people. As the Social Security (FICA) tax is currently set up, the rate of 7.51 percent applies only to earnings up to $45,000. This means the rich have been given an immense advantage. While the majority of citizens have to pay this tax on all or most of their income, the wealthy do not pay this tax at all on the great bulk of their income. Simply removing the ceiling on the Social Security tax alone would add $13 billion per year to the national budget.

Thus, although the World Policy plan would raise taxes, it would target that segment of our population which has been enriched by the policies of the last decade. This seems only just, given the rapid rise of relative and absolute income inequality that has taken place within the past fifteen years within our society. The vested interests of the wealthy, as well as pork-barrel defense contracts, are at stake. The World Policy budget and tax plan addresses the burning issues facing our nation. It pinpoints the fat in the budget. The plan is honest—in admitting that America must brace itself for more taxes to pay for the excesses of the past. In the last analysis, the World Policy plan sets forth a clear blueprint that could help bring a sustainable economy back to life in America.

Whatever plan eventually takes shape to preserve the American economy and our individual standards of living, the government must deal from the top of the deck. Economic decisions affect us all. At this point in our democracy, however, as citizens, voters, and workers, we have been shut out of the major policy-making that affects our economy. The plans of presidents and prime ministers, CEOs, and bankers all ignore the citizens who are most affected by their decisions. We seem to be expendable pawns in the world of international finance and the multinational mega-deals which occur in the world marketplace. Yet, the financial status quo is not chiseled in stone. The average American need not remain powerless. There can be a fairer and more equitable way to generate and use income within our society.

Many contemporary studies looking at the malaise of the U.S. economy are emphatic in their call for more industrial democracy in our nation. This concept goes far beyond simply involving workers in decisions about production or permitting unionization. It involves every worker and citizen in all walks of life. How our economy is structured and how firms conduct business both within and outside our borders have major repercussions for every person. Democratic economic planning raises an annoying question which challenges monolithic economic powers. Whose interests are met by the decisions being made? Economic democracy questions the belief that an unfettered and unplanned market economy is the best means to meet the social and economic needs of the nation. It asks what corporations and industries are rewarded by development and expansion policies (generally via the Pentagon), and who pays for the bills once they come due (e.g., the taxpayer bailout of Chrysler Corporation). What it involves, in the view of Falk and Lyson, is the chance for ordinary people to gain more control of their lives:

> In its boldest form, economic democracy calls for a rising standard of living for working people; an adequate supply of socially useful goods and services, unmindful of their profitability; a more hospitable, less authoritarian, and safer work environment; and increased participation by workers in the day-to-day running of the economy.[43]

This is indeed different thinking from the profit-driven and privativistic model so dominant in the market system. It raises the point that all should benefit from the workings of the economy—if not equally, at least to the point where minimal needs are met. It focuses on activities of concern to all of us that the private sector has been unable or unwilling to deal with. The list is lengthy and includes such activities as recycling, developing alternative energy sources, promoting mass transportation (light rail), guaranteeing basic health care for every person, providing a widespread system of day care, promoting a sustainable and ecologically responsible system of agriculture geared to family farms, promoting sunrise industries by guaranteeing startup/development capital for promising technology, and helping to cushion the effects of dying industries through policies which regulate plant closures, retraining, aid for employee buyouts of folding businesses, etc.

Above all, economic democracy is skeptical of the notion, "What is good for General Motors is good for America." This shopworn idea, prevalent in the 1950s, no longer "plays well in Peoria." Americans are becoming more astute and aware that the de facto military/industrial complex is failing them. As an engine of economic growth, it is inefficient and can no longer earn its way in a global economy. Economic democracy questions whether the real interests of Americans can be served by policies aimed at maximizing the profits of huge, conglomerate corporations. It asks the embarassing question: Is the overseas expansion of American multinational firms of any benefit to U.S. citizens? Does it instead harm us, reduce our incomes, and increase inequality?

We can no longer assume that U.S. corporations doing business abroad will have the best interests of the American people and government at heart. In fact, there is evidence to the contrary. The heads of multinational firms have been remarkably candid in admitting that their corporations come first. These global enterprises are now shedding any vestige of American identity as they develop world markets and reduce their dependency on home sales. One *New York Times* article has found that the executives of American multinationals

> increasingly speak as if the United States were no longer home port. "The United States does not have an automatic call on our resources," said Cyrill Siewart, chief financial officer at the Colgate-Palmolive Co., which sells more toothpaste, soaps, and other toiletries outside the United States than inside. "There is no mindset that puts this country first." . . . More and more high-paying jobs, including those for engineers and other professionals, are going abroad, instead of being kept at home. . . . Many executives say the global strategy supersedes preferential treatment for U.S. employees. . . . Many executives also distance themselves from the trade issues that are stirring so much concern in Congress and the Bush administration. Motorola and the Hewlett-Packard Co. say they

will not be directly affected if the United States does not outdistance other countries in the development of high-definition television. . . . "Whatever the technology that is developed, in whatever country, we'll be going after it for our products," said John Young, chief executive of Hewlett-Packard. These products include semiconductors and electronic instruments made in several countries.[44]

Such policies are a direct threat to the economic well-being of the great majority of Americans. In effect, our country has helped pay for the overseas expansion of multinationals through generous tax policies. As a result, investment capital needed at home is now gushing out of the country at an alarming rate. Along with the capital flight have gone countless jobs that would now exist here if more modern, up-to-date, competitive factories had been built within our borders. One direct consequence has been the decline in the U.S. standard of living. Personal income in America is decreasing in comparison to other industrial countries. As voting citizens in a democracy we need to resist the continuation of de facto policies which directly threaten our financial security. We need to support political candidates and policies which aim to rebuild the manufacturing base here at home. We must call for a more active involvement of government—at all levels—to ensure that the living standards of our citizens are no longer sacrificed to the profit needs of huge corporations with no allegiance to the United States.

Personal Actions

All too frequently, studies of American economic decline stop at this point, after advocating reforms and action at the macroeconomic and societal level. This is not enough. We are all aware that writing letters to our congressmen or the local newspaper, by itself, has little effect. To be sure, publicly supporting certain actions and policies is of great importance. Yet the strength of the huge economic actors with strong vested interests tends to keep the economic status quo from changing. It would be foolish to expect that simply expressing an opinion will change things. We can do much more on our own through individual actions.

Paul Thompson, who has formed a regional group called *Ski to End Hunger,* is fond of stating a truism that too frequently goes unrecognized: "Think globally—act locally!" By this phrase he conveys how we can overcome the feeling of helplessness we experience in seeing how global and national forces affect us. It is crucial that we see the connection between the world economy and how it has reduced our income on a personal level. But in so doing, we may feel overwhelmed, because the actors are so gigantic and powerful. What I can do as one person to change things for the better seems pitifully inadequate. The truth is, however, that there is much I can do acting alone and by joining forces with those who have similar beliefs.

Paul's group, for example, builds awareness of global and local inequities by focusing on a basic human need: the lack of food internationally and at home. The group helps host an annual media event/seminar/conference/celebration on World Food Day (October 15) every year in the Minneapolis-St. Paul area. Paul also has conducted well-publicized fasts to end hunger. He has imaginatively put together events where people downhill ski (as they now do by walking, running, and bicycling) as a means of getting funds pledged to end hunger. Proceeds go to local food shelves and charities, with some international contributions. Personal actions like these are effective ways of helping the poor that a few people have put together. Fighting poverty does not necessarily have to be grim.

One of the best sources for information at the national level is Food First (Institute for Food and Development Policy).[45] This organization was formed by Joseph Collins and Frances Moore Lappé to work toward social and economic justice in the Third World, especially as it relates to helping feed people. They are partly a think-tank dedicated to raising the awareness of people in the United States through studies and publications, but they are also active in advocating reforms and helping the poor directly. Other issues in the economic and social justice arena need active help as well. One of the best and most up-to-date sources for these issues has been compiled by Lappé and Collins in *World Hunger: Twelve Myths*.[46] Their roster of organizations deals with the farm crisis, children's issues, basic nutrition, local economics, poverty, pesticide abuse, apartheid, peace in Central America, and so on.

Local church and civic groups always need willing volunteers to solicit donations, to help with telephone campaigns, to drum up publicity, and to sit on committees. Community food shelves and programs such as "Loaves and Fishes," which directly feed the poor, appreciate all the help they can get. Past-President Jimmy Carter is an active leader in a well-organized group that helps rehabilitate housing in cities. He can be seen at one location or another with a hammer or saw in hand, getting the job done. The list of jobs and agencies is endless. We can do a great deal for the poor in our country or in LDCs as volunteers donating our time and money.

Another obvious solution to protect our income is to consume less, to refuse to buy products we do not need or want. This is difficult in a culture that bombards us with advertising. Ads play upon our fears of inadequacy, of rejection, of not fitting-in with the crowd. We are urged to buy the latest fashion, the trendy perfume, the ultimate car, the fashionable house in a costly upscale neighborhood we may not even like. There are no easy answers for building up an immunity to advertising. But this is still a *choice* that we can make. In the words of Nancy Reagan, "Just say no!"

A number of journals and magazines exist which can help you unhook from our consumer culture while offering a refreshing and healthy substitute to big business media. The best of the "alternative press," in my opinion, is the *Utne Reader.*[47] Founder and chief editor, Eric Utne, has unabashedly vowed to make his magazine the *"Reader's Digest* of the alternative press." The most incisive, informative articles from other magazines are reprinted in his journal, along with book reviews, consumer information, and lifestyle stories. The *Utne Reader* also provides detailed descriptions of and ordering information for other like-minded publications. This media is not beholden to large business interests or greatly dependent upon mass advertising revenues—both of which can influence what stories are covered and how they are written up.

Another welcome alternative to official government pronouncements on economic trends, which tend to be slanted to support the political agenda of whoever is in power, is *Dollars & Sense.*[48] This journal focuses on economic issues, but attempts to describe them in a clear, jargon-free manner. Its emphasis is also on economic justice, the fight against inequality, and problems of fairness in the distribution of income.

We can also use the market system to advance our own values and interests, rather than those of multinational corporations. One way to do this is to shop and work at food coops, which can be found in most major cities. A large portion of an individual's income generally goes to buy food, so where we spend our food allowance can have an impact. Many coops have policies forbidding the selling of anything but organically grown, wholesome food. For the most part, this cuts out the large agribusiness firms that import pesticide-laced fruit, vegetables, and meat from Mexico, the Phillipines, and Central America. Your pocket book can benefit as well as your health. Price reductions are typically earned through volunteer, part-time work. Food coops are great places to meet concerned people who wish to lead healthy and less wasteful lives. They can provide an important network to meet local activists working to solve a large variety of problems in your particular community and in the country as a whole.

The policy of boycotting irresponsible companies for damaging the environment, promoting nuclear power plants, plunging blindly into heavy defense contracting without considering the larger consequences, and the like is now being supplemented by a newer, more positive strategy. Coop America is an organization formed to assist today's concerned buyers in making an intelligent choice of what firms and whose products should be rewarded through purchases.[49] This organization investigates the positions taken by major U.S. companies on a variety of issues ranging from heavy defense procurement, minority hiring practices, and investment in South Africa, to environmental cleanliness—and publishes rankings. Their sole purpose is to help you as a consumer make every dollar count where it means the most to corporations—the profit line. For $1.00 you can order their *Alternative Catalog,* which lists products that have passed the test for being socially and environmentally responsible. The organization also gives information on networking tools, travel, investments, health insurance, and other topics in its magazine.

One of my favorites among the products which make use of the market system to combat economic injustice is Working Assets.[50] This organization has a money fund dedicated to socially responsible investments that has gone through explosive growth—doubling from $100 million to $200 million in the matter of a few years. Though critics said it would be impossible to combine a social conscience with investment, the fund has been attractive to many people. Working Assets offers check-writing, and reduced long-distance telephone charges, and travel arrangements may be made through their agency.

Best of all, Working Assets offers a VISA card. Every time the card is used, a nickel is donated to causes that you vote on each year as a cardholder. Two dollars are donated when you join. This may seem a paltry sum, yet there are now 90,000 Working Asset VISA holders who charge items several times a month. Each time I use the card I know at least some of my money is going to work against the injustices an unrestrained market system has spawned—much of it because of plastic credit cards!

The field of social investment has grown at an explosive rate in the last decade, and is also being used as a weapon against the corporate abuses and destruction of income caused by the loss of good-paying jobs in American industry. Severyn Bruyn argues that social investment can halt the decline of industry in America if it is directed at exemplary firms.[51] These are corporations that choose to stay in the United States in an effort to revitalize our manufacturing base, that encourage worker self-management/involvement, and that promote the flexibility and flat organizational hierarchies needed to compete effectively in the global economy. Bruyn believes that the profit motive operating alone in the world marketplace does not serve the needs of most people. Investment based upon both profit and more humane considerations, on the other hand, can lead to greater democracy, personal power, and economic justice.

Even if a person does not have the money to contribute to an "Invest in America" program, there is still a great deal that he or she can do. On a personal level, we can confront our own values and those of others. All too frequently negative stereotypes and group jealousies hinder group coalition building. This in turn weakens the political campaigns we must mount to bring about fundamental changes.

Sexism is one problem, for example, that we should all work to eradicate. Yet we should not be blind to the fact that men and women are together in the same rapidly sinking boat. Families suffer equally from plant shutdowns that throw men out of work and from the continuation of "traditional" low wages for women and blacks, who have no other job options.

At bottom, the destruction of the social wage and the slide in real income are part of the same process brought on by a system that takes advantage of any chink in the armor of worker unity. It is a system that has effectively pitted blacks against whites, men against women, native-born against recent immigrants, South against North, core against periphery. The constant, ever present goal of industry has been to pay the lowest wage possible. To attain this objective, our prejudices, fears, and biases have been used against us by unscrupulous employers. When we define others as the "enemy," as being the "cause" leading to the loss of income, we fail to grasp who is really benefiting from our declining standard of living.

One of the most distressing tendencies that accompanies a lowered standard of living is racial bigotry. America is now witnessing an epidemic rise in right-wing, paramilitary, Fascist groups who base their existence on hatred of blacks and Jews. In particular, "skinheads" (named for their closely shaven heads), a group composed of young adult and teenage white males, are becoming a major force in large cities.[52] These angry young men, incapable of earning a decent living because of poor education and lack of jobs that pay a livable wage, are taking out their frustrations on innocent black victims and "peacenik punkers." Low-scale warfare has broken out within the inner cities of major metropolitan areas. Gangs of skinheads now roam the streets with chains and baseball bats. They often beat their victims senseless, which invites retaliation from black ghetto youths who attack their white targets with the same ferocity.

In the meantime, in debt-ridden Louisiana, where a deep and prolonged five-year recession has slashed personal income to the bone, the Ku Klux Klan is making a comeback. David Duke, one of the state's newly elected legislators, has become a folk hero to many white residents in the area.⁵³ He was swept to power on a tide of fear and racial scapegoating. Before his election, voters had full knowledge of his past ties to the KKK and his active involvement in the National Association for the Advancement of White People. Duke ran for president in 1988 under a far-right Populist party platform which stressed that the major issue in America is "preserving our very bloodline." He has been active in promoting the Holocaust-as-myth theory, which argues that the Nazi slaughter of Jews was an historical hoax. Political contributions from ultra-conservative interests are now pouring into Duke's campaign chest from all over the country. The latest rumor is that he will run for a seat in the U.S. House of Representatives. With a lot of money backing him plus racial hatred fueled by declining income in the state, he may have a good chance of being propelled into a national position of power.

These are the consequences which befall a nation that suffers from a decline of income and rising inequality. The similarities to Germany before Hitler was swept to power through a Nazi party that feasted on racial hatred is truly frightening. When the people of a country are forced to undergo economic meltdown, the fallout seems to promote bigotry and violence.

At the start of this book, research evidence was cited that indicated that an increase in violence and political instability results when societies experience high degrees of inequality. This is now starting to happen in the United States. But we are capable of turning this negative trend around, both as a nation and as individual citizens. One of the differences between economics and sociology is the emphasis given to power. Traditional economics continues to stress the operation of an impersonal marketplace; the theories of this field tend to be conservative and oriented toward maintaining the status quo. Yet we are not on a level playing field to begin with. All economic actors do not participate as equals. In the competitive struggle for income, this is a fact we should never forget. Huge and powerful vested interests act to help the wealthy survive and flourish, sometimes at the expense of the middle class and poor. We are going through such a period now. The slide of income has been going on for quite some time. The rise of inequality is both real and profound. While the rich continue to amass greater wealth, middle-income groups and the poor become more destitute.

Yet we do not need to accept this situation as an accomplished fact. The power we have as workers and citizens remains with our votes and our pocket books. By being aware, joining forces, confronting issues, and taking personal action, it is possible to turn back the rising tide of inequality which threatens to engulf our nation. If we relinquish the belief that we can make a difference, then the forces of greed will have won. To paraphrase Franklin Delano Roosevelt: "The only thing we have to fear is believing we are helpless!"

In the final analysis, every person in our society should be able to lead a productive life free from want. We need to guarantee that each American has the basic health care, food, and shelter to survive. This can be accomplished if we are willing to use the power that has been within us all along.

APPENDIX A
MULTIPLE REGRESSION RESULTS

TABLE A1　　Standardized Betas for Stepwise Regressions of Average
Annual Percent Growth in GNP Per Person (1965–86)
with Development Variables, by World System Position

Economic Indicator	All World Countries	Core Countries	Semi-Pheriphery Countries	Periphery Countries
Multinational Corporate Penetration (PEN)	− .30		− .66	− .48
Gross Domestic Investment as Percent of GDP, 1986 (GDIOFGDP)	.43	.61	.34	.34
Exports as Percent of GDP, 1986 (XPORTGDP)	.25		.63	
Total Energy Consumed Per Person in Kilograms of Oil, 1986 (LOGSIZE)	.32			
Flow of Foreign Direct Investment, 1973 (FDI)				.20
GNP per person, 1986 (LOGGNP)				.60
GNP Per Person Squared (LOGNPSQ)				
Adjusted R Square	.54	.33	.78	.59
Sample Size	90	16	18	54

(All variables significant at .05)

TABLE A2   Standardized Betas for Stepwise Regressions of Average
Annual Percent Growth in GNP Per Person (1965–86) with
Development and Debt Variables, by World System Position

Economic Indicator	Semi- and Periphery Countries	Semi- Periphery Countries	Periphery Countries
Multinational Corporate Penetration (PEN)	−.35	−.55	−.30
Gross Domestic Investment as Percent of GDP, 1986 (GDIOFGDP)	.44	.39	.40
Flow of Foreign Direct Investment, 1973 (FDI)			
GNP per person, 1986 (LOGGNP)	.42		.44
GNP Per Person Squared (LOGNPSQ)			
Total Debt as Percent of GNP, 1986 (DEBTGNP)	−.24		−.30
Debt Service as Percent of GNP, 1986 (DEBTSERV)		.49	
Total Debt Per Person, 1986 (DEBTPRSN)			
Adjusted R Square	.62	.76	.60
Sample Size	64	14	49

(All variables significant at .05)

TABLE A3   Regressions of Household Income Inequality (Gini Ratios) with Standardized Betas of Variables, by World System Position[a]

Development Indicator	All World Countries	Core Countries	Periphery[b] Countries	Periphery[c] Countries
Multinational Corporate Penetration	.39	.30	.51	.72
GNP Per Person Squared, 1986 (Logged Value)	−.71	−.06	−.59	−.39
Average Balance of Payments, 1986	−.05	−.41	.03	NA
Total Debt as Percent of GNP, 1986	NA	NA	NA	−.11
Adjusted R Square	.65	.16	.44	.37
Sample Size	44	14	29	24

a. Semi-periphery, periphery, and unclassified countries were combined to enable analysis because of low sample size.
b. Regression run with balance-of-payment but without debt.
c. Regression run with debt but without balance-of-payment.
NA = Not Applicable or Not Available.

TABLE A4   Standardized Betas for Regressions of Basic Human Needs
            with Economic Development and World System Variables

Economic Development and World System Indicators	Population/ Doctor	Percent in High School	Percent Spent on Welfare	Life Expectancy	Infant Death	Average Calories
GNP Per Person, 1986 (LOGGNP)	−.66**	.84**	.75**	.85**	−.82**	.78**
World System Position and Multinational Penetration (POSINTER)	−.27**	−.19**	−.20**	−.01	−.004	−.24**
Average Balance of Payments Per Person, 1986 (AVBOP86)	−.06	−.03	.08	.05	−.05	−.10*
Average Annual Percent Growth in GNP per Person, 1965–86 (GROWGNP)	−.08	−.07	−.24**	.08	−.05	−.03
Exports as Percent of Gross Domestic Product, 1986 (XPORTGDP)	.12	.12*	.23**	.04	−.10**	.10
Adjusted R Square	.39	.76	.67	.81	.78	.72
Sample Size	80	84	60	90	90	90

**Beta is at least 2 times its Standard Error
*Beta is at least 1.5 times it Standard Error

TABLE A5   Standardized Betas for Regressions of Basic Human Needs
             with Economic Development, World System, and Household
             Income Inequality Variables: 1986

Economic Development and World System Indicators	Population/ Doctor	Percent in High School	Percent Spent Welfare	Life Expectancy	Infant Death	Average Calories
GNP Per Person, 1986 (LOGGNP)	−.82★★	.60★★	.55★★	.76★★	−.62★★	.58★★
World System Position and Multinational Penetration (POSINTER)	−.04	.02	.005	.12	−.25★	−.04
Household Gini, 1986 (HHGINI)	−.09	−.36★★	−.28	−.19	.37★★	−.26
Average Annual Percent Growth in GNP per Person, 1965–86 (GROWGNP)	−.08	.11	−.14	.21★★	−.21★★	−.006
Exports as Percent of Gross Domestic Product, 1986 (XPORTGDP)	.10	−.09	.21★	−.08	.05	−.06
Adjusted R Square	.51	.78	.65	.79	.74	.57
Sample Size	41	43	36	44	44	44

★★Beta is at least 2 times its Standard Error
 ★Beta is at least 1.5 times its standard Error

TABLE A6   Stepwise Regressions of Median Family Income with
Standardized Betas for Development, Human Capital,
and Regional Indicators: 1980

Predictive Variables	All U.S. Counties	Southern Counties	Non-Southern Counties
Percent High School Graduates	.435	.492	.271
Percent of Population Living on Farms	−.198	−.119	−.123
Region (0 = So./1 = Non-S.)	.073	NA	NA
Percent of Labor Force in Manufacturing Jobs	.216	.174	.253
Percent of Female-Headed Households	−.199	−.081	−.216
Percent Urban	.178	.053	.240
Percent of Labor Force that is Female	−.106	−.183	Not Signif.
In Metropolitan Area	.151	.141	.156
Percent Employed	.186	.308	.123
High Black Presence	−.039	Not Signif.	−.040
Percent Over 64 Years	−.236	−.229	−.313
Adjusted R Square	.703	.727	.669
Sample Size	3136	1424	1712

NA = Not Applicable

TABLE A7   Stepwise Regressions of Household Income Inequality Gini
             Scores with Standardized Betas for Development, Human
             Capital, and Regional Indicators: 1980

Predictive Variables	All U.S. Counties	Southern Counties	Non-Southern Counties
Percent High School Graduates	− .262	− .291	− .110
Percent of Population Living on Farms	Not Signif.	.069	.137
Region (0 = So./1 = Non-S.)	− .188	NA	NA
Percent of Labor Force in Manu-facturing Jobs	− .358	− .325	− .419
Percent of Female-Headed Households	.263	.297	.203
Percent Urban	.086	.130	Not Signif.
Percent of Labor Force that is Female	.054	Not Signif.	.233
In Metropolitan Area	− .150	− .167	− .107
Percent Employed	Not Signif.	.060	− .146
High Black Presence	Not Signif.	Not Signif.	− .055
Percent Over 64 Years	.388	.385	.395
Mean Household Income	.325	.388	1.016
(Household Income)^2	Not Signif.	Not Signif.	− .733
Adjusted R Square	.344	.342	.267
Sample Size	3136	1424	1712

NA = Not Applicable

APPENDIX B
FAMILY INCOME IN DOLLARS

Family Dollar Income

▤   7170-14322 (Low 25%)
▨   14323-18906 (Mid 50%)
■   18907-40236 (Top 25%)

Maine Median Family Income: 1979

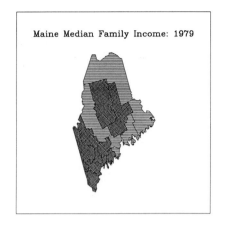

Vermont Median Family Income: 1979

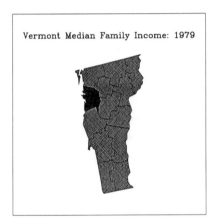

Massachusetts Median Family Income: 1979

New Hampshire Median Family Income: 1979

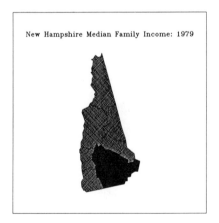

Connecticut Median Family Income: 1979

Family Dollar Income

- 7170-14322 (Low 25%)
- 14323-18906 (Mid 50%)
- 18907-40236 (Top 25%)

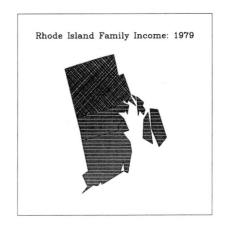

Rhode Island Family Income: 1979

New York Median Family Income: 1979

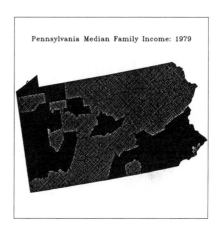

Pennsylvania Median Family Income: 1979

New Jersey Median Family Income: 1979

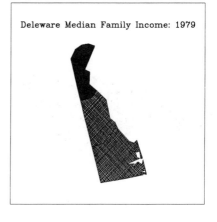

Deleware Median Family Income: 1979

Maryland Median Family Income: 1979

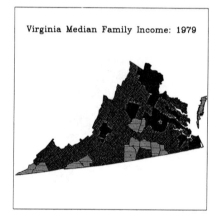

Family Dollar Income

▤ 7170-14322 (Low 25%)
▨ 14323-18906 (Mid 50%)
■ 18907-40236 (Top 25%)

West Virginia Median Family Income: 1979

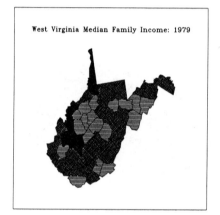

Virginia Median Family Income: 1979

North Carolina Median Family Income: 1979

South Carolina Median Family Income: 1979

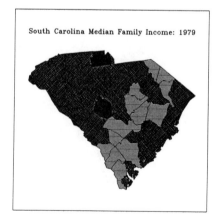

Florida Median Family Income: 1979

Family Dollar Income

- ▤ 7170-14322 (Low 25%)
- ▨ 14323-18906 (Mid 50%)
- ■ 18907-40236 (Top 25%)

Georgia Median Family Income: 1979

Kentucky Median Family Income: 1979

Tennessee Median Family Income: 1979

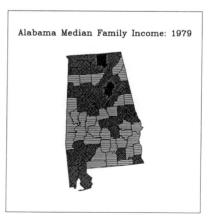

Alabama Median Family Income: 1979

Family Dollar Income

▤ 7170-14322 (Low 25%)
▦ 14323-18906 (Mid 50%)
■ 18907-40236 (Top 25%)

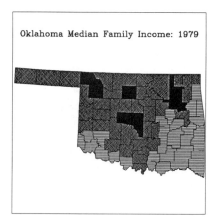

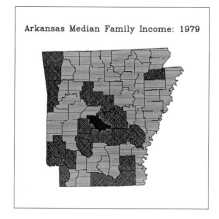

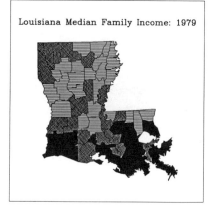

Family Dollar Income

▤   7170-14322 (Low 25%)
▨ 14323-18906 (Mid 50%)
■ 18907-40236 (Top 25%)

Michigan Median Family Income: 1979

Wisconsin Median Family Income: 1979

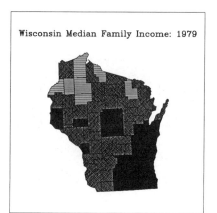

Ohio Median Family Income: 1979

Illinois Median Family Income: 1979

Indiana Median Family Income: 1979

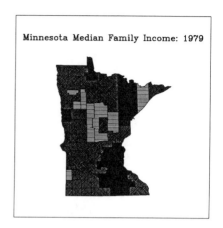

Minnesota Median Family Income: 1979

Family Dollar Income

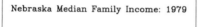

7170-14322 (Low 25%)
14323-18906 (Mid 50%)
18907-40236 (Top 25%)

Nebraska Median Family Income: 1979

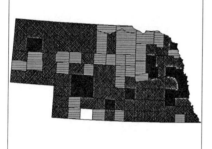

Iowa Median Family Income: 1979

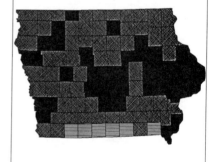

Kansas Median Family Income: 1979

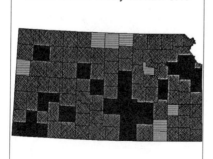

Missouri Median Family Income: 1979

Family Dollar Income

▤ 7170-14322 (Low 25%)
▨ 14323-18906 (Mid 50%)
■ 18907-40236 (Top 25%)

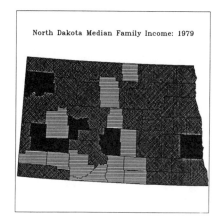

North Dakota Median Family Income: 1979

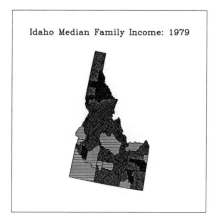

Idaho Median Family Income: 1979

South Dakota Median Family Income: 1979

Montana Median Family Income: 1979

Wyoming Median Family Income: 1979

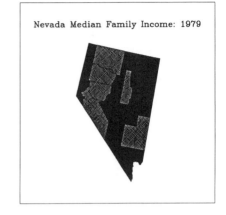

Nevada Median Family Income: 1979

Family Dollar Income

▤ 7170-14322 (Low 25%)
▨ 14323-18906 (Mid 50%)
■ 18907-40236 (Top 25%)

Utah Median Family Income: 1979

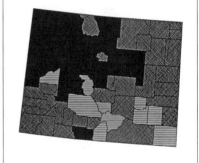

Colorado Median Family Income: 1979

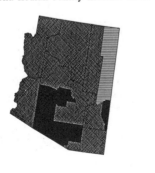

Arizona Median Family Income: 1979

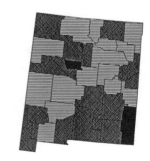

New Mexico Median Family Income: 1979

Family Dollar Income

☰ 7170-14322 (Low 25%)
▨ 14323-18906 (Mid 50%)
■ 18907-40236 (Top 25%)

Alaska Median Family Income: 1979

Washington Median Family Income: 1979

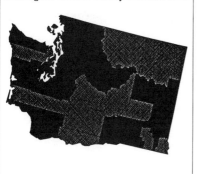

Oregon Median Family Income: 1979

California Median Family Income: 1979

Hawaii Median Family Income: 1979

APPENDIX C
RANGE OF GINI SCORES

Range of Gini Scores

☰	.2693-.3617 (Low 25%)
▨	.3618-.3939 (Mid 50%)
■	.3940-.6675 (Top 25%)

Range of Gini Scores

≣ .2693-.3617 (Low 25%)
▨ .3618-.3939 (Mid 50%)
■ .3940-.6675 (Top 25%)

Rhode Island Gini Scores: 1979

New York Gini Scores: 1979

Pennsylvania Gini Scores: 1979

New Jersey Gini Scores: 1979

Delaware Gini Scores: 1979

Range of Gini Scores

▤ .2693-.3617 (Low 25%)
▨ .3618-.3939 (Mid 50%)
■ .3940-.6675 (Top 25%)

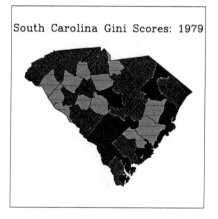

Maryland Gini Scores: 1979

West Virginia Gini Scores: 1979

Virginia Gini Scores: 1979

North Carolina Gini Scores: 1979

South Carolina Gini Scores: 1979

Florida Gini Scores: 1979

Range of Gini Scores

▤ .2693-.3617 (Low 25%)
▨ .3618-.3939 (Mid 50%)
■ .3940-.6675 (Top 25%)

Georgia Gini Scores: 1979

Kentucky Gini Scores: 1979

Tennessee Gini Scores: 1979

Alabama Gini Scores: 1979

Range of Gini Scores

▤ .2693-.3617 (Low 25%)
▨ .3618-.3939 (Mid 50%)
■ .3940-.6675 (Top 25%)

Mississippi Gini Scores: 1979

Oklahoma Gini Scores: 1979

Arkansas Gini Scores: 1979

Texas Gini Scores: 1979

Louisiana Gini Scores: 1979

Michigan Gini Scores: 1979

Range of Gini Scores

.2693-.3617 (Low 25%)
.3618-.3939 (Mid 50%)
.3940-.6675 (Top 25%)

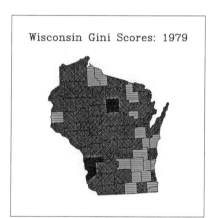

Wisconsin Gini Scores: 1979

Ohio Gini Scores: 1979

Illinois Gini Scores: 1979

Indiana Gini Scores: 1979

Range of Gini Scores

▤ .2693-.3617 (Low 25%)
▨ .3618-.3939 (Mid 50%)
■ .3940-.6675 (Top 25%)

Minnesota Gini Scores: 1979

Nebraska Gini Scores: 1979

Iowa Gini Scores: 1979

Kansas Gini Scores: 1979

Missouri Gini Scores: 1979

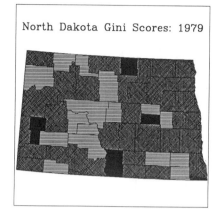

North Dakota Gini Scores: 1979

Range of Gini Scores

- .2693-.3617 (Low 25%)
- .3618-.3939 (Mid 50%)
- .3940-.6675 (Top 25%)

Idaho Gini Scores: 1979

South Dakota Gini Scores: 1979

Montana Gini Scores: 1979

Wyoming Gini Scores: 1979

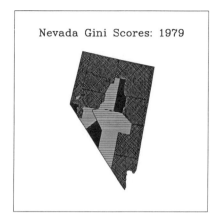

Nevada Gini Scores: 1979

Range of Gini Scores

▤	.2693-.3617 (Low 25%)
▨	.3618-.3939 (Mid 50%)
■	.3940-.6675 (Top 25%)

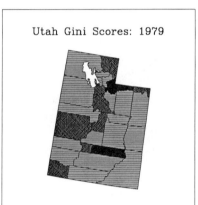

Utah Gini Scores: 1979

Colorado Gini Scores: 1979

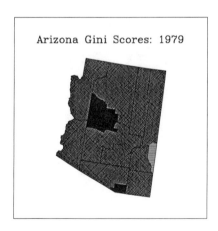

Arizona Gini Scores: 1979

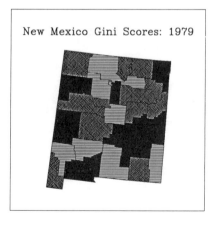

New Mexico Gini Scores: 1979

Range of Gini Scores

- .2693-.3617 (Low 25%)
- .3618-.3939 (Mid 50%)
- .3940-.6675 (Top 25%)

Alaska Gini Scores: 1979

Washington Gini Scores: 1979

Oregon Gini Scores: 1979

California Gini Scores: 1979

Hawaii Gini Scores: 1979

NOTES

Chapter 1

1. Bergen Evans, *Dictionary of Quotations* (New York: Delacorte, 1968), p. 85. The quotation was first recorded by Rousseau and attributed to an unknown princess, who said it well before Marie Antoinette was born. Even though Marie may not have originated these words, another calloused member of the aristocracy did. These words serve to illustrate the indifference of a privileged economic elite to the suffering of common people.

2. Barry Bluestone and Bennett Harrison, *The Deindustrialization of America* (New York: Basic Books, 1982).

3. Monroe W. Karmin, "Is Middle Class Really Doomed to Shrivel Away?" *U.S. News and World Report* 9(Aug. 20, 1984):65.

4. Robert J. Samuelson, "The Myth of the Missing Middle," *Newsweek* (July 1, 1985):50.

5. William Baldwin, "Chicken Little's Income Statistics," *Forbes* 137(March 24, 1986):68–69.

6. Jerry Flint, "Too Much Ain't Enough," *Forbes* 140 (July 13, 1987):92 ff.

7. Charlotte Salkowski, "Growth in Living Standard Slows for the American Middle Class," *Christian Science Monitor* (Jan. 8, 1986):1ff.

8. Robert Kuttner, "A Shrinking Middle Class Is a Call to Action," *Business Week* (Sept. 16, 1985):16.

9. "Is the Middle Class Shrinking?" *Time* (Nov. 3, 1986):54–56.

10. Paul Blustein, "The Great Jobs Debate," *Washington Post National Weekly Edition* (Sept. 5–11, 1988):20–21.

11. Barbara Ehrenreich, "Is the Middle Class Doomed?" *New York Times Magazine* 135 (Sept. 7, 1986):44ff.

12. Ibid., p. 63.

13. Edward A. Muller, "Income Inequality, Regime Repressiveness, and Political Violence," *American Sociological Review* 50(1985):47–61.

14. Edward A. Muller, "Democracy, Economic Development, and Income Inequality," *American Sociological Review,* 53(1988):66.

15. Bennett Harrison and Barry Bluestone, *The Great U-Turn: Corporate*

317

Restructuring and the Polarization of America (New York: Basic Books, 1988), pp. 112–13. See also David Kotz, "Feeling Overworked? Here's Why," *Utne Reader,* 28 (July/Aug. 1988), pp. 56–60.

16. Frank Levy, *Dollars and Dreams: The Changing American Income Distribution* (New York: Russell Sage, 1987), pp. 79–80.

17. Lenore Weitzman, *The Divorce Revolution* (New York: Free press, 1985), p. 323.

18. William P. O'Hare, *America's Welfare Population: Who Gets What* (Washington, DC: Population Reference Bureau, 1987); William P. O'Hare, "Poverty in America: Trends and New Patterns," *Population Bulletin* 40, 3(1985).

19. Sheldon Danziger and Peter Gottshalk, "Families with Children Have Fared Worse," *Challenge* 29(March–April 1986):40–47.

20. Ravi Batra, *The Great Depression of 1990* (New York: Dell, 1988).

21. Daniel B. Radner and Denton R. Vaughn, "Wealth, Income, and the Economic Status of Aged Households," in Edward N. Wolff (ed.), *International Comparisons of the Distribution of Household Wealth* (New York: Oxford University Press, 1987), pp. 93–120.

22. Daphne T. Greenwood, "Age, Income, and Household Size: Their Relation to Wealth Distribution in the United States," in Wolff, *Distribution of Household Wealth,* pp. 121–40.

23. Harold R. Kerbo, *Social Stratification and Inequality: Class Conflict in the United States* (New York: McGraw-Hill, 1983), pp. 36–37.

24. Batra, *Great Depression of 1990,* pp. 133–34.

25. Ibid., pp. 136–37.

26. Edward N. Wolff, *International Comparisons of the Distribution of Household Wealth* (New York: Oxford University Press, 1987), pp. 5–7.

27. William Wilson, *The Declining Significance of Race: Blacks and Changing American Institutions* (Chicago: University of Chicago Press, 1980); ibid., *The Truly Disadvantaged: The Inner City, the Underclass, and Public Policy* (Chicago: University of Chicago Press, 1987); William P. O'Hare, *America's Welfare Population: Who Gets What* (Washington, DC: Population Reference Bureau, 1987); William P. O'Hare, "Poverty in America: Trends and New Patterns," *Population Bulletin* 40, 3(1985).

28. One of the best available is Harold R. Kerbo, *Social Stratification and Inequality: Class Conflict in the United States* (New York: McGraw-Hill, 1983).

29. "Corporate America's Most Powerful People," *Forbes* (May 30, 1988): 154 ff.

30. Apparently, the old axiom that education will pay off in future earnings is a misnomer when it comes to top corporate executives. *Forbes* reports that the eighty-seven chief executives who hold no college degree earned a median $735,000 in 1987 versus a median $746,000 for the 378 with an undergraduate college degree. The 323 executives with graduate degrees earned a median of $773,000—leading to the inescapable conclusion that at this level it simply does not pay to pursue higher education. The "increase" in salary between a non-college and college graduate CEO comes to a paltry 1.5 percent per year.

31. Stock ownership is an indication of capitalism par excellance. A number of studies performed on a much wider scale (Wright 1978; Wright and Per-

onne 1977) show that income is actually predicted more accurately by Marxian class position, i.e., whether one owns the means of production—capital and stocks—versus having to earn one's living by selling one's labor (working for an employer). Status attainments that many of us rely on to increase our income, such as acquiring education or entering a lucrative profession, are simply less relevant in explaining income differences between people. Stock owners have higher incomes than nonowners with the same education, occupation, age, job tenure, etc. In essence, being a capitalist—regardless of educational and occupational factors—brings more income (Aldrich and Weiss 1981). Furthermore, when persons are examined within class categories, there are not many differences by race and sex with respect to income. The large differences between men and women or blacks and whites is really due to class position: women and blacks simply have higher proportions within the working class. Empirical research using national samples within the United States and England (Robinson and Kelley 1979) also corroborates Wright's research. With this evidence in mind, the lack of correspondence between performance and education of corporate executives on the one hand, and their job performance on the other, should not be too surprising.

32. Graef S. Crystal, "The Wacky, Wacky World of CEO Pay," *Fortune* (June 6, 1988):68 ff.

33. For those who are statistical tyros, the term "multiple regression" conjures up fear and anxiety. This reaction need not be the typical response. One does not need to know complex formulas and mathematical nuances to understand the results of regression analysis. In a word, we try to predict change in a dependent variable (CEO compensation in this example) by use of several independent variables (tenure with the corporation, company performance, CEO's ownership of company stock, etc.). The procedure is useful in isolating what variables are most important in causing change in the subject we are interested in. For the most part, income inequality will nearly always be the dependent variable predicted in this book. I have tried to interpret regression results throughout the book in generalized layman terms. For scholars wishing to delve more deeply into the labyrinth of statistical results, I have included more detailed tables in the appendices.

34. Amanda Bennett, "A Great Leap Forward for Executive Pay," *Wall Street Journal* (April 24, 1989):B1.

35. David Kirkpatrick. "Abroad, It's Another World," *Fortune* (June 1988):78.

36. Crystal, "Wacky World," p. 74.

37. U.S. Internal Revenue Service, *Statistics of Income Bulletin* (Winter 1984–1985) (Washington, DC: U.S. Government Printing Office, 1985).

38. No one, it seems, ever states that "the rich are always with us." The implicit value assumption is that it is in the nature of things to have persons living under poverty, that their presence is perhaps a curse that we must accept with fatalism, that there is nothing we could possibly do to alleviate their suffering, that the natural order precludes a society from doing something so that poverty can be eradicated. In essence, there is a heavy status-quo orientation to the assumption that "the poor are always with us." Conversely, nothing is ever

mentioned about eradicating extreme affluence. Somehow this condition is seen as right and just, and that to have large segments of the population living what could only be described as opulent lifestyles has no bearing upon the presence of the poor. In a word, if someone gets a bigger piece of the pie—someone else will inevitably get a smaller piece—all things being unequal. One could argue that this is not necessarily the case when the pie itself gets bigger over time. As we have seen, however, the pie has been contracting since 1973—making the increasing inequities doubly painful.

Chapter 2

1. James R. Kluegel and Eliot R. Smith, *Beliefs about Inequality: Americans' Views of What Is and What Ought to Be* (Hawthorne, NY: Aldine De Gruyter, pp. 75–89, esp. p. 83.

2. Unfortunately, documenting the ideological biases present in our culture would take enough space to form another book. But, there are a number of excellent books that discuss the ideological mindset of American life as it is defined for us by our major institutions—particularly in the support of free enterprise, the market system, and capitalism. Michael Parenti is keenly insightful at the level of major U.S. institutions, especially education and spectator sports (1978). The media and public opinion also figure prominently in his analysis (1985). Ben H. Bagdikian (1987) has the most thoroughly detailed current account of how major corporations systematically distort the news and analyses of major media outlets in support of conservative, big-business values. It is also true, however, that ideological bias is present in other societies. Shlapentokh (1987) recounts case after case of state pressure, coercion, and intimidation of academicians, the media, and average citizens within the Soviet Union in favor of Marxist thought. Any deviation from orthodoxy or possible recognition that personal economic self-interest and market forces could motivate people to work harder have been rigidly repressed in this society. Glimmerings of recognition for these basic forces are just now being permitted under Gorbachev's new era of *glasnost*.

3. Gerhard Lenski, *Power and Privilege* (New York: McGraw-Hill, 1966), pp. 3–17.

4. Robert Gilpin, *The Political Economy of International Relations* (Princeton, NJ: Princeton University Press, 1987), p. 41.

5. Michael Parenti, *The Sword and the Dollar: Imperialism, Revolution, and the Arms Race* (New York: St. Martin's Press, 1989), pp. 1–6, 135–51.

6. Karl Marx, *Capital: A Critique of Political Economy,* 3 vols. (New York: Vintage Books, 1981); Karl Marx, *The Grundrisse* (New York: Vintage Books, 1973).

7. Many scholars would energetically dispute the notion of a rather complacent, benign, and nonmilitant labor union movement. A knowledge of the bloody and savage strike-breaking activity in early twentieth century America seems to contradict this image (Gutman 1988), but concessions by big business to labor in the 1930s quickly resulted in a status quo of high wages in heavy

industry for low political consciousness and/or a conservative ethos on the part of labor. The ease with which the Reagan administration was able to bust unions also suggests an absence of working-class consciousness and identification within American labor. There is certainly lack of unity, as unions themselves have increasingly permitted two-tier contracts among their own workers, avoided strikes by agreeing to wage rollbacks, crushed any wildcat strikes or other opposition initiatives, etc. Moreover, there has always been a division within American labor between much wealthier, larger "core" firms of heavy industry (e.g., General Motors or Ford)—where workers have been granted comparatively high wages—and noncore firms in small, specialized, and transitory industries with less hope of survival (textiles). Even within the core, relatively cohesive unions have not been able to prevent the erosion of earnings of male workers over the past two decades (Tigges 1987).

8. Michael Harrington, *The Twilight of Capitalism* (New York: Simon and Schuster, 1976); Erick O. Wright, *Class, Crisis and the State* (New York: Schocken Books, 1978).

9. Gilpin, *Political Economy*, p. 53.

10. Max Weber, *The Protestant Ethic and the Spirit of Capitalism*, translated by Talcott Parsons (New York: Scribner's, 1958).

11. Max Weber, "Class, Status, Party," in Seymour M. Lipset and Reinhard Bendix (eds.), *Class, Status and Power* (New York: Free Press, 1958), pp. 21–28.

12. Kingsley Davis and Wilbert E. Moore, "Some Principles of Stratification," *American Sociological Review* 10(1945):242–49.

13. Melvin Tumin, "Some Principles of Stratification: A Critical Analysis," *American Sociological Review* 18(1953):387–94.

14. Harold R. Kerbo, *Social Stratification and Inequality: Class Conflict in the United States* (New York: McGraw-Hill, 1983), p. 132.

15. Randal Collins, *Conflict Sociology* (New York: Academic Press, 1975), p. 420.

16. Christopher Jencks, et al., *Who Gets Ahead? The Determinants of Economic Success in America* (New York: Basic Books 1979), pp. 214–17.

17. J. A. Brittain, *The Inheritance of Economic Status* (Washington, DC: Brookings Institution, 1977), p. 72.

18. For basic treatments of pro-capitalist, free-market economics, see Milton Friedman, *Capitalism and Freedom* (Chicago: University of Chicago Press, 1962) and Paul Samuelson, *Economics,* 11th ed. (New York: McGraw-Hill, 1980).

19. Milton Friedman, "Choice, Chance, and the Personal Distribution of Income," *Journal of Political Economy* 61, 4(Aug. 1953):277–90.

20. G. Becker, *Human Capital* (New York: Columbia University Press, 1964).

21. Lars Osberg, *Economic Inequality in the United States* (New York: M. E. Sharpe, 1984), p. 135.

22. Ibid., p. 136.

23. Ibid., p. 158.

24. Charles Lindblom, *Politics and Markets: The World's Political-Economic Systems* (New York: Basic Books, 1977).

25. P. B. Doeringer, and M. J. Piore, *Internal Labor Markets and Manpower Analysis* (Lexington, MA: D.C. Heath, 1971), pp. 41–42.

26. Lester Thurow, *Generating Inequality: Mechanisms of Distribution in the U.S. Economy* (New York: Basic Books, 1975), p. 79.

27. Education can be an important means of maintaining class boundaries. The gradual educational upgrading of occupations over time has not been due to any increase in technical skills needed for these jobs. Rather, as more persons attained a high school education in our society, a college degree was redefined as necessary for middle-class occupations to keep entrants from flooding the market (Collins 1971). What developed, of course, was a different flooding of college graduates on the labor market, which resulted in under-employment and a critical questioning of higher education's role for both economic production and occupational attainment (Smith 1986). Social-class bias is replete within elementary and secondary education. The home environment of children from higher classes prepares them through role modeling, encouragement, and resources such as books and educational toys to do well in school (Jencks 1972). Teachers expect more from children of higher-class families (Stein 1971; Good and Brophy 1973), leading to their better performance in a self-fulfilling prophecy. Tracking students between vocational (blue collar) and college-preparatory curriculums (middle and upper class)—practiced in 85% of public schools—is frequently determined by class background (Jencks et al 1972; Alexander, Cook, and McDill 1978; McPortland 1968). Among high-intelligence high school students, 91% attend college compared to 40% of highly intelligent lower-class students (Sewell and Shah 1968). Conversely, 58% of students with low intelligence but higher-class backgrounds attend college compared to 9% of low intelligence, lower-class high school students. No matter what their intelligence, 84% of students from higher-class backgrounds go to college but only 21% from lower-class families do so (Featherman and Hauser 1978). Recent evidence comparing twins continues to corroborate an independent effect due to family background apart from schooling on subsequent earnings (Hauser and Sewell 1986). Intergenerational data from the Panel Study of Income Dynamics also reveal significant effects of parental family income on the completed schooling and wage rates of adult children (Hill and Duncan 1987). Moreover, the educational payoff is diminished very greatly for Hispanics and nonwhites in labor markets with a large share of minority workers; this drop in earnings is sharpest for black men and greater among workers with college educations (Tienda and Lii 1987). Even for women, the payoff for enhanced family income via a college education is found more through marriage than through using their education in the labor market (Glenn 1984). College attendance continues to be important, of course, even if a person does not acquire skills needed for the job market. Those who finish college have a nearly 50% occupational advantage over those who do not (Jencks et al. 1979) Differences in personal human capital attributes do help explain initial career position, although not subsequent upward occupational mobility among male workers in low-income areas (Rosenberg 1980). Although a college degree has considerable impact upon a worker's subsequent earnings

within core industries, this is not true within more marginal, nonunionized periphery industries (Beck et al. 1978). Lastly, Bowles and Gintis (1976) argue that the most important lessons taught in school are implicit: being on time and obeying authority are emphasized in working-class schools and curriculums, while self-direction and expectation for success are stressed in the education of upper-class students. Thus, while one segment is socialized for factory labor, the other inculcates the habits of command needed for corporate management.

28. Osberg, *Economic Inequality,* p. 169.

29. Edward N. Wolff, and D. Bushe, *Age, Education and Occupational Earnings Inequality* (New York: National Bureau of Economic Research, 1976); J. C. Riley, "Testing the Educational Screening Hypothesis," *Journal of Political Economy* 87,5 (Oct., 1979):S227–52; Sam Rosenberg, "Male Occupational Standing and the Dual Labor Market," *Industrial Relations* 19, 1 (Winter 1980):34–48.

30. Arne L. Kalleberg, Michael Wallace, and Robert P. Althauser, "Economic Segmentation, Worker Power, and Income Inequality," *American Journal of Sociology* 87, 3(Nov. 1981):651–83.

31. E. M. Beck, Patrick M. Horan, and Charles M. Tolbert, II, "Stratification in a Dual Economy: A Sectoral Model of Earnings Determination," *American Sociological Review* 43 (Oct. 1978):704–20; Barry Bluestone, William M. Murphy, and Mary Stevenson, *Low Wages and the Working Poor* (Ann Arbor: Institute of Labor and Industrial Relations, University of Michigan, 1973); R. C. Edwards, M. Reich, and D. Gordon, eds., *Labor Market Segmentation* (Lexington, MA: D. C. Heath, 1975).

32. Lynne G. Zucker and Carolyn Rosenstein, "Taxonomies of Institutional Structure: Dual Economy Reconsidered," *American Sociological Review* 46 (Dec. 1981):869–84.

33. Bluestone et al., *Low Wages,* pp. 28–29.

34. A number of radical writers (Edwards 1975; Bowles and Gintis 1976) agree with the idea that the U.S. labor market is segmented and that many are relegated to low pay on the basis of such ascriptive characteristics as sex and race, but they see more Machiavellian intent with regard to how capitalists develop their production technology. Not only profit motivates business leadership, but also a desire to keep control of production out of the hands of workers. By building giant corporations with centralized control, worker/management relationships must necessarily be authoritarian and remotely impersonal. Work is broken up into very small tasks which are seemingly meaningless to those on the assembly line. The laborer loses touch with the final product, while pride of craftsmanship rapidly disappears. Moreover, it may be that the gaps between differentiated labor within the factory or even between market segments is more artificial and arbitrary than real. Such a system helps to perpetuate false barriers between workers, who seem pitted against one another in competition and are thus unable to develop a collective identity or build resistance through class consciousness. While this orientation may seem extreme, it should be remembered that corporations such as Volvo have successfully reconstituted their factory workplace by forming worker production teams to build cars. Productivity may rise when workers share in decision-making and when production tasks are not so minutely divided—i.e., traditional approaches are not necessary for high ef-

ficiency. Recent evidence (Tigges 1986) corroborates the fact that type of industrial production is an important dimension of workers' earnings over and above a segmented labor force divided between a typology of core and periphery industries. Lastly, U.S. corporations steer the direction of research and development toward high-tech defense projects through their influence on the federal government—i.e., they do "choose" the direction of production technology in determining what and how things will be manufactured.

35. Beck et al., "Stratification in a Dual Economy" p. 78. The challenge did not go unnoticed. One critic who is identified with the human capital school (Hauser 1980) dismissed the study by Beck and his associates as essentially false because they included ninety-nine cases as haveing zero income when they should have been deleted from the analysis. A reanalysis when this is done destroys many of their findings, although a core vs. periphery distinction in earnings does remain, and at quite a large level at that. Beck et al. (1980) replied that their use of the suspect ninety-nine was theoretically justified, an argument I tend to agree with. At any rate, critics of the dual economy approach have been hard put to explain why core/periphery distinctions remain—especially with reference to income earnings—no matter how the data is manipulated and massaged. Recent evidence does indicate that the dual economy has been eroding over the past two decades, however, and has less impact today in explaining earnings inequality than previously (Tigges 1986, 1987). In the end, however, the very loss of explanatory power for the dual economy has been supplanted by other macro-economic and social structural variables: deindustrialization, capital flight from the United States, trade and export battles, restructured taxation schemes that benefit the very rich, skewed Reaganomic budgets, etc. Very few scholars, it seems, continue to be swayed by the human capital viewpoint.

36. Nevertheless, there is *some* awareness of class self-interest and political cohesiveness/activism, especially on the part of the upper class (Edsall 1985). Research indicates that greater income consistently results in conservative economic policy preferences (Knocke et al. 1987) whereas lesser income produces a tendency to believe that poverty results from the structure of society and social institutions (Oropesa 1986).

37. Gallup Poll, "U.S. Citizens, British Hold Differing Views of Haves, Have-Nots," *Minneapolis Tribune* (Aug., 1988), p. 22A.

38. G. William Domhoff, *Who Rules America Now?* (Englewood Cliffs, NJ: Prentice-Hall, 1983), pp. 126–29. See also C. Wright Mills, *The Power Elite* (New York: Oxford University Press, 1956) and Thomas R. Dye, *Who's Running America?* (Englewood Cliffs, NJ: Prentice Hall, 1979).

39. Leonard Beeghly, *The Structure of Social Stratification in the United States* (Boston: Allyn and Bacon, 1989), pp. 206–11. See also Thomas B. Edsall, *The New Politics of Inequality* (New York: Norton, 1985).

40. Domhoff, *Who Rules America Now?* pp. 131–43. For an in-depth study, refer to G. William Domhoff, *The Powers That Be* (New York: Vintage Press, 1979).

41. David R. Simon and D. Stanley Eitzen, *Elite Deviance* (Boston: Allyn and Bacon, 1982).

42. V. I. Lenin, *Imperialism: The Highest Stage of Capitalism* (New York: International Pub., 1939).

43. Gilpin, *Political Economy*, p. 40.

44. For the reader who is interested in a more detailed and sophisticated theoretical framework regarding the multiplicity of contending economic forces in the modern world, an excellent beginning point is Chilcote (1984). A full theoretical development was not made because of space and time limitations. Apologies are made for the neglect of competing and/or complementary theories to the World System approach, especially Barran (1960, 1969), Barran and Sweezy (1966), and André Gunder Frank (1967, 1969, 1979, 1981a, 1981b).

45. Immanuel Wallerstein, *The Modern World System: Capitalist Agriculture and the Origins of the European World-Economy in the Sixteenth Century* (New York: Academic Press, 1974).

46. Christopher Chase-Dunn and Richard Rubinson, "Toward a Structural Perspective on the World-System," *Politics and Society* 7, 4(1977):453–76.

47. Ibid., pp. 472–73.

48. Ibid., pp. 475–76.

49. David Snyder and Edward L. Kick, "Structural Position in the World System and Economic Growth, 1955–1970: A Multiple-Network Analysis of Transnational Interactions," *American Journal of Sociology* 84, 5:1096–126.

50. Ibid., pp. 1106–7.

51. World Bank, *World Development Report 1988* (New York: Oxford University Press, 1988), Table 1, pp. 222–23.

52. Snyder and Kick report an intriguing serendipitous finding from their analysis. A separate examination of the impact of the four networks upon subsequent economic growth for core countries revealed that only the impact of military interventions was negative. In essence, while trade dominance, diplomatic initiatives, and treaty-making all work to enrich core nations, military interventionism within poorer countries actually has the opposite effect—it costs the core country a great deal without yielding any financial benefits. Moreover, the economic impact upon countries receiving military intervention is negligible. It neither hurts them nor helps them, at least as measured solely in economic terms. The lesson for core countries should be obvious: military interventionism is a nonproductive form of power maintenance. It should not be used other than in a purely defensive capacity—at least if it is seen as the only viable means for enriching the core. Military intervention, of course, may be dictated by less direct economic motivation and in less measurable dollars and cents payoffs. It can be used to maintain a nation's political hegemonic dominance, and/or to prevent the "threat of a good example" by labeling a nation's development as communist and thus an evil force that must be resisted at all costs (Chomsky 1988).

53. Kenneth Bollen, "World System Position, Dependency, and Democracy: The Cross-National Evidence," *American Sociological Review* 48 (Aug. 1983):468–79.

54. Christopher Chase-Dunn, *Global Formation: Structures of the World Economy* (New York: Basil Blackwell, 1989).

55. Willy Brandt, *Arms and Hunger* (Cambridge, MA: MIT Press, 1986), pp. 1–2, 19–48.

56. Theotonio Dos Santos, "The Structure of Dependence," in Mitchell A. Seligson, *The Gap Between Rich and Poor* (Boulder, CO: Westview, 1984), pp. 95–104.

57. Ibid., p. 100.

58. Ibid., p. 101.

59. Alejandro Portes, "On the Sociology of National Development: Theories and Issues," *American Journal of Sociology* 82 (July 1976):55–85.

60. S. Lall, "Is 'Dependence' a Useful Concept in Analyzing Underdevelopment?" *World Development* 3(1979):799–810; Tony Smith, "The Underdevelopment of the Development Literature: The Case of Dependency Theory," *World Politics,* 31(1979):247–88; Richard Rubinson and Deborah Holtzman, "Comparative Dependence and Economic Development," *International Journal of Comparative Sociology* 22(1981):86–101.

61. Tony Smith, *The Pattern of Imperialism: The United States, Great Britain, and the Late Industrializing World since 1815* (Cambridge: Cambridge University Press, 1981), pp. 69–84.

62. See Evans (1979) for a revision of dependency meant to explain these exceptions and the refutations of Brewer (1980) and Kuo et al. (1981).

63. Henrik Marcussen and Jens Torp, *Internationalization of Capital—Prospects for the Third World: A Re-Examination of Dependency Theory* (London: Zed Press, 1982), pp. 10–12.

64. Bill Warren. *Imperialism: Pioneer of Capitalism* (New York: Routledge, Chapman and Hall, 1980), pp. 7–10, 163–65.

65. Bruce Russett, "International Interactions and Processes: The Internal vs. External Debate Revisited," in Ada W. Finifter (ed.), *Political Science—The State of the Discipline* (Washington, DC: Political Science Association, 1983).

66. Giorgio Gagliani, "Income Inequality and Economic Development," *Annual Review of Sociology* 13(1987):313–34.

67. Robert W. Jackman, "Dependence on Foreign Investment and Economic Growth in the Third World," *World Politics* 34(Jan. 1982):175–97.

68. Lloyd G. Reynolds, "The Spread of Economic Growth to the Third World, 1850–1950," *Journal of Economic Literature* 21(1983):941–80.

69. David Morawetz, "The Gap Between Rich and Poor Countries," in Mitchell Seligson (ed.), *The Gap Between Rich and Poor: Contending Perspectives on the Political Economy of Development* (Boulder, CO: Westview, 1984), p. 11.

70. Mitchell Seligson, "The Dual Gaps: An Overview of Theory and Research," in Seligson, *Gap Between Rich and Poor,* p. 3.

71. W. A. Lewis, "Development and Distribution," in A. Cairncross and M. Puri (eds.), *Employment, Income Distribution and Development Strategy* (London: Macmillan, 1976), p. 26; H. F. Lydall, *Income Distribution During the Process of Development* (Geneva: International Labour Office, (1977), pp. 13–14.

72. Simon Kuznets, "Economic Growth and Income Inequality," *American Economic Review* 45 (March 1955):1–28; Simon Kuznets, "Quantitative Aspects of the Economic Growth of Nations: Distribution of Income by Size" *Economic Development and Cultural Change* 11, 2 (Jan. 1963):1–80.

73. Roger D. Hansen, "The Emerging Challenge: Global Distribution of Income and Economic Opportunity," in James W. Howe, *The U.S. and World Development Agenda for Action 1975* (New York: Praeger, 1975), p. 61.

74. Montak S. Ahluwalia, "Inequality, Poverty, and Development," *Journal of Development Economics* 3(1976):307–42.

75. Gilpin, *Political Economy*, p. 269.

76. Ronald H. Chilcote, *Theories of Development and Under-Development* (Boulder, CO: Westview, 1984), p. 11.

77. Shirley Ceresoto, "Socialism, Capitalism, and Inequality," *Insurgent Sociologist* 11, 2 (Spring 1982):8.

78. W. A. Lewis, "Development and Distribution," pp. 28–29.

79. Francis Moore Lappé and Joseph Collins, *World Hunger: Twelve Myths* (New York: Grove Press, 1986), pp. 85–94.

80. Francis Moore Lappé, Rachel Shurman, and Kevin Danaher, *Betraying the National Interest: How U.S. Foreign Aid Threatens Global Security by Undermining the Political and Economic Stability of the Third World* (New York: Grove Press, 1987), pp. 15–55.

81. Susan George, *A Fate Worse Than Debt* (New York: Grove Press, 1988), pp. 58–73.

82. In fairness, this position is and will continue to be intensely controversial. To begin with, many LDCs are currently attempting to divorce themselves from dependence upon IMF and World Bank loans, multinational corporate investment, etc. in recognition of their capital flight problems (Mason 1988:117). World Bank (1984) figures suggest the point may become moot, noting that among nonindustrialized countries in the 1970–81 period 79% of gross domestic investment came from gross national savings. Interestingly, criticism of development aid has come from both ends of the political spectrum (Toye 1987). Conservatives argue that aid which focuses upon questions of poverty, basic human needs, and income inequality needs to be challenged; nations can only grow economically through freely operating markets with a hands-off policy by their governments. The other problems will then be eventually eradicated through increasing affluence. On the whole, however, some review compendiums of development research find that on balance most recipient countries have benefited from such assistance (Riddell 1987). Although not all countries do benefit, and not all types of development aid are helpful, most aid succeeds in meeting its objectives and in yielding respectable rates of economic return (Cassen et al. 1986). This is particularly true with reference to family planning and population control programs that have reduced runaway birth rates, enabling poorer countries to invest more in the future rather than being forced to feed and clothe a burgeoning dependent population. Especially for LDCs, reduced fertility and smaller family size has produced higher savings rates which can be used in national economic development (Mason 1988). The effect of multinational corporate investment, however, on development within periphery countries is much more doubtful and will be addressed in the next chapter. London (1988) found with respect to fertility decline that multinational corporate penetration did significantly retard development in periphery countries. For a radically different view of abuses "development aid" can produce, i.e., to block fundamental

needed change while mounting a pacification effort, U.S. involvement with Central America has provided many recent examples (Barraclough and Scott 1988; Barry and Preusch 1988).

83. George, *Fate Worse Than Debt*, pp. 63, 73.

84. Ibid., p. 15.

85. Bradley P. Bullock, "Cross-National Research and the Basic Needs Approach to Development: A New Direction," paper presented at the American Sociological Association conference, Chicago, 1987; Paul Streeten, et al., *First Things First: Meeting Basic Needs in Developing Countries* (New York: Oxford University Press, 1981).

86. Lee Soltow, *Patterns of Wealthholding in Wisconsin since 1850* (Madison, WI: Wisconsin University Press, 1971).

87. Shirley Kuo, Gustav Ranis, and John C. Fei, *The Taiwan Success Story: Rapid Growth with Improved Distribution in the Republic of China, 1952–1979* (Boulder, CO: Westview, 1981).

Chapter 3

1. John Whalley, "The Worldwide Income Distribution: Some Speculative Calculations," *Review of Income and Wealth* 25(1979):261–76.

2. Cuomo Commission on Trade and Competitiveness, *The Cuomo Commission Report: A New American Formula for a Strong Economy* (New York: Simon & Shuster, 1988), pp. 26–27.

3. Ibid., p. 32.

4. Barry Bluestone and Bennett Harrison, *The Deindustrialization of America: Plant Closings, Community Abandonment, and the Dismantling of Basic Industry* (New York: Basic Books, 1982), pp. 113–14.

5. Robert W. Jackman, "Dependence on Foreign Investment and Economic Growth in the Third World," *World Politics* 34 (Jan. 1982):175–97.

6. Cuomo Commission, *Report*, p. 59.

7. Stephen D. Krasner, *Structural Conflict: The Third World Against Global Liberalism* (Berkeley: University of California Press, 1985), pp. 97, 101.

8. P. T. Bauer, "The Vicious Circle of Poverty," in Mitchell A. Seligson (ed.), *The Gap Between Rich and Poor* (Boulder, CO: Westview, 1984), p. 324.

9. These differences are statistically significant at the .05 level for GNP per person comparing industrial countries to all others, and significant on percentage increase of GNP per person comparing industrial countries to low-income countries. Strictly speaking, because we are dealing with an entire population of world countries rather than a sample, the level of significance does not matter. It does give some idea about the degree of difference, however, between these groups of countries.

10. Susan George, *A Fate Worse Than Debt: The World Financial Crisis and the Poor* (New York: Grove Press, 1988), p. 73.

11. Mitchell A. Seligson, "The Dual Gaps: An Overview of Theory and Research," in Mitchell A. Seligson (ed.), *The Gap Between Rich and Poor: Contending Perspectives on the Political Economy of Development* (Boulder, CO: Westview, 1984), p. 3.

12. Unfortunately, the fourteen countries not presently classified under this system indicate the necessity of an updated categorization. The populous nation of Bangladesh, with over 100 million people, has not been placed nor have two go-go economies (Hong Kong and Singapore), which especially may not belong in the periphery. Research by Modern World Systems theorists should work to clear up these ambiguities.

13. Again, the differences between GNP per person in core countries is statistically significant at the .05 level with each of the other two groups.

14. Albert Berry, Francois Bourguignon, and Christian Morrisson, "Changes in the World Distribution of Income Between 1950 and 1977," *Economic Journal* 93 (June 1983):331–50.

15. Ibid., p. 340.

16. Ibid.

17. World Bank, *The World Development Report 1988* (New York: Oxford University Press, 1988), pp. 46–54, 111–20.

18. Harry Makler, *The New International Economy* (Beverly Hills, CA: Sage, 1982), p. 16.

19. Andrew Reding, "Mexico at a Crossroads," *World Policy Journal* 5, 4 (Fall 1988):633.

20. William R. Cline, *International Debt and the Stability of the World Economy* (Washington, DC: Institute for International Economics, 1983), pp. 20–21.

21. George, *A Fate Worse Than Debt,* pp. 60–61.

22. Ibid., p. 63.

23. A. Kent MacDougall, "In Third World, All But the Rich Are Poorer," *Los Angeles Times* (Nov. 4, 1984):1.

24. Cuomo Commission, *Report,* pp. 53–54.

25. International Monetary Fund, *Direction of Trade Statistics Yearbook* (Washington, DC: International Monetary Fund, 1987), p. 405.

26. Bennett Harrison and Barry Bluestone, *The Great U-Turn: Corporate Restructuring and the Polarizing of America* (New York: Basic Books, 1988), pp. 154–55.

27. Robert Gilpin, *The Political Economy of International Relations* (Princeton, NJ: Princeton University Press, 1987), pp. 330, 344.

28. David M. Gordon, "Private Debt Dwarfs Uncle Sam's," *Los Angeles Times* (Jan. 20, 1987):3.

29. Harrison and Bluestone, *The Great U-Turn,* pp. 149, 151–52, report that consumer debt doubled during the Reagan years of 1981–86 in a desperate attempt by average people to keep abreast of stagnation and decline in real income. The use of "plastic money" expanded at even more astronomical rates. Revolving installment credit owed to Visa, Mastercard, Sears, etc. nearly tripled during the same period. By 1986, the typical American family owed $11,500, not counting their home mortgage. If this amount is calculated to the norm of a three-year loan at 12% interest, the average monthly payment in 1986 on past debt comes to $380. With after-tax monthly household income of $1,930 during the same year, this means that the normal American family is paying one-fifth of its monthly income just to pay off its old debts—not including the house payment!

30. Cuomo Commission, *Report,* p. 5.

31. Walter Mossberg, "Cost of Paying the Foreign Piper," *Wall Street Journal* (Jan. 18, 1988):3.

32. Bob Rast, "U.S. Banks Lose Top Status in Global Financial Markets" *Minneapolis Star Tribune* (Nov. 27, 1988):1D.

33. Gilpin, *Political Economy,* p. 329.

34. IMF, *Trade Statistics Yearbook,* pp. 243, 404.

35. Harrison and Bluestone, *The Great U-Turn,* p. 147.

36. David K. Henry, and Richard P. Oliver, "The Defense Buildup, 1977–85: Effects on Production and Employment," *Monthly Labor Review* (Aug. 1987):6.

37. Council of Economic Advisers, *Economic Report of the President* (Washington, DC: U.S. Government Printing Office, 1987), Appendix B.

38. Cuomo Commission, *Report,* pp. 61, 64.

39. Associated Press, "Study Says Deficit Cost 5.1 Million Jobs," *Minneapolis Star Tribune* (Oct. 16, 1988):3A.

40. Hobart Rowen, "Capital Economics: Candidates in Blunderland" *Washington Post National Weekly* (Oct. 10–16, 1988):5.

41. Gilpin, *Political Economy,* pp. 336, 346–49.

42. Howard M. Wachtel, *The Money Mandarins: The Making of a Supranational Economic Order* (New York: Pantheon Books, 1986), p. 128. It is quite true that the rich do save and invest more than the poor. The implication is that the poor are less thrifty—in addition to being lazy and shiftless—than a less careless and thoughtless upper class. A moment's reflection leads to the realization, however, that the poor simply do not have excess funds to invest after meeting the basic necessities of life.

43. George, *A Fate Worse Than Debt,* pp. 171–77.

44. Ibid., p. 177.

45. Steven Stack, "The Effect of Direct Government Involvement in the Economy on the Degree of Income Inequality: A Cross-National Study," *American Sociological Review* 43(Dec. 1978):880–88.

46. P. A. Della, and N. Oguchi, "Distribution, the Aggregate Consumption Function, and the Level of Economic Development: Some Cross-Country Results," *Journal of Political Economy* 84, 6 (Dec. 1976):1325–34; Asfaque Khan, "Aggregate Consumption Function and Income Distribution Effect: Some Evidence from Developing Countries," *World Development* 15, 10/11 (1987):1369–74.

47. Manuel Pastor, Jr., "The Effects of IMF Programs in the Third World: Debate and Evidence from Latin America," *World Development* 15, 2(1987):259. One recent study (Helleiner 1987) even documents the failure of Tanzania, with a government outspokenly sympathetic and concerned for the well-being of its people, to protect its citizens from the erosion and financial deterioration caused by an IMF-induced austerity plan. Despite the best of intentions, therefore, some doubt remains whether a country could ward off the evil effects of these adjustment packages and protect its inhabitants—even if it were inclined to do so.

48. Alan Riding, "Debt Fears Realized with Venezuela Unrest," *Minneapolis Star Tribune* (March 2, 1989):4A.

49. News Services, "Venezuela President Blames Debt for Riots," *Minneapolis Star Tribune* (March 4, 1989):3A.

50. Economy in Numbers, "The High Cost of Debt," *Dollars & Sense* 144 (March, 1989):23.

51. World Bank, *World Development Report 1988,* pp. 223, 273.

52. Montek S. Ahluwalia, "Income Inequality: Some Dimensions of the Problem," in Mitchell A. Seligson (ed.), *The Gap Between the Rich and Poor: Contending Perspectives on the Political Economy of Development* (Boulder, CO: Westview, 1984), pp. 14–21.

53. William Loehr, "Some Questions on the Validity of Income Distribution." Seligson (ed.), *Gap Between the Rich and Poor,* pp. 283–91. The difficulties in drawing international comparisons on income inequality are compounded by shifts between sample coverage (e.g., national, urban only, rural only, etc.), the unit of analysis (such as families, households, income recipients, economically active population), and a wide variation in the years in which the data are compiled between countries. In a detailed analysis of what biases could result from ill-considered mixing of these data groups, Menard (1986) found that household income and personal income distributions are essentially equivalent, as are personal income distributions based on urban-only samples with national-level data. He also discovered very little effect in averaging income inequality data for a single period of time, but only within recent years (estimates based upon data gathered prior to 1960 are largely invalid). On the whole, however, he recommends that researchers avoid combining different data sets on income inequality for the same country that are more than five years apart.

54. World Bank, *World Development Report 1988* (New York: Oxford University Press, 1988), pp. 272–73. The World Bank correctly points out that the collection of income distribution data is not systematically organized within many countries and that some data may be derived from surveys conducted for other purposes—most frequently consumer buying studies. Although the estimates they use are considered the best available, in some cases the coverage of the surveys may be too unreliable to make nationwide estimates of income distribution. Nonetheless, the figures compiled by the World Bank are for both rural and urban areas, which is a crucial source of error if both sectors are not represented. The surveys are also relatively recent, which is a major strength in comparison to the ILO study. Yet the ILO review also included some rare household income distribution data for Senegal, Iran, and Columbia that, added to the World Bank figures, raised the total number of countries analyzed to forty-seven.

55. Edward N. Muller, "Democracy, Economic Development, and Income Inequality," *American Sociological Review* 53 (Feb. 1988):50–68. Strangely, however, Muller chooses not to control for unit of analysis but instead mixes individual with household data. This would be acceptable if the individual data were not for workers or economically active persons but for all income recipients. It is impossible to tell directly from his data.

56. Lars Osberg, *Economic Inequality in the United States* (Armonk, NY: M. E. Sharpe, 1984), p. 19.

57. It is crucial to keep in mind that, although LDCs have greater *internal*

inequality than core countries, the great majority of their problem stems from the huge differences between their average incomes and those of industrial nations. Average per capita income is 7.6 times higher in developed countries than in LDCs, while over half of worldwide income inequality comes because of this gap. Only 18% is attributable to internal income inequality within LDCs (Berry et al. 1983). Put another way, Whalley (1979) believes that if one had to choose between attacking income inequality between countries versus eradicating income inequality within countries—be they LDCs or industrial nations—equalizing incomes between countries would be the most effective way to reduce worldwide income inequality.

58. M. O. Lorenz, "Methods of Measuring the Concentration of Wealth," *Quarterly Publications of the American Statistical Association* 9(1905):205–19.

59. Of course, no one actually draws the Lorenz curves to estimate the Gini ratio. A full discussion of this and other income inequality measurements can be found in Schwartz and Winship (1979). The formulas for the Gini ratio vary, depending upon whether grouped data or continuous data are being used. The calculations for grouped data in my analysis follow Morgan (1962). Aiker (1965) has the clearest explanation of this procedure. Also, the methodology now exists to calculate Gini ratios using grouped data by drawing Lorenz curves with microcomputers (Brown and Mazzarino 1984).

60. Age has an effect upon the ratio, so that the simple aging of a population could increase inequality quite apart from any structural change (Morgan, 1962). Although Paglin (1975) introduced a modification to the traditional Gini ratio which eliminates about one-third of the inequality, it has not been widely adopted in subsequent research (for a modification, see Formberg and Seaks 1980). A popular method of computing Gini scores utilizes census income categories. The assumption is made that the mean income of each income category is the midpoint of that interval. Cumulative percentages are then calculated, frequently with an adjustment using a Pareto curve (Knott 1970) for the open-ended interval at the top. This is not always done, however, which can lead to inconsistent comparisons between different sets of data constructed at different times. Moreover, the number of income intervals differ from one census to another (14 in 1950, 13 in 1960, 15 in 1970, and 9 in 1980). Even within the same Census year, the Gini may vary between publications. In 1970, the Bureau used 15 income classes in its published state reports but 19 classes were used to compute the Gini (Knott 1970). It has been shown that the Gini coefficient will be reduced to the degree that the number of income intervals also declines (Sale 1974). At times, the reduction in accuracy because of the number and/or nature of the income groups may be misleadingly low. Murphy reports that based upon Irish income data, there is a 1 to 2% underestimation of the actual Gini ratio—which seems innocuous. It is especially when Gini ratios are decomposed for separate analytical groups, however, that error becomes quite large. For example, in 1980 the underestimation of the Gini coefficient for Ireland was 1.7% for direct income, for households with employed heads it was 3.3%, and for households with three or more earners it was 25.5%. It is also true that the Gini ratio is not sensitive to nonmoney income components and differential price indices between states. Jonish and Kau (1973: 180) conclude that this exaggerates income inequal-

ities in rural areas. Budd (1970) directs his criticism of the Gini coefficient against its relative insensitiveness, which can be quite serious for researchers making comparisons between various dates. Quite simply, the Gini coefficient is more responsive to changes in the distribution of income among the middle class rather than among the rich or poor (Osberg 1984:29; Allison 1978:868). This may perhaps be why the Gini coefficient shows such stability over long periods of time in the United States. Soltow's study of Wisconsin income data (1971), for example, shows no great change in the Gini coefficient over one hundred years while Reynolds and Smolensky (1977) show no U.S. change between 1950 and 1970 despite massive taxation and welfare shifts.

61. Denny Braun, "Multiple Measurements of U.S. Income Inequality," *Review of Economics and Statistics* 70, 3(Aug. 1988):398–405.

62. Osberg, *Economic Inequality,* p. 29; Paul D. Allison, "Measures of Inequality," *American Sociological Review* 43 (Dec. 1978):868.

63. MacDougall, "In Third World," pp. 1, 3, 8.

64. Reding, "Mexico at a Crossroads," p. 630.

65. James M. Cypher, "The Party's Over: Debt, Economic Crisis Undermine Mexico's PRI," *Dollars & Sense* 142 (Dec. 1988):9–11.

66. Stephen G. Bunker, *Underdeveloping the Amazon: Extraction, Unequal Exchange, and the Failure of the Modern State* (Chicago: University of Illinois Press, 1985).

67. Benedict J. Clements, *Foreign Trade Strategies, Employment, and Income Distribution in Brazil* (New York: Praeger, 1988), pp. 31–33.

68. David Denslow, Jr., and William Tyler, "Perspectives on Poverty and Income Inequality in Brazil," *World Development* 12, 10(1984):1019–28.

69. Jose Camargo, "Income Distribution in Brazil:1960–1980," monograph, Pontificia Universidade Catolica do Rio De Janeiro, 1984.

70. Helga Hoffman, "Poverty and Property in Brazil: What Is Changing?" in Edmar Bocha and Herbert S. Klein (eds.), *Incomplete Transition: Brazil since 1945* (Albuquerque, NM: University of New Mexico Press, 1989), pp. 197–231.

71. Albert Fishlow, "A Tale of Two Presidents: The Political Economy of Crisis Management," in Alfred Stepan (ed.), *Democratizing Brazil: Problems of Transition and Consolidation* (New York: Oxford University Press, 1989), pp. 83–119.

72. Ibid., p. 99.

73. Peter Evans, *Dependent Development: The Alliance of Multinational, State, and Local Capital in Brazil* (Princeton, NJ: Princeton University Press, 1979), pp. 81–83, 159–62, 214–24, 278–88.

74. Ibid., pp. 96–97, 288.

75. Jan Knippers Black, *United States Penetration of Brazil* (Philadelphia, University of Pennsylvania Press, 1977), p. 241.

76. Clements, *Foreign Trade Strategies,* pp. 143–44.

77. Fishlow, "A Tale of Two Presidents," pp. 83–119.

78. MacDougall, "In Third World," pp. 3, 8.

79. Albert Fishlow, "Brazilian Size Distribution of Income," *American Economic Review* 62 (May 1972):391–401; Denslow and Tyler, "Perspectives on Inequality in Brazil," p. 1024.

80. Gary S. Fields, "Who Benefits from Economic Development? A Reexamination of Brazilian Growth in the 1960s," *American Economic Review* 67, 4 (Sept. 1977):570–82.

81. Hoffman, "Poverty and Property in Brazil," pp. 197–231.

82. Camargo, "Income Distribution in Brazil," pp. 19–20.

83. Black, *United States Penetration of Brazil.*

84. Ibid., p. 236.

85. Ibid., pp. 238–39. Originally in Marcio Moreira Alves, *A Grain of Mustard Seed: The Awakening of the Brazilian Revolution* (New York: Doubleday, 1973), pp. 164–65.

86. Evans, *Dependent Development,* pp. 287–95, 314–29.

87. Albert Fishlow, "Some Reflections on Post-1964 Brazilian Economic Policy," in Alfred Stepan (ed.), *Authoritarian Brazil* (New Haven: Yale University Press, 1973), p. 90.

88. Harry Makler, Alberto Martinelli, and Neil Smelser (eds.), *The New International Economy* (Beverly Hills, CA: Sage, 1982), p. 22.

89. Edmar L. Bacha, "External Shocks and Growth Prospects: The Case of Brazil, 1973–89," *World Development* 14, 8(1986):919–36.

90. In particular, see Rudolfo Hoffman, "A Distribuicao da Renda No Brasil Em 1985, 1986 e 1987." The paper can be obtained from: Instituto de Planejamento Economico e Social, Avenida Presidente Antonio Carlos, 51, Rio de Janeiro-RJ-20020, Brazil.

91. George, *A Fate Worse Than Debt,* pp. 122–23.

92. Eul-Soo Pang, "Debt, Adjustment, and Democratic Cacophony in Brazil." In Barbara Stallings and Robert Kaufman (ed.), *Debt and Democracy in Latin America* (Boulder, CO: Westview, 1989), pp. 127–42.

93. Charles H. Wood and José Alberto Magno de Carvaho, *The Demography of Inequality in Brazil* (New York: Cambridge University Press, 1988), pp. 184–200.

94. Ibid., p. 258.

95. Walter Russel Mead, "The United States and the World Economy," *World Policy Journal* 6, 1(Winter 1989):1–46; Jerry W. Sanders, "America in the Pacific Century," *World Policy Journal* 6, 1(Winter 1989):47–80; Robert Gilpin, *The Political Economy of International Relations* (Princeton, NJ: Princeton University Press, 1987).

96. Roger Cohen, "Rio's Murder Wave Takes on the Aura of a Class Struggle," *Wall Street Journal* (May 9, 1989): A1, A15.

97. Ibid., p. A15.

98. For example, Ben Bagdikian (*The Media Monopoly* 1987) points out that General Electric—the tenth largest U.S. corporation—owns RCA, which in turn owns NBC. Bagdikian does a commendable job in providing a great deal of evidence showing a right-wing, pro-business, conservative bias to U.S. news, advertising, and general media content. For further details on the conservative bias of American media caused by big business, see Noam Chomsky and Edward S. Herman, *Manufacturing Consent: The Political Economy of the Mass Media* (New York: Pantheon, 1989), pp. 3–18.

Chapter 4

1. Simon Kuznets, "Economic Growth and Income Inequality," *American Economic Review* 45, 1(March 1955):1–28.

2. David A. Smith, "Overurbanization Reconceptualized: A Political Economy of the World-System Approach," *Urban Affairs Quarterly* 23, 2 (Dec. 1987):270–94.

3. Felix Paukert, "Income Distribution at Different Levels of Development: A Survey of the Evidence," *International Labour Review* (Aug.–Sept. 1973):97–125.

4. A great division exists among the variety of studies which examine the effect of economic development as it changes relative income inequality such as Gini ratios. Economic development has been measured either as Gross Domestic Product (GDP) per person or Gross National Product (GNP) per person. GDP is different from GNP because GDP includes payments made abroad to other nations and corporations, as well as repatriated profits and loans being paid back to the home country. While GNP includes only financial transactions among citizens of a given country, GDP encompasses a much broader spectrum of economic actors—including flows to and from overseas through prior loans and corporate foreign subsidiaries. Thus, GNP per person is a better measurement of economic activity going on within a country that is not directly effected by foreign investors or international trade imbalances.

5. Montek S. Ahluwalia, "Income Inequality: Some Dimensions of the Problem," in H. Chenery et al., *Redistribution with Growth* (London: Oxford University Press, 1974), pp. 3–37.

6. Jacques Lecaillon, et al., *Income Distribution and Economic Development: An Analytical Survey* (Geneva: International Labour Office, 1984), p. 12.

7. Ibid., p. 41.

8. The statistical significance level of .05 was used to compare the means among all five groups on all three measurements of income inequality. Differences between Group 3 and the poorer country Groups 1 and 2 are only significant with the household Gini measurement, but they are significant on all three inequality scores between Group 3 and the core countries in Group 1. It is at this point levels of significance do become important since the countries in each level (especially Groups 1 through 3) are "samples" representing many more countries where information is simply not available.

9. W. Beckerman, "Some Reflections on Redistribution with Growth," *World Development* Aug. 1977):665–76.

10. Lecaillon, et al., *Income Distribution,* pp. 14–15.

11. Jerry Cromwell, "The Size Distribution of Income: An International Comparison," *Review of Income and Wealth* (Sept. 1977): pp. 291–308.

12. As measured by the annual percentage increase in Gross Domestic Product between 1965–80 (6.04%) and 1980–86 (2.80%), this is certainly true. But measuring development as the annual percentage increase in GNP per person, as some studies do, shows Group 3 countries slightly behind Groups 4 and 5 combined, at rates of 2.58% and 2.63% respectively. Lastly, among countries

where Gini scores cannot be computed for households because of lack of data, Group 3 countries show a lower annual rate of GDP per person increase (6.26%) than countries in Groups 4 and 5 (7.17%).

13. Lecaillon, et al., *Income Distribution* p. 82.

14. Harold R. Kerbo, *Social Stratification and Inequality* (New York: McGraw-Hill, 1983), p. 437.

15. Michael Taylor and Nigel Thrift, *The Geography of Multinationals* (New York: St. Martin's Press, 1982), p. 25.

16. Barry Bluestone and Bennett Harrison, *The Deindustrialization of America* (New York: Basic Books, 1982), pp. 143–47.

17. Taylor and Thrift, *Geography of Multinationals*, p. 1.

18. Robert Gilpin, *The Political Economy of International Relations* (Princeton, NJ: Princeton University Press, 1987), pp. 238–39.

19. John Burgess, "When the Product Is America Instead of American Products," *Washington Post National Weekly Edition* (Oct. 24–30, 1988):21.

20. Gilpin, *Political Economy*, p. 257.

21. Bluestone and Harrison, *Deindustrialization*, pp. 42, 113–114, 172, 176.

22. John Pearson, "Strong Dollar or No, There's Money to Be Made Abroad," *Business Week* (March 1985), p. 155.

23. "The 100 Largest U.S. Multinationals," *Forbes* (July 25, 1988), pp. 248–50.

24. Howard M. Wachtel, *The Money Mandarins: The Making of a New Supranational Economic Order* (New York: Pantheon, 1986), pp. 153–78.

25. Neil Smelser, et al., *The New International Economy* (Beverly Hills, CA: Sage, 1982), pp. 18–19, 21–22.

26. Taylor and Thrift, *Geography of Multinationals*, p. 142.

27. Bluestone and Harrison, *Deindustrialization*, pp. 129–30.

28. Ibid., pp. 130–32.

29. Cuomo Commission, *The Cuomo Commission Report* (New York: Simon and Schuster, 1988), p. 41.

30. Bluestone and Harrison, *Deindustralization*, pp. 171–72.

31. Bennett Harrison and Barry Bluestone, *The Great U-Turn: Corporate Restructuring and the Polarizing of America* (New York: Basic Books, 1988), p. 30.

32. Andrew Reding, "Mexico at a Crossroads," *World Policy Journal* 5, 4 (Fall 1988):643.

33. Harrison and Bluestone, *The Great U-Turn*, p. 32.

34. Motor Vehicle Manufacturers Association, *Minneapolis Star Tribune* (Nov. 13, 1988):1J.

35. Steve Lohr, "'Global Office' Changing White-Collar Work World," *Minneapolis Star Tribune* (Oct. 23, 1988):1J.

36. Taylor and Thrift, *Geography of Multinationals*, p. 3.

37. Margaret Shapiro, "Empire of the Sun," *Washington Post National Weekly Edition* (Oct. 31–Nov. 6, 1988):6–7.

38. World Bank, *World Development Report 1988* (New York: Oxford University Press, 1988), p. 21.

39. Wachtel, *Money Mandarins*, p. 162.

40. For one of the more sympathetic portrayals of the difficulties and pit-

falls typically encountered by multinational expansion, see Theodore H. Moran, *Multinational Corporations: The Political Economy of Foreign Direct Investment* (Lexington, MA: D. C. Heath, 1985) and/or Robert Gilpin, Political Economy, pp. 231–305.

41. Francis Moore Lappé and Joseph Collins, *World Hunger: Twelve Myths* (New York: Grove Press, 1986), pp. 85–94.

42. World Bank, *Report,* p. 25.

43. Lappé and Collins, *World Hunger,* pp. 91, 93.

44. Moran, *Multinational Corporations,* p. 4.

45. Walden Bello, "U.S.-Phillipine Relations in the Aquino Era," *World Policy Journal* 5, 4 (Fall 1988):688.

46. Taylor and Thrift, *Geography of Multinationals,* p. 154.

47. Volker Bornschier, Christopher Chase-Dunn, and Richard Rubinson, "Cross-national Evidence of the Effects of Foreign Investment and Aid on Economic Growth and Inequality: A Survey of Findings and a Reanalysis," *American Journal of Sociology* 84, 3(1978):651–83.

48. Richard Rubinson, "The World-Economy and the Distribution of Income Within States: A Cross-National Study," *American Sociological Review* 41 (Aug. 1976):638–59.

49. Robert W. Jackman, "Dependence on Foreign Investment and Economic Growth in the Third World," *World Politics* 34 (Jan. 1982):175–97.

50. Erich Weede and Horst Tiefenbach, "Some Recent Explanations of Income Inequality," *International Studies Quarterly* 25 (June 1981):255–82; Erich Weede, "Beyond Misspecification in Sociological Analyses of Income Inequality," *American Sociological Review* 45 (June 1980): 497–501.

51. Edward N. Muller, "Financial Dependence in the Capitalist World Economy and the Distribution of Income Within Nations," in Mitchel Seligson, (ed.), *The Gap Between Rich and Poor* (Boulder, CO: Westview, 1984), pp. 256–82.

52. Bruce London, "Dependence, Distorted Development, and Fertility Trends in Noncore Nations: A Structural Analysis of Cross-National Data," *American Sociological Review* 53 (Aug. 1988):608 n.2.

53. Volker Bornschier and Christopher Chase-Dunn, *Transnational Corporations and Underdevelopment* (New York: Praeger, 1985).

54. Specifically replying to the devastating critique of their early work by Weede and Tiefenbach (1981), Bornschier and Chase-Dunn point out that their original research was unfairly replicated. It was not surprising that no effect for multinational penetration was found on income inequality because Weede and Tiefenbach did not use measurement of penetration at an early enough time to actually estimate its effect upon subsequent growth or decline in GNP per person; nor was there any attempt to differentiate between penetration as measured by long-term stock ownership versus current flows of investment.

55. World Bank, *World Development Report 1988,* Tables 16, 18, 19, 22. By leaving out the "advanced" core countries, the implication is given that Third World countries are really the ones with the debt problems—not industrial nations. Given the performance of the U.S. economy within the past decade, including the staggering leap to a mountain of debt, this assumption is very du-

bious. Future reports from the World Bank would do well to include data for core countries, if only for greater fairness and objectivity.

56. Bornschier and Chase-Dunn, *Transnational Corporations,* pp. 109–10.

57. Although the authors give no evidence either way, it may be surmised that multinational agribusiness may be found in greater proportion among smaller, very poor nations than among the richer, more industrial LDCs. Thus, the fact that agribusiness penetration is unrelated to relative income inequality may be due to the type of country they set up shop in rather than the type of product they produce.

58. Harland Prechel, "The Effects of Exports, Public Debt, and Development on Income Inequality," *Sociological Quarterly* 26, 2(1985): 213–34.

59. A reader desiring more information about the great variety of high quality publications can contact these organizations: Institute for Food and Development Policy (Food First), 145 Ninth Street, San Francisco, CA 94103–3584, Tel. (415) 864–8555; Institute for Policy Studies/Transnational Institute, 1901 Q Street NW, Washington, DC 20009, Tel. (202) 234–9382

60. Rati Ram, "Physical Quality of Life and Inter-Country Economic Inequality," *Economic Letters* 5(1980):195–99. Norman L. Hicks and Paul P. Streeten, "Indicators of Development: The Search for a Basic Needs Yardstick," *World Development* 7(1979):576–77.

61. Shirley Ceresoto, "Socialism, Capitalism, and Inequality," *Insurgent Sociologist* 11, 2(Spring 1982):5–29.

62. Bruce London and Bruce A. Williams, "Multinational Corporate Penetration, Protest, and Basic Needs Provision in Non-Core Nations: A Cross-National Analysis," *Social Forces* 66, 3 (March 1988):747–73.

63. Norman L. Weatherby et al., "Development, Inequality, Health Care, and Mortality at the Older Ages: A Cross-National Study," *Demography* 20, 1 (Feb., 1983):27–43. For a detailed discussion of the impact that relative income inequality has as an independent or intervening causative variable, see especially Bornschier and Chase-Dunn, *Transnational Corporations,* pp. 131–47.

64. Frances Moore Lappé, et al., *Betraying the National Interest* (New York: Grove Press, 1987); Noam Chomsky, *The Culture of Terrorism* (Boston: South End Press, 1988).

65. Bruce London and Thomas D. Robinson, "The Effect of International Dependence on Income Inequality and Political Violence," *American Sociological Review* 54, 2 (April 1989): 305–8.

Chapter 5

1. Cuomo Commission, *The Cuomo Commission Report* (New York: Simon & Schuster, 1988), p. 142.

2. John Agnew, *The United States in the World Economy: A Regional Geography* (New York: Cambridge University Press, 1987), p. 70.

3. Frank Levy, *Dollars and Dreams: The Changing American Income Distribution* (New York: Russell Sage Foundation, 1987), pp. 3–4;

4. Bennett Harrison and Barry Bluestone, *The Great U-Turn: Corporate*

Restructuring and the Polarizing of America (New York: Basic Books, 1988), pp. 4–5.

5. John M. Berry, "The Legacy of Reaganomics: Underlying Flaws Threaten the Successes," *Washington Post National Weekly Edition* (Dec. 19–25, 1988):7.

6. Paul Blustein, "Peace for All, Prosperity for Some: The Reagan Expansion Is an Uneven Affair," *Washington Post National Weekly Edition* (Oct. 3–9, 1988):8.

7. Bureau of the Census, *Housing in America, 1985–86,* H 121, No. 19 (Washington, DC: U.S. Government Printing Office, 1989), p. 52.

8. Blustein, "Peace for All," p. 8.

9. Berry, "Legacy of Reaganomics," p. 7.

10. Agnew, *United States in the World Economy,* p. 150.

11. Graphed from data in Harrison and Bluestone, *Great U-Turn,* pp. 8–9.

12. Cuomo Commission, *Report,* pp. 13–14.

13. Agnew, *United States and the World Economy,* pp. 142–45.

14. Council of Economic Advisors, *Economic Report of the President: 1987* (Washington, DC: U.S. Government Printing Office, 1988), p. 360.

15. Associated Press, "Despite 4th Quarter Rise, Trade Deficit Down in '88," *Minneapolis Star Tribune* (March 1, 1989), p. 3D.

16. "Financial Games Reduce R&D Spending," *Dollars & Sense* 145 (April 1989):5.

17. Cuomo Commission, *Report,* pp. 10–13.

18. I. Magaziner and R. B. Reich, *Minding America's Business: The Decline and Rise of America's Economy* (New York: Vintage Press, 1982), p. 52.

19. Robert Kuttner, "Why We Don't Make TVs Anymore," *Washington Post National Weekly Edition* (Oct. 24–30, 1988):29.

20. Bob Davis, "Firms Plan to Seek U.S. Aid to Develop High-Definition TV," *Wall Street Journal* (May 5, 1989): A16.

21. Evelyn Richards, "The Pentagon Plans to Get into Television," *Washington Post National Weekly Edition* (Dec. 26, 1988–Jan. 1, 1989):32.

22. Harrison and Bluestone, *Great U-Turn,* pp. 125, 144–50.

23. Magaziner and Reich, *Minding America's Business,* p. 36. Specifically, average annual increases were in this order: West Germany (5.0%), Belgium (4.9%), France (4.8%), Netherlands (4.2%), Denmark (4.1%), Japan (3.8%), Canada (2.5%), Italy (2.4%), Sweden (1.8%), U.S. (.9%), United Kingdom (.1%).

24. Harrison and Bluestone, *Great U-Turn,* p. 178.

25. Tom Riddell, "The Political Economy of Military Spending," in *The Imperiled Economy: Through the Safety Net* (New York: Union for Radical Political Economics, 1988), p. 232.

26. Ibid.

27. Bruce M. Russett, *What Price Vigilance?* (New Haven, CT: Yale University Press, 1970), pp. 140–41.

28. Riddell, "Military Spending," p. 232.

29. For a detailed discussion of this relationship plus earlier data of a similar

nature, see R. W. DeGrasse, "The Military: Short-Changing the Economy," *Bulletin of the Atomic Scientists* (May 1984): 39–43.

30. Agnew, *United States in the World Economy,* p. 151.

31. Harrison and Bluestone, *Great U-Turn,* p. 154.

32. John Burgess, "When the Product Is America Instead of American Products," *Washington Post National Weekly Edition* (Oct. 24–30, 1988):21.

33. Cuomo Commission, *Report,* p. 8. According to the General Accounting Office, the $325 billion necessary to close or sell failed savings institutions is greater than the annual Pentagon budget. Comptroller General Charles Bowsher believes this could rise to $500 billion if an economic recession occurs. See "Congress Warned S and L Bailout Could Reach $500 Billion," *Minneapolis Star Tribune* (April 7, 1990):12D.

34. William P. O'Hare, *Poverty in America: Trends and New Patterns* (Washington, DC: Population Reference Bureau, 1985), p. 7.

35. Bureau of the Census, *Current Population Reports,* Consumer Income: "Money Income and Poverty Status in the United States: 1987," Series P-60, No. 161 (March 1988), p. 7.

36. O'Hare, *Poverty in America,* p. 9.

37. This surface tranquility is very misleading. A number of reports show great leaps forward for educated blacks, but severe decline for those left in an "underclass" within our major metropolitan areas (Wilson 1987). Wilson points out that the real improvements for some blacks, brought on by the civil rights movement, helped an upwardly mobile group escape inner-city life. What remained were the "truly disadvantaged." These ill-educated poor are haunted by violence, crime, drugs, joblessness, and welfare dependency. A recent RAND report notes that conditions are worsening for under-educated blacks and single black women with children (Smith and Welch 1986). Such findings are also echoed and corroborated in a study documenting a decline in per capita income in female-headed black households (Farley and Bianchi 1985).

38. Bureau of the Census, Census of Population, 1980, *General Social and Economic Characteristics: United States Summary,* PC80-1-C1 (Washington, DC: U.S. Government Printing Office, 1983), table 245. The year 1980 is the last date that poverty statistics are available by state.

39. Joint Economic Committee, *Poverty, Income Distribution, the Family and Public Policy* (Washington, DC: U.S. Government Printing Office, 1986), pp. 56–63.

40. Timothy Smeeding, Barabara B. Torrey, and Martin Rein, "Patterns of Income and Poverty: The Economic Status of Children and the Elderly in Eight Countries," in *The Vulnerable* (Washington, DC: Urban Institute Press, 1988), pp. 95–98.

41. O'Hare, *Poverty in America,* p. 18.

42. Committee on Ways and Means, U.S. House of Representatives, *Background Material and Data on Programs within the Jurisdiction of the Committee on Ways and Means* (Washington, DC: U.S. Government Printing Office, 1989), p. 881.

43. Ibid., pp. 878–908.

44. Ibid., pp. 958–83.

45. Gwen Hill, "It Is Becoming a Permanent Issue," *Washington Post National Weekly Edition* (March 27—April 2, 1989): 8.

46. Arthur Haupt, "Another Winter for the Homeless," *Population Today* 17, 2 (Feb. 1989): 3–4.

47. Chris Spolar, "No Home–and Not Much More," *Washington Post National Weekly Edition* (March 27–April 2): 7.

48. Committee on Ways and Means, *Background Material,* pp. 1060–63.

49. Bureau of the Census, "Money Income and Poverty Status: 1987," p. 10.

50. William P. O'Hare, *America's Welfare Population: Who Gets What?* (Washington, DC: Population Reference Bureau, 1987), p. 10, and Kristin Moore, "The Effect of Government Policies on Out-of-Wedlock Sex and Pregnancy," *Family Planning Perspectives* 94, 4 (1977):164–69. For greater detail, see Kristin Moore and Martha Burt, *Private Crisis, Public Cost: Policy Perspectives on Teenage Childbearing* (Washington, DC: Urban Institute, 1982), and Kristin Moore and Steven Caldwell, *Out-of-Wedlock Pregnancy and Childbearing* (Washington, DC: Urban Institute, 1976).

51. Isabell V. Sawhill, "Poverty in the U.S.: Why Is It So Persistent? *Journal of Economic Literature* 26 (Sept. 1988):1104.

52. O'Hare, *America's Welfare Population,* p. 10

53. Irwin Garfinkel and Sara McLanahan, *Single Mothers and Their Children: A New American Dilemma* (Washington, DC: Urban Institute, 1986), pp. 62–63.

54. O'Hare, *Poverty in America,* pp. 17–18.

55. Michael Harrington, *The New American Poverty* (New York: Holt, Rinehart, and Winston, 1984).

56. Sheldon Danziger and Peter Gottschalk, "Do Rising Tides Lift All Boats? The Impact of Secular and Cyclical Changes on Poverty," *American Economic Review* 76, 2 (May 1986):405–10.

57. Peter Gottschalk and Sheldon Danziger, "A Framework for Evaluating the Effects of Economic Growth and Transfers on Poverty," *American Economic Review* 75, 1 (March 1985):153–61.

58. Sawhill, "Poverty in the U.S.," p. 1112.

59. Edward M. Gramlich and Deborah S. Laren, "How Widespread Are Income Losses in a Recession?" in D. Lee Bawdin (ed.), *The Social Contract Revisited* (Washington, DC: Urban Institute, 1984), pp. 157–80.

60. Council of Economic Advisers, *Economic Report of the President, 1989* (Washington, DC: U.S. Government Printing Office, 1989), p. 433.

61. David Wessel, "If a Recession Hits, Is U.S. Prepared for It?" *Wall Street Journal* (April 17, 1989): 1.

62. Charles Murray, *Losing Ground: American Social Policy 1950–1980* (New York: Basic Books, 1984).

63. Richard Vedder and Lowell Gallaway, "AFDC and the Laffer Principle," *Wall Street Journal* (March 26, 1986), p. 30, and Lowell Gallaway, Richard Vetter, and Therese Foster, "The New Structural Poverty: A Quantitative Anal-

ysis," in Joint Economic Committee, *War on Poverty: Victory or Defeat* (Washington, DC: U.S. Government Printing Office, 1986).

64. Sanford F. Schram and Paul H. Wilken, "It's No 'Laffer' Matter: Claim That Increasing Welfare Aid Breeds Poverty and Dependence Fails Statistical Test," *American Journal of Economics and Sociology* 48, 2 (April 1989):203–17.

65. Sawhill, "Poverty in the U.S.," p. 1113.

66. Patricia Horn, "Measure for Measure: Deciphering the Statistics on Income and Wages," *Dollars & Sense* 143 (Jan./Feb. 1989):10.

67. Council of Economic Advisors, *Report of the President, 1989*, Table B-45.

68. Ibid., p. 358.

69. Bureau of the Census, *Statistical Abstract of the United States: 1987* (Washington, DC: U.S. Government Printing Office, 1988), Table 676.

70. Horn, "Measure for Measure," pp. 10–11.

71. Council of Economic Advisors, *Report of the President, 1989*, p. 433.

72. Alfred L. Malabre, Jr., "The Outlook: Is the Bill Arriving for the Free Lunch?" *Wall Street Journal* (Jan. 9, 1989): 1.

73. Harrison and Bluestone, *Great U-Turn*, pp. 117–28.

74. Levy, *Dollars and Dreams*, pp. 78–80.

75. Harrison and Bluestone, *Great U-Turn*, p. 120.

76. Linda LeGrande, "The Service Sector: Employment and Earnings in the 1980s," Report No. 85-167 E (Aug. 15, 1985), p. 5; Congressional Research Service, Library of Congress.

77. Levy, *Dollars and Dreams*, pp. 86–87.

78. Barry Bluestone and Bennett Harrison, *The Great American Job Machine: The Proliferation of Low-Wage Employment in the U.S. Economy* (Washington, DC: Joint Economic Committee, 1986), p. 3.

79. Lester C. Thurow, "A Surve in Inequality," *Scientific American* 256, 5 (May 1987): 34.

80. Harrison and Bluestone, *Great U-Turn*, p. 120.

81. Martin Dooley and Peter Gottschalk, "The Increasing Proportion of Men with Low Earnings in the United States," *Demography* 22, 1 (Feb. 1985): 25–34; Martin Dooley and Peter Gottschalk, "Earnings Inequality among Males in the United States: Trends and the Effect of Labor Force Growth," *Journal of Political Economy* 92, 1(1984):59 ff.

82. Bluestone and Harrison, *Great American Job Machine*, p. 6.

83. Harrison and Bluestone, *Great U-Turn*, pp. 121–23. For an analogous treatment, see Patrick J. McMahon and John H. Tschetter, "The Declining Middle Class: A Further Analysis," *Monthly Labor Review* 1 (Sept. 1986):22–27.

84. Harrison and Bluestone, *Great U-Turn*, pp. 126–28.

85. Leann M. Tigges, "Age, Earnings, and Change Within the Dual Economy," *Social Forces* 66, 3 (March 1988):676–98.

86. Leann M. Tigges, "Dueling Sectors: The Role of Service Industries in the Earnings Process of the Dual Economy," in George Iarkas and Paula England (eds.), *Industries, Firms, and Jobs: Sociological and Economic Approaches* (New York: Plenum, Press, 1988), pp. 281–301.

87. Lynn A. Karoly, "Changes in the Distribution of Individual Earnings in the United States: 1967–1986" (Santa Monica, CA: RAND Corp., 1989). See also W. Norton Grubb and Robert H. Wilson, "The Distribution of Wages and Salaries, 1960–1980: The Contributions of Gender, Race, Sectoral Shifts and Regional Shifts," Lyndon B. Johnson School of Public Affairs, The University of Texas at Austin, Working Paper No. 39. Grubb and Wilson largely corroborate the fact that earnings inequality has been on the rise for over twenty years within race, industry, and regional groups. Their data stop before it became possible to observe the increase of earnings inequality for women as well as men. Decomposing inequality with the Theil index led them to agree with Bluestone and Harrison that increases in part-time work were partly responsible for the growth of earnings inequality. They also uncovered much support for the idea that shifts away from industrial production toward service employment has led to an increase of earnings inequality.

88. For quite some time it seemed that the experience of women in the U.S. labor force was doubly blessed. Although they have consistently made less money than men, we have seen a continued increase in their real earnings. At least until 1980, their earnings were also much more equal on a relative basis in comparison to men. Looking at Gini scores for earnings of men and women separately shows a decline of inequality for women between 1958 to 1977 (Henley and Ryscavage 1980). Yet figures through 1986 strongly indicate that relative earnings inequality is now probably on the rise for women as well as men (Harrison and Bluestone 1988; Karoly 1989).

89. Agnew, *United States in the World-Economy;* Bluestone and Harrison, *Deindustrialization of America;* Harrison and Bluestone, *Great U-Turn.*

90. Linda LeGrande and Mark Jickling, "Earnings as a Measure of Regional Economic Performance," No. 87-377 E, Congressional Research Service, Library of Congress, p. 2. Earnings in this report were defined as wage and salary disbursements, other labor income (e.g., employer contributions to pension funds), and proprietors' income (income of the self-employed). In essence, this study tracks income earnings from a much wider variety of sources than we have been considering to this point. The widened spectrum also includes the private (including farm) and public (including military) sectors.

91. Agnew, *United States in the World Economy,* p. 162.

92. Ibid., p. 172.

93. Harrison and Bluestone, *Great U-Turn,* pp. 21–52.

94. Richard S. Belous, "Two-Tier Wage Systems in the U.S. Economy," No. 85-165 E (1985), Congressional Research Service, Library of Congress.

95. Harrison and Bluestone, *Great U-Turn,* pp. 44–47.

96. Bureau of the Census, *Statistical Abstract 1987,* pp. 408–9.

97. Harrison and Bluestone, *Great U-Turn,* p. 118.

98. Council of Economic Advisors, *Report of the President, 1989,* p. 429.

99. Bureau of the Census, "Money Income and Poverty Status," p. 1. The Census Bureau defines a family as a group of two or more persons related by birth, marriage, or adoption, who are living together. All persons in such a relationship are considered members of a family.

100. Bureau of the Census, *Current Population Reports:* "Money Income of Households, Families, and Persons in the United States: 1986," Series P-60, No. 159 (Washington, DC: U.S. Government Printing Office, 1987), pp. 36–38.

101. Bureau of the Census, "Money Income and Poverty Status," Table 3.

102. Levy, *Dollars and Dreams,* pp. 160, 143.

103. McKinley L. Blackburn and David E. Bloom, "Family Income Inequality in the United States: 1967–1984," Paper no. 1294 (Cambridge, MA: Harvard Institute of Economic Research, 1987), Table 4.

104. Judith Treas, "The Effect of Women's Labor Force Participation on the Distribution of Income in the United States," *Annual Review of Sociology,* 13 (1987):283.

105. The methodology used to construct this data followed that used by Harrison and Bluestone, *Great U-Turn,* p. 223n.32.

106. Congressional Budget Office, *Trends in Family Income: 1970–1986* (Washington, DC: U.S. Government Printing Office, 1988), Tables A-1, A-11.

107. Kenneth Cahill, "The Distribution of Income among Families with Children, 1968–1984," No. 85-1017 EPW (1985), pp. 8–12, Congressional Research Service, Library of Congress.

108. Blackburn and Bloom, "Family Income Inequality," Table 2.

109. McKinley L. Blackburn and David E. Bloom, "What Is Happening to the Middle Class?" *American Demographics* (Jan. 1985): 21.

110. Cahill, "Distribution of Income," p. 18.

111. Committee on Ways and Means, *Background Material,* pp. 983–1018. This research used an adjusted family income, meaning that poverty thresholds were used to calculate the differing "needs" that families would have as their size changed. For example, the indices show that a family of four needs only about twice as much income (not four times) as that of a single person living alone since some costs can be shared by many persons more efficiently when they live together, e.g., housing. In this way, the estimates take account of the savings implicit in larger units (shared clothing, bulk food discounts, etc.). The research also kept all comparisons in constant 1987 dollars to remove the effect of inflation over the years. Lastly, the adjustment used a modified inflation index which has diminished the importance of mortgage costs, interest rates, etc. By doing so, in my view, the crash of income that befell America within the past decade is understated in the data. Yet the more conservative figures still bare eloquent witness to an undeniable growth in income inequality.

112. Levy, *Dollars and Dreams,* pp. 151–91.

113. For an analogous treatment, see Congressional Budget Office, *Trends in Family Income: 1970–1986* (Washington, DC: U.S. Government Printing Office, 1988).

114. Levy, *Dollars and Dreams,* p. 196.

115. Judith Treas, "The Effect of Women's Labor Force Participation on the Distribution of Income in the United States," *Annual Review of Sociology* 13 (1987):278, 282.

116. Judith Treas, "Trickle Down or Transfers? Postwar Determinants of Family Income Inequality," *American Sociological Review* 48 (Aug. 1983):546–59;

Judith Treas, "U.S. Income Stratification: Bringing Families Back In," *Sociology and Social Research* 66, 3 (March 1982):231–51.

117. Congressional Budget Office, *Trends in Family Income,* pp. 6–9.

118. Katherine L. Bradbury, "The Shrinking Middle Class," *New England Economic Review* (Sept./Oct. 1986):41–55.

Chapter 6

1. Frank Levy, *Dollars and Dreams: The Changing American Income Distribution* (New York: Russell Sage Foundation, 1987), pp. 27–30.

2. Bureau of the Census, *Current Population Reports:* "Money Income and Poverty Status in the United States: 1987," Series P-60, No. 161 (March 1988):3.

3. James C. Cobb, *Industrialization and Southern Society, 1877–1984* (Lexington: University of Kentucky Press, 1984), pp. 57–58.

4. Gary P. Green, *Finance Capital and Uneven Development* (Boulder, CO: Westview, 1987), p. 86.

5. William J. Wilson, *The Declining Significance of Race: Blacks and Changing American Institutions* (Chicago: University of Chicago Press, 1980). See especially chapters 2 and 3, which contain a cogent summary of race relations and the Southern economy after the Civil War.

6. Cobb, *Industrialization and Southern Society,* p. 63.

7. John Agnew, *The United States in the World-Economy: A Regional Geography* (New York: Cambridge University Press, 1987), pp. 110–29.

8. Green, *Finance Capital,* pp. 80–83.

9. William W. Falk and Thomas A. Lyson, *High Tech, Low Tech, No Tech: Recent Industrial and Occupational Change in the South,* (Albany: State University of New York Press, 1988), p. 85.

10. Ibid., p. 2.

11. Ibid., pp. 27–37.

12. To be fair, such advanced industrial foreign countries have only been responding to the constant wooing of southern industrial expansionists as well. By the 1970s, European and Japanese industrialists were as likely to be courted by southern development agencies as the reverse. Georgia has actually established state development branch offices in Brussels, Tokyo, Sao Paulo, and Toronto. Within the South, both North and South Carolina have been the most successful in attracting foreign plants. The latter saw 40% of its yearly industrial investment come from abroad. By the end of the 1970s, there was more West German capital in South Carolina than anywhere else in the world except West Germany (Cobb, *Industrialization and Southern Society,* p. 58).

13. Falk and Lyson, *High Tech, Low Tech,* p. 22.

14. Cobb, *Industrialization and Southern Society,* p. 161.

15. Ibid., p. 136.

16. Ibid., p. 137.

17. William H. Frey and Alden Speare, Jr., *Regional and Metropolitan Growth and Decline in the United States* (New York: Russell Sage Foundation, 1988), p. 474.

18. Cobb, *Industrialization and Southern Society,* p. 139.

19. Agnew, *United States in the World Economy*, pp. 199–200.

20. Falk and Lyson, *High Tech, Low Tech*, p. 152.

21. Green, *Finance Capital*, pp. 92–93.

22. Ibid., p. 93.

23. Cobb, *Industrialization and Southern Society*, p. 60.

24. K. Sale, *Power Shift: The Rise of the Southern Rim and Its Challenge to the Eastern Establishment* (New York: Vintage, 1975), pp. 17–53.

25. Falk and Lyson, *High Tech, Low Tech*, pp. 152–53.

26. Morris S. Thompson, "Clouds in the Sunbelt: Signs of Economic Deceleration Appear in the Southeast," *Washington Post National Weekly Edition* (Nov. 21–27, 1988): 21.

27. Green, *Finance Capital*, p. 92.

28. Falk and Lyson, *High Tech, Low Tech*, pp. 135–36.

29. Gunnar Myrdal, *Economic Theory and Underdeveloped Regions* (London: Duckworth & Co., 1957).

30. David M. Smith, *Where the Grass Is Greener: Living in an Unequal World* (Baltimore, MD: Johns Hopkins University Press, 1982), p. 119.

31. Lionel J. Beaulieu, (ed.), *The Rural South in Crisis: Challenges for the Future* (Boulder, CO: Westview, 1988), pp. 2–4.

32. Stuart A. Rosenfeld, "The Tale of Two Souths," in Beaulieu, *Rural South in Crisis*, pp. 51–71.

33. Stuart A. Rosenfeld, Edward Bergman, and Sara Rabin, *After the Factories: Changing Employment Patterns in the Rural South* (Research Triangle Park, NC: Southern Growth Policies Board, 1985), p. 53.

34. Daniel T. Lichter, "Race and Underemployment: Black Employment Hardship in the Rural South," in Beaulieu, *Rural South in Crisis*, pp. 181–97.

35. Jerry Wilcox and Wade C. Roof, "Percent Black and Black-White Status Inequality: Southern Versus Nonsouthern Patterns," *Social Science Quarterly* 59, 3 (Dec. 1978):421–34.

36. Stuart Holland, *The Regional Problem* (New York: St. Martin's Press, 1976), pp. 96–120.

37. Eric A. Hanushek, "Regional Differences in the Structure of Earnings," *Review of Economics and Statistics* 55, 2 (May 1973):204–13.

38. The definition of a Metropolitan Statistical Area, for the most part, consists of a central city of at least 50,000 people, the county it is located in, and any adjacent counties that display a high degree of social and economic integration with the central city nucleus. Part of this integration is measured by commuting ties. In 1980, there were 734 metropolitan counties, or nearly one-fourth of all U.S. counties.

39. Toby L. Parcel, "Race, Regional Labor Markets and Earnings," *American Sociological Review* 44 (April 1979):262–79.

40. The Census Bureau defines people as urban if they are living in a place of 2,500 people or more. To confuse matters, the concept is different from the metropolitan definition—which throws all residents of a county into the category whether they live in an urban place or not. It is theoretically possible to have a heavily urbanized county that is not metropolitan, or a metropolitan county that is not very urbanized. Fortunately, however, this is seldom the case.

It is especially at the other end that the concepts are in agreement. Rural counties are rarely very urban or connected with metropolitan areas. They also stand in sharp contrast to areas dominated by city life. They are qualitatively different from urban and/or metropolitan counties. Rural counties are deeply branded with low income.

41. Jerry R. Skees and Louis E. Swanson, "Farm Structure and Local Society Well-Being in the South," Beaulieu, *Rural South in Crisis*, pp. 141–57.

42. E. Yvonne Beauford and Mack C. Nelson, "Social and Economic Conditions of Black Farm Households: Status and Prospects," in Beaulieu, *Rural South in Crisis*, pp. 99–119.

43. Louis E. Swanson, "The Human Dimension of the Rural South in Crisis," in Beaulieu, *Rural South in Crisis*, pp. 91–93.

44. Levy, *Dollars and Dreams*, pp. 103–106, 164. The impact has been especially positive for blacks, which started during World War II (pp. 31–33, 136).

45. See especially chapter 5 of Falk and Lyson, *High Tech, Low Tech.*

46. Smith, *Where the Grass Is Greener.*

47. Denny Braun, "Multiple Measurements of U.S. Income Inequality," *Review of Economics and Statistics* 70, 3 (Aug. 1988):398–405. Scores for 1949, 1959, and 1969 were taken from Tom S. Sale, "Interstate Analysis of the Size Distribution of Family Income, 1950–1970," *Southern Economic Journal* 40 (Jan. 1974):434–41. Scores for the District of Columbia were taken from James F. Jonish and James B. Kau, "State Differentials in Income Inequality," *Review of Social Economy* 31 (Oct. 1973):179–90.

48. Starting with the most recent see: Braun, "Multiple Measurements," pp. 398–405; Joel I. Nelson, "Income Inequality: The American States," *Social Science Quarterly* 65, 3(1984):854–60; David Ruthenberg and Miron Stano, "The Determinants of Interstate Variation in Income Distribution," *Review of Social Economy* 35, 1(April 1977):55–66; Sale, "Interstate Analysis," pp. 434–41; Jonish and Kau, "State Differentials in Income Inequality," pp. 179–90; D. J. Aigner and A. J. Heins, "On the Determinants of Income Inequality," *American Economic Review* 57 (March 1967):175–84; Ahmad Al-Samarrie and Herman P. Miller, "State Differentials in Income Concentration," *American Economic Review* 57 (March 1967):59–72; John Conlisk, "Some Cross-State Evidence on Income Inequality," *Review of Economics and Statistics* 49 (Feb. 1967):115–18; David I. Verway, "A Ranking of States by Inequality Using Census and Tax Data," *Review of Economics and Statistics* 48, 3 (Aug. 1966):314–21.

49. H. E. Frech and L. S. Burns, "Metropolitan Interpersonal Income Inequality: A Comment," *Land Economics* 47 (Feb. 1971):104–6; Michael D. Betz, "The City as a System Generating Income Inequality," *Social Forces* 51 (Dec. 1972):192–98; Sheldon Danziger, "Determinants of the Level and Distribution of Family Income in Metropolitan Areas, 1969," *Land Economics* 52 (Nov. 1976):467–78.

50. Charles T. Haworth, James E. Long, and David W. Rasmussen, "Income Distribution, City Size, and Urban Growth," *Urban Studies* 15 (Feb. 1978):1–7; James E. Long, David W. Rasmussen, and Charles T. Haworth, "Income Inequality and City Size," *Review of Economics and Statistics* 59 (May 1977):244–46; Gasper Garofalo and Michael S. Fogarty, "Urban Income Distri-

bution and the Urban Hierarchy-Equality Hypothesis," *Review of Economics and Statistics* 61 (Aug. 1979):381–88; Stephen Nord, "Income Inequality and City Size: An Examination of Alternative Hypotheses for Large and Small Cities," *Review of Economics and Statistics* 62 (Nov. 1980):502–8.

51. Garey C. Durden and Ann V. Schwarz-Miller, "The Distribution of Individual Income in the U.S. and Public Sector Employment," *Social Science Quarterly* 63, 1 (March 1982):39–47; John W. Foley, "Trends, Determinants and Policy Implications of Income Inequality in U.S. Counties," *Sociology and Social Research* 61, 4(1977):441–61.

52. In the data set analyzed, which was derived from the 1983 *County and City Data Book,* family income categories were not available. Although this has been the favored unit of analysis at the national level, it was impossible to replicate using the data available for all 3,186 counties. Hence, household income was used. As explained before, families are units where members are related by matrimonial or blood ties. They are in a household if they live with one another. Households are also made up of people who are not necessarily related: roommates, cohabiting couples who are not married, etc. Although important differences exist between the two units on a number of different dimensions, for the purpose of this analysis the differences are not crucial. For example, the correlation between household income Gini scores and family income Gini scores among U.S. states was .9433 in 1980.

53. Cobb, *Industrialization and Southern Society,* pp. 136–64.

54. Agnew, *United States in the World Economy,* pp. 178–89.

55. Smith, *Where the Grass Is Greener,* p. 121.

Chapter 7

1. Robert W. Cox, "The Core-Periphery Structure of Production and Jobs: The Internationalizing of Production," in Edward Weisband (ed.), *Poverty Amidst Plenty: World Political Economy and Distributive Justice* (Boulder, CO: Westview, 1989), pp. 186–96.

2. James S. Henry, "Poor Man's Debt, Rich Man's Loot," *Washington Post National Weekly Edition,* Dec. 19–25, 1988, pp. 24–25.

3. Ibid., p. 24.

4. Alvaro Umana, "Costa Rica's Debt-for-Nature Swaps Come of Age," *Wall Street Journal* (May 26, 1989).

5. Sandra Postel and Lori Heise, "Reforesting the Earth," in Lester R. Brown (ed.), *State of the World 1988* (New York: Norton, 1988), pp. 83–100.

6. Edward C. Wolf, "Avoiding a Mass Extinction of Species," in Brown, *State of the World 1988,* pp. 101–17.

7. Lester Brown and Christopher Flavin, "The Earth's Vital Signs," in Brown, *State of the World 1988,* p. 21.

8. Pat Aufderheide and Bruce Rich, "Environmental Reform and the Multilateral Banks," *World Policy Journal* 5, 2 (Spring 1988):317.

9. Hobart Rowen, "Trading Debt for Nature," *Washington Post National Weekly Edition* (April 10–16, 1989):5.

10. Michael Renner, "Enhancing Global Security," in Brown, *State of the World 1989*, p. 133.

11. Ibid., p. 151.

12. One of the best books on how arms and military assistance feeds a dependency-relationship between the United States and the Third World is Frances Moore Lappé, Rachel Schurman, and Kevin Danaher, *Betraying the National Interest* (New York: Grove Press, 1987).

13. Felix Lecaillon, *Income Distribution and Economic Development* (Geneva, Switzerland: International Labour Office, 1984), pp. 115–99.

14. Edward C. Wolf, "Raising Agricultural Productivity," in Brown, *State of the World 1987*, pp. 139–56.

15. Shirley W. Y. Kuo, Gustav Ranis, and John C. H. Fei, "Rapid Growth with Improved Income Distribution: The Taiwan Success Story," in Mitchell A. Seligson (ed.), *The Gap Between Rich and Poor* (Boulder, CO: Westview, 1984), pp. 379–91.

16. Tim Wise, "Land Reform for the Landed: Philippine Congress Frustrates Peasant Demands," *Dollars & Sense* (Nov. 1988):12–15.

17. Walden Bello, *Brave New World: Strategies for Survival in the Global Economy* (San Francisco, CA: Institute for Food and Development Policy, 1989).

18. *Los Angeles Times,* "South American Presidents Vow to Try Again for Regional Common Market," *Minneapolis Star Tribune* (May 27, 1989): 12A.

19. Jeff Faux, "The Austerity Trap and the Growth Alternative," *World Policy Journal,* 5, 3 (Summer 1988):367–414.

20. Economy in Numbers, "Where the Federal Deficit Comes From," in *Real World Macro: A Macroeconomics Reader from Dollars & Sense,* 5th ed. (Somerville, MA: Economic Affairs Bureau, 1988), p. 14.

21. Randy Albelda, "Let Them Pay Taxes: The Growing Tax Burden on the Poor," *Dollars & Sense* (April 1988).

22. Ibid.

23. Economic Affairs Bureau, "Tax Reform Hoopla: Do Lower Rates and Fewer Loopholes Equal Reform?" in *Real World Macro,* pp. 32–34.

24. Joseph A. Pechman, "But Reduction Would Favor the Rich, Damage Tax Equity," *Minneapolis Star Tribune* (Feb. 13, 1989):9A.

25. Jeffrey H. Birnbaum, "Merging a Lower Capital Gains Rate with a Rise in Gasoline Tax Would Leave the Poor the Losers," *Wall Street Journal* (May 8, 1989):A16.

26. Tom Riddell, "The Political Economy of Military Spending," in *The Imperiled Economy, Book II: Through the Safety Net* (New York: Union for Radical Political Economics, 1988), p. 232.

27. Lester R. Brown, "Redefining National Security," in Brown, *State of the World 1986*, p. 201.

28. Michael Renner, "Enhancing Global Security," in Brown, *State of the World 1989*, p. 139.

29. John Agnew, *The United States in the World-Economy: A Regional Geography* (New York: Cambridge University Press, 1987), p. 216.

30. Peter Truell and Alan Murray, "Singled Out: Designation of Japan as

Unfair Trader Holds Promise But Much Risk," *Wall Street Journal* (May 26, 1989):A3, A6.

31. Art Pine, "New U.S. Trade Weapon May Backfire," *Minneapolis Star Tribune* (May 22, 1989):4D.

32. John Berry, "The Legacy of Reaganomics: Underlying Flaws Threaten Successes," *Washington Post National Weekly Edition* (Dec. 19–25, 1988):6–7.

33. Bennett Harrison and Barry Bluestone, *The Great U-Turn: Corporate Restructuring and the Polarizing of America* (New York: Basic Books, 1988), pp. 169–96.

34. Cuomo Commission, *The Cuomo Commission Report* (New York: Simon & Schuster, 1988), pp. 120–121.

35. Michael L. Dertouzos, *Made in America: Regaining the Productive Edge* (Cambridge, MA: MIT Press, 1989), p. 20.

36. Harrison and Bluestone, *Great U-Turn,* p. 185.

37. Dertouzos, *Made in America.*

38. Harrison and Bluestone, *Great U-Turn,* p. 189.

39. Dertouzos, *Made in America,* pp. 84–85.

40. Cuomo Commission, *Report,* p. 123.

41. Barbara Vobejda, "Class, Color and College: Higher Education's Role in Reinforcing the Social Hierarchy," *Washington Post National Weekly Edition* (May 15–21, 1989):6–8.

42. Richard J. Barnet, et al., "American Priorities in a New World Era," *World Policy Journal* 2 (Spring 1989):203–38.

43. William W. Falk and Thomas A. Lyson, *High Tech, Low Tech, No Tech: Recent Industrial and Occupational Change in the South* (Albany, NY: State University of New York Press, 1988), pp. 145–46.

44. Louis Uchitelle, "U.S. Companies Are Globalizing Their Resources," *Minneapolis Star Tribune* (May 30, 1989):5B.

45. Institute for Food and Development Policy, 145 Ninth Street, San Francisco, CA 94103, (415) 864–8555.

46. Frances M. Lappé and Joseph Collins, *World Hunger: Twelve Myths* (New York: Grove Press, 1986), pp. 203–8.

47. Utne Reader, Subscriber Services, P.O. Box 1974, Marion, OH, 43306-2074.

48. The Economic Affairs Bureau, Inc., One Summer Street, Somerville, MA, 02143, (617) 628–8411.

49. Co-op America, 2100 M Street, N.W., Suite 310, Washington, DC, 20063, (800) 424-COOP.

50. Working Assets Visa, 230 California Street, San Francisco, CA, 94111, 1-800-52-APPLY.

51. Severyn T. Bruyn, *The Field of Social Investment* (Cambridge: Cambridge University Press, 1987).

52. Jeff Coplon, "Skinhead Reich," *Utne Reader* 33 (May/June 1989):80–83, 85–89; "The Roots of Skinhead Violence: Dim Economic Prospects for Young Men," *Utne Reader* 33 (May/June 1989):84.

53. Jason Berry, "In Louisiana, the Hazards of Duke," *Washington Post National Weekly Edition* (May 22–28, 1989):25.

REFERENCES

Agnew, John. 1987. *The United States in the World Economy: A Regional Geography.* New York: Cambridge University Press.

Ahluwalia, Montek S. 1984. "Income Inequality: Some Dimensions of the Problem." In Mitchell A. Seligson (Ed.), *The Gap Between the Rich and Poor: Contending Perspectives on the Political Economy of Development,* pp. 14–21. Boulder, CO: Westview Press.

Ahluwalia, Montek S. 1976. "Inequality, Poverty, and Development." *Journal of Development Economics,* 3:307–42.

Aigner, D. J. and A. J. Heins. 1967. "On the Determinants of Income Inequality." *American Economic Review,* 57 (March):175–84.

Aiker, Hayward R., Jr. 1965. *Mathematics and Politics.* New York: Macmillan.

Al-Samarrie, Ahmad and Herman P. Miller. 1967. "State Differentials in Income Concentration." *American Economic Review,* 57 (March):59–72.

Albelda, Randy. 1988. "Let Them Pay Taxes: The Growing Tax Burden on the Poor." *Dollars & Sense* (April).

Aldrich, Howard and Jane Weiss. 1981. "Differentiation Within the U.S. Capitalist Class: Workforce Size and Income Differences." *American Sociological Review,* 46:279–89.

Alexander, Karl, Martha Cook, and Edward McDill. 1978. "Curriculum Tracking and Educational Stratification: Some Further Evidence." *American Sociological Review,* 43:47–66.

Allison, Paul D. 1978. "Measures of Inequality." *American Sociological Review,* 43 (Dec.):865–80.

Associated Press. 1988. "Study Says Deficit Cost 5.1 Million Jobs." *Minneapolis Star Tribune* (Oct. 16):3A.

Associated Press. 1989. "Despite 4th Quarter Rise, Trade Deficit Down in '88." *Minneapolis Star Tribune* (March 1):3D.

Associated Press. 1990. "Congress Warned S and L Bailout Could Reach $500 Billion." *Minneapolis Star Tribune* (April 7):12D.

Aufderheide, Pat and Bruce Rich. 1988. "Environmental Reform and the Multilateral Banks." *World Policy Journal,* 5, 2 (Spring): 317.

351

Bacha, Edmar L. 1986. "External Shocks and Growth Prospects: The Case of Brazil, 1973–89." *World Development,* 14, 8:919–36.

Bagdikian, Ben H. 1987. *The Media Monopoly* (2d ed.). Boston, MA: Beacon Press.

Baldwin, William. 1986. "Chicken Little's Income Statistics." *Forbes,* 137 (March 24):68–69.

Barnet, Richard J. et al. 1989. "American Priorities in a New World Era." *World Policy Journal,* 6, 2 (Spring): 203–38.

Barraclough, Solon L. and Michael F. Scott. 1988. *The Rich Have Already Eaten: Roots of Catastrophe in Central America.* Amsterdam: Transnational Institute.

Barran, Paul A. 1960. *The Political Economy of Growth.* New York: Prometheus.

Barran, Paul A. 1969. *The Longer View: Essays Toward a Critique of Political Economy.* New York: Monthly Review Press.

Barran, Paul A. and Paul M. Sweezy. 1966. *Monopoly Capital: An Essay on the American Economic and Social Order.* New York: Monthly Review Press.

Barry, Tom and Deb Preusch. 1988. *The Soft War: The Uses and Abuses of U.S. Economic Aid in Central America.* New York: Grove Press.

Batra, Ravi. 1988. *The Great Depression of 1990.* New York: Dell.

Bauer, P. T. 1984. "The Vicious Circle of Poverty." In Mitchell A. Seligson (Ed.), *The Gap Between Rich and Poor.* Boulder, CO: Westview Press.

Beauford, E. Yvonne and Mack C. Nelson. 1988. "Social and Economic Conditions of Black Farm Households: Status and Prospects." In Lionel J. Beaulieu (Ed.) *The Rural South in Crisis,* pp. 99–119. Boulder, CO: Westview Press.

Beaulieu, Lionel J. (Ed.). 1988. *The Rural South in Crisis: Challenges for the Future.* Boulder, CO: Westview Press.

Beck, E. M., Patrick M. Horan, and Charles M. Tolbert II. 1978. "Stratification in a Dual Economy: A Sectoral Model of Earnings Determination." *American Sociological Review,* 43 (Oct.): 704–20.

Beck, E. M., Patrick M. Horan, and Charles M. Tolbert II. 1980. "Social Stratification in Industrial Society: Further Evidence from a Structural Perspective (Reply to Hauser)." *American Sociological Review,* 45, 4 (Aug.):712–19.

Becker, G. 1964. *Human Capital.* New York: Columbia University Press.

Beckerman, W. 1977. "Some Reflections on Redistribution with Growth." *World Development,* (Aug.):665–76.

Beeghly, Leonard. 1989. *The Structure of Social Stratification in the United States.* Boston: Allyn and Bacon.

Bello, Walden. 1988. "U.S.-Phillipine Relations in the Aquino Era." *World Policy Journal,* 5, 4 (Fall):688.

Bello, Walden. 1989. *Brave New World: Strategies for Survival in the Global Economy.* San Francisco, CA: Institute for Food and Development Policy.

Belous, Richard S. 1985. "Two-Tier Wage Systems in the U.S. Economy." No. 85-165E. Congressional Research Service, Library of Congress.

Bennett, Amanda. 1989. "A Great Leap Forward for Executive Pay." *Wall Street Journal* (April 24):B1.

Berry, Albert, Francois Bourguignon, and Christian Morrisson. 1983. "Changes in the World Distribution of Income Between 1950 and 1977." *Economic Journal,* 93 (June):331–50.

Berry, Albert. 1983. "The Level of World Inequality: How Much Can One Say?" *Review of Income and Wealth,* 29, 3 (Sept.):217–41.

Berry, Jason. 1989. "In Louisiana, the Hazards of Duke." *Washington Post National Weekly Edition* (May 22–28): 25.

Berry, John M. 1988. "The Legacy of Reagonomics: Underlying Flaws Threaten the Successes." *Washington Post National Weekly Edition* (Dec. 19–25): 6–7.

Betz, Michael D. 1972. "The City as a System Generating Income Inequality." *Social Forces,* 51 (Dec.): 192–98.

Birnbaum, Jeffrey H. 1989. "Merging a Lower Capital Gains Rate with a Rise in Gasoline Tax Would Leave the Poor the Losers." *Wall Street Journal* (May 8): A16.

Black, Jan K. 1977. *United States Penetration of Brazil.* Philadelphia: University of Pennsylvania Press.

Blackburn, McKinley L. and David E. Bloom. 1985. "What Is Happening to the Middle Class?" *American Demographics* (Jan.): 18–25.

Blackburn, McKinley L. and David E. Bloom. 1987. "Family Income Inequality in the United States: 1967–1984." No. 1294. Cambridge, MA: Harvard Institute of Economic Research.

Bluestone, Barry, William M. Murphy, and Mary Stevenson. 1973. *Low Wages and the Working Poor.* Ann Arbor, MI: Institute of Labor and Industrial Relations, University of Michigan.

Bluestone, Barry and Bennett Harrison. 1982. *The Deindustrialization of America.* New York: Basic Books.

Bluestone, Barry and John Havens. 1985. *Reducing the Federal Deficit Fair and Square.* Chestnut Hill, MA: Social Welfare Research Institute.

Blumberg, Paul. 1979. "White Collar Status Panic." *New Republic* (Dec. 1).

Blumberg, Paul. 1980. *Inequality in an Age of Decline.* New York: Oxford University Press.

Blustein, Paul. 1988a. "The Great Jobs Debate." *Washington Post National Weekly Edition,* 5, 46 (Sept. 5–11): 20–21.

Blustein, Paul. 1988b. "Peace for All, Prosperity—For Some." *Washington Post National Weekly Edition* (Oct. 3–9): 8.

Bollen, Kenneth. 1983. "World System Position, Dependency, and Democracy: The Cross-National Evidence." *American Sociological Review,* 48 (Aug.): 468–79.

Bornschier, Volker and Christopher Chase-Dunn. 1985. *Transnational Corporations and Underdevelopment.* New York: Praeger.

Bornschier, Volker, Christopher Chase-Dunn, and Richard Rubinson. 1978. "Cross-national Evidence of the Effects of Foreign Investment and Aid on Economic Growth and Inequality: A Survey of Findings and a Reanalysis." *American Journal of Sociology,* 84, 3:651–83.

Bowles, Samuel and Herbert Gintis. 1976. *Schooling in Capitalist America: Educational Reform and the Contradictions of Economic Life.* New York: Basic Books.

Bradbury, Katherine L. 1986. "The Shrinking Middle Class." *New England Economic Review* (Sept./Oct.): 41–55.

Brandt, Willy. 1986. *Arms and Hunger.* Cambridge, MA: MIT Press.

Braun, Denny. 1988. "Multiple Measurements of U.S. Income Inequality." *Review of Economics and Statistics,* 70, 3 (Aug.): 398–405.

Brewer, Anthony. 1980. *Marxist Theories of Imperialism.* London: Routledge and Kegan Paul.

Brittain, J. A. 1977. *The Inheritance of Economic Status.* Washington, D.C.: Brookings Institution.

Brown, J. A. C. and G. Mazzarino. 1984. "Drawing the Lorenz Curve and Calculating the Gini Concentration Index from Grouped Data by Computer." *Oxford Bulletin of Economics and Statistics,* 46, 3:273–78.

Brown, Lester R. 1986. "Redefining National Security." In Lester R. Brown (Ed.) *State of the World 1986,* p. 201. New York: W. W. Norton.

Brown, Lester and Christopher Flavin. 1988. "The Earth's Vital Signs." In Lester R. Brown (Ed.), *State of the World 1988,* p. 21. New York: W. W. Norton.

Bruyn, Severyn T. 1987. *The Field of Social Investment.* Cambridge: Cambridge University Press.

Budd, Edward C. 1970. "Postwar Changes in the Size Distribution of Income in the U.S." *American Economic Review* (May): 247–60.

Bullock, Bradley P. 1987. "Cross-National Research and the Basic Needs Approach to Development: A New Direction." Paper presented at the American Sociological Association conference, Chicago.

Bunker, Stephen G. 1985. *Underdeveloping the Amazon: Extraction, Unequal Exchange, and the Failure of the Modern State.* Chicago: University of Illinois Press.

Burgess, John. 1988. "When the Product Is America Instead of American Products." *Washington Post National Weekly* (Oct. 24–30):21.

Cahill, Kenneth. 1985. "The Distribution of Income among Families with Children, 1968–1984." No. 85-1017 EPW. Congressional Research Service, Library of Congress.

Camargo, Jose M. 1984. "Income Distribution in Brazil: 1960–1980." Rio de Janeiro: Pontificia Universidade Catolica do Rio de Janeiro.

Cassen, Robert et al. 1986. *Does Aid Work? Report to an Intergovernmental Task Force.* Oxford: Clarendon Press.

Cerresoto, Shirley. 1982. "Socialism, Capitalism, and Inequality." *Insurgent Sociologist,* 11, 2 (Spring):5–38.

Chase-Dunn, Christopher. 1989. *Global Formation: Structures of the World Economy.* New York: Basil Blackwell.

Chase-Dunn, Christopher and Richard Rubinson. 1977. "Toward a Structural Perspective on the World-System." *Politics and Society,* 7, 4:453–76.

Chilcote, Ronald H. 1984. *Theories of Development and Underdevelopment.* Boulder, CO: Westview Press.

Chomsky, Noam. 1988. *The Culture of Terrorism.* Boston, MA: South End Press.

Chomsky, Noam and Edward S. Herman. 1989. *Manufacturing Consent: The Political Economy of the Mass Media.* New York: Pantheon.

Clements, Benedict J. 1988. *Foreign Trade Strategies, Employment, and Income Distribution in Brazil.* New York: Praeger.

Cline, William. 1983. *International Debt and the Stability of the World Economy.* Washington, D.C.: Institute for International Economics.

Cobb, James C. 1984. *Industrialization and Southern Society: 1877–1984.* Lexington: University Press of Kentucky.

Cohen, Roger. 1989. "Rio's Murder Wave Takes on the Aura of a Class Struggle." *Wall Street Journal* (May 9): A1, A15.

Collins, Randal. 1971. "Functional and Conflict Theories of Educational Stratification." *American Sociological Review*, 36:1002–19.

Collins, Randal. 1975. *Conflict Sociology.* New York: Academic Press.

Commission on International Development. 1969. *Partners in Development.* New York: Praeger.

Committee on Ways and Means, U.S. House of Representatives. 1989. *Background Material and Data on Programs Within the Jurisdiction of the Committee on Ways and Means.* Washington, D.C.: U.S. Government Printing Office.

Congressional Budget Office. 1988. *Trends in Family Income: 1970–1986.* Washington, D.C.: U.S. Government Printing Office.

Conlisk, John. 1967. "Some Cross-State Evidence on Income Inequality." *Review of Economics and Statistics*, 49 (Feb.): 115–18.

Coplon, Jeff. 1989. "Skinhead Reich." *Utne Reader*, 33 (May/June): 80–83, 85–89.

Council of Economic Advisors. 1987. *Economic Report of the President.* Washington, D.C.: U.S. Government Printing Office.

Council of Economic Advisors. 1989. *Economic Report of the President, 1989.* Washington, D.C.: U.S. Government Printing Office.

Cox, Robert W. 1989. "The Core-Periphery Structure of Production and Jobs: The Internationalizing of Production." In Edward Weisband (Ed.), *Poverty Amidst Plenty: World Political Economy and Distributive Justice*, pp. 186–96. Boulder, CO: Westview Press.

Cromwell, Jerry. 1977. "The Size Distribution of Income: An International Comparison." *Review of Income and Wealth* (Sept.):291–308.

Crystal, Graef S. 1988. "The Wacky, Wacky World of CEO Pay." *Fortune* (June 6):68ff.

Cuomo Commission on Trade and Competitiveness. 1988. *The Cuomo Commission Report: A New American Formula for a Strong Economy.* New York: Simon & Schuster.

Cypher, James M. 1988. "The Party's Over: Debt, Economic Crisis Undermine Mexico's PRI." *Dollars & Sense* (Dec.) 142:9–11, 21.

Danziger, Sheldon. 1976. "Determinants of the Level and Distribution of Family Income in Metropolitan Areas, 1969." *Land Economics*, 52 (Nov.):467–78.

Danziger, Sheldon and Peter Gottschalk. 1986a. "Do Rising Tides Lift All Boats? The Impact of Secular and Cyclical Changes on Poverty." *American Economic Review*, 76, 2 (May):405–10.

Danziger, Sheldon, and Peter Gottschalk. 1986b. "Families with Children Have Fared Worse." *Challenge*, 29 (March-April):40–47.

Davis, Bob. 1989. "Firms Plan to Seek U.S. Aid to Develop High-Definition TV." *Wall Street Journal,* (May 5):A16.

Davis, Kingsley and Wilbert E. Moore. 1945. "Some Principles of Stratification." *American Sociological Review,* 10:242–49.

DeGrasse, R. W. 1984. "The Military: Shortchanging the Economy." *Bulletin of the Atomic Scientists,* (May):39–43.

Della, P. A. and N. Oguchi. 1976. "Distribution, the Aggregate Consumption Function, and the Level of Economic Development: Some Cross-Country Results." *Journal of Political Economy,* 84, 6 (Dec.):1325–34.

Denslow, Jr., David and William Tyler. 1984. "Perspectives on Poverty and Income Inequality in Brazil." *World Development,* 12, 10:1019–28.

Dertouzos, Michael L. et al. 1989. *Made in America: Regaining the Productive Edge.* Cambridge, MA: MIT Press.

Doeringer, P. B. and M. J. Piore. 1971. *International Labor Markets and Manpower Analysis.* Lexington, MA: D. C. Heath.

Dollars & Sense. 1989. "The Roots of Skinhead Violence: Dim Economic Prospects for Young Men." *Utne Reader,* no. 33 (May/June):84.

Domhoff, G. William. 1970. *The Higher Circles.* New York: Random House.

Domhoff, G. William. 1979. *The Powers That Be.* New York: Vintage Press.

Domhoff, G. William. 1983. *Who Rules America Now?* Englewood Cliffs, NJ: Prentice-Hall.

Dooley, Martin and Peter Gottschalk. 1984. "Earnings Inequality among Males in the United States: Trends and the Effect of Labor Force Growth." *Journal of Political Economy,* 92, 1:59ff.

Dooley, Martin and Peter Gottschalk. 1985. "The Increasing Proportion of Men with Low Earnings in the United States." *Demography,* 22, 1 (Feb.):25–34.

Dos Santos, Theotonio. 1970. "The Structure of Dependence." *American Economic Review,* 6: 231–36.

Durden, Garey C. and Ann V. Schwarz-Miller. 1982. "The Distribution of Individual Income in the U.S. and Public Sector Employment." *Social Science Quarterly,* 63, 1 (March):39–47.

Dye, Thomas R. 1979. *Who's Running America?* Englewood Cliffs, NJ: Prentice-Hall.

Economic Affairs Bureau. 1988. "Tax Reform Hoopla: Do Lower Rates and Fewer Loopholes Equal Reform?" In *Real World Macro: A Macroeconomics Reader from Dollars & Sense* (5th ed.). Somerville, MA: Economic Affairs Bureau.

Economy in Numbers. 1988. "Where the Federal Deficit Comes From." In *Real World Macro: A Macroeconomics Reader from Dollars & Sense* (5th ed.). Somerville, MA: the Economic Affairs Bureau.

Economy in Numbers. 1989. "The High Cost of Debt." *Dollars & Sense.* 144 (March):23.

Edsall, Thomas B. 1985. *The New Politics of Inequality.* New York: W. W. Norton.

Edwards. R. C., M. Reich, and D. Gordon, Eds. 1975. *Labor Market Segmentation.* Lexington, MA: D. C. Heath.

Ehrenreich, Barbara. 1986. "Is the Middle Class Doomed?" *New York Times Magazine,* 135 (Sept. 7):44ff.

Evans, Bergen, 1968. *Dictionary of Quotations.* New York, NY: Delacorte.

Evans, Peter. 1979. *Dependent Development: The Alliance of Multinational, State, and Local Capital in Brazil.* Princeton, NJ: Princeton University Press.

Falk, William W. and Thomas A. Lyson. 1988. *High Tech, Low Tech, No Tech: Recent Industrial and Occupational Change in the South.* Albany: State University of New York Press.

Farley, Reynolds and Suzanne M. Bianchi. 1985. "Social Class Polarization: Is It Occurring among Blacks?" *Research in Race and Ethnic Relations,* 4:1–31.

Faux, Jeff. 1988. "The Austerity Trap and the Growth Alternative." *World Policy Journal,* 5, 3 (Summer):367–414.

Featherman, David and Robert Hauser. 1978. *Opportunity and Change.* New York: Academic Press.

Fields, Gary S. 1977. "Who Benefits from Economic Development? A Re-examination of Brazilian Growth in the 1960s." *American Economic Review,* 67, 4 (Sept.):570–82.

Fishlow, Albert. 1972. "Brazilian Size Distribution of Income." *American Economic Review,* 62 (May):391–401.

Fishlow, Albert. 1973. "Some Reflections on Post-1964 Brazilian Economic Policy." In Alfred Stepan (Ed.), *Authoritarian Brazil.* New Haven, CT: Yale University Press.

Fishlow, Albert. 1989. "A Tale of Two Presidents: The Political Economy of Crisis Management." In Alfred Stepan (Ed.), *Democratizing Brazil: Problems of Transition and Consolidation.* New York: Oxford University Press.

Flint, Jerry. 1987. "Too Much Ain't Enough." *Forbes,* 140 (July 13):92ff.

Foley, John W. 1977. "Trends, Determinants and Policy Implications of Income Inequality in U.S. Counties." *Sociology and Social Research,* 61, 4:441–61.

Forbes. 1988a. "The 100 Largest U.S. Multinationals." (July 25):248–50.

Forbes. 1988b. "Corporate America's Most Powerful People." (May 30):154 ff.

Formberg, J. P., and T. G. Seaks. 1980. "Paglin Gini Measure of Inequality—A Modification." *American Economic Review,* 70, 3:479–82.

Frank, André Gunder. 1967. *Capitalism and Underdevelopment in Latin America: Historical Studies of Chile and Brazil.* New York: Monthly Review Press.

Frank, André Gunder. 1969. *Latin America—Underdevelopment or Revolution: Essays on the Development of Underdevelopment and the Immediate Enemy.* New York: Monthly Review Press.

Frank, André Gunder. 1979. *Dependent Accumulation and Underdevelopment.* New York: Monthly Review Press.

Frank, André Gunder. 1981a. *Crisis in the Third World.* New York: Holmes and Meier.

Frank, André Gunder. 1981b. *Reflections on the World Crisis.* New York: Monthly Review Press.

Frech, H. E. and L. S. Burns. 1971. "Metropolitan Interpersonal Income Inequality: A Comment." *Land Economics,* 47 (Feb.):104–6.

Frey, William H. and Alden Speare, Jr. 1988. *Regional and Metropolitan Growth and Decline in the United States.* New York: Russell Sage Foundation.

Friedman, Milton. 1953. "Choice, Chance, and the Personal Distribution of Income." *Journal of Political Economy,* 61, 4 (Aug.):277–90.

Friedman, Milton. 1962. *Capitalism and Freedom.* Chicago, IL: University of Chicago Press.

Friedman, Milton. 1979. *Free to Choose.* New York: Avon Books.

Gagliani, Giorgio. 1987. "Income Inequality and Economic Development." *Annual Review of Sociology,* 13:313–34.

Gallaway, Lowell, Richard Vetter, and Therese Foster. 1986. "The New Struc-
tural Poverty: A Quantitative Analysis." In Joint Economic Committee,
War On Poverty: Victory or Defeat? Washington, DC: U.S. Government
Printing Office.

Gallup Poll. 1988. "U.S. Citizens, British Hold Differing Views of Haves, Have-
Nots." *Minneapolis Tribune* (Aug. 14).

Garfinkel, Irwin and Sara McLanahan. 1986. *Single Mothers and Their Children:
A New American Dilemma.* Washington, DC: Urban Institute.

Garofalo, Gasper and Michael S. Fogarty. 1979. "Urban Income Distribution
and the Urban Hierarchy-Equality Hypothesis." *Review of Economics and
Statistics,* 61 (Aug.):381–88.

George, Susan. 1988. *A Fate Worse Than Debt: The World Financial Crisis and the
Poor.* New York: Grove Press.

Gilpin, Robert. 1987. *The Political Economy of International Relations.* Princeton,
NJ: Princeton University Press.

Glenn, Norvall D. 1984. "Education and Family Income." *Social Forces,* 63,
1:169–83.

Good, T. and J. Brophy. 1973. *Looking in Classrooms.* New York: Harper &
Row.

Gottschalk, Peter and Sheldon Danziger. 1985. "A Framework for Evaluating
the Effects of Economic Growth and Transfers on Poverty." *American Economic Review,* 75, 1 (March):153–61.

Gordon, David M. 1987. "Private Debt Dwarfs Uncle Sam's." *Los Angeles Times*
(Jan. 20).

Gramlich, Edward M. and Deborah S. Laren. 1984. "How Widespread Are Income Losses in a Recession?" In D. Lee Bawdin (Ed.), *The Social Contract
Revisited,* pp. 157–80. Washington, DC: Urban Institute.

Green, Gary P. 1987. *Finance Capital and Uneven Development.* Boulder, CO:
Westview Press.

Greenwood, Daphne T. 1987. "Age, Income, and Household Size: Their Relation to Wealth Distribution in the United States. In Edward N. Wolff
(Ed.), *International Comparisons of the Distribution of Household Wealth,* pp.
121–40. New York: Oxford University Press.

Grubb, W. Norton and Robert H. Wilson. 1987. *The Distribution of Wages and
Salaries, 1960–1980: The Contributions of Gender, Race, Sectoral Shifts and
Regional Shifts.* Lyndon B. Johnson School of Public Affairs, The Univer-
sity of Texas at Austin, Working Paper No. 39.

Gutman, Herbert G. 1988. *Power and Culture: Essays on the American Working
Class.* New York: Pantheon Books.

Hansen, Roger D. 1975. "The Emerging Challenge: Global Distribution of Income and Economic Opportunity." In James W. Howe (Ed.), *The U.S. and World Development Agenda for Action 1975.* New York: Praeger.

Hanushek, Eric A. 1973. "Regional Differences in the Structure of Earnings." *Review of Economics and Statistics,* 55, 2 (May):204–13.

Harrington, Michael. 1976. *The Twilight of Capitalism.* New York: Simon and Schuster.

Harrington, Michael. 1984. *The New American Poverty.* New York: Holt, Rinehart and Winston.

Harrison, Bennett and Barry Bluestone. 1986. *The Great American Job Machine: The Proliferation of Low Wage Employment in the U.S. Economy.* Washington, DC: Joint Economic Committee.

Harrison, Bennett and Barry Bluestone. 1988. *The Great U-Turn: Corporate Restructuring and the Polarizing of America.* New York: Basic Books.

Haupt, Arthur. 1989. "Another Winter for the Homeless." *Population Today,* 17, 2 (Feb.):3–4.

Hauser, Robert M. 1980. "On 'Stratification in a Dual Economy' (Comment on Beck et al., ASR, Oct. 1978)." *American Sociological Review,* 45, 4 (Aug.):702–12.

Hauser, Robert M. and William H. Sewell. 1986. "Family Effects in Simple Models of Education, Occupational Status, and Earnings: Findings from the Wisconsin and Kalamazoo Studies." *Journal of Labor Economics,* 4, 3:S83ff.

Haworth, Charles T., James E. Long, and David W. Rasmussen. 1978. "Income Distribution, City Size, and Urban Growth." *Urban Studies,* 15 (Feb.):1–7.

Helleiner, Gerald K. 1987. "Stabilization, Adjustment, and the Poor." *World Development,* 15, 12:1499–513.

Henle, Peter and Paul Ryscavage. 1980. "The Distribution of Earned Income among Men and Women, 1958–1977." *Monthly Labor Review,* 103, 4 (April):3–10.

Henry, David K. and Richard P. Oliver. 1987. "The Defense Buildup, 1977–85: Effects on Production and Employment." *Monthly Labor Review,* 110, 8. (Aug.).

Henry, James S. 1988. "Poor Man's Debt, Rich Man's Loot." *Washington Post National Weekly Edition* (Dec. 19–25):24–25.

Hicks, Norman L. and Paul P. Streeten. 1979. "Indicators of Development: The Search for a Basic Needs Yardstick." *World Development,* 7:576–77.

Hill, Gwen. 1989. "It Is Becoming a Permanent Issue." *Washington Post National Weekly Edition* (March 27-April 2):8.

Hill, Martha S. and Greg J. Duncan. 1987. "Parental Family Income and the Socioeconomic Attainment of Children." *Social Science Research,* 16, 1 (March):39–73.

Hodson, Randy D. 1981. "How Workers' Earnings Are Determined by Corporate and Industry Level Economic Structure." Paper presented at the American Sociological Association Conference.

Hoffman, Helga. 1989. "Poverty and Property in Brazil: What Is Changing?" In Edmar Bacha and Herbert S. Klein (Eds.), *Incomplete Transition: Brazil Since 1945.* Albuquerque: University of New Mexico Press.

Hoffman, Rudolfo. 1988. "A Distribuicao da Renda No Brasil Em 1985, 1986 e 1987." Rio de Janeiro: Instituto de Planejamento Economico e Social.

Holland, Stuart. 1976. *The Regional Problem.* New York: St. Martin's Press.

Horn, Patricia. 1989. "Measure for Measure: Deciphering the Statistics on Income and Wages." *Dollars & Sense,* 143 (Jan./Feb.):10.

International Monetary Fund. 1987. *Direction of Trade Statistics Yearbook.* Washington, D.C.: IMF.

"Is the Middle Class Shrinking?" 1986. *Time,* 128 (Nov. 3):54–56.

Jackman, Robert W. 1982. "Dependence on Foreign Investment and Economic Growth in the Third World." *World Politics,* 34 (Jan.):175–97.

Jencks, Christopher et al. 1972. *Inequality: A Reassessment of the Effect of Family and Schooling in America.* New York: Harper and Row.

Jencks, Christopher et al. 1979. *Who Gets Ahead? The Determinants of Economic Success in America.* New York: Basic Books.

Joint Economic Committee. 1986. *Poverty, Income Distribution, The Family and Public Policy.* S.Prt. 99–199. Washington, DC: U.S. Government Printing Office.

Jonish, James F. and James B. Kau. 1973. "State Differentials in Income Inequality." *Review of Social Economy,* 31 (Oct.):179–90.

Kalleberg, Arne L., Michael Wallace, and Robert P. Althauser. 1981. "Economic Segmentation, Worker Power, and Income Inequality." *American Journal of Sociology,* 87, 3 (Nov.):651–83.

Karmin, Monroe W. 1984. "Is the Middle Class Really Doomed to Shrivel Away?" *U.S. News and World Report,* 9 (Aug. 20):65.

Karoly, Lynn A. 1989. "Changes in the Distribution of Individual Earnings in the United States: 1967–1986." Santa Monica, CA: RAND Corp.

Kerbo, Harold R. 1983. *Social Stratification and Inequality: Class Conflict in the United States.* New York: McGraw-Hill.

Khan, Ashfaque. 1987. "Aggregate Consumption Function and Income Distribution Effect: Some Evidence From Developing Countries." *World Development,* 15, 10/11:1369–74.

Kirkpatrick, David. 1988. "Abroad, It's Another World." *Fortune,* (June):78.

Kluegel, James R. and Eliot R. Smith. 1986. *Beliefs about Inequality: Americans' Views of What Is and What Ought to Be.* Hawthorne, NY: Aldine De Gruyter.

Knocke, David, Lawrence Raffalovich, and William Erskine. 1987. "Class, Status, and Economic Policy Preferences." *Research in Social Stratification and Mobility,* 6:141–58.

Knott, Joseph J. 1970. "The Index of Income Concentration in the 1970 Census of Population and Housing." Working paper, Population Division, U.S. Bureau of the Census.

Kotz, David. 1988. "Feeling Overworked? Here's Why." *Utne Reader,* 28 (July/Aug.):56–60.

Krasner, Stephen D. 1985. *Structural Conflict: The Third World Against Global Liberalism.* Berkeley: University of California Press.

Kuo, Shirley W. Y., Gustav Ranis and John C. H. Fei. 1984. "Rapid Growth with Improved Income Distribution: The Taiwan Success Story." In

Mitchell A. Seligson (Ed.), *The Gap Between Rich and Poor*, pp. 379–91. Boulder, CO: Westview Pess.

Kuo, Shirley, Gustav Ranis, and John C. Fei. 1981. *The Taiwan Success Story: Rapid Growth with Improved Distribution in the Republic of China, 1952–1979.* Boulder, CO: Westview Press.

Kuznets, Simon. 1955. "Economic Growth and Income Inequality." *American Economic Review,* 45 (March):1–28.

Kuznets, Simon. 1963. "Quantitative Aspects of the Economic Growth of Nations: Distribution of Income by Size." *Economic Development and Cultural Change,* 11, 2 (Jan.):1–80.

Kuttner, Robert. 1985. "A Shrinking Middle Class Is a Call to Action." *Business Week,* (Sept. 16):16.

Kuttner, Robert. 1988. "Why We Don't Make TVs Anymore." *Washington Post National Weekly Edition* (Oct. 24–30):29.

Lappé, Francis M. and Joseph Collins. 1986. *World Hunger: Twelve Myths.* New York: Grove Press.

Lappé, Francis M., Rachel Schurman, and Kevin Danaher. 1987. *Betraying the National Interest: How U.S. Foreign Aid Threatens Global Security by Undermining the Political and Economic Stability of the Third World.* New York: Grove Press.

Lall, S. 1979. "Is 'Dependence' a Useful Concept in Analyzing Underdevelopment?" *World Development,* 3:799–810.

Lecaillon, Jacques, Felix Paukert, Christian Morrisson, and Dimitri Germidis. 1984. *Income Distribution and Economic Development: An Analytical Survey.* Geneva: International Labour Office.

LeGrande, Linda. 1985. "The Service Sector: Employment and Earnings in the 1980s." No. 85–167 E. Congressional Research Service, Library of Congress.

LeGrande, Linda and Mark Jickling. 1987. "Earnings as a Measure of Regional Economic Performance." No. 87-377 E. Congressional Research Service, Library of Congress.

Lenin, V. I. 1939. *Imperialism: The Highest Stage of Capitalism.* New York: International Pub.

Lenski, Gerhard. 1966. *Power and Privilege.* New York: McGraw-Hill.

Levy, Frank. 1987. *Dollars and Dreams: The Changing American Income Distribution.* New York: Russell Sage Fdn.

Levy, Frank and Richard C. Michel. 1983. "The Way We'll Be in 1984: Recent Changes in the Level and Distribution of Disposable Income." Washington, DC: Urban Institute.

Lewis, W. A. 1976. "Development and Distribution." In A. Cairncross and M. Puri (Eds.), *Employment, Income Distribution and Development Strategy.* London: Macmillan.

Lichter, Daniel T. 1988. "Race and Underemployment: Black Employment Hardship in the Rural South." In Lionel J. Beaulieu (Ed.), *The Rural South in Crisis,* pp. 181–97. Boulder, CO: Westview Press.

Lindblom, Charles. 1977. *Politics and Markets: The World's Political-Economic Systems.* New York: Basic Books.

Leohr, William. 1984. "Some Questions on the Validity of Income Distribution." In Mitchell A. Seligson (Ed.), *The Gap Between Rich and Poor*, pp. 283–91. Boulder, CO.: Westview Press.

Lohr, Steve. 1988. " 'Global Office' Changing White-Collar Work World." *Minneapolis Star Tribune* (Oct. 23):1J.

London, Bruce. 1988. "Dependence, Distorted Development, and Fertility Trends in Noncore Nations: A Structural Analysis of Cross-National Data." *American Sociological Review*, 53 (Aug.):606–18.

London, Bruce and Bruce A. Williams. 1988. "Multinational Corporate Penetration, Protest, and Basic Needs Provision in Non-Core Nations: A Cross-National Analysis." *Social Forces*, 66, 3 (March):747–73.

London, Bruce and Thomas D. Robinson. 1989. "The Effect of International Dependence on Income Inequality and Political Violence." *American Sociological Review*, 54, 2 (April): 305–8.

Long, James E., David W. Rasmussen, and Charles T. Haworth. 1977. "Income Inequality and City Size." *Review of Economics and Statistics*, 59 (May): 244–46.

Lorenz, M. O. 1905. "Methods of Measuring the Concentration of Wealth." *Quarterly Publications of the American Statistical Association*, 9:205–19.

Los Angeles Times. 1989. "South American Presidents Vow to Try Again for Regional Common Market." *Minneapolis Star Tribune* (May 27): 12A.

Lydall, H. F. 1977. *Income Distribution During the Process of Development*. Geneva: International Labour Office.

McMahon, Patrick J. and John H. Tschetter. 1986. "The Declining Middle Class: A Further Analysis." *Monthly Labor Review*, 1 (Sept.): 22–27.

McPortland, J. 1968. *The Segregated Students in Desegregated Schools: Sources of Influence on Negro Secondary Students*. Baltimore, MD: Johns Hopkins University Press.

MacDougall, A. Kent. 1984. "In Third World, All but the Rich Are Poorer." *Los Angeles Times*, 6 (Nov. 4).

Macedo, Roberto. 1977. *Distribuicao Funcional na Industria de Transformacao: do Trabalho*. Sao Paulo: Tese de Livre Docecia.

Magaziner, I. and R. B. Reich. 1982. *Minding America's Business: The Decline and Rise of America's Economy*. New York: Vintage Press.

Malabre, Jr., Alfred L. 1989. "The Outlook: Is the Bill Arriving for the Free Lunch?" *Wall Street Journal* (Jan. 9):1.

Marcussen, Henrik and Jens Torp. 1982. *Internationalization of Capital—Prospects for the Third World: A Re-Examination of Dependency Theory*. London: Zed Press.

Marx, Karl. 1981. *Capital: A Critique of Political Economy*, 3 vols. New York: Vintage Books.

Marx, Karl. 1973. *The Grundrisse*. New York: Vintage Books.

Mason, Andrew. 1988. "Saving, Economic Growth, and Demographic Change." *Population and Development Review*, 14, 1 (March): 113–44.

Mead, Walter R. 1989. "The United States and the World Economy." *World Policy Journal*, 6, 1 (Winter): 1–46.

Menard, Scott. 1986. "A Research Note on International Comparisons of Inequality of Income." *Social Forces,* 64,3 (March):778–93.

Miller, S. M. 1988. Review of "Dollars and Dreams: The Changing American Income Distribution," by Frank Levy. *Contemporary Sociology: An International Journal of Reviews,* 17, 4 (July): 456.

Mills, C. Wright. 1956. *The Power Elite.* New York: Oxford University Press.

Moore, Kristin. 1977. "The Effect of Government Policies on Out-of-Wedlock Sex and Pregnancy." *Family Planning Perspectives,* 94, 4:164–69.

Moore, Kristin and Martha Burt. 1982. *Private Crisis, Public Cost: Policy Perspectives on Teenage Childbearing.* Washington, DC: Urban Institute.

Moore, Kristin and Steven Caldwell. 1976. *Out-of-Wedlock Pregnancy and Childbearing.* Washington, DC: Urban Institute.

Moran, Theodore H. 1985. *Multinational Corporations: The Political Economy of Foreign Direct Investment.* Lexington, MA: D. C. Heath.

Morgan, James. 1962. "The Anatomy of Income Distribution." *Review of Economics and Statistics,* 44 (Aug.):270–83.

Mossberg, Walter. 1988. "Cost of Paying the Foreign Piper." *Wall Street Journal* (Jan. 18).

"Motor Vehicle Manufacturers Association." 1988. *Minneapolis Star Tribune* (Nov. 13):1J.

Muller, Edward A. 1985. "Income Inequality, Regime Repressiveness, and Political Violence." *American Sociological Review,* 50:47–61.

Muller, Edward A. 1988. "Democracy, Economic Development, and Income Inequality." *American Sociological Review,* 53:50–68.

Muller, Edward N. 1984. "Financial Dependence in the Capitalist World Economy and the Distribution of Income Within Nations." In Mitchel Seligson (Ed.), *The Gap Between Rich and Poor,* pp. 256–82. Boulder, CO: Westview Press.

Murphy, D. C. 1985. "Calculation of Gini and Theil Inequality Coefficients for Irish Household Incomes in 1973 and 1980." *Economic and Social Review,* 16 (April):225–49.

Myrdal, Gunnar. 1957. *Economic Theory and Underdeveloped Regions.* London: Duckworth.

Nelson, Joel I. 1984. "Income Inequality: The American States." *Social Science Quarterly,* 65, 3:854–60.

Nord, Stephen. 1980. "Income Inequality and City Size: An Examination of Alternative Hypotheses for Large and Small Cities." *Review of Economics and Statistics,* 62 (Nov.):502–8.

Noyelle, Thierry J. and Thomas M. Stanback, Jr. 1984. *The Economic Tranformation of American Cities.* Totowa, NJ: Rowman and Allanheld.

O'Hare, William P. 1987. *America's Welfare Population: Who Gets What.* Washington, DC: Population Reference Bureau.

O'Hare, William P. 1985. "Poverty in America: Trends and New Patterns." *Population Bulletin,* 40, 3.

Oropesa, R. S. 1986. "Social Class, Economic Marginality, and the Image of Stratification." *Sociological Focus,* 19, 3 (Aug.):229–43.

Osberg, Lars. 1984. *Economic Inequality in the United States*. New York: M. E. Sharpe.

Paglin, M. 1975. "The Measurement and Trend of Inequality: A Basic Revision." *American Economic Review*, 65,4 (Sept.): 598–609.

Pang, Eul-Soo. 1989. "Debt, Adjustment, and Democratic Cacophony in Brazil." In Stallings, Barbara and Robert Kaufman (Eds.), *Debt and Democracy in Latin America*, pp. 127–42. Boulder, CO: Westview Press.

Parcel, Toby L. 1979. "Race, Regional Labor Markets and Earnings." *American Sociological Review*, 44 (April):262–79.

Parenti, Michael. 1985. *Inventing Reality: Politics and the Mass Media*. New York: St. Martin's Press.

Parenti, Michael. 1978. *Power and the Powerless*. New York: St. Martin's Press.

Parenti, Michael. 1989. *The Sword and the Dollar: Imperialism, Revolution, and the Arms Race*. New York: St. Martin's Press.

Pastor, Jr., Manuel. 1987. "The Effects of IMF Programs in the Third World: Debate and Evidence from Latin America." *World Development*, 15, 2.

Paukert, Felix. 1973. "Income Distribution at Different Levels of Development: A Survey of the Evidence." *International Labour Review* (Aug.-Sept.):97–125.

Pearson, John. 1985. "Strong Dollar or No, There's Money to Be Made Abroad." *Business Week* (March):155.

Pechman, Joseph A. 1989. "But Reduction Would Favor the Rich, Damage Tax Equity." *Minneapolis Star Tribune* (Feb. 13):9A.

Pen, Jan. 1971. *Income Distribution*. New York: Penguin Books.

Pine, Art. 1989. "New U.S. Trade Weapon May Backfire." *Minneapolis Star Tribune* (May 22):4D.

Portes, Alejandro. 1976. "On the Sociology of National Development: Theories and Issues." *American Journal of Sociology*, 82 (July):55–85.

Postel, Sandra and Lori Heise. 1988. "Reforesting the Earth." In Lester R. Brown (Ed.), *State of the World 1988*, pp. 83–100. New York: W. W. Norton.

Prechel, Harland. 1985. "The Effects of Exports, Public Debt, and Development on Income Inequality." *Sociological Quarterly*, 26, 2:213–34.

Radner, Daniel B. and Denton R. Vaughan. 1987. "Wealth, Income, and the Economic Status of Aged Households." In Edward N. Wolff (Ed.), *International Comparisons of the Distribution of Household Wealth*, pp. 93–120. New York: Oxford University Press.

Ram, Rati. 1980. "Physical Quality of Life and Inter-Country Economic Inequality." *Economic Letters*, 5:195–99.

Rast, Bob. 1988. "U.S. Banks Lose Top Status in Global Financial Markets." *Minneapolis Star Tribune* (Nov. 27):1D.

Reding, Andrew. 1988. "Mexico at a Crossroads." *World Policy Journal*, 5, 4 (Fall):615–50.

Renner, Michael. 1989. "Enhancing Global Security." In Lester R. Brown (Ed.), *State of the World 1989*. New York: W. W. Norton.

Reynolds, Lloyd G. 1983. "The Spread of Economic Growth to the Third World, 1850–1950." *Journal of Economic Literature*, 21:941–80.

Reynolds, Morgan and Eugene Smolensky. 1977. *Public Expenditures, Taxes, and the Distribution of Income.* New York: Academic Press.

Richards, Evelyn. 1989. "The Pentagon Plans to Get into Television." *Washington Post National Weekly Edition* (Dec. 26, 1988–Jan. 1, 1989).

Riddell, Roger C. 1987. *Foreign Aid Reconsidered.* Baltimore, MD: Johns Hopkins University Press.

Riddell, Tom. 1988. "The Political Economy of Military Spending." *The Imperiled Economy: Through the Safety Net.* New York: Union for Radical Political Economics.

Riding, Alan. 1989. "Debt Fears Realized with Venezuela Unrest." *Minneapolis Star Tribune* (March 2):4A.

Riley, J. C. 1979. "Testing the Educational Screening Hypothesis." *Journal of Political Economy,* 87, 5 (Oct.):S227–52.

Robinson, Robert and Jonathan Kelley. 1979. "Class as Conceived by Marx and Dahrendorf: Effects on Income Inequality, Class Consciousness, and Class Conflict in the United States and Great Britain." *American Sociological Review,* 44:38–58.

Rosenberg, Sam. 1980. "Male Occupational Standing and the Dual Labor Market." *Industrial Relations,* 19, 1 (Winter):34–48.

Rosenfeld, Stuart A. 1988. "The Tale of Two Souths." In Lionel J. Beaulieu (Ed.), *The Rural South in Crisis.* Boulder, CO: Westview Press.

Rosenfeld, Stuart A., Edward Bergman, and Sara Rabin. 1985. *After the Factories: Changing Employment Patterns in the Rural South.* Research Triangle Park, NC: Southern Growth Policies Board.

Rowen, Hobart. 1988. "Capital Economics: Candidates in Blunderland." *Washington Post National Weekly Edition.* (Oct. 10–16).

Rowen, Hobart. 1989. "Trading Debt for Nature." *Washington Post National Weekly Edition* (April 10–16, 1989):5.

Rubinson, Richard. 1976. "The World-Economy and the Distribution of Income Within States: A Cross-National Study." *American Sociological Review,* 41 (Aug.):638–59.

Rubinson, Richard and Deborah Holtzman. 1981. "Comparative Dependence and Economic Development." *International Journal of Comparative Sociology,* 22:86–101.

Russett, B. 1970. *What Price Vigilance?* New Haven, CT: Yale University Press.

Russett, Bruce. 1983. "International Interactions and Processes: The Internal vs. External Debate Revisited." In Ada W. Finifter (Ed.), *Political Science— The State of the Discipline.* Washington, DC: Political Science Association.

Ruthenberg, David and Miron Stano. 1977. "The Determinants of Interstate Variation in Income Distribution." *Review of Social Economy,* 35, 1 (April): 55–66.

Sale, K. 1975. *Power Shift: The Rise of the Southern Rim and Its Challenge to the Eastern Establishment.* New York: Vintage.

Sale, Tom S. 1974. "Interstate Analysis of the Size Distribution of Family Income 1950–1970." *Southern Economic Journal,* 40 (Jan.):434–41.

Salkowski, Charlote. 1986. "Growth in Living Standard Slows for the American Middle Class." *Christian Science Monitor* (Jan. 8):1ff.

Samuelson, Paul. 1980. *Economics* (11th ed.). New York: McGraw-Hill.

Samuelson, Robert J. 1985. "The Myth of the Missing Middle." *Newsweek,* (July 1):50.

Sanders, Jerry W. 1989. "America in the Pacific Century." *World Policy Journal,* 6, 1 (Winter):47–80.

Sawhill, Isabel V. 1988. "Poverty in the U.S.: Why Is It So Persistent?" *Journal of Economic Literature,* 26 (Sept.):1073–119.

Schram, Sanford F. and Paul H. Wilken. 1989. "It's No 'Laffer' Matter: Claim That Increasing Welfare Aid Breeds Poverty and Dependence Fails Statistical Test." *American Journal of Economics and Sociology,* 48, 2 (April):203–17.

Seligson, Mitchell A. 1984. *The Gap Between Rich and Poor: Contending Perspectives on the Political Economy of Development.* Boulder, CO: Westview Press.

Shapiro, Margaret. 1988. "Empire of the Sun." *Washington Post National Weekly Edition* (Oct. 31–Nov. 6):6–7.

Shlapentokh, Vladimir. 1987. *The Politics of Sociology in the Soviet Union.* Boulder, CO: Westview Press.

Schwarz, Joseph and Christopher Winship. 1979. "The Welfare Approach to Measuring Inequality." In Karl F. Schuessler (Ed.), *Sociological Methodology 1980.* San Francisco, CA: Jossey-Bass.

Simon, David R. and D. Stanley Eitzen. 1982. *Elite Deviance.* Boston, MA: Allyn and Bacon.

Skees, Jerry R. and Louis E. Swanson. 1988. "Farm Structure and Local Society Well-Being in the South." In Lionel J. Beaulieu (Ed.), *The Rural South in Crisis,* pp. 141–57. Boulder, CO: Westview Press.

Smeeding, Timothy, Barabara B. Torrey, and Martin Rein. 1988. "Patterns of Income and Poverty: The Economic Status of Children and the Elderly in Eight Countries." In Timothy Smeeding, John L. Palmer, and Barbara Torrey (Eds.), *The Vulnerable.* Washington, DC: Urban Institute Press.

Smelser, Neil, Harry Makler, and Alberto Martinelli. 1982. *The New International Economy.* Beverly Hills, CA: Sage Publications.

Smith, David A. 1987. "Overurbanization Reconceptualized: A Political Economy of the World-System Approach." *Urban Affairs Quarterly,* 23, 2 (Dec.):270–94.

Smith, David M. 1982. *Where the Grass Is Greener: Living in an Unequal World.* Baltimore, MD: Johns Hopkins University Press.

Smith, Herbert L. 1986. "Overeducation and Underemployment: An Agnostic Review." *Sociology of Education,* 59, 2 (April):85–99.

Smith, James and Finis R. Welch. 1986. *Closing the Gap: Forty Years of Economic Progress for Blacks.* Santa Monica, CA: RAND Corp.

Smith, Tony. 1979. "The Underdevelopment of the Development Literature: The Case of Dependency Theory." *World Politics,* 31:247–88.

Smith, Tony. 1981. *The Pattern of Imperialism: The United States, Great Britain, and the Late Industrializing World since 1815.* Cambridge: Cambridge University Press.

Snyder, David and Edward L. Kick. 1979. "Structural Position in the World System and Economic Growth, 1955–1970: A Multiple-Network Analysis of Transnational Interactions." *American Journal of Sociology*, 84, 5:1096–126.

Soltow, Lee. 1971. *Patterns of Wealthholding in Wisconsin since 1850*. Madison: Wisconsin University Press.

Spolar, Chris. "No Home—And Not Much More." *Washington Post National Weekly Edition* (March 27–April 2):6–7.

Stack, Steven. 1978. "The Effect of Direct Government Involvement in the Economy on the Degree of Income Inequality: A Cross-National Study." *American Sociological Review* (Dec.) 43:880–88.

Stein, A. 1971. "Strategies for Failure." *Harvard Educational Review*, 41:158–204.

Stowsky, Jay. 1986. "Beating Our Plowshares into Double-Edged Swords: The Impact of Pentagon Policies on the Commercialization of Advanced Technologies." Berkeley Roundtable on the International Economy, Working Paper No. 17 (April).

Streeten, Paul, Shahid Javed Burki, Mahbub W. Haq, Norman Hicks, and Frances Stewart. 1981. *First Things First: Meeting Basic Needs in Developing Countries*. New York: Oxford University Press.

Swanson, Louis E. 1988. "The Human Dimension of the Rural South in Crisis." In Lionel J. Beaulieu (Ed.), *The Rural South in Crisis*, pp. 91–93. Boulder, CO: Westview Press.

Taylor, Michael and Nigel Thrift. 1982. *The Geography of Multinationals*. New York: St. Martin's Press.

Thompson, Morris S. 1988. "Clouds in the Sunbelt: Signs of Economic Deceleration Appear in the Southeast." *Washington Post National Weekly Edition* (Nov. 21–27): 21.

Thurow, Lester. 1975. *Generating Inequality: Mechanisms of Distribution in the U.S. Economy*. New York: Basic Books.

Thurow, Lester. 1987. "A Surge in Inequality." *Scientific American*, 256 (May):30–37.

Tienda, Marta and Ding-Tzann Lii. 1987. "Minority Concentration and Earnings Inequality: Blacks, Hispanics, and Asians Compared." *American Journal of Sociology*, 93, 1 (July):141–65.

Tigges, Leann M. 1986. "Dueling Sectors: The Role of Service Industries in the Earnings Process of the Dual Economy." Paper presented at the American Sociological Association Conference.

Tigges, Leann M. 1987. "Age, Earnings, and Change Within the Dual Economy." Paper presented at the American Sociological Association Conference.

Tigges, Leann M. 1988a. "Age, Earnings, and Change Within the Dual Economy." *Social Forces*, 66, 3 (March):676–98.

Tigges, Leann M. 1988b. "Dueling Sectors: The Role of Service Industries in the Earnings Process of the Dual Economy. In George Iarkas and Paula England (Eds.), *Industries, Firms, and Jobs: Sociological and Economic Approaches*, pp. 281–301. New York: Plenum Press.

Toye, John. 1987. *Dilemmas of Development*. Oxford: Basil Blackwell.

Treas, Judith. 1982. "U.S. Income Stratification: Bringing Families Back In." *Sociology and Social Research*, 66, 3 (March): 231–51.

Treas, Judith. 1983. "Trickle Down or Transfers? Postwar Determinants of Family Income Inequality." *American Sociological Review*, 48 (Aug.):546–59.

Treas, Judith. 1987. "The Effect of Women's Labor Force Participation on the Distribution of Income in the United States." *Annual Review of Sociology 1987*, 13:259–88.

Truell, Peter and Alan Murray. 1989. "Singled Out: Designation of Japan as Unfair Trader Holds Promise But Much Risk." *Wall Street Journal* (May 26): A3, A6.

Tumin, Melvin. 1953. "Some Principles of Stratification: A Critical Analysis." *American Sociological Review*, 18:387–94.

Turner, Jonathan and Charles Starnes. 1976. *Inequality: Privilege and Poverty in America*. Santa Montica, CA: Goodyear.

Uchitelle, Louis. 1989. "U.S. Companies Are Globalizing Their Resources." *Minneapolis Star Tribune* (May 30):5B.

Umana, Alvaro. 1989. "Costa Rica's Debt-for-Nature Swaps Come of Age." *Wall Street Journal* (May 26):A11.

Updates. 1989. "Financial Games Reduce R&D Spending." *Dollars & Sense*, 145 (April):5.

Urban Institute. 1984. *An Analysis of Time on Welfare*. Washington, DC.

U.S. Census Bureau. 1983. *General Social and Economic Characteristics: United States Summary*. 1980 Census of Population, PC80–1–C1. Washington, DC: U.S. Government Printing Office.

U.S. Census Bureau. 1987. "Current Population Reports: Money Income of Households, Families, and Persons in the United States: 1986." Series P-60, no. 159. Washington, DC: U.S. Government Printing Office.

U.S. Census Bureau. 1988a. "Current Population Reports: Money Income and Poverty Status in the United States: 1987 (Advance Report)." Series P-60, no. 161. Washington, DC: U.S. Government Printing Office.

U.S. Census Bureau. 1988b. *Statistical Abstract of the United States: 1987*, Washington, DC: U.S. Government Printing Office.

U.S. Census Bureau. 1989. *Housing in America, 1985–86*. Washington, DC: U.S. Government Printing Office.

U.S. Congress, House of Representatives. 1989. *Background Material and Data on Programs Within the Jurisdiction of the Committee on Ways and Means*. Washington, DC: U.S. Government Printing Office.

U.S. Internal Revenue Service. 1985. *Statistics of Income Bulletin*. Washington, DC: U.S. Government Printing Office.

Vedder, Richard and Lowell Gallaway. 1986. "AFDC and the Laffer Principle." *Wall Street Journal* (March 26).

"Venezuela President Blames Debt for Riots." *Minneapolis Star Tribune* (March 4):3A.

Verway, David I. 1966. "A Ranking of States by Inequality Using Census and Tax Data." *Review of Economics and Statistics*, 48, 3 (Aug.):314–21.

Vobejda, Barbara. 1989. "Class, Color and College: Higher Education's Role in

Reinforcing the Social Hierarchy." *Washington Post National Weekly Edition* (May 15–21):6–8.

Wachtel, Howard M. 1986. *The Money Mandarins: The Making of a Supranational Economic Order.* New York: Pantheon Books.

Wallerstein, Immanuel. 1974. *The Modern World System: Capitalist Agriculture and the Origins of the European World-Economy in the Sixteenth Century.* New York: Academic Press.

Warren, Bill. 1980. *Imperialism: Pioneer of Capitalism.* New York: Routledge, Chapman, and Hall.

Weatherby, Norman L., Charles B. Nam, and Larry W. Isaac. 1983. "Development, Inequality, Health Care, and Mortality at the Older Ages: A Cross-National Study." *Demography,* 20, 1 (Feb.):27–43.

Weber, Max. 1958a. *The Protestant Ethic and the Spirit of Capitalism.* Translated by Talcott Parsons. New York: Scribner's.

Weber, Max. 1958b. "Class, Status, Party." In Seymour M. Lipset and Reinhard Bendix (Eds.), *Class, Status and Power.* New York: Free Press.

Weede, Erich and Horst Tiefenbach. 1981. "Some Recent Explanations of Income Inequality." *International Studies Quarterly,* 25 (June):255–82.

Weede, Erich. 1980. "Beyond Misspecification in Sociological Analyses of Income Inequality." *American Sociological Review,* 45 (June):497–501.

Weitzman, Lenore. 1987. *The Divorce Revolution.* New York: Free Press.

Wessel, David. 1989. "If a Recession Hits, Is U.S. Prepared for It?" *Wall Street Journal* (April 17):1.

Whalley, John. 1979. "The Worldwide Income Distribution: Some Speculative Calculations." *Review of Income and Wealth,* 25:261–76.

Wilcox, Jerry and Wade C. Roof. 1978. "Percent Black and Black-White Status Inequality: Southern Versus Nonsouthern Patterns." *Social Science Quarterly,* 59, 3 (Dec.):421–34.

Wilson, William. 1980. *The Declining Significance of Race: Blacks and Changing American Institutions.* Chicago, IL: University of Chicago Press.

Wilson, William J. 1987. *The Truly Disadvantaged: The Inner City, the Underclass, and Public Policy.* Chicago, IL: University of Chicago Press.

Wise, Tim. 1988. "Land Reform for the Landed: Philippine Congress Frustrates Peasant Demands." *Dollars & Sense* (Nov.):12–15.

Wolf, Edward C. 1987. "Raising Agricultural Productivity." In Lester R. Brown (Ed.), *State of the World 1987,* pp. 139–56. New York: W. W. Norton.

Wolf, Edward C. 1988. "Avoiding a Mass Extinction of Species." In Lester R. Brown (Ed.), *State of the World 1988,* pp. 101–17. New York: W. W. Norton.

Wolff, Edward N. 1987. *International Comparisons of the Distribution of Household Wealth.* New York: Oxford University Press.

Wolff, Edward N. and D. Bushe. 1976. *Age, Education and Occupational Earnings Inequality.* New York: National Bureau of Economic Research.

Wood, Charles H. and José Alberto Magno de Carvaho. 1988. *The Demography of Inequality in Brazil.* New York: Cambridge University Press.

World Bank. 1984. *World Tables,* 3d ed. Baltimore, MD: Johns Hopkins University Press.

World Bank. 1988. *World Development Report 1988.* New York: Oxford University Press.

Wright, Erick O. 1978a. "Race, Class, and Income Inequality." *American Journal of Sociology,* 83:1368–88.

Wright, Erick O. 1978b. *Class, Crisis and the State.* New York: Schocken Books.

Wright, Erick and Lucca Perrone. 1977. "Marxist Class Categories and Income Inequality." *American Sociological Review,* 42:32–55.

Zucker, Lynne G. and Carolyn Rosenstein. 1981. "Taxonomies of Institutional Structure: Dual Economy Reconsidered." *American Sociological Review,* 46 (Dec.):869–84.

INDEX